Human Resource Management

Shahbaz
Anita

ATLANTIC
PUBLISHERS & DISTRIBUTORS (P) LTD

Published by
ATLANTIC
PUBLISHERS & DISTRIBUTORS (P) LTD
7/22, Ansari Road, Darya Ganj,
New Delhi-110002
Phones : +91-11-40775252, 23273880, 23275880, 23280451
Fax : +91-11-23285873
Web : www.atlanticbooks.com
E-mail : info@atlanticbooks.com

Branch Office
5, Nallathambi Street, Wallajah Road,
Chennai-600002
Phones : +91-44-64611085, 32413319
E-mail : chennai@atlanticbooks.com

ISBN 978-81-269-1324-4

Printed in India at Glorious Printers, A-13, D.S.I.D.C, Jhilmil Industrial Area, Delhi-110095

Acknowledgements

We are highly indebted for visionary contribution to our management guru Dr. Ratan Sharma, IIM MBA, PhD., Director Bhartiya Vidya Bhawan's Usha Lakshmi Mittal Institute of Management, New Delhi. Special thanks are due to our parents and family members for their valuable support rendered generously all the time. We are obliged to Dr. Monir Ashraf Joffery Sir and J.S. Gill Sir for the insight and professional acumen they drilled into us that never faded.

We also put on record our sincere thanks to Sanjeev Sir, MD, Akums for his cooperation. We are thankful to our teachers and friends and team members of Atlantic Publishers and Distributors (P) Ltd. We extend our gratitude to Almighty God for giving us an opportunity to write this book.

Shahbaz
Anita

Preface

Human Resource Management is the nerve centre of any organisation. For the growth of a company both financial capital and human capital are equally important. Efficient and smooth functioning of these two is crucial for the progress of the company.

HRM is purely a knowledge-based management and it is vital for the success of any company. Now, most of the companies have their own full-fledged HR department but earlier this department was taken care of by marketing people only. This domain has really taken a paradigm shift in recent years in India and at global level as well. Here, many new terminologies, concepts and theories have been introduced to augment profitability of the organisation by improving efficiency of the employees.

HRM is closely linked to the corporate vision and goals. Human Resource provides essential support to attract, develop and retain talent, who will deliver better business outcomes. It derives sustainable business performance through competitive remuneration while satisfying the highest requirements of corporate governance. It helps to evolve a culture of mutual respect and inclusion, work actively to promote diversity of employees at all levels and finally manage the integrity. Effective Human Resource planning gives optimal productivity in terms of timeliness and quality of deliverables.

The book *Human Resource Management* offers an insight into a highly competitive professional environment of HRM today and in days to come. It aims at accomplishing three objectives: (1) to provide updated Human Resource terminologies, theories and concepts; (2) to analyze decision alternatives and criteria in these areas; and (3) to inform about real world situation of HR profession and its industry trend.

The book is loaded with current HR terminologies, concepts and theories which have been presented in easy-to-understand language. It attempts to solve most of HR related queries. It provides guidelines and formats as a ready assistance. This book will surely improve readers' efficiency level in Human Resource Management and build confidence in pursuing their professional career. Undoubtedly, the book will serve as a manual in day-to-day HR practices.

The book will be highly useful to the students, teachers and researchers of management. It will also find favour with the management professionals, business executives, entrepreneurs and HR managers working in various organisations in public as well as private sector.

Shahbaz
Anita

Contents

1

New Horizon in HRM

Why People Join HR Profession?

Only five years back from now specialization in HR was not so demanding because every company was used to appoint one HR people or marketing manager was taking extra HR responsibility. Like every profession HR domain has got tremendous facelift and in present scenario there are lots of jobs with lucrative salary packages. Second point which obviously comes to every professional that HR duty is very flexible and it requires only 8 hours. Most of the companies offering 5-day working as well. There is no target sort of things linked to this profession and this is totally an office job. Most of the females join this profession because they want to work and this is the only "decent job" in corporate world which, gives them respect and dignity. They don't want to join "field jobs" (Marketing). This is the only profession where time suits them...as per the family needs and restrictions. What more you need, you are getting good salary; flexible office timing and you are taking care of your family as per your plan and desire.

What Others Think about This Profession?

Those who are not working they still have so many myths about this profession. They think that this is a very easy going job and doesn't require MBA qualification. Even a graduate can do this job. Oh ho HR job is that Na...which involves filling and maintaining so many forms, and settling the claims. These days HR is a synonym of recruitment. Tell anybody that you are in HR and they will reply, "Oh, ok so you are a recruiter". But they have underrated HR job. It is because HR responsibility was taken by simply marketing people and accounting people. Marketing people was also involved in conducting interview, manpower planning and recruitment and preparation of salary was covered by accounts fellow.

Old days and bad days for HR professionals have gone and now HR people have got a paradigm shift in terms of job responsibility, job opening, salary package and profit generation for the organization. Now retention of employee is one of the biggest problems for small and medium size companies. It is directly linked with the globalization and boom in jobs market especially due to lots of job opening into banking sectors, life insurance sectors, call centers, telecommunication sectors and many more sectors.

Image of HR Profession in Society

Image of HR profession in the public or in the corporate world is very good and we are really doing much to improve the same. Frankly speaking HR professionals have the top corporate secrets and much more associated with the organization in comparision with the other employees. I feel sad when people ask queries like: What is the difference between HRM and HRD? What is the concept of CTC? What is the difference between Offer-Letter and Appointment-Letter? How much amount should be deducted for P.F. and E.S.I. from salary? How many leaves we should give to our employees? How to calculate attrition rate or rate per hire? What components of salary are taxable? And many more questions that play a pivotal role and that are directly linked with image of HR professionals.

Why Should You Join HR Profession?

There are top ten reasons why should you join HR profession as a career which are summarized as follows:

1. It is not necessary that you should have third eyes like "Chankaya"; clever like "Birbal" and visionary like Lord Krishna (A mythological character), but you should have sharp eyes for recognizing the talent,

talent identification, talent management and talent development.

2. You should be an excellent motivator and can motivate any person to get best out of him in a stipulated time period.
3. You should have a talent to motivate and inspire a non-performer in such a way that over a period of time that person gets counted in the high-performers in your organization and starts getting rewards for his performance.
4. You are great in crisis management. If there is any incident or accident in the organization; if there is any rumour in the organization or any crisis...you can ensure that a minimum possible damage is caused... keeping in mind the interests of the organization and its people but remember one thing, decision should always be in favour of the organization.
5. You have to rule on emotion of the employees and always try to show them achievable dream plan.
6. You should design career map linked with performance, attitude, skills and knowledge.
7. You don't think from your heart and understand the way people think.
8. You are a problem solver and solve both personal and professional problems of employee so that they can concentrate more on assigned job.
9. It is important to note that when you are hiring people be smiling, talk less and listen more but when you are firing don't let them explain, talk more, don't listen and try to change your face with more aggression.
10. Be caring, smiling but don't be sharing with other employees.

Outlook of Global HR Industry

In the globalized era, organizations have realized that the need of the hour is to have skilled, well-trained and highly motivated staff to help the growth of the company.

Organizations invest time and money in the welfare and benefit of the employees because they see merit in such activities. All this and more has led this part of an organization's activity to be called Human Resource Management.

The human resource marketplace is a highly competitive and fragmented industry that is poised for enormous growth in the next 10 years as companies and countries around the world invest in their human resources infrastructure.

The human capital marketplace is a multi-hundred billion dollar industry encompassing tens of thousands of suppliers selling hundreds of different products and services including recruitment and staffing, employee benefits, payroll, training and development and more. When you consider virtually every company purchases at least one HR product or service, you can appreciate the total size of this unique marketplace. In fact, in a given year an estimated $785 billion is spent on employee benefit products and services alone (Thomas Weisel Partners).

If you are a human resources supplier, aggressively targeting the human resources industry, today is critical to secure your portion of this marketplace.

Understanding the Human Resources Marketplace

Before you can claim your target market you should have an overall understanding of how the human resources industry is organized.

In general, the human resources function of an organization is responsible for all the practices and processes that impact the companies most important asset—their employees. And while admittedly there are many ways of categorizing the human resources industry, we believe the simplest and most logical method is to organize the industry within the following HR pillars:

Recruitment and Staffing: This includes searching for and hiring new employees and a wide variety of services from job boards to staffing and relocation firms, testing and assessment technologies, applicant tacking technologies, executive search/ placement firms, background checking services, etc. For the most part, this category ends when the employee is hired.

Compensation/Payroll: This includes everything from payroll processing companies to companies specializing in specific payroll and compensation services, compensation design, and salary statistics services.

Employee Benefits: This category encompasses a wide variety of employee benefit and related services from traditional health and welfare benefits to worksite/voluntary products, pharmacy benefit programs, benefits administration and communication software, third-party administrators, retirement plan services, and workers' compensation/disability insurance services.

Talent Management/Employee Relations: This category includes all the human resources services related to managing the individual once they are hired as an employee—appraisal, evaluation, recognition, promotion, retention, and succession planning services.

Training and Development: This category includes many products and services related to training and developing employees from instructor-based training to e-Learning solutions.

Compliance: This category includes all the services related to complying with and managing the various aspects of labor laws, labor relations, legislation, litigation, alternative dispute services. In addition to these specific human resources categories, it is also important to highlight services that are cross-functional in nature and relate to one or all the HR pillars:

Consulting Services: This cross-functional category includes the thousands of consulting firms that can help HR departments with one or all aspects of human resources management and process improvement.

HRIS/ERP/ATS Solutions: At one time, this might have been considered a separate pillar within HR but today, technology is integrated and impacts all aspects of HR from applicant tracking to e-Learning. The Internet and other technologies are fundamentally changing the human capital marketplace as companies strive to become more efficient.

Technology allows HR to automate processes and eliminate many of the more labor-intensive transactional and administrative processes that have burdened HR professionals for years.

Outsourcing: Any and all aspects of HR can be outsourced. According to research by Gartner, Inc., 80 per cent of companies now outsource at least one HR activity, and the number is swiftly growing. For this reason, we do not consider outsourcing as a functional pillar within HR, but rather cross-functional. Increasing numbers of organizations are turning to specialized firms to supplement various aspects of human resource management. While outsourcing makes sense for many reasons, the primary benefit is containment/reduction of costs of routine transactional and administrative work. Another key reason is the belief that a company should outsource all non-mission critical aspects of its business.

HR Managers and Specialists Nature of Work

Every organization wants to attract the most qualified employees and match them to jobs for which they are best suited. However, many enterprises are too large to permit close contact between top management and employees. Human resources, training, and labor relations managers and specialists provide this connection. In the past, these workers performed the administrative functions of an organization, such as handling employee benefits questions or recruiting, interviewing, and hiring new staff in accordance with policies established by top management. Today's human resources workers manage these tasks, but increasingly, they also consult with top executives regarding strategic planning. They have moved from behind-the-scenes staff work to leading the company in suggesting and changing policies.

In an effort to enhance morale and productivity, limit job turnover, and help organizations increase performance and improve business results, these workers also help their firms effectively use employee skills, provide training and development opportunities to improve those skills, and increase employees' satisfaction with their jobs and working conditions. Although some jobs in the human resources field require only limited contact with people outside the human resources office, dealing with people is an important part of the job.

There are many types of human resources, training, and labor relations managers and specialists. In a small organization, a *human resources generalist* may handle all aspects of human resources work, and thus require an extensive range of knowledge. The responsibilities of human resources generalists can vary widely, depending on their employer's needs.

In a large corporation, the *director of human resources* may supervise several departments, each headed by an experienced manager who most likely specializes in one human resources activity, such as employment and placement; compensation, and benefits; training and development; or labor relations. The director may report to a top human resources executive.

Employment and Placement. *Employment and placement managers* supervise the hiring and separation of employees. They also supervise employment, recruitment, and placement specialists, including recruitment specialists and employment interviewers. *Employment, recruitment and placement specialists* recruit and place workers.

Recruiters maintain contacts within the community and may travel considerably, often to college campuses, to search for promising job applicants. Recruiters screen, interview, and occasionally test applicants. They also may check references and extend job offers. These workers must be thoroughly familiar with the organization and its human resources policies in order to discuss wages, working conditions, and promotional opportunities with prospective employees. They also must stay informed about equal employment opportunity (EEO) and affirmative action guidelines and laws, such as the Americans with Disabilities Act.

Employment Interviewers—whose many job titles include human resources consultants, human resources development specialists, and human resources coordinators—help to match employers with qualified jobseekers. Similarly, employer relations representatives, who usually work in government agencies, maintain working relationships with local employers and promote the use of public employment programs and services.

Compensation, Benefits, and Job Analysis. Compensation, benefits, and job analysis specialists conduct compensation programs for employers and may specialize in specific areas such as pensions or position classifications. For example, job analysts, occasionally called position classifiers, collect and examine detailed information about job duties in order to prepare job descriptions. These descriptions explain the duties, training, and skills that each job requires. Whenever a large organization introduces a new job or reviews existing jobs, it calls upon the expert knowledge of the job analyst.

Occupational analysts conduct research, usually in large firms. They are concerned with occupational classification systems and study the effects of industry and occupational trends on worker relationships. They may serve as technical liaison between the firm and other firms, government, and labor unions.

Establishing and maintaining a firm's pay system is the principal job of the ***compensation manager***. Assisted by staff specialists, compensation managers devise ways to ensure fair and equitable pay rates. They may conduct surveys to see how their firm's rates compare with others, and they ensure that the firm's pay scale complies with changing laws and regulations. In addition, compensation managers often manage their firm's performance evaluation system, and they may design reward systems such as pay-for-performance plans.

Employee benefits managers and specialists manage the company's employee benefits program, notably its health insurance and pension plans. Expertise in designing and administering benefits programs continues to take on importance as employer-provided benefits account for a growing proportion of overall compensation costs, and as benefit plans increase in number and complexity. For example, pension benefits might include a 401K or thrift savings, profit-sharing, and stock ownership plans; health benefits might include long-term catastrophic illness insurance and dental insurance. Familiarity with health benefits is a top priority for employee benefits managers and specialists, as more firms struggle to cope with the rising cost of health care for employees and retirees. In addition to health insurance and pension coverage, some firms offer employees life and accidental death and dismemberment insurance, disability insurance, and relatively new benefits designed to meet the needs of a changing workforce, such as parental leave, child and elder care, long-term nursing home care insurance, employee assistance and wellness programs, and flexible benefits plans. Benefits managers must keep abreast of changing central and state regulations and legislation that may affect employee benefits.

Employee assistance plan managers, also called *employee welfare managers*, are responsible for a wide array of programs. These include occupational safety and health standards and practices; health promotion and physical fitness, medical examinations, and minor health treatment, such as first aid; plant security; publications; food service and recreation activities; carpooling and transportation programs, such as transit subsidies; employee suggestion systems; child care and elder care; and counseling services. Child care and elder care are increasingly significant because of growth in the number of dual-income households and the elderly population. Counseling may help employees deal with emotional disorders, alcoholism, or marital, family, consumer, legal, and financial problems. Some employers offer career counseling as well. In large firms, certain programs, such as those dealing with security and safety, may be in separate departments headed by other managers.

Training and Development. *Training and development managers and specialists* conduct and supervise training and development programs for employees. Increasingly, management recognizes that training offers a way of developing skills, enhancing productivity and quality of work, and building worker loyalty to the firm, and most importantly, increasing individual and organizational performance to achieve business results. Training is widely accepted as an employee benefit and a method of improving employee morale, and enhancing employee skills has become a business imperative. Increasingly, managers and leaders realize that the key to business growth and success is through developing the skills and knowledge of its workforce.

Other factors involved in determining whether training is needed include the complexity of the work environment, the rapid pace of organizational and technological change, and the growing number of jobs in fields that constantly generate new knowledge, and thus, require new skills. In addition, advances in learning theory have provided insights into how adults learn, and how training can be organized most effectively for them.

Training managers provide worker training either in the classroom or onsite. This includes setting up teaching materials prior to the class, involving the class, and issuing completion certificates at the end of the class. They have the responsibility for the entire learning process, and its environment, to ensure that the course meets its objectives and is measured and evaluated to understand how learning impacts business results.

Training specialists plan, organize, and direct a wide range of training activities. Trainers respond to corporate and worker service requests. They consult with onsite supervisors regarding available performance improvement services and conduct orientation sessions and arrange on-the-job training for new employees. They help all employees maintain and improve their job skills, and possibly prepare for jobs requiring greater skill. They help supervisors improve their interpersonal skills in order to deal effectively with employees. They may set up individualized training plans to strengthen an employee's existing skills or teach new ones. Training specialists in some companies set up leadership or executive development programs among employees in lower level positions. These programs are designed to develop leaders, or "groom" them, to replace those leaving the organization and as part of a succession plan. Trainers also lead programs to assist employees with job transitions as a result of mergers and acquisitions, as well as technological changes. In government-supported training programs, training specialists function as case managers. They first assess the training needs of clients and then guide them through the most appropriate training method. After training, clients may either be referred to employer relations representatives or receive job placement assistance.

Planning and program development is an essential part of the training specialist's job. In order to identify and assess training needs within the firm, trainers may confer with managers and supervisors or conduct surveys. They also evaluate training effectiveness to ensure that the training employees receive helps the organization meet its strategic business goals and achieve results.

Depending on the size, goals, and nature of the organization, trainers may differ considerably in their responsibilities and in the methods they use. Training methods include on-the-job training; operating schools that duplicate shop conditions for trainees prior to putting them on the shop floor; apprenticeship training; classroom training; and electronic learning, which may involve interactive Internet-based training, multimedia programs, distance learning, satellite training, other computer-aided instructional technologies, videos, simulators, conferences, and workshops.

Employee Relations. An organization's *director of industrial relations* forms labor policy, oversees industrial labor relations, negotiates collective bargaining agreements, and coordinates grievance procedures to handle complaints resulting from management disputes with unionized employees. The director of industrial relations also advises and collaborates with the director of human resources, other managers, and members of their staff, because all aspects of human resources policy—such as wages, benefits, pensions, and work practices—may be involved in drawing up a new or revised union contract.

Labor relations managers and their staff implement industrial labor relations programs. Labor relations specialists prepare information for management to use during collective bargaining agreement negotiations, a process that requires the specialist to be familiar with economic and wage data and to have extensive knowledge of labor law and collective bargaining trends. The labor relations staff interprets and administers the contract with respect to grievances, wages and salaries, employee welfare, health care, pensions, union and management practices, and other contractual stipulations. As union membership continues to decline in most industries, industrial relations personnel are working more often with employees who are not members of a labor union.

Dispute resolution—attaining tacit or contractual agreements—has become increasingly significant as parties to a dispute attempt to avoid costly litigation, strikes, or other disruptions. Dispute resolution also has become more complex, involving employees, management, unions, other firms, and government agencies. Specialists involved in dispute resolution must be highly knowledgeable and experienced, and often report to the director of industrial relations. *Conciliators*, or *mediators*, advise and counsel labor and management to prevent and, when necessary, resolve disputes over labor agreements or other labor relations issues. *Arbitrators,* occasionally called umpires or referees, decide disputes that bind both labor and management to specific terms and conditions of labor contracts. Labor relations specialists who work for unions perform many of the same functions on behalf of the union and its members.

EEO *officers, representatives,* or *affirmative action coordinators* handle EEO matters in large organizations. They investigate and resolve EEO grievances, examine corporate practices for possible violations, and compile and submit EEO statistical reports.

Other emerging specialties in human resources include *international human resources managers*, who handle human resources issues related to a company's foreign operations; and *human resources information system specialists*, who develop and apply computer programs to process human resources information, match job seekers with job openings, and handle other human resources matters.

Work environment. Human resources work usually takes place in clean, pleasant, and comfortable office settings. Arbitrators and mediators may work out of their homes.

Although most human resources, training, and labor relations managers and specialists work in the office, some travel extensively. For example, recruiters regularly attend professional meetings and visit college campuses to interview prospective employees; arbitrators and mediators often must travel to the site chosen for negotiations.

Many human resources, training, and labor relations managers and specialists work a standard 35- to 40-hour week. However, longer hours might be necessary for some workers—for example, labor relations managers and specialists, arbitrators, and mediators—when contract agreements are being prepared and negotiated.

Training, Other Qualifications, and Advancement

The educational backgrounds of human resources, training, and labor relations managers and specialists vary considerably, reflecting the diversity of duties and levels of responsibility. In filling entry-level jobs, many employers seek college graduates who have majored in human resources, human resources administration, or industrial and labor relations. Other employers look for college graduates with a technical or business background or a well-rounded liberal arts education.

Education and training. Many colleges and universities have programs leading to a degree in personnel, human resources, or labor relations. Some offer degree programs in human resources administration or human resources management, training and development, or compensation and benefits. Depending on the school, courses leading to a career in human resources management may be found in departments of business administration, education, instructional technology, organizational development, human services, communication, or public administration, or within a separate human resources institution or department.

Because an interdisciplinary background is appropriate in this field, a combination of courses in the social sciences, business, and behavioral sciences is useful. Some jobs may require a more technical or specialized background in engineering, science, finance, or law, for example. Most prospective human resources specialists should take courses in compensation, recruitment, training and development, and performance appraisal, as well as courses in principles of management, organizational structure, and industrial psychology. Other relevant courses include business administration, public administration, psychology, sociology, political science, economics, and statistics. Courses in labor law, collective bargaining, labor economics, labor history, and industrial psychology also provide a valuable background for the prospective labor relations specialist. As in many other fields, knowledge of computers and information systems also is useful.

An advanced degree is increasingly important for some jobs. Many labor relations jobs require graduate study in industrial or labor relations. A strong background in industrial relations and law is highly desirable for contract negotiators, mediators, and arbitrators; in fact, many people in these specialties are lawyers. A background in law also is desirable for employee benefits managers and others who must interpret the growing number of laws and regulations. A master's degree in human resources, labor relations, or in business administration with a concentration in human resources management is highly recommended for those seeking general and top management positions.

The duties given to entry-level workers will vary, depending on whether the new workers have a degree in human resource management, have completed an internship, or have some other type of human resources-related experience. Entry-level employees commonly learn the profession by performing administrative duties—helping to enter data into computer systems, compiling employee handbooks, researching information for a supervisor, or answering the phone and handling routine questions. Entry-level workers often enter formal or on-the-job training programs in which they learn how to classify jobs, interview applicants, or administer employee benefits. They then are assigned to specific areas in the human resources department to gain experience. Later, they may advance to a managerial position, supervising a major element of the human resources program—compensation or training, for example.

Other qualifications. Previous experience is an asset for many specialties in the human resources field, and is essential for more advanced positions, including managers, arbitrators, and mediators. Many employers prefer entry-level workers who have gained some experience through an internship or work-study program while in school. Human resources administration and human resources development require the ability to work with individuals as well as a commitment to organizational goals. This field also demands other skills that people may develop elsewhere—using computers, selling, teaching, supervising, and volunteering, among others. The field offers clerical workers opportunities for advancement to professional positions. Responsible positions occasionally are filled by experienced individuals from other fields, including business, government, education, social services administration, and the military.

The human resources field demands a range of personal qualities and skills. Human resources, training, and labor relations managers and specialists must speak and write effectively. The growing diversity of the workforce requires that they work with or supervise people with various cultural backgrounds, levels of education, and experience. They must be able to cope with conflicting points of view, function under pressure, and demonstrate discretion, integrity, fair-mindedness, and a persuasive, congenial personality.

Certification and advancement. Most organizations specializing in human resources offer classes intended to enhance the skills of their members. Some organizations offer certification programs, which are signs of competence and credibility and can enhance one's advancement opportunities. For example, the International Foundation of Employee Benefit

Plans confers a designation in three distinct areas of specialization—group benefit, retirement, and compensation—to persons who complete a series of college-level courses and pass exams. Candidates can earn a designation in each of the specialty tracks and, simultaneously, receive credit toward becoming a Certified Employee Benefits Specialist (CEBS). The American Society for Training and Development (ASTD) Certification Institute offers professional certification in the learning and performance field. Addressing nine areas of expertise, it requires passing a knowledge-based exam and successful work experience. In addition, ASTD offers 16 short-term certificate and workshop programs covering a broad range of professional training and development topics. The Society for Human Resource Management offers two levels of certification, including the Professional in Human Resources (PHR) and the Senior Professional in Human Resources (SPHR). Additionally, the organization offers the Global Professional in Human Resources for those with international and cross-border responsibilities and the California Certification in Human Resources for those who plan to work in the State and are unfamiliar with California's labor and human resource laws. All designations require experience and a passing score on a comprehensive exam. World at Work Society of Certified Professionals offers four levels of designations in the areas of compensation, benefits, work life, and total rewards management practices. Through the Society, candidates can obtain the designation of Certified Compensation Professional (CCP), Certified Benefits Professional (CBP), Global Remuneration Professional (GRP), and Work-Life Certified Professional (WLCP).

Exceptional human resources workers may be promoted to director of human resources or industrial relations, which can eventually lead to a top managerial or executive position. Others may join a consulting or outsourcing firm or open their own business. A Ph.D. is an asset for teaching, writing, or consulting work. Other matters related to the Nation's public employees:

Job Outlook. Employment of human resources, training, and labor relations managers and specialists is expected to grow faster than the average for all occupations. College graduates who have earned certification should have the best job opportunities.

Employment change. Overall employment is projected to grow by 17 per cent between 2006 and 2016, faster than the average for all occupations. Legislation and court rulings setting standards in various areas—occupational safety and health, equal employment opportunity, wages, health care, pensions, and family leave, among others—will increase demand for human resources, training, and labor relations experts. Rising health care costs should continue to spur demand for specialists to develop creative compensation and benefits packages that firms can offer prospective employees.

Employment of labor relations staff, including arbitrators and mediators, should grow as firms become more involved in labor relations and attempt to resolve potentially costly labor-management disputes out of court. Additional job growth may stem from increasing demand for specialists in international human resources management and human resources information systems.

Job growth could be limited by the widespread use of computerized human resources information systems that make workers more productive. Like other workers, employment of human resources, training, and labor relations managers and specialists, particularly in larger firms, may be adversely affected by corporate downsizing, restructuring, and mergers and acquisitions.

Demand may be particularly strong for certain specialists. For example, employers are expected to devote greater resources to job-specific training programs in response to the increasing complexity of many jobs and technological advances that can leave employees with obsolete skills. Additionally, as highly trained and skilled baby boomers retire, there should be strong demand for training and development specialists to impart needed skills to their replacements. In addition, increasing efforts throughout industry to recruit and retain quality employees should create many jobs for employment, recruitment, and placement specialists.

Among industries, firms involved in management, consulting, and employment services should offer many job opportunities, as businesses increasingly contract out human resources functions or hire human resources specialists on a temporary basis in order to deal with the increasing cost and complexity of training and development programs. Demand for specialists also should increase in outsourcing firms that develop and administer complex employee benefits and compensation packages for other organizations.

Job prospects. College graduates who have earned certification should have the best job opportunities. Graduates with a bachelor's degree in human resources, human resources administration, or industrial and labor relations should be in demand; those with a technical or business background or a well-rounded liberal arts education also should find opportunities. Demand for human resources, training, and labor relations managers and specialists is governed by the staffing needs of the firms for which they work. A rapidly expanding business is likely to hire additional human resources workers—either as permanent employees or consultants—while a business that has experienced a merger or a reduction in its workforce will require fewer of these workers. Also, as human resources management becomes increasingly important to the success of an organization, some small and medium-size businesses that do not have a human resources department may assign employees various human resources duties together with other unrelated responsibilities.

In addition to human resources management and specialist jobs created over the 2006-16 projection period, many job openings will arise from the need to replace workers who transfer to other occupations, retire, or leave the labor force for other reasons.

Working Conditions. HR staff members generally work in functional, pleasant offices. HR workers for large corporations frequently travel within the country to recruit. A bonus for those working for international companies is the opportunity to travel outside the country.

Job Opportunities. Job opportunities will occur as companies place greater emphasis on quality and productivity and hire HR trainers to meet training and development needs. Specialists will also be needed to deal with the increasing complexity of legal requirements, court rulings and new legislation. Those seeking entry level and generalist HR positions are likely to face competition because of the large number of qualified college graduates.

Entrance Requirements and Training. Entry-level professional positions in Human Resources normally require a four year college degree. The preferred degree could vary from business administration with a human resources specialization to industrial relations or sociology. Some employers may look for a well-rounded background and choose liberal arts graduates. Certain jobs may also require additional background in such fields as engineering, finance, health or law. Graduate work is becoming increasingly important for specialists in labor relations.

Advancement. Human resources workers usually rotate to different areas within the department to broaden their background and learn more about other specialties. HR specialists also have the opportunity to advance to managerial ranks such as a department supervisor or director. Some HR Specialists work as consultants or open their own business.

Finding the Job. College students would be well advised to join a student association of a human resources professional organization to learn more about the field and network with HR professionals. Such contacts provide job seekers with job leads. Students should also register with their college placement office and read classified ads. Job seekers can apply directly to government and private agencies and register with the Employment Development Department's Workforce Services Offices.

What do You do in a Human Resources Specialist Career?

A human resources specialist in training and development leads a new employee orientation. A human resources specialist is responsible for a specific type of human resources work in an organization. HR specialists are far more common in large companies than in small ones, and also frequently work in HR consulting firms, such as Mercer, Buck and Aon.

A human resources specialist's work depends upon the specialty, though there is often some amount of overlap. Human resources managers also frequently transfer between specialist and generalists roles depending on their interests, exposure and place of work. The Bureau of Labor Statistics lists five human resources specialties:

Employment and Recruiting: Work with hiring manager to develop ideal candidate criteria, collaborate with private headhunters and peruse job boards to find employees, attract qualified employees and match them to jobs, coordinate relocation.

Labor and Employee Relations: Serve as liaisons between employees and management, negotiate with unions over contracts and grievances, resolve disputes, direct employee health and safety programs.

Training and Development: Organize and conduct new employee orientation, provide ongoing education for staff, determine what training is necessary, design materials and workshops for presentations.

Job Analysis: Identify and document job duties and requirements and their relative importance, use data to develop training materials and methods, determine compensation, develop job titles, and descriptions and application materials.

Benefits and Compensation: Prepare benefits and salary packages, ensure benefits fit the needs of employees, design performance reviews, establish bonus and stock options plans, develop pay structure, serve as liaisons between company, employees, and insurance carriers.

A bachelor's degree in human resources includes courses that will prepare you for a general career in human resources, but as the demand for HR resources specialists has grown, many universities have begun to offer more focused programs of study. Subsequently, higher level HR specialist positions now generally require post-graduate education within the specialty. To begin working towards a human resources specialist career, find a human resources bachelor's, master's or MBA degree.

Human Resources Specialist Career Path

Entry Level: Roles entail benefits specialist, placement specialist, negotiations specialist. Qualification required is degree or diploma in MBA with HR and experience should be 0-4 years. Course work should tie in to specialty: statistics and economics for benefits, social and behavioral sciences for negotiations. Salary varies according to specialty and the present salary package in India is INR-20,000-50,000 and in international market it ranges in between $21,000-45,000.

Mid Level: Roles include compensation manager, hiring manager, labor relations manager, training supervisor. Qualification required is HR or general business masters or MBA, with associated post-graduate specialty in training, excellent people skills & excellent communication skills. Rest all entry-level requirements along with 5-10 years. Current salary package in India is INR-50,000-1,00,000 and in international market it ranges in between $49,000-90,000

Senior Level: Major roles or designations are director of employee benefits, employee relations director, director of human resources development. All mid-level requirements with post-graduate specialty course work, multi-faceted, creative problem solving skills and confident decision maker. Current salary package in India is INR-1,00,000-2,00,000 and in international market it ranges in between $90,000-120,000.

Salary depends strongly on the type of organization as well as the HR specialty. The highest paying HR specialty, according to Bureau of Labor Statistics, is training and development, and the lowest paying is employment and recruiting. It is noteworthy, salary package also depends on your involvement and performance. Up to entry level you behave like an employee but from mid level you start to behave like an employer and finally at senior level your thinking will match with employer and your thinking, behavior and attitude will be similar to your employer. If you gradually change positively like this then you will decide your salary package without any hesitation. Wipro has recently fired one of his executive who was getting CTC INR-8,0000000 and he was highest paid executive in India. In senior level, you should perform with six sigma quality (Error free) and organizational benefits should be above all things in this world.

15 Steps of HR Practices

Save money, reduce turnover and improve morale by re-examining these commonly overlooked, but detrimental practices.

Someone said it's a lot cheaper to learn from the mistakes of others. The 15 HR practices that follow are in place at a surprising number of organizations—make sure yours isn't one of them.

1. *Less Money When on Vacation*

Some companies highlight vacation as earned time off, but then pay vacation time at the day rate. Therefore, employees who receive a shift differential (normally work the second or third shift) receive less money. The practice is legal—but is it worth the savings? Remember, vacation is a benefit.

2. *Vacation Pay After Discharge*

Most companies do not view earned, unused vacation and personal time as time owed upon termination. However, companies often pay for these hours if the employee resigns in good standing.

What is surprising is the number of companies that pay vacation and personal hours to employees who are discharged for cause.

3. *New Employees Need not Apply*

Organizations often brag about their practice of promoting from within. So does it make sense to prohibit certain groups from this benefit, for example, probationary employees, or those who have worked less than one year? Managers respond by explaining the negative impact a transfer will have on their departments. I question the signal the prohibition gives to existing employees. Would it be better for an employee to quit and apply for the other position?

4. *Free Work that isn't*

What manager would say no to a non-exempt employee who is willing to work extra hours for free? Every manager should. The problem is that the employer is obligated by the federal Fair Labor Standards Act to pay for the time, even if overtime is not authorized. The employee's willingness to forgo pay does not exempt the employer from payment requirements.

5. *Confusing Discipline Categories*

Some companies try to help managers by categorizing infractions and then prescribing appropriate disciplinary action. What is intended to be helpful ends up causing more confusion. For example, one company defined infractions as critical, major, severe and minor. The company viewed sexual harassment as a critical offense with discharge prescribed for the first offense. In contrast, use of abusive language and breach of professional ethics were listed as severe offenses that warranted a written warning for the first offense. Both may be correct. However, depending on the facts, a sexual harassment case may justify only a written warning, and breach of professional ethics or use of abusive language could warrant more than a written warning. Unfortunately, company guidelines do not allow for such flexibility.

It's almost impossible to make the "art" of labor relations into an exact "science". There are too many variables to be considered. Simply classifying offenses and prescribing disciplinary action will only guarantee additional confusion.

6. *Discipline that Reduces Morale*

A practice of progressive discipline by infraction, instead of cumulative discipline regardless of infraction, can lead to morale problems. An employee could be suspended for absenteeism, and later receive a written warning (instead of discharge) for a different type of violation (work performance, for example). This practice places an undue burden on managers, and allows violators of company policies considerable latitude. Is it any wonder morale suffers when disciplinary action is not cumulative?

7. *Get Paid, then Work*

Many companies advance payment of paid time off—vacation, personal and sick time—before it is earned. These same companies say employees must repay time owed if they leave before earning the advanced time. What happens if the employee does not fully repay the debt? Many companies write off the time. Even if the employee repays the full amount, the company lent the money interest free.

8. *Not a Necessary Cost*

Unemployment compensation is often viewed as a "cost of doing business". It's like FICA tax—you just have to pay it. Not so! Even if your state awards a claimant payment, do not overlook the benefit of appealing the case by requesting a hearing—you do not necessarily need a lawyer to represent you.

9. *Managers with Hourly Mind-set*

Going from hourly to exempt status is like a leap of faith. Changing how you view your paycheck is a major mind stretch. It's no longer "What is my hourly rate" but "What is my salary?" Who cares how many "extra" hours you work—it comes with the territory. Failure to change mind-set will impede a new manager's success. Managers shouldn't record extra hours worked as "comp" time on their time cards, nor should managers be given a day off with pay after they accumulated eight of these "comp" hours. This practice sends a mixed signal.

10. *Information Leaks*

It's an occupational hazard. If you work in HR, then you may be a suspect if "sensitive" information is leaked. HR staff might leak information; however, there is another way leaks could occur. If you use volunteers to file and do other work that enables them to see salaries and related information, add them to your "suspect" list.

11. *Guaranteed Extra Work*

Most employers process paperwork before an employee terminates. However, some employers handle all processing by mail. If you fall into the latter category, you will spend an inordinate amount of time tracking down eligible employees.

12. *No Bids for Benefits*

Complacency breeds expensive benefits. Especially if you have one agent of record for your group insurance plans. You might be pleasantly surprised at the amount of savings you'll realize by obtaining competitive bids. Competition has a way of lowering costs, or at least ensuring you are receiving the best buy possible.

13. *Free Benefits that Cost You*

Does this sound familiar? The insurance company offers a "free" benefit to your organization. They will do all the work; HR only has to distribute information and allow employees to pay for the benefit through payroll deduction.

I'm not against expanding benefits; however, even "free" benefits cost time and money. By distributing information, HR endorses the product. Who will answer employee questions if the vendor isn't responsive? What happens if the employee is dissatisfied with the service or product? Finally, there is a payroll cost. If you are offered a "free" benefit, you may want to request a processing fee from the insurance company for offering their service or product.

14. *Keep the Overpayment*

It's common for organizations to reimburse employees for the underpayments. Would you believe some companies are reluctant to request payment if an employee was overpaid?

15. *Requiring a Doctor's Note*

Many organizations require a doctor's note to verify legitimacy of an illness if an employee is out for more than three work days. Some organizations require a doctor's note for every illness, or if they suspect an employee is abusing time. They believe they "got" the abuser. Think again.

A doctor's note policy may give the abuser a legitimate out if he or she can easily obtain a note. Also, you may be unfair to good attenders if you require a doctor's note for all illnesses. Using a doctor's note as part of a disciplinary process could also involve you in a discrimination complaint. Controlling absenteeism is not as simple as a "doctor's note".

2

Basic Concept of HRM

Evolution of HRM

The human resource function and human resource profession have undergone tremendous change over the past 5-10 years world over. Many years ago, large organizations looked to the "Personnel Department", mostly to manage the paperwork around hiring and paying people.

Now human resource department has taken a paradigm shift. In medium to large size companies' human resource department is well equipped with specialized managers for example, HR manager-generalized, Recruitment manager, Performance manager, Human resource development manager, Trainer and Counselor, etc. More recently, organizations consider the "HR Department" as playing a major role in staffing, training and helping to manage people so that people and the organization are performing at maximum capability in a highly fulfilling manner.

Human resource (or personnel) management, in the sense of getting things done through people, is an essential part of every manager's responsibilities, but many organizations find it advantageous to establish a specialist division to provide an expert service dedicated to ensuring that the human resource function is performed efficiently.

"People are our most valuable asset" is a cliché which no member of any senior management team would disagree with. Yet, the reality for many organizations is that their people remain under-valued, under-trained and under-utilized.

The rate of change facing organizations has never been greater and organizations must absorb and manage change at a much faster rate than in the past. In order to implement a successful business strategy to face this challenge, organizations, large or small, must ensure that they have the right people capable of delivering the strategy.

The market place for talented, skilled people is competitive and expensive. Taking on new staff can be disruptive to existing employees. Also, it takes time to develop 'cultural awareness', product/process/organization knowledge and experience for new staff members.

As organizations vary in size, aims, functions, complexity, construction, the physical nature of their product, and appeal as employers, so do the contributions of human resource management. But, in most the ultimate aim of the function is to: "ensure that at all times the business is correctly staffed by the right number of people with the skills relevant to the business needs", that is, neither overstaffed nor understaffed in total or in respect of any one discipline or work grade.

Human Resource Management (HRM)/Human Resource Development (HRD) is a center nerve to any organization. For the establishment of a company we require two major capital—financial capital and human capital. Circulation of both the capital should be maintained regularly without fail like blood in our body, and then only a company will hugely progress beyond the expectation.

Human Resources Management is actively linked to the corporate vision and goals. The HR approach is through Total Employee Development Focus. While achieving the heights of business and customer satisfaction, quality of management, innovativeness, employee talent dynamism, cost saving and social responsibility are proving to be as important as effective operations.

Human Resource provides essential support to attract, develop and retain talent, who will deliver sustainable business outcomes. To achieve these outcomes we recruit and develop people to deliver sustainable business results. Optimise individual, team and organizational performance through appropriate consultation, use of proven tools, techniques and processes. Provide competitive remuneration that drives sustainable business performance while satisfying the highest requirements of corporate governance and reporting. Enable a culture of mutual respect and inclusion, work activity to promote diversity of employees at all levels and finally manage the integrity.

Vision Building and Innovation

One of the powerful tools of taking the organization in leaps and bounds, Vision Building is considered to be of top relevance for today's dynamic organization. It should be compulsory to engage executives across all levels, including shop-floor and frontline executives to the senior strategy makers of the organization in fruitful Vision-Building exercise and Idea sharing for business growth.

Structuring/Restructuring of the Organization

Continuous review and revamping at appropriate junctures is the key for keeping away from imbalances in organizational structure leading to inefficiency and delays. It should be renewed internally the need for restructuring and also engaging outside expertise on occasional basis for keeping a balanced and efficient structure.

Systems Development and Managing Change

HRM has a very crucial role in development and implementation of systems in an organization. It can be a powerful catalyst in managing change in the organization. Company should enter into Enterprise Resource Planning (ERP) by way of networking all its major functional areas and will be drastically reducing the manual administrative work.

Succession and Career Planning

Implementing a succession plan is important to the health of an organization as it ensures availability of future leaders at key positions and effective co-ordination. It also allows for creative development of personnel to "fit" within the organization at the middle and upper management level. A meticulous Succession Planning for the top 3-4 layers of the organization is worked out and reviewed at regular intervals for implementation.

Employee Development

Organizations that support employee development are better able to attract and retain talented people, especially in this era where employability has taken priority over the old promise of secure employment. The following HRD sub-systems should very well established.

Training and Development

A systematic top down approach is being followed in Training & Development activities, which are very aptly designed for all levels and are being carried out on a continuous basis. Modular Training concept has been introduced at all levels including managers and workmen, designed to provide uniform inputs at different employee levels leading to positive change in organizational performance, overall quality of manpower and organizational culture.

Employee Involvement and Commitment

Continuous efforts for encouraging employee involvement at different levels as the following lead to enhanced commitment of workforce at OD Interventions like Quality Circles, Suggestion Scheme, TQM, Best employee Awards, etc.

Performance linked Compensation (Profit Sharing).

Best Employee Retention.

Counseling Services for Employees.

Manpower Audit

(Rightsizing/Redeployment/Retraining Needs/Recruitment)

In view of the competitive environment which is forcing organizations all over the world to review their structures and manpower strength, systematic internal review is needed for restructuring for maintaining a balanced and efficient structure. Manpower redeployment and retraining is given priority over possibilities of retrenchment.

Study of Present Status of Manpower Allocation in various Departments.

Analytical study of Optimum Manpower in various Departments.

Identification of Redeployable manpower Retraining Scheme for employees identified for redeployment Developing Scheme for non-redeployable employees (VRS etc.).

Commercialization of HRM

HR manager should be commercially expert to make a decision boldly. Designing, developing and implementing need based HR policy is our strength.

The HRM function includes a variety of activities, and key among them is deciding what staffing needs you have and whether to use independent contractors or hire employees to fill these needs, recruiting and training the best employees, ensuring they are high performers, dealing with performance issues, and ensuring your personnel and management practices conform to various regulations. Activities also include managing your approach to employee benefits and compensation, employee records and personnel policies. Usually small businesses (for-profit or nonprofit) have to carry out these activities themselves because they can't yet afford part or full-time help. However, they should always ensure that employees have—and are aware of—personnel policies which conform to current regulations. These policies are often in the form of employee manuals, which all employees have.

It is very important to understand the primary and secondary functions of HRM. It is more important to know that HRD is a part of HRM, but now HR is broadly divided into HRM and HRD. The primary function of HRM includes HR planning, Staffing (recruitment and selection), equal employment opportunity, compensation and benefits, employee and labour relations, health, safety, and security, HRD. Performance management and job specification is the secondary management function.

Functional Overview of HRM

These sets of resources are offered to promote thought, stimulate discussion, diagnose the organizational environment and develop a sound human resource management strategy for your organization. The four major functions of HRM are categorized as follows:

1. Manpower Planning

The penalties for not being correctly staffed are costly. Understaffing loses the business economies of scale and specialization, orders, customers and profits. Overstaffing is wasteful and expensive, if sustained, and it is costly to eliminate because of modern legislation in respect of redundancy payments, consultation, minimum periods of notice, etc.

Very importantly, overstaffing reduces the competitive efficiency of the business. Staffing level planning requires that an assessment of present and future needs of the organization be compared with present resources and future predicted resources. Appropriate steps then be planned to bring demand and supply into balance.

Thus, the first step is to take a 'satellite picture' of the existing workforce profile (numbers, skills, age, flexibility, sex, experience, forecast capabilities, character, potential, etc. of existing employees) and then to adjust this for 1, 3 and 10 years ahead by amendments for normal turnover, planned staff movements, retirements, etc. in line with the business plan for the corresponding time frames.

The result should be a series of crude supply situations as would be the outcome of present planning if left unmodified. (This, clearly, requires a great deal of information accretion, classification and statistical analysis as a subsidiary aspect of personnel management.)

What future demands will be is only influenced in part by the forecast of the personnel manager, whose main task may well be to scrutinize and modify the crude predictions of other managers. Future staffing needs will derive from:

- Sales and production forecasts.
- The effects of technological change on task needs.
- Variations in the efficiency, productivity, flexibility of labor as a result of training, work study, organizational change, new motivations, etc.

- Changes in employment practices (e.g. use of subcontractors or agency staffs, hiring-off tasks, buying in, substitution, etc.).
- Variations, which respond to new legislation, e.g. payroll taxes or their abolition, new health and safety requirements.
- Changes in Government policies (investment incentives, regional or trade grants, etc.).

What should emerge from this 'blue sky gazing' is a 'thought out' and logical staffing demand schedule for varying dates in the future which can then be compared with the crude supply schedules. The comparisons will then indicate what steps must be taken to achieve a balance.

That, in turn, will involve the further planning of such recruitment, training, retraining, labor reductions (early retirement/redundancy) or changes in workforce utilization as will bring supply and demand into equilibrium, not just as a one-off but as a continuing workforce planning exercise the inputs to which will need constant varying to reflect 'actual' as against predicted experience on the supply side and changes in production actually achieved as against forecast on the demand side.

2. Recruitment and Selection of Employees

Recruitment of staff should be preceded by:

An analysis of the job to be done (i.e. an analytical study of the tasks to be performed to determine their essential factors) written into a job description so that the selectors know what physical and mental characteristics applicants must possess, what qualities and attitudes are desirable and what characteristics are a decided disadvantage:

- In the case of replacement of staff a critical questioning of the need to recruit at all (replacement should rarely be an automatic process).
- Effectively, selection is 'buying' an employee (the price being the wage or salary multiplied by probable years of service) hence bad buys can be very

expensive. For that reason some firms (and some firms for particular jobs) use external expert consultants for recruitment and selection. Equally some small organizations exist to 'head hunt', i.e. to attract staff with high reputations from existing employers to the recruiting employer. However, the 'cost' of poor selection is such that, even for the mundane day-to-day jobs, those who recruit and select should be well trained to judge the suitability of applicants.

The main sources of recruitment are:

- Internal promotion and internal introductions (at times desirable for morale purposes).
- Careers officers (and careers masters at schools).
- University appointment boards.
- Agencies for the unemployed.
- Advertising (often via agents for specialist posts) or the use of other local media (e.g. commercial radio).

Where the organization does its own printed advertising it is useful if it has some identifying logo as its trade mark for rapid attraction and it must take care not to offend the sex, race, etc. antidiscrimination legislation either directly or indirectly. The form on which the applicant is to apply (personal appearance, letter of application, completion of a form) will vary according to the posts vacant and numbers to be recruited.

It is very desirable in many jobs that claim about experience and statements about qualifications are thoroughly checked and that applicants unfailingly complete a health questionnaire (the latter is not necessarily injurious to the applicants chance of being appointed as firms are required to employ a percentage of disabled people).

Before letters of appointment are sent, any doubts about medical fitness or capacity (in employments where hygiene considerations are dominant) should be resolved by requiring applicants to attend a medical examination. This is especially so where, for example in the case of apprentices, the recruitment is for a contractual period or involves the firm in training costs.

Interviewing can be carried out by individuals (e.g. supervisor or departmental manager), by panels of interviewers or in the form of sequential interviews by different experts and can vary from a five minute 'chat' to a process of several days. Ultimately personal skills in judgment are probably the most important, but techniques to aid judgment include selection testing for:

- Aptitudes (particularly useful for school leavers)
- Attainments
- General intelligence

(All of these need skilled testing and assessment.) In more senior posts other techniques are:

- Leaderless groups
- Command exercises
- Group problem solving

(These are some common techniques—professional selection organizations often use other techniques to aid in selection.)

Training in interviewing and in appraising candidates is clearly essential to good recruitment. Largely the former consists of teaching interviewers how to draw out the interviewee and the latter how to rate the candidates. For consistency (and as an aid to checking that) rating often consists of scoring candidates for experience, knowledge, physical/mental capabilities, intellectual levels, motivation, prospective potential, leadership abilities, etc. (according to the needs of the post). Application of the normal curve of distribution to scoring eliminates freak judgments.

3. Employee Motivation

To retain good staff and to encourage them to give of their best while at work requires attention to the financial and psychological and even physiological rewards offered by the organization as a continuous exercise.

Basic financial rewards and conditions of service (e.g. working hours per week) are determined externally (by national bargaining or government minimum wage legislation) in many occupations but as much as 50 per cent of the gross pay of manual workers is often the result of local negotiations and details (e.g. which particular hours shall be worked) of conditions of service are often more important than the basics. Hence, there is scope for financial and other motivations to be used at local levels.

As staffing needs will vary with the productivity of the workforce (and the industrial peace achieved) so good personnel policies are desirable. The latter can depend upon other factors (like environment, welfare, employee benefits, etc.) but unless the wage packet is accepted as 'fair and just' there will be no motivation.

Hence, while the technicalities of payment and other systems may be the concern of others, the outcome of them is a matter of great concern to human resource management.

Increasingly, the influences of behavioral science discoveries are becoming important not merely because of the widely-acknowledged limitations of money as a motivator, but because of the changing mix and nature of tasks (e.g. more service and professional jobs and far fewer unskilled and repetitive production jobs).

The former demand better-educated, mobile and multi-skilled employees much more likely to be influenced by things like job satisfaction, involvement, participation, etc. than the economically dependent employees of yesteryear.

Hence, human resource management must act as a source of information about and a source of inspiration for the application of the findings of behavioral science. It may be a matter of drawing the attention of senior managers to what is being achieved elsewhere and the gradual education of middle managers to new points of view on job design, work organization and worker autonomy.

4. Employee Evaluation

An organization needs constantly to take stock of its

workforce and to assess its performance in existing jobs for three reasons:

- To improve organizational performance via improving the performance of individual contributors (should be an automatic process in the case of good managers) but (about annually) two key questions should be posed:
  - What has been done to improve the performance of a person last year?
  - And what can be done to improve his or her performance in the year to come?
- To identify potential, i.e. to recognize existing talent and to use that to fill vacancies higher in the organization or to transfer individuals into jobs where better use can be made of their abilities or developing skills.
- To provide an equitable method of linking payment to performance where there are no numerical criteria (often this salary performance review takes place about three months later and is kept quite separate from 1. and 2. but is based on the same assessment).

On-the-spot managers and supervisors, not HR staffs, carry out evaluations. The personnel role is usually that of:

- Advising top management of the principles and objectives of an evaluation system and designing it for particular organizations and environments.
- Developing systems appropriately in consultation with managers, supervisors and staff representatives. Securing the involvement and cooperation of appraisers and those to be appraised.
- Assistance in the setting of objective standards of evaluation/assessment, for example:
  - Defining targets for achievement;
  - Explaining how to quantify and agree objectives;
  - Introducing self-assessment;
  - Eliminating complexity and duplication.

- Publicizing the purposes of the exercise and explaining to staff how the system will be used.
- Organizing and establishing the necessary training of managers and supervisors who will carry out the actual evaluations/appraisals. Not only training in principles and procedures but also in the human relations skills necessary. (Lack of confidence in their own ability to handle situations of poor performance is the main weakness of assessors.)
- Monitoring the scheme—ensuring it does not fall into disuse, following up on training/job exchange, etc. recommendations, reminding managers of their responsibilities.

Full-scale periodic reviews should be a standard feature of schemes since resistance to evaluation/appraisal schemes is common and the temptation to water down or render schemes ineffectual is ever present (managers resent the time taken if nothing else).

Basically an evaluation/appraisal scheme is a formalization of what is done in a more casual manner anyway (e.g. if there is a vacancy, discussion about internal moves and internal attempts to put square pegs into 'squarer holes' are both the results of casual evaluation). Most managers approve merit payment and that too calls for evaluation. Make a standard routine task, it aids the development of talent, warns the inefficient or uncaring and can be an effective form of motivation.

Employee Evaluation and Selection

Employee evaluation and selection process will enable you to conduct effective job interviews, focusing you on the interview questions you need to ask in order to ascertain candidate appropriateness for the important job dimensions you have analyzed as being important to success.

This technique of first dimensioning a position, then evaluating and comparing each person against the position constructs is not only beneficial when hiring people from outside the organization. It can easily be applied inter alia other instances such as:

- Developing employees for internal promotion.
- Constructing training and development programs for individuals and groups.
- In team building, constructing a project team having key skill, knowledge and experience bases.
- Employee surveys, where you wish to compare an ideal situation, with the situation perceived by employees.

Also, one of the traits of an effective manager is his/her ability to extract information from informal conversations (management by wandering around) as he or she goes about daily routine. Such a manager would be able to use the technique of profile analysis to build a profile of key constructs in his/her area of responsibility (not covered by normal performance reporting, like say morale) and measure this over time.

Employee selection process—Who makes the selection decision, the roles of operating management/human resource management specialists, general selection criteria, and the reliability and validity of job interviews are explored.

Job analysis—Job analysis can be defined as the determination of the essential characteristics of a job in order to produce a job specification. In this section, we explain the use of job analysis in the employee selection process.

Job interviews—purpose and validity. The two-fold purpose of job interview are explained, as well as a critical look at their validity is explored.

Establishing job constructs for the job interview—The job constructs (dimensions) and the sub-dimensions, against which applicants are to be evaluated for suitability and compatibility are shown below:

- Communication skills,
- Self-motivation,
- Setting of work standards—self/others,

- Interpersonal/ability to sell self and ideas,
- Leadership potential and skills,
- Decision making abilities,
- Judgment abilities,
- Knowledge bases/technical skills, and
- Management abilities.

Profile analysis—Profile analysis is a tool to maximize the probability of matching people to job positions. In this 'how to' section, the construction of position profiles and imposing data collected from applicants, is explained.

Profile analysis has other uses in human resource management, and these are expounded on.

Job interview outline guide—The mechanics of conducting a professional job interview are explained. There are some informal do's and don'ts for the job interview; they are listed in this article.

Chronological job interview guide—This places all of the above together in an organized and planned methodology so that you will be able to individualize interview questions to the unique experiences of each prospective candidate, for each of the key constructs for the job being interviewed for.

Job Analysis

Job analysis can be defined as the determination of the essential characteristics of a job in order to produce a job specification. A job specification is a written statement of the essential characteristics of a job including necessary qualifications, duties, responsibilities and degree of authority of the job holder.

The purposes for which a job analysis is required can be

- To establish criteria for selection and performance appraisal,
- To establish training and development programs,
- For job evaluation,
- Remuneration purposes,

- To assist in job design, and
- For organizational restructuring purposes.

Job analysis also has important implications for fair employment practices.

In order to demonstrate job relatedness in employee selection, the criteria utilized should be directly related to, or embody constructs associated with job performance.

Therefore, the purpose of the job analysis will determine which information is considered important, and which HR specialist skills (e.g. training, selection, and job evaluation) would be most relevant.

The nature of the information elicited from job analysis incorporates the following:

- The nature of the work activities, including work procedures or processes, human behavior, physical job demands, personal responsibility and accountability.
- The machinery and equipment used.
- The nature of the work inputs and outputs, e.g. raw materials and finished goods.
- Work performance, including productivity standards and product quality specifications.
- Job context, incorporating the work, the organizational environment, societal context, compensation and motivational factors.
- Personal requirements of incumbents, including requisite knowledge and skills, aptitudes, physical and psychological characteristics.

Thus, in analyzing a job, an attempt is made to measure various aspects of that job. As mentioned previously, effective measurement requires reliable and valid measures. To ensure this, more than one rater or rating technique should be used, eliciting both qualitative and quantitative data. Methods of collecting this data include:

- Job interviews and/or observing employees at their workplace, using structured or unstructured approaches.
- Interviewing individual workers away from their workplace.
- Interviewing groups of workers.
- Interviewing supervisors and technical specialists.
- Utilizing structured or open-ended questionnaires.
- Requiring workers to complete self-report diaries.

Focus on the Job

A factor that should be emphasized is that job analysis typically focuses on the job itself, rather than on the incumbent. However, the incumbent cannot be ignored. A total focus on the work itself would imply that following a job analysis, a job would be designed to ensure optimal productivity, and that the incumbent would merely be required to perform the job.

However, this rather mechanistic approach ignores two factors:

- First, the ideal incumbent might not exist or be available for placement.
- A second, individual difference between people necessitates some adjustment of the job to accommodate the individual needs of the incumbent.

Application of Job Analysis

Job analysis is used for three important purposes in the employment process:

- First, it provides information for compiling job descriptions. A Job description typically contains a brief summary of the nature of the job, and lists the duties and responsibilities thereof.
- Second, job analysis assists in the compiling of job specifications. Job specifications set out the traits and characteristics considered to be essential for successful job performance. These include, education

level, relevant experience, skill level or physical characteristics. Job descriptions and specifications are generally used in combination for recruitment purposes. They enable accurate information dissemination, which, in turn, maximizes the number of appropriate applicants.

- The third purpose, for which job analysis is used, is in the development of selection criteria, criterion measures and predictors.

In doing job analysis, the tasks are extracted from the job description, if available, and listed in a column. The line manager together with the personnel specialist and the immediate supervisor of the person to be recruited then complete the skills and knowledge column.

In this manner a very clear picture emerges of the total job. Based on this information both HR and line management are in a better position to structure a job interview that could lead to an effective selection decision; one where the most appropriate person is hired.

Purpose and Validity of the Employee Evaluation and Selection Process

The specific purposes of an employee evaluation interview are:

- To assist in the assessment of candidates capacity and motivation to perform a particular job within an organization, to the satisfaction of the organization.
- To help the candidates formulate her/his own assessment of the job and the organization.

The interview may be the only tool which is used for selection, or it may form one stage in a sequence of eliminating hurdles. These can include medical checks, school reports, references, intelligence tests, personality tests, aptitude tests and group assessment techniques.

Validity of the Employee Evaluation and Selection Process

Much has been written about the validity of the interview as a selection tool. It is regarded by some as being so subjective as to be totally worthless. Interviewer bias, prejudice and the halo/horn effect undermine, so the argument goes, any pretence of an objective assessment of the candidates suitability. The proponents of this view advocate scrapping the interview in favor of tests.

Some interviewers, on the other hand, will confess to no such human frailty. They maintain and that they can tell as soon as the candidate has walked through the door of the interview room, whether the person is suitable or not. "When you've been in the game as long as I have you can spot them straight away," they say.

Such interviewers, with implicit faith in their own judgment, tend to assume that their own highly personalized methods are the right answer to their (and everyone else) problems. For them, the sophistication of testing is wasted on an exercise as simple as summing up another person's character and abilities.

Undoubtedly, a properly conducted job interview should have a place, and a fairly significant one, in any selection process. But properly conducted, means something rather less hit and miss than the "I can spot them..." approach.

A properly conducted selection interview is one where the interviewer does not pretend to be free from bias and prejudice and susceptibility to the halo effect. It is one where the interviewer has examined his own attitudes sufficiently thoroughly to be aware when these forces may be coming into play, and to make allowance for them.

Even where the candidate will ultimately be required to work with the interviewer, this principle holds good. It is in the nature of such misconceptions that they are eventually found to be either ill-founded or illegal.

Employee Evaluation and Selection Process Requirements

What is required during the employee evaluation and selection interview in particular is interviewer discipline. Discipline to work out what it is that interviewer (or more appropriately what the organization) is looking for and why is he looking for it:

- To consider how he will recognize it when he sees it;
- How he will judge whether it is there in sufficient quantity;
- And to assess each employee or potential employee strictly in terms of the qualities and attributes he has described, rather than in terms of his own likes and dislikes.

This discipline can only be achieved with effort. It is after all, much easy to say "I just did not take to him", but you may have lost the organization an effective worker or even potential savior. So, we start with discipline and the embodiment of this will be found in the stages of preparation for employee evaluation and selection interviewing that will be described shortly.

Self-discipline is but one factor. It would be foolish to discount the power of gut instinct. If at the end of a detailed and objective assessment the interviewer finds that there is something that just does not fit, he/she should beware. He/she should reevaluate his/her data, search his/her inner self afresh to be sure that it is not the accent with which the interviewee speaks, or the way he parts his hair that is reminiscent of someone who holds unfortunate associations for him/her.

If he/she is still not satisfied, if there is still something he/she cannot quite put his/her finger on, he/she should either seek a second opinion, through references or a second interview with an unprepared colleague or, if neither of these is feasible, write a polite letter rejecting the candidate.

Importance of Employee Evaluation

Putting square pegs into round has never been good employment practice, and can have a very adverse effect on the organizations performance if multiplied by a sufficiently high number.

Today, it is positively detrimental for all concerned, not least the square peg. It is a truism which the law seems to be making constantly truer; that it is a lot easier to get square pegs in, than get them out. They may only be eased out finally after a considerable amount of humiliation and bitterness, which helps neither the employer nor the employee.

Correct selection is therefore of crucial importance. And correct selection must mean that both parties to the selection decision, interviewer and interviewee, are satisfied, in all circumstances, the right decisions has been made. The candidate who has been subjected to a battery of tests, however thoroughly validated, will not necessarily feel this if he/she has never had a chance to talk to a member of the organization.

Similarly, the interviewer who has never met the candidate cannot be sure that the approved ingredients detected by the tests do really go to make up an acceptable whole whose appearance and impact on others match his/her test scores and whose tenacity and motivation augur well for success in the job.

3

Manpower Planning

Planning is nothing but using the available assets for the effective implementation of the production plans. After preparing the plans, people are grouped together to achieve organizational objectives. Planning is concerned with coordinating, motivating and controlling of the various activities within the organization. Time required for acquiring the material, capital and machinery should be taken into account. Manager has to reasonably predict future events and plan out the production. The basic purpose of the management is to increase the production, so that the profit margin can be increased. Manager has to guess the future business and to take timely and correct decisions in respect of company objectives, policies and cost performances. The plans need to be supported by all the members of the organization.

Planning is making a decision in advance what is to be done. It is the willpower of course of action to achieve the desired results. It is a kind of future picture where events are sketched. It can be defined as a mental process requiring the use of intellectual faculty, imagination, foresight and sound judgment. It involves problem-solving and decision-making. Management has to prepare for short-term strategy and measure the achievements, while the long-term plans are prepared to develop the better and new products, services, expansion to keep the interest of the owners.

Personnel Management

Personnel management is productive exploitation of manpower resources. This is also termed as 'Manpower Management'. Manpower management is choosing the proper type of people as and when required. It also takes into account the upgrading of existing people. Manpower management starts with manpower planning. Every manager in an organization is a personnel man, dealing with people.

Manpower Planning

Manpower Planning is a process of optimum utilization of human resource or human capital for organizational benefit. Manpower planning is also known as human capital planning. Manpower management is choosing the proper type of people as and when required. It also takes into account the upgrading of existing people. Manpower management starts with manpower planning. Every manager in an organization is a personnel man, dealing with people. Therefore human resource management is productive exploitation of manpower resources.

Manpower planning enables a department to project its short to long-term needs on the basis of its departmental plans so that it can adjust its manpower requirements to meet changing priorities. The more changing the environment the department is in, the more the department needs manpower planning to show:

- The number of recruits required in a specified timeframe and the availability of talent.
- Early indications of potential recruitment or retention difficulties.
- Surpluses or deficiencies in certain ranks or grades.
- Availability of suitable qualified and experienced successors.

Manpower planning in Human Resource Management is a core factor. Here the penalties for not being correctly staffed are costly. Understaffing loses the business economies of scale and specialization, orders, customers and profits. Overstaffing is wasteful and expensive, if sustained, and it is costly to eliminate because of modern legislation in respect of redundancy payments, consultation, minimum periods of notice, etc. Very importantly, overstaffing reduces the competitive efficiency of the business.

Planning sufficiently

Planning staff levels requires that an assessment of present and future needs of the organization be compared with present resources and future predicted resources. Appropriate steps then be planned to bring demand and supply into balance.

See the pros and cons

Thus, the first step is to take a clear and average view of the existing workforce profile such as numbers, skills, ages, flexibility, gender, experience, forecast capabilities, character, potential, etc. of existing employees and then to adjust this for one or three and ten years ahead by amendments for normal turnover, planned staff movements, retirements, etc. in line with the business plan for the corresponding time frames.

The result should be a series of crude supply situations as would be the outcome of present planning if left unmodified. This, clearly, requires a great deal of information accretion, classification and statistical analysis as a subsidiary aspect of personnel management.

Future plan

The future demands will be only influenced in part by the forecast of the personnel manager, whose main task may well be to scrutinize and modify the crude predictions of other managers.

Staffing in the future needs is derived due to some factors:

1. Variations in the efficiency, productivity, flexibility of labor as a result of training, work study, organizational change, new motivations, etc.
2. Changes in employment practices (e.g. use of subcontractors or agency staffs, hiving-off tasks, buying in, substitution, etc.).
3. Sales and production forecasts.

4. Variations, which respond to new legislation, e.g. payroll taxes or their abolition, new health and safety requirements.
5. The effects of technological change on task needs.
6. Changes in Government policies (investment incentives, regional or trade grants, etc.).

What we understand from the above factors is that a thought out and logical staffing demand schedule for varying dates in the future which can then be compared with the crude supply schedules. The comparisons will then indicate what steps must be taken to achieve a equilibrium.

Conclusion

It will involve the further planning of such recruitment, training, retraining, labor reductions such as early retirement/redundancy or changes in workforce utilization as will bring supply and demand into equilibrium, not just as a one-off but as a continuing workforce planning exercise the inputs to which will need constant varying to reflect actual as against predicted experience on the supply side and changes in production actually achieved as against forecast on the required surface.

Advantages of Manpower Planning

Manpower planning ensures optimum use of available human resources:

1. It is useful both for organization and nation.
2. It generates facilities to educate people in the organization.
3. It brings about fast economic developments.
4. It boosts the geographical mobility of labor.
5. It provides smooth working even after expansion of the organization.
6. It opens possibility for workers for future promotions, thus providing incentive.
7. It creates healthy atmosphere of encouragement and motivation in the organization.

8. Training becomes effective.
9. It provides help for career development of the employees.
10. It saves cost.

Steps in Manpower Planning

1. Predict manpower plans.
2. Design job description and the job requirements.
3. Find adequate sources of recruitment.
4. Give boost to youngsters by appointment to higher posts.
5. Best motivation for internal promotion.
6. Look after the expected losses due to retirement, transfer and other issues.
7. See for replacement due to accident, death, dismissals and promotion.

Factors which Affect the Efficiency of Labor

1. *Inheritance*: Persons from good collection are bound to work professionally. The quality and rate of physical as well as mental development, which is dissimilar in case of different individuals is the result of genetic differences.
2. *Climate*: Climatic location has a definite effect on the efficiency of the workers.
3. *Health of worker*: Worker's physical condition plays a very important part in performing the work. Good health means the sound mind, in the sound body.
4. *General and technical education*: Education provides a definite impact in the working ability and efficiency of the worker.
5. *Personal qualities*: Persons with dissimilar personal qualities bound to have definite differences in their behavior and methods of working. The personal qualities influence the quality of work.
6. *Wages*: Proper wages guarantees certain reasons in standard of living, such as cheerfulness, discipline,

etc. and keep workers satisfy. This provides incentive to work.

7. *Hours of work*: Long and tiring hours of work exercise have bad effect on the competence of the workers.

Downsizing of Manpower

Downsizing of manpower gives the correct picture about the number of people to be employed to complete given task in the predetermined period. It is used for achieving fundamental growth in the concern. It can work out the correct price by the resource building or capacity building. It aims at correct place, correct man on a correct job. Thus manpower planning is must to make the optimum utilization of the greatest resource available, i.e. manpower for the success of any organization.

Key Components of Manpower Planning

Succession Planning

Succession planning assesses the likely turnover in key posts, identifies suitable candidates to fill these posts in future, and ensures that they have the right training and exposure for their future work. Given the effort and support required for undertaking succession planning, it is normally confined to the directorate and those ranks immediately below, plus any grades with high turnover or anticipated expansion.

Succession planning is a very important exercise because it minimizes the impact of turnover in these key ranks and gives a branch or department early warning of any skill shortages or likely difficulties in finding suitable candidates. Ideally a succession plan should cover 3 to 5 years. The succession plan should identify:

- key posts and possible successors,
- causes of turnover,
- competencies of successors and the training required for them, and
- posts for which no apparent successor exists and the remedial action planned.

The information derived from the succession plan should feed into the training and development of the individuals concerned by ensuring that they attend the necessary training and are posted to jobs that will provide them with the experience for their intended role.

Turnover

Turnover refers to retirement, resignation and redundancy. While a department cannot plan turnover because there are factors, such as resignation, which are beyond its control, it can monitor turnover carefully to ensure the department will have minimal difficulties in retaining staff. If such difficulties are envisaged or experienced, the department will find out the causes for them and take early steps to address them by improving, for example, motivation or training and development opportunities.

When addressing the aspects of succession and turnover, the department also needs to consider other manpower planning factors.

External Factors

A number of factors may affect whether talent is available in the market to fill posts in a department. These include the availability of the required personnel with the necessary qualifications, skills and experience at a specified time, the relative job opportunities in the private sector and the general outlook of the economy.

Internal Factors

Departmental Plan: A department assesses the number of staff it requires at different levels, at specified timeframes, in the light of its present and planned future work commitments. This may lead to an increase or decrease of the current manpower.

Cost to Company

Cost to Company (CTC) is a term used to describe an investment without return. Travel expenditures, interviewing, spending time with potential customers can all be interpreted as CTC's.

Cost to Company can also be used to refer to the total cost that an organization is spending towards their employee including the Salary, Perks, Cost related to benefits, Cost related to hiring, Training, Retirals, Statutory Contributions, etc.

Cost to Company is a buzz word to describe how the company can slowly pay you less and less, and remove all your benefits, until you are "self funded"—in other words you pay for all your "benefits" yourself, while the company receives the tax benefits for these payments. This improves their profit ratio, and if this system is extrapolated, you will eventually pay the company to work there. So you'll need a second job to fund this.

Cost to company is a trick of a company and HR department, to show we are paying a big salary, but unfortunatly it is just bubble. They overload total expenses of human resorces on salary, and show that they are paying this much salary to the staff, but actually they pay less and show more. For example, your salary is 6 lacs p.a. it means you are getting 50,000/- per month. But actually person gets only 25,000/- per month...all other money is deducted for facilities. This means we are paying for getting facilities, but company shows they are giving us good facilities in the organization. In short, we pay from our salary for getting facilities, but company says they are giving good facilities to their staff. So you are paying for even unwanted facilities which you don't need. Before deciding CTC, ask for breakup of facilities.

How to Calculate Your Compensation?

Total compensation includes the value of all the perks and benefits one gets from the Company in addition to one's salary. Calculating Annual Cost to the Company is important while changing jobs as it more often than not determines what your compensation will be in the new Company. At the same time all the components are not always apparent. In order to arrive at a comprehensive figure one has to carefully add the value of all components or their cash equivalent. Given below is a format which may be filled up to arrive at the Annual Cost to the Company.

	Components	Applicability	Amount
1.	**SALARY DETAILS**		
	Basic Salary	Yes/No	
	House Rent Allowance	Yes/No	
	Company Leased Accommodation	Yes/No	
	Daily Allowance	Yes/No	
	City Compensatory Allowance	Yes/No	
	Special Allowance	Yes/No	
	Conveyance Allowance	Yes/No	
	Lunch Allowance	Yes/No	
	Entertainment Allowance	Yes/No	
	Books/Periodicals Allowance	Yes/No	
	Education Allowance	Yes/No	
	House Maintenance Allowance	Yes/No	
	Furnishing Allowance	Yes/No	
	Dress/Uniform Allowance	Yes/No	
	Other Allowances	Yes/No	
2.	**BENEFITS/PERKS/ REIMBURSEMENTS**		
	Value of Company Car	Yes/No	
	Car Subsidy(or equivalent tax savings)	Yes/No	
	Driver's Salary	Yes/No	
	Maintenance and Petrol Expenses	Yes/No	
	Leave Travel Allowance	Yes/No	
	Canteen Subsidy	Yes/No	
	Telephone Expenses	Yes/No	
	Mobile Phone	Yes/No	
	Club Membership	Yes/No	
	Electricity/Gas	Yes/No	
	Servant/Gardener	Yes/No	
	Credit Cards	Yes/No	
	Furnishings/Durables	Yes/No	
	Holiday Facilities	Yes/No	
	Medical Reimbursements	Yes/No	
	Medical Insurance	Yes/No	
	Personal Accident Scheme	Yes/No	

	Others Benefits	Yes/No
3.	**RETIRALS**	
	Provident Fund	Yes/No
	Superannuation Fund	Yes/No
	Gratuity	Yes/No
4.	**BONUS**	
	Fixed Bonus	Yes/No
	Productivity Linked Variable Bonus(*)	Yes/No
	Any Other Performance Oriented Incentive including Stock Option Plan(*)	Yes/No
5.	**SOFT LOANS**	
	Interest Subsidy	Yes/No
	GROSS COMPENSATION	

(*) Please take the average value of the amounts received by you in the present grade, to reach at a fair estimate.

Source: *Times News*, New York.

Calculating Employee Attrition

A high attrition reflects poorly on an organization's ability to hold on to its people. Attrition is unfortunately viewed as a management flaw when in fact it could well be a recruitment error. The high attrition rate in the IT, call center and in the field job has always been its greatest concern and a subject of much analysis and debate. Organizations use different methodologies for calculating their turnover rate. Ideally, attrition should be calculated on a monthly basis for companies that have over 50 employees for the first five years of its business. Subsequently, a quarterly index should be applied till a company's 10th anniversary. After this, annual attrition figures should be measured and accounted for. Hiding attrition rate is never a solution for good retention strategy. Attrition rate can be summarized as follows:

- Attrition: Number of employees who left in the year/ average employees in the year × 100. Thus, if the company had 1,000 employees in April 2007, 2,000 in March 2008, and 300 quit in the year, then the average employee strength is 1,500 and attrition is

100 × (300/1500) = 20 per cent. A graded system can probably depict the true picture.

- Many firms may not include attrition of freshers who leave because of higher studies or within three months of joining.

Organizations aim to reduce voluntary attrition of productive employees and encourage unproductive staff to leave its fold. "It makes way for career progression, new thinking and innovation. However, what that number should be again differs from industry to industry and from country to country as economies vary. What is considered a healthy attrition number in an industry in India may not be so in a more stagnant economy where no new jobs are being created."

In India, the average attrition rate in the BPO sector is approximately 30-35 per cent. It is true that this is far less than the prevalent attrition rate in the US market (around 70 per cent). If a person leaves after the training it costs the company about Rs. 60,000. For a 300-seater call centre facing the normal 30 per cent attrition, this translates into Rs. 60 lakh per annum. Normally the attrition rate in India is 18%, US 42%, Europe 24%, Australia 29% and Global Average 24%.

Components to be taken into consideration, while calculating attrition rate. If calculating in monetary terms, it includes the following:

Costs Due to a Person Leaving

1. Calculate the cost of the person(s) who fills in while the position is vacant. Calculate the cost of lost productivity at a minimum of 50 per cent of the person's compensation and benefits cost for each week the position is vacant, even if there are people performing the work. Calculate the lost productivity at 100 per cent if the position is completely vacant for any period of time.
2. Calculate the cost of conducting an exit interview to include the time of the person conducting the interview, the time of the person leaving, the

administrative costs of stopping payroll, benefit deductions, benefit enrollments.

3. Calculate the cost of the manager who has to understand what work remains, and how to cover that work until a replacement is found.
4. Calculate the cost of training your company has invested in this employee who is leaving.
5. Calculate the impact on departmental productivity because the person is leaving. Who will pick up the work, whose work will suffer, what departmental deadlines will not be met or delivered late.
6. Calculate the cost of lost knowledge, skills and contacts that the person who is leaving is taking with them out of your door. Use a formula of 50 per cent of the person's annual salary for one year of service, increasing each year of service by 10 per cent.
7. Subtract the cost of the person who is leaving for the amount of time the position is vacant.

Recruitment Costs

1. The cost of advertisements; agency costs; employee referral costs; internet posting costs.
2. The cost of the internal recruiter's time to understand the position requirements, develop and implement a sourcing strategy, review candidates backgrounds, prepare for interviews, conduct interviews, prepare candidate assessments, conduct reference checks, make the employment offer and notify unsuccessful candidates. This can range from a minimum of 30 hours to over 100 hours per position.
3. Calculate the cost of the various candidate pre-employment tests to help assess candidates' skills, abilities, aptitude, attitude, values and behaviors.

Training Costs

1. Calculate the cost of orientation in terms of the new person's salary and the cost of the person who

conducts the orientation. Also include the cost of orientation materials.

2. Calculate the cost of departmental training as the actual development and delivery cost plus the cost of the salary of the new employee. Note that the cost will be significantly higher for some positions such as sales representatives and call center agents who require 4-6 weeks or more of classroom training.
3. Calculate the cost of the person(s) who conduct the training.
4. Calculate the cost of various training materials needed including company or product manuals, computer or other technology equipment used in the delivery of training.

Lost Productivity Costs

As the new employee is learning the new job, the company policies and practices, etc. they are not fully productive. Use the following guidelines to calculate the cost of this lost productivity:

1. Upon completion of whatever training is provided, the employee is contributing at a 25 per cent productivity level for the first 2-4 weeks. The cost therefore is 75 per cent of the new employees full salary during that time period.
2. During weeks 5-12, the employee is contributing at a 50 per cent productivity level. The cost is therefore 50 per cent of full salary during that time period.
3. During weeks 13-20, the employee is contributing at a 75 per cent productivity level. The cost is therefore 25 per cent of full salary during that time period.
4. Calculate the cost of mistakes the new employee makes during this elongated indoctrination period.

New Hire Costs

Calculate the cost of bringing the new person on board including the cost to put the person on the payroll, establish computer and security passwords and identification cards, telephone hookups, cost of establishing email accounts, or leasing other equipment such as cell phones, automobiles.

Calculate the cost of a manager's time spent developing trust and building confidence in the new employee's work.

Lost Sales Costs

1. Calculate the revenue per employee by dividing total company revenue by the average number of employees in a given year. Whether an employee contributes directly or indirectly to the generation of revenue, their purpose is to provide some defined set of responsibilities that are necessary to the generation of revenue. Calculate the lost revenue by multiplying the number of weeks the position is vacant by the average weekly revenue per employee.

Conclusion: It is clear that there are massive costs associated with attrition or turnover and, while some of these are not visible to the management reporting or budget system, they are none the less real. The 'rule of thumb' appears to be very inaccurate indeed and, while it depends upon the category of staff, it is probably better to estimate around 80 per cent of salary as a truer rule of thumb—and this will be on the conservative side. What does this mean? Well, it means that if a company has 100 people doing a certain job paid 25,000 and that turnover or attrition is running at 10 per cent, the cost of attrition is:

(Total staff × attrition rate %) × (annual salary × 80%)

1. Hundred staff at 10 per cent attrition means 10 people leave and are replaced each year.
2. A replacement cost of 80 per cent of a salary of 25,000 means the cost of each replacement is 20,000.
3. The cost of turnover is therefore 10 × 20,000 or 200,000 a year.
4. The oncost to the overall salary bill is 8 per cent.

(Saving 8% of salary costs would make the average HR manager a hero).

Manpower Planning for the Future

Business is creation of customer, retention of customer and encashment of customer. Creation of customer is comparatively not very challenging but retaining and encashing customer is main crux of business. If we will develop loyal employees over the time then they can maintain and retain loyal customer for future profit generation. If we will provide better salary package, challenging job profile and job security then only we can retain 40 per cent employees confidently those who are really performer. In nutshell, loyal employee begets loyal customer and gives message to the world about happy chain that lures others to come and join the team. Business growth and stability of an organization depends on future workforce planning. Strategic workforce planning is not limited to hiring and retaining talent, but anticipating future manpower needs of an organization.

D.C. Jain, CMD of Akums Drugs and Pharmaceuticals Ltd.

"Manpower needs, if planned properly, in terms of profile required, numbers, time and place, will give the company mileage over competitors in terms of consistency in output."

Ashwin Thacker, Managing Director, Flamingo Pharma

"You need educated, skilled manpower for sales, product management, R&D and production. There will be a shortage of such people in the future" also critical to the process.

Kris Lakshmikanth, CEO, The Headhunters India

"The need for contingency plan would come during market fluctuations, stringent deadline, natural calamity, change in technology and an unexpected opportunity."

Geeta A. Sundrani, Director, Oasis Executive Search

The best strategy to formulate a backup plan includes grooming fresh talent and creating a second line at all functions. "Building second line personnel in the organization, coupled with robust systems, will ensure that company gets a competitive edge over other market players."

Sanjeev Jain, MD of Akums Drugs and Pharmaceuticals Ltd.

"Working closely with the business groups and keeping an active talent inventory and effective churning the internal employee database (from skills availability and referencing programme perspective) is the key. Identifying the skill matrix of the internal talent pool and putting to good use during business exigency optimises the manpower utilization at any given point."

Fadi, MD Golden Suns Real Estate, Dubai

India and Philippines are the best hub for the most economical skilled and non-skilled manpower but it won't be for a longer period of time because of globalization.

B.M. Munjal, CMD Hero Honda Group

Finally, Old days have gone when there was monopoly and discrimination of employer in terms of salary package and all other facilities to the employees. Entry of new MNCs, banking sector, call centers require people for production, development, sales and product management. On the retail front, all big retail groups—Future Group, Reliance, RPG, etc. are setting up pharmacies across India. Subhiksha, Guardian and Apollo already exist in north India and are set for expansion. These stores will require trained people and the best are obviously available in pharma companies. Clinical research organization and clinical data management organisation, which requires specialists, is increasingly shifting to India. The salaries of such people have gone up significantly in the last two to three years. Most B.Sc. graduates who were the prime source of supply will shift to clinical research/trials as it offers them better salaries and greater chances of career development. Quality young people will be lost to such companies. Finally, many of the pharmaceuticals companies are expanding fast, both in India as well as abroad, further aggravating the war for talent.

Conclusion

In a dynamic business scenario, manpower planning is critical to organizational growth and stability. It is integral to recruiting, retaining, retraining and redeployment of talent. Linked to business needs of the organization, the process is much more complicated than it seems, primarily because it also involves developing skills and competencies of existing employees to meet market demands which can change with time.

"Business needs are achieved from effective management of materials, machines, money and manpower. Manpower needs, if planned properly, in terms of profile required, numbers, time and place, will give the company mileage over competitors in terms of consistency in output. Effective Human Resources planning gives optimal productivity in terms of timelines and quality of deliverables." It will not only improve people competency, but will also ensure that people grow with the company. This helps arrest the attrition rate.

HR manager should give close attention to why attrition is occurring in the present. To ignore why people are leaving the organization is to ignore the organization greatest assets—its people. People in organization are needed to perform the task; but they are not just machine but more than that. They are organization dreams, hopes, ambitions, creativity and innovation. And to retain these valuable assets is one of the surest ways to build an organization rather than just to go in global markets. And this is the only way an organization can lower its attrition rate.

Employees are human capital and one of the best assets of the organization. It cannot be ignored even for a short period of time. Now this is an era, when employees eagerly wish to leave the organization, let them go for better future with full-fledged bound and this bound should be family for ever. Give them one month advance salary and come back facility and welcome them if it happens. These types of employees would set example for others and can reduce employees' turnover. If they won't come back and they were good employees then send them birth day and marriage anniversary card regularly. This technique will help to make good image in the industry and make family members happier.

4

Recruitment and Selection

Recruitment refers to the process of finding possible candidates for a job or desired function. OR

It is a process of taking on professional with desired amount of skills and knowledge to serve an organization for the augmentation of profitability of the company.

Recruiting and selecting the right people is of paramount importance to the continued success of the organization. Before a department takes steps to employ staff, it should work out the type of staff it needs in terms of grade and rank, and the time scale in which the staff are required. The general principles underpinning recruitment within the civil service are that recruitment and it should:

- Use procedures which are clearly understood by candidates and which are open to public scrutiny,
- Be fair, giving candidates who meet the stipulated minimum requirements equal opportunity for selection; and select candidates on the basis of merit and ability.

Key Components

Deciding on Terms of Appointment

Terms of Appointment: Having decided on the grade and rank of the staff required, and the timing concerned, the department should consider what the most appropriate terms of appointment would be. This should take into account the nature of the duties to be performed and the overall manpower deployment of the department. The different terms of appointment that can be offered are:

- Permanent and pensionable.
- Agreement terms.
- Temporary terms (month-to-month or day-to-day).
- Part-time.
- Non-civil service appointment, and
- Consultancy.

Guides to Appointment: Entry requirements of staff in each rank and grade are agreed between the Head of Grade/Department concerned and the Civil Service Branch, taking into account the advice of the Standing Commission on Civil Service Salaries and Conditions of Service or other relevant advisory bodies. These requirements are periodically reviewed and laid down in Guides to Appointments.

Selection of Candidates

Advertising: Vacancies in the civil service are normally advertised in newspapers and through circulars.

Screening and Selection: Departments screen applications to see if the applicants meet the specified qualifications and other requirements of the post. Suitable candidates are then short listed for subsequent examination and/or interviews. Not all grades/departments would require candidates to undergo examination, but candidates would normally be required to be interviewed by a recruitment board or an officer from the recruitment team.

Roles and Responsibilities: The Civil Service Branch recruits staff of some General Grades while Heads of Grades/ Departments recruit staff of their own grade/department. For recruitment to middle and senior ranks, the advice of the Public Service Commission has to be sought before appointment is offered.

Flexibility: To minimize recruitment difficulties as well as attract and retain the best people, there are flexibilities which include recruitment overseas, offer of agreement terms, lowering entry qualifications and granting incremental credit for experience.

Probation: During probation staffs are introduced to the mission, objectives and values of the civil service and their departments. Probation is a serious process which provides regular feedback on performance and assesses suitability for employment in the civil service. It includes:

On-the-job training: Staff should be exposed to the different duties required for their rank. In this way they can learn the skills expected of them and managers can verify their long-term suitability.

Supervision and guidance: Staff should receive close and sympathetic supervision and guidance to enable problems and difficulties to be identified early and timely counseling or other action to be taken. Newly joined staff must be told the length of their probationary period, which varies with the requirements of each grade. If there are indications that staff is not suitable for confirmation, they must be counseled and then warned in writing if the problem persists. Confirmation is the step whereby a member of staff on probation is found suitable for the job and employed on permanent and pensionable terms.

Phases of Recruitment

Phases of recruitment vary from company to company because style of human resource functioning varies. There are five phases of recruitment as follows.

The Generic Overview

Phase-1 Identification of Prospective Candidate

- Job boards
- Candidate's references
- Application received for job
- Postings

Phase-2 Candidates Profiling & Assessment

- Skill set & degree of difficulty
- Level of experience

- Market acceptance for the skills
- Candidate expectation

Phase-3 Candidate selection

- Technical screening
- Taking references
- Making the offer

Phase-4 Candidate Induction Process

- Sending the employment
- Agreement
- Assessing the candidate for desired level

Phase-5 Candidate Hand Holding & on Project Support

- Preparing for interview
- Conducting mock interview
- Just in time training on cutting edge technology
- Looped feedback mechanism while at client site to ensure "null redundancy"

Recruitment Steps

Recruitment steps can be understood easily through the following ways.

Job Description

A job description is a key document in the recruitment process, and must be finalised prior to taking any other steps in the process. It should clearly and accurately set out the duties and responsibilities of the job and must include:

- The job title (which must be sex neutral)
- The location of the job i.e. department/faculty/division/research group
- Grade of the post
- The post to whom the postholder is responsible
- Any posts reporting to the postholder
- Main purpose of the job
- Main duties and responsibilities

- Any special working conditions (e.g. unsocial or shift working patterns, the requirement—for clinical posts—to obtain health clearance. Items that should be included in job descriptions are:
  - A note that indicates that, as duties and responsibilities change, the job description will be reviewed and amended in consultation with the postholder.
  - An indication that the postholder will carry out any other duties as are within the scope, spirit and purpose of the job as requested by the line manager or Head of Department/Division.
  - A statement that the postholder will actively follow company policies including Equal Opportunities policies.
  - An indication that the postholder will maintain an awareness and observation of Fire and Health & Safety Regulations.

The language in job descriptions should:

- Avoid jargon and unexplained acronyms and abbreviations.
- Be readily understandable to potential applicants for the post.
- Avoid ambiguity about responsibilities and be clear about the postholder's accountability for resources, staff, etc.

Person Specification

The person specification is of equal importance to the job description and informs the selection decision. The person specification details the skills, experience, abilities and expertise that are required to do the job. It should be drawn up after the job description and, with the job description, should inform the content of the advert. The person specification should be specific, related to the job, and not unnecessarily restrictive—for example only qualifications strictly needed to do the job should be specified. The inclusion of criteria that cannot be justified as essential for the performance of the job may be deemed discriminatory under race and sex discrimination law, if equal proportions of men and women and those from different racial groups could not meet them.

The person specification must form part of the further particulars of a vacancy along with the job description in order that applicants have a full picture of what the job entails. The person specification enables potential applicants to make an informed decision about whether to apply and those who do apply, to give sufficient relevant detail of their skills and experience in their application. The person specification forms the basis of the selection decision and enables the selection panel to ensure objectivity in their selection. Elements of the person specification are as follows:

- knowledge (including necessary qualifications)
- skills and abilities
- experience
- aptitudes

The person specification details are required to do the job, specifying which are essential and which are desirable; obviously, these may be different from the attributes of the previous postholder.

Essential criteria are those without which an appointee would be unable to adequately perform the job; Desirable criteria are those that may enable the candidate to perform better or require a shorter familiarisation period.

Criteria which are subjective and for which little evidence is likely to be obtained through the selection process should be avoided (for example, 'a flexible approach' is often too vague to be of any help in the selection process).

Knowledge can be derived in a number of ways, for example, through education, training, or experience:

- For some jobs a particular qualification(s) may be essential, while for others no single qualification may be appropriate and a particular type of experience may be just as relevant as a formal qualification.

Where qualifications are deemed essential, these should reflect the minimum requirements necessary to carry out the job to an acceptable standard. The Human Resources Division can assist in advising on the equivalence of particular overseas qualifications.

- Candidates will increasingly come forward with National Vocational Qualifications (NVQs). These qualifications recognise the achievement of employment-led standards of competence.
- The type of experience required of applicants should be specified; but stipulating the length of experience should be avoided if possible, because the quality of experience is more important than its length. It is also important to remember that experience is sometimes transferable from one area of work to another, in which case specifying skills is likely to be more effective than specifying a narrow definition of experience.

Required abilities should be expressed in terms of the standards required, not just in terms of the task to be undertaken. For example, avoid statements such as 'Ability to write reports'; instead, indicate the expected standard, such as 'Ability to write detailed financial reports that encompass departmental budgeting, annual variances, and forecasting'.

Extreme care must be taken if physical requirements are specified. The Disability Discrimination Act requires employers to make reasonable adjustments to jobs to make them suitable for people with a disability. It is, therefore, important that any physical requirement is stated in terms of the job that needs to be done. For example, a job may require that the appointee 'must be able to travel to a number of different locations on company business'. For driving jobs, it will be appropriate to specify the ability to drive.

Personal qualities may affect the ability of an individual to do the job, but they should not be seen as substitutes for skills. For example, the ability to deal effectively with frustrated customers is a skill. Simply possessing patience (a personal quality) will not be enough.

Details for Applicants

The details of a vacancy or 'further particulars' of a post must include the job description and person specification for the post together with any other important information that a potential applicant needs to decide whether to apply. The purpose of advertising a post is to attract the widest range of high calibre applicants possible and, therefore, the further particulars sent to or accessed by applicants must give a clear picture of the post, the department, and as an employer.

Further particulars should include the following:

- Details of the main terms and conditions of employment (including holiday and pension arrangements, entitlement to apply for sabbatical leave if appropriate, working hours, call-out or shift patterns arrangements if appropriate, etc.).
- Details of any relocation benefits—relocation expenses, relocation supplements where they apply, etc.
- Information about *company* and the department (including details about the research strategy or research interests within the department).
- The Equal Opportunity Policy statement and Equal Opportunities monitoring form.
- Guidelines about completing the application form, including the number of referees and whether there is an intention to seek references before interview.
- Where a CV is required, candidates should be advised that it must include: education history (institution name, start and end dates of courses, qualification gained), details of membership of any professional organizations, details of current or most recent employer (name and address of current organization, job title, salary and duties, details of previous employment and how the applicants' knowledge, skills, and abilities meet the job requirements.

Publicising the Vacancy

All posts must be advertised with entitled 'Opportunities' to ensure that vacancies are open to external applicants. The majority of posts, however, will also be concurrently advertised in other specialist, national or international media to maximise the chances of attracting the best candidate. Attention is drawn to the specific requirements in relation to advertising for work permit purposes.

It is very important, therefore, that all posts are advertised as widely as possible and that all applicants are dealt with in the same way and given the same information and opportunity to make an application.

To ensure that applicants are fully informed about the vacancy for which they are applying and to ensure that they provide with all the information we require, adverts must direct applicants to the further particulars, which will provide more information including how to apply.

An advertisement is written from the job description and person specification and should contain the following points:

- Title of vacancy and salary structure.
- Brief details of the job.
- Key details of the person specification.
- The necessity of a criminal records check, if required, or an Occupational Health Assessment.
- The period of the initial grant (if grant funded).
- How to obtain further particulars of the vacancies.
- Closing date for applications (sufficient time should be allowed to enable applicants to consider the further particulars and make their application).
- Where known, date of interview.
- A statement reflecting company's commitment to equality of opportunity is automatically included in all recruitment advertisements.

Assistance with drafting advertisements is available on request from the Human Resources Division.

Heads of Departments must ensure that permission to fill a post has been obtained before seeking to publicise a vacancy; details are available from the appropriate section of the Finance Division—Planning & Management Accounts in respect of non-research posts and Research Administration in respect of research posts.

All job advertisements must be placed through the Human Resources website to ensure compliance with this policy and because the contract with company's advertising agency is dependent on significant volume discounts.

Processing Applications

Heads of Departments must make their staff aware that when dealing with enquiries about vacancies it is unlawful to state or imply that applications from one sex or from a particular racial group/regional group would be preferred and to do so may lead to a complaint of race or sex discrimination against company.

Care must also be taken when initiating contacts with applicants that all are treated in the same way, for example with regard to invitations to visit the department, informal meetings to discuss the vacancy, and provision of information.

The confidentiality of applications must be respected by all of those involved in the selection process.

Selecting the Interview Panel

All interviews must be conducted by a panel. The Head of Department/Line Manager should select interview panel members prior to the closing date. This allows panel members to assist in the shortlisting process. Familiarity with the vacancy and preparation for the interview is a key to successful interviewing.

Panels must:

- Consist of a minimum of three people including the immediate Line Manager of the vacant post, a colleague who is familiar with the area of work and a third person, preferably from outside the department to balance the panel's perspective.

- Consist of staff who have received training in fair recruitment.
- Consider if the appointment is to a department providing services to the rest of the college, of inviting an end user of these services to join the panel.
- Reflect a sex and ethnicity balance wherever possible —the make up of panels will be monitored to assess how regularly this is achieved.
- Declare if they already know a candidate.
- Be willing and able to attend all interviews for the duration of the recruitment process, to maintain consistency and to ensure fair treatment of all candidates.

Monitoring

It is mandatory to monitor the ethnic origin of applicants for all posts, those shortlisted and appointees, and has also decided to monitor sex and disability status. This informs about company how its Equal Opportunities Policy is working in practice and whether its recruitment practices are having a discriminatory effect on any particular groups.

Shortlisting

After the closing date has passed, the interview panel should assess the applications to determine which applicants are to be called for interview. At least two members of the interview panel, including the immediate Line Manager, should undertake the task of shortlisting. Where the panel has an external member, that person should take part in the shortlisting wherever practicable. Shortlisting decisions should be based on evidence that the applicant has met the requirements of the person specification. Shortlisting panel members should avoid dismissing applicants who appear to be over-qualified. Assumptions should not be made about their reasons for applying for the post as they may eliminate an otherwise exemplary candidate. The selection criteria pro-forma can assist with the task of shortlisting.

The original applications for all applicants, together with a written note of reasons for shortlisting or rejecting applicants must be retained for a minimum of 6 months from the date that an appointment decision is notified, in case of complaint to an Employment Tribunal.

Arrangements for Interviews

Letters or e-mails to Shortlisted Candidates should include:

- Date, time and place of their interview.
- Instructions on how to find their way to the interview venue.
- A request that they contact the author of the letter/message if they have any special requirements in relation to the interview (related to access to the venue or any other special need related to a disability).
- If appropriate, details of any test or presentation they will be required to take or anything they should bring with them (e.g. examples of work or proof of qualifications that are essential to the post).

It is best practice to write to candidates who have not been shortlisted, but if this is not possible due to limited resources, the further particulars for the post should make clear that after a certain period, if they have not heard from company, applicants should consider themselves not to have been shortlisted.

Interviewing

All members of the interview panel must have received training in fair recruitment. In addition to being available to offer advice on any stage of the recruitment process, HR staff can join an interview panel, if requested in advance. Interviews should be scheduled as soon after the closing date as reasonably possible, as delays are likely to lead to a loss of candidates.

The structure of interviews should be decided in advance by determining who will chair the panel and what areas of questioning are required to cover all of the elements of the person specification. The question areas to be explored by each panel member should be agreed in advance to avoid overlap or repetition and panels may find it helpful to discuss their expectations of full answers to the questions, prior to the interview. The interview panel may decide to schedule a number of one-to-one interviews between individual panel members and each candidate. In this situation, each individual panel member should keep notes of each interview.

The same areas of questioning should be covered with all candidates and assumptions should not be made regarding the expertise or abilities of candidates because of their employment history. Interview questions should be phrased so that they do not favour any one candidate or group of candidates. Supplementary questions should be used to probe for further information or clarification where answers are incomplete or ambiguous. Care must be taken to avoid questions that could be construed as discriminatory (e.g. questions about personal circumstances that are unrelated to the job). It is, for example, legitimate to ask for confirmation of whether individuals can comply with the working patterns of the post, but not to ask details of their domestic or child care arrangements, etc. It is the responsibility of the Chair of the panel to ensure that such questions are not asked.

Staff conducting interviews must be aware that, although questions asked may not in themselves be discriminatory, the interpretation of answers by the panel could exhibit prejudice. For example, if indications of ambition were to be regarded as a worthy characteristic in applicants of one sex or ethnic group but not in another. Information regarding personal circumstances which is offered in a CV or at interview must not be taken into consideration in reaching a selection decision. For example, the fact that a male candidate shares details of his domestic circumstances with the panel but a female candidate chooses not to (or vice versa), should not be taken into account.

Interview panels act for company in making selection decisions and are accountable for them. Interview notes must be taken to help the panel to make an informed decision based on the content of the interviews. Such notes must relate to how candidates demonstrate their knowledge, skills, experience and abilities in relation to the person specification.

Where the candidate being interviewed has a disability for which adjustments may need to be considered, the candidate's requirements should be discussed with him/her once the planned questioning is complete. The outcome of these discussions must not influence the consideration of the candidate's application. If the disabled candidate best meets the person specification, urgent advice must be sought after the interview from the HR Division regarding what would be considered 'reasonable adjustments' to accommodate the disability in question for example, HR may seek assistance from Facilities Division to ascertain the likely cost of any required adaptations. In the event that on consideration of the needs of the potential appointee, it is considered that the adaptations needed would not be deemed to be 'reasonable'.

It is good practice to offer internal applicants feedback after interviews and it is company policy to respond to requests for feedback from external applicants. Feedback should be specific, relating to the person specification, and honest. In letting disappointed applicants down gently it can be helpful to balance the applicants' weaknesses with some positive feedback.

Selection Tests and Presentations

Consideration should be given to using job-related selection tests or asking candidates to give presentations as part of the selection process if there are some elements of the person specification that are difficult to test at interview. If selection tests or presentations are to be used, all candidates should be given the same written information as to how long they will take, the topic area(s) they will cover, and what—if anything—they should prepare in advance. Psychometric tests may only be given by trained test administrators and any department wishing to use psychometric tests must contact HR Division for advice. In all cases care should be taken to ensure that job-related tests are well explained in writing for candidates, in plain language, that all candidates are subject to the same tests under exactly the same conditions, and that presentation topics do not favour any one candidate. It is very important that selection tests are not unfairly discriminatory. Advice is available from the Human Resources Division for those wishing to develop selection tests.

Making a Decision After Interview

The information obtained in the application, the interview, any selection tests and in references (if obtained prior to interview) will allow candidates to be assessed against the person specification and a selection decision to be made. The Chair of the panel must ensure that a written note of the reasons for selecting the successful candidate and rejecting others is made and placed on the recruitment file, together with the original applications and notes of all panel members, for a minimum of 6 months after the appointment decision has been notified to the candidates.

If a member of a selection panel feels that there has been any irregularity in the recruitment and selection procedure and the panel cannot resolve the matter at the time, they must report the matter without delay to the Director of Human Resources.

Interview proceedings are confidential and interviewers are free to divulge to others the decision reached only once the appointee has accepted the post.

If references have not been taken up prior to the appointment decision, the Human Resources Division will make a provisional offer to the preferred candidate subject to satisfactory references being received and criminal records or occupational health clearance, where appropriate.

References

The further particulars for a post should make clear to candidates the number and status of referees required and whether the panel intends to seek references before interview. References from relatives or friends should not be accepted. Appropriate referees are those who have direct experience of a candidate's work, education or training: preferably in a supervisory capacity and a reference must be obtained from the current or previous employer. Where an applicant indicates that she does not wish his/her current employer to be contacted prior to a provisional offer being made, this should be respected.

When requesting references, it is helpful to seek precise information and confirm facts, such as length of employment, relationship of the applicant to the referee, job title, brief details of responsibilities, reasons for leaving, sickness record, performance, and any other relevant information. It is helpful to the referee to include a copy of the job description and person specification of the post to which you are recruiting. Do not make requests that only elicit generalisations about candidates' attendance, honesty, or subjective information as to the applicant's suitability for the job. The value of unsolicited references submitted by candidates and addressed 'To Whom It May Concern' is very limited and should be disregarded.

Telephone references should be avoided but, where time pressures or the location of referees dictate that this may be appropriate, recruiters should ensure that they are certain as to the identity of the person to whom they are speaking. When conducting telephone references, it is helpful to plan the conversation beforehand and to have a list of questions ready. A file note should be made at the time of the telephone conversation and written confirmation should always be requested.

References are confidential and must be sought 'in confidence'. Any request for disclosure of references must be forwarded to the Human Resources Division. References should only be used for the purpose for which they were intended and their confidentiality must be maintained. Panel members must return all copies of any references with the application forms and their interview notes to the Chair on completion of the recruitment exercise. References must only be kept on the recruitment file and the personal file held by the Human Resources Division.

Criminal Reference Checks

The company will not discriminate unfairly against

applicants who possess a criminal record; for company's policy on the recruitment of staff with criminal records and the use of criminal record checks under the Rehabilitation of Offenders Act. However certain types of posts, particularly those that involve working with children or vulnerable adults or in other positions of trust or sensitive areas, are exempt from these provisions, and in these cases all convictions must be declared.

Appointment

Only the Human Resources Division issues letters of appointment and places individuals on the payroll (other than very limited exceptions). If the job offer is conditional on completion of a qualification or health screening, this will be made clear in the appointment letter.

Academic qualifications and any others considered essential for the post must be verified by the Department. If requested, Human Resources can advise on the equivalence of overseas qualifications.

The Asylum and Immigration Act makes it an offence to employ anyone who does not have permission to be in, or work in, the country. To avoid making assumptions about such permission, it is the Department's responsibility to ask all appointees for evidence of eligibility to work in the country. It is unlawful racial discrimination to carry out checks only on potential employees who by their appearance or accent seem to be other than Indian. It is, therefore, useful to ask all candidates attending for interview to bring with them evidence of their right to work in the India.

Evidence may be presented in the form of:

- An Indian passport.
- A passport or other travel document endorsed to show that the holder can stay indefinitely in the country or that they can stay in the country and are allowed to undertake the type of work that they are being offered (for further advice, contact Human Resources).
- An Application Registration Card issued by the Home Office stating that the holder is permitted to take employment.

Induction and Probation

It is the company policy that all staff who are new to the company undergo a probationary period during which they will be introduced to the main duties and responsibilities of their post.

Recruitment Process

The eight steps recruitment process is as follows:

1. A vacancy arises. Sometimes this is due to the creation of a new job, on other occasions it may be because an existing member of staff has been promoted or is retiring.
2. The job description is updated and an employee specification is written. The job description lists the duties of the job whilst the employee specification gives details of the experience, skills and abilities needed to carry out the job.
3. A vacancy advertisement is written and is circulated via Walsall Council's weekly bulletin, *Job Shop Weekly*. Other media can be used including newspapers, internet recruitment sites, specialist publications and the Employment Service.
4. Application forms are sent out along with copies of the job description and employee specification and must be returned on or before the closing date that has been set. See our applying for jobs page for further information.
5. A shortlist is compiled of applicants who are going to be invited to attend for interview. This is done by the recruitment panel who compare each application form with the requirements of the employee specification. Feedback can be provided (upon request) to those not shortlisted and applicants have the right to complain if they feel they have been unfairly treated.
6. Interviews are held. The panel will use the same set of questions with each interviewee. The interview may include a selection test. Feedback can be provided

(upon request) and unsuccessful applicants have the right to complain if they feel they have been unfairly treated. See our interviews page for further information.

7. References will be requested. The successful applicant for jobs working in certain areas, including working with children or vulnerable adults, will be asked to apply for a criminal disclosure check through the Criminal Records Bureau.
8. Appoint the successful candidate and arrange induction training.

Recruiting the wrong kind of people can become a serious issue for any company. A defined recruitment process needs to be followed to ensure that the right person reaches the right place.

A general recruitment process involves identifying vacancies, prepare job description and person specification, advertising, managing the response, short-listing, arranging interviews, conducting interviews, decision-making, convey the decision and appointment action. This means that a lot of time and resources have to be invested.

Interviews are an important and a crucial part of recruitment process. The person taking the interview of the candidate has to be well prepared in advance. Concerns like the location of the interview, the time table, the structure of the question strategy, style of taking the interview needs to be decided beforehand so that nothing is left ambiguous.

A general recruitment process may include a written test to judge particular skills of a candidate. In this case, the test should be prepared carefully, not deviating from the subject. A lot can be judged about the candidate from his CV. A proper presentation of his CV in an organized and refined manner speaks a lot about the individual. His mindset and attitude can be judged according to his CV.

There are a few things that need to be kept in mind during the recruitment process. Until the final decision about a certain candidate is taken, it is important to keep in regular touch with the candidate. The decision-making process should not take very long to avoid the candidate from taking up some other opportunity. A candidate should be duly informed once the decision is taken. He should be told the complete process of his appointment clearly with details of all the documents that he needs to submit. A record file should be maintained of the candidate for any future reference.

The recruitment process must be robust and justifiable and should stand up to external scrutiny. Only a good recruitment agency with good understanding can perform the same with a good understanding.

Recruitment Management System

It is absolutely new management system that helps in finding out the Return on Investment (ROI) on Recruitment. How many organizations expect sensible questions about the return on recruitment investment to be answered? The truth is that very few really do. Recruitment is evaluated on the basis of the speed with which positions are filled, the feedback from participants and the percentages of candidates who end up being employed. Very few organizations expect that the true impact on business performance can ever be proven, or recruitment processes fine-tuned to deliver precisely the business benefits required. Instead, recruitment is allowed to carry on without anyone ever knowing if it is delivering the goods, or if opportunities are being missed. Because recruitment is not an exact science, it is allowed to continue (often very thoroughly) without proving its true value.

But is it really so unrealistic to believe that we can measure the business impact of different approaches to recruitment? More and more organizations are asking these questions, and the ones who can respond effectively are achieving surprising business results through their HR functions. A wide range of organizations in western countries, have invested in examining the business success of their recruitment practices, and achieved clear returns. Organizations are starting to find that, with some skill, it is possible to assess the return on investment. It is possible to define the business benefits required, and track the results. This is not just a bean-counting exercise aimed at proving that we are right—it points the way to improve results, and deliver business performance through HR.

What should a Recruitment/Hiring Manager do to calculate the return on investments on recruitment?

1. Start off with a clear analysis of the organizational and commercial outcomes required from recruitment. What is the business trying to achieve, and what part will successful candidates need to play?
2. Develop clear ways of tracking and measuring these outcomes.
3. Carry out an objective and open-minded analysis of the qualities people need to perform. Ruthlessly avoid your judgment being colored by past practice or "knowing what works from experience". If doing this well seems expensive in the short run, it's never as expensive as doing it badly in the long run!
4. Ensure that you assess the full range of qualities needed for success—include personality, motivation and aptitude as well as experience.
5. Ensure that everyone involved in recruitment is trained to the highest possible standards.
6. Carefully connect recruitment to induction, training, management and performance management—to ensure that the business does not just get the right people, but nurtures and capitalizes in them as well.

These approaches deliver returns of investment because

- They identify people who perform,
- Reduce the risk of employing people who cannot (or will not) perform,
- Cut the costs of recruitment and development, and
- Play a major part in driving forwards organizational change.

In common with all people processes, recruitment is there to deliver tangible human and business benefits. Devoting a little time to considering the return on investment is not a nebulous luxury—it is essential to delivering the results the organization needs. It is also a powerful way of positioning HR at the heart of the business. You will not regret.

The need to have Recruitment Management System, its importance in streamlining recruitment process and calculating the Return on Investment. As we are in 21st century, which is being governed by Information Management System and wherein we are talking about Systems, be it Performance Management System, Compensation and Benefits Management Systems, etc. we also have Recruitment Management System, hope you all know about it.

Technology has ushered in new ways of thinking about and executing on talent attraction, selection, and acquisition.

- Applicants can be processed more efficiently and with greater care.
- Candidate relationship management, once reserved for top-tier professional applicants, can be realized across every level of job seeker.
- Proprietary talent communities provide companies with opportunities for targeted marketing and can ultimately reduce time-to-fill and cost-per-hire while increasing the value of the employment brand.

These benefits provide a foundation for talent management to be in play at a broad and individual level.

Don't be mistaken if the biggest pain point in your recruiting process today is that you have no way to track applicants electronically.

For most recruiters, a basic applicant tracking system, even if it starts as an Excel spreadsheet or Access database, is a key to survival and certainly to efficiency. If anything, the urgency to implement even a basic system has only increased in the past few years, as the internet has made it so easy for candidates to apply for jobs. If you don't have an automated way to capture and search for candidate information, your job is going to be defined by performing administrative tasks that consume a significant portion of your available time—time that could almost certainly be better spent on higher-level activities. The good news is that if you're just getting started with applicant tracking, there are many good systems available today to fit almost any budget.

Recruitment Management picks up where applicant tracking left off. Tracking your applicants efficiently is no longer a self-sustaining hiring process and you will inevitably start focusing on the following areas to raise your recruiting process to the next level:

- Tight integration between the hiring management system and corporate recruitment site. This is key because it is the basis for ensuring a consistent and positive job seeker experience, and the most visible aspect of the online employment brand interface. The hiring management system needs to support the integrity of the company's brand first and foremost —which, depending on the company, plays out at varying levels of complexity. An intuitive, flexible interface, supported by data capture, provides insight into the job seeker and drives the overall effectiveness of the system.
- Engaging above-average talent by providing a streamlined and user-friendly online application process—one that candidates tell you is better than your competitors'.
- The ability to seamlessly pre-screen candidates by asking job-specific questions in addition to collecting their resumes. This component should also add value to the applicant's experience while supporting recruiter productivity. If done well, a well-thought-out approach integrated into your Hiring Management System can serve as a self-screen or job preview.
- The ability, at a glance, to see how a candidate fits with the job he or she has applied for, individually and in comparison with all other applicants.
- Making it easy for your recruiters to communicate and build relationships with candidates throughout the recruiting process.

- Additional recruiter productivity enhancement tools.
- The ability to extract data from your system to make decisions that support continuously improving your recruiting and talent attraction process.

Conclusion

At the end, I like to say that HR professional is having a big responsibility to hire a best person from the available talent pool. At the same time, one needs to be cost conscious. It is a good practice in recruitment to be objective and seek to identify the candidates' abilities. Judge on individual merits and set the same standards for all. Whereas generalized assumptions made about ability or ambition, based on applicant's sex, caste, age, religious belief, sexual orientation or any disability, is a bad practice. One need to use the technology, to get the best results from recruitment process.

E-recruitment

Online recruitment facilitates just-in-time hiring. When an organization needs a candidate it can access the database of job portals, screen resumes and send a mass mail. It can also shortlist people based on skills, location, salary and availability and move on to the interview stage.

Online recruitment offers candidates the advantage of knowing the job profile, responsibilities expected and the nature of the organization, which are well-defined at the outset. Regular communication with potential employees in the manual recruitment process is almost nil, whereas communication with job seekers and within the team is seamless in online recruitment. "It takes a while for the manual recruitment process to become operational and yield results whereas in e-recruitment, one can look at the first response to a job advertisement in just 20 minutes.

Online Recruitment Techniques

- To measure the effectiveness of online recruitment, set up the metrics for recruitment spending.
- A detailed job description should be given while posting jobs to attract candidates with the right skill sets.

- Give a precise and unambiguous questionnaire to reduce time in searching for a suitable candidate.
- Ensure that all the approaches related to recruitment are linked to and centered on your own recruitment site.
- Integrate e-recruitment into your overall recruitment strategy.
- Applicant tracking system should be of a high quality and should be integrated with the back-office.
- Develop a comprehensive website to receive and process job applications whether through direct or online advertising.

Advantage of Online Recruitment

- It is much faster than traditional modes of recruitment.
- One can post a job online in just 20 minutes and receive resumes within minutes of the job going live.
- Access an online pool of resumes on a 24 × 7 basis.
- It allows the hiring manager to screen out unqualified candidates in an automated way, which saves over 65 per cent of the hiring time.
- One can track the progress that the candidate is making in various stages of the hiring process.

Recruitment Process Outsourcing (RPO)

It is modern recruitment style for recruiting offshore candidate for world market. It is very common in India. Recruitment Process Outsourcing grew in India with Business Process Outsourcing (BPO). This new recruitment process opened the door for talented employees and employers round the globe.

5
Interviews

Interviews are an important and a crucial part of recruitment process. The person taking the interview of the candidate has to be well prepared in advance. Concerns like the location of the interview, the time table, the structure of the question strategy, style of taking the interview needs to be decided beforehand so that nothing is left ambiguous in.

All job interviews have the same objective, but employers reach that objective in a variety of ways. You might enter the room expecting to tell stories about your professional successes and instead find yourself selling the interviewer a bridge or editing code at a computer. One strategy for performing your best during an interview is to know the rules of the particular game you are playing when you walk through the door. The types of interview are as follows:

The Screening Interview

Companies use screening tools to ensure that candidates meet minimum qualification requirements. Computer programs are among the tools used to weed out unqualified candidates. (This is why you need a digital resume that is screening-friendly. See our resume center for help.) Sometimes human professionals are the gatekeepers. Screening interviewers often have honed skills to determine whether there is anything that might disqualify you for the position. Remember they do not need to know whether you are the best fit for the position, only whether you are not a match. For this reason, screeners tend to dig for dirt. Screeners will hone in on gaps in your employment history or pieces of information that look inconsistent. They also will want to know from the outset whether you will be too expensive for the company.

Some tips for maintaining confidence during screening interviews:

- Highlight your accomplishments and qualifications.
- Get into the straightforward groove. Personality is not as important to the screener as verifying your qualifications. Answer questions directly and succinctly. Save your winning personality for the person making hiring decisions!
- Be tactful about addressing income requirements. Give a range, and try to avoid giving specifics by replying, "I would be willing to consider your best offer."
- If the interview is conducted by phone, it is helpful to have note cards with your vital information sitting next to the phone. That way, whether the interviewer catches you sleeping or vacuuming the floor, you will be able to switch gears quickly.

The Informational Interview

On the opposite end of the stress spectrum from screening interviews is the informational interview. A meeting that you initiate, the informational interview is underutilized by job-seekers who might otherwise consider themselves savvy to the merits of networking. Jobseekers ostensibly secure informational meetings in order to seek the advice of someone in their current or desired field as well as to gain further references to people who can lend insight. Employers that like to stay apprised of available talent even when they do not have current job openings, are often open to informational interviews, especially if they like to share their knowledge, feel flattered by your interest, or esteem the mutual friend that connected you to them. During an informational interview, the jobseeker and employer exchange information and get to know one another better without reference to an employment.

Specific Job Opening

This takes off some of the performance pressure, but be intentional nonetheless:

- Come prepared with thoughtful questions about the field and the company.
- Gain references to other people and make sure that the interviewer would be comfortable if you contact other people and use his or her name.
- Give the interviewer your card, contact information and resume.
- Write a thank you note to the interviewer.

The Directive Style

In this style of interview, the interviewer has a clear agenda that he or she follows unflinchingly. Sometimes companies use this rigid format to ensure parity between interviews; when interviewers ask each candidate the same series of questions, they can more readily compare the results. Directive interviewers rely upon their own questions and methods to tease from you what they wish to know. You might feel like you are being steam-rolled, or you might find the conversation develops naturally. Their style does not necessarily mean that they have dominance issues, although you should keep an eye open for these if the interviewer would be your supervisor.

Either way, remember:

- Flex with the interviewer, following his or her lead.
- Do not relinquish complete control of the interview. If the interviewer does not ask you for information that you think is important to proving your superiority as a candidate, politely interject it.

The Meandering Style

This interview type, usually used by inexperienced interviewers, relies on you to lead the discussion. It might begin with a statement like "tell me about yourself", which you can use to your advantage. The interviewer might ask you another broad, open-ended question before falling into silence. This interview style allows you tactfully to guide the discussion in a way that best serves you.

The following strategies, which are helpful for any interview, are particularly important when interviewers use a non-directive approach:

- Come to the interview prepared with highlights and anecdotes of your skills, qualities and experiences. Do not rely on the interviewer to spark your memory-jot down some notes that you can reference throughout the interview.
- Remain alert to the interviewer. Even if you feel like you can take the driver's seat and go in any direction you wish, remain respectful of the interviewer's role. If he or she becomes more directive during the interview, adjust.
- Ask well-placed questions. Although the open format allows you significantly to shape the interview, running with your own agenda and dominating the conversation means that you run the risk of missing important information about the company and its needs.

The Stress Interview

Astounding as this is, the Greek hazing system has made its way into professional interviews. Either employers view the stress interview as a legitimate way of determining candidates' aptness for a position or someone has latent maniacal tendencies. You might be held in the waiting room for an hour before the interviewer greets you. You might face long silences or cold stares. The interviewer might openly challenge your believes or judgment. You might be called upon to perform an impossible task on the fly-like convincing the interviewer to exchange shoes with you. Insults and miscommunication are common. All this is designed to see whether you have the mettle to withstand the company culture, the clients or other potential stress.

Besides wearing a strong anti-perspirant, you will do well to:

- Remember that this is a game. It is not personal. View it as the surreal interaction that it is.
- Prepare and memorize your main message before walking through the door. If you are flustered, you will better maintain clarity of mind if you do not have to wing your responses.
- Even if the interviewer is rude, remain calm and tactful.
- Go into the interview relaxed and rested. If you go into it feeling stressed, you will have a more difficult time keeping a cool perspective.

The Behavioral Interview

Many companies increasingly rely on behavior interviews since they use your previous behavior to indicate your future performance. In these interviews, employers use standardized methods to mine information relevant to your competency in a particular area or position. Depending upon the responsibilities of the job and the working environment, you might be asked to describe a time that required problem-solving skills, adaptability, leadership, conflict resolution, multi-tasking, initiative or stress management. You will be asked how you dealt with the situations.

Your responses require not only reflection, but also organization. To maximize your responses in the behavioral format:

- Anticipate the transferable skills and personal qualities that are required for the job.
- Review your resume. Any of the qualities and skills you have included in your resume are fair game for an interviewer to press.
- Reflect on your own professional, volunteer, educational and personal experience to develop brief stories that highlight these skills and qualities in you. You should have a story for each of the competencies on your resume as well as those you anticipate the job requires.

- Prepare stories by identifying the context, logically highlighting your actions in the situation, and identifying the results of your actions. Keep your responses concise and present them in less than two minutes.

The Audition

For some positions, such as computer programmers or trainers, companies want to see you in action before they make their decision. For this reason, they might take you through a simulation or brief exercise in order to evaluate your skills. An audition can be enormously useful to you as well, since it allows you to demonstrate your abilities in interactive ways that are likely familiar to you. The simulations and exercises should also give you a simplified sense of what the job would be like. If you sense that other candidates have an edge on you in terms of experience or other qualifications, requesting an audition can help level the playing field.

To maximize on auditions, remember to:

- Clearly understand the instructions and expectations for the exercise. Communication is half the battle in real life, and you should demonstrate to the prospective employer that you make the effort to do things right the first time by minimizing confusion.
- Treat the situation as if you are a professional with responsibility for the task laid before you. Take ownership of your work.
- Brush up on your skills before an interview if you think they might be tested.

The Group Interview

Interviewing simultaneously with other candidates can be disconcerting, but it provides the company with a sense of your leadership potential and style. The group interview helps the company get a glimpse of how you interact with peers—are you timid or bossy, are you attentive or do you seek attention, do others turn to you instinctively, or do you compete for authority? The interviewer also wants to view what your tools of persuasion are: do you use argumentation and careful reasoning to gain support or do you divide and conquer? The interviewer might call on you to discuss an issue with the other candidates, solve a problem collectively, or discuss your peculiar qualifications in front of the other candidates.

This environment might seem overwhelming or hard to control, but there are a few tips that will help you navigate the group interview successfully:

- Observe to determine the dynamics the interviewer establishes and try to discern the rules of the game. If you are unsure of what is expected from you, ask for clarification from the interviewer.
- Treat others with respect while exerting influence over others.
- Avoid overt power conflicts, which will make you look uncooperative and immature.
- Keep an eye on the interviewer throughout the process so that you do not miss important cues.

The Tag-Team Interview

Expecting to meet with Ms. Jain, you might find yourself in a room with four other people: Ms. Jain, two of her staff, and the Sales Director. Companies often want to gain the insights of various people when interviewing candidates. This method of interviewing is often attractive for companies that rely heavily on team cooperation. Not only does the company want to know whether your skills balance that of the company, but also whether you can get along with the other workers. In some companies, multiple people will interview you simultaneously. In other companies, you will proceed through a series of one-on-one interviews. Some helpful tips for maximizing on this interview format:

- Treat each person as an important individual. Gain each person's business card at the beginning of the meeting, if possible, and refer to each person by name. If there are several people in the room at once, you might wish to scribble down their names on a sheet of paper according to where each is sitting.

Make eye contact with each person and speak directly to the person asking each question.

- Use the opportunity to gain as much information about the company as you can. Just as each interviewer has a different function in the company, they each have a unique perspective. When asking questions, be sensitive not to place anyone in a position that invites him to compromise confidentiality or loyalty.
- Bring at least double the anecdotes and sound-bites to the interview as you would for a traditional one-on-one interview. Be ready to illustrate your main message in a variety of ways to a variety of people.
- Prepare psychologically to expend more energy and be more alert than you would in a one-on-one interview. Stay focused and adjustable.

The Mealtime Interview

For many, interviewing over a meal sounds like a professional and digestive catastrophe in the making. If you have difficulty chewing gum while walking, this could be a challenge. With some preparation and psychological readjustment, you can enjoy the process. Meals often have a cementing social effect-breaking bread together tends to facilitate deals, marriages, friendships, and religious communion. Mealtime interviews rely on this logic, and expand it.

Particularly when your job requires interpersonal acuity, companies want to know what you are like in a social setting. Are you relaxed and charming or awkward and evasive? Companies want to observe not only how you handle a fork, but also how you treat your host, any other guests, and the serving staff.

Some basic social tips help ease the complexity of mixing food with business:

- Take cues from your interviewer, remembering that you are the guest. Do not sit down until your host does. Order something slightly less extravagant than your interviewer. If he badly wants you to try a particular dish, oblige him. If he recommends an appetizer to you, he likely intends to order one himself. Do not begin eating until he does. If he orders coffee and dessert, do not leave him eating alone.

- If your interviewer wants to talk business, do so. If she and the other guests discuss their upcoming travel plans or their families, do not launch into business.
- Try to set aside dietary restrictions and preferences. Remember, the interviewer is your host. It is rude to be finicky unless you absolutely must. If you must, be as tactful as you can. Avoid phrases like: "I do not eat mammals," or "Shrimp makes my eyes swell and water."
- Choose manageable food items, if possible. Avoid barbeque ribs and spaghetti.
- Find a discrete way to check your teeth after eating. Excuse yourself from the table for a moment.
- Practice eating and discussing something important simultaneously.
- Thank your interviewer for the meal.

The Follow-up Interview

Companies bring candidates back for second and sometimes third or fourth interviews for a number of reasons. Sometimes they just want to confirm that you are the amazing worker they first thought you to be. Sometimes they are having difficulty deciding between a short-list of candidates. Other times, the interviewer's supervisor or other decision makers in the company want to gain a sense of you before signing a hiring decision.

The second interview could go in a variety of directions, and you must prepare for each of them. When meeting with the same person again, you do not need to be as assertive in your communication of your skills. You can focus on cementing rapport, understanding where the company is going and how your skills mesh with the company vision and culture.

Still, the interviewer should view you as the answer to their needs. You might find yourself negotiating a compensation package. Alternatively, you might find that you are starting from the beginning with a new person.

Some tips for managing second interviews:

- Be confident. Accentuate what you have to offer and your interest in the position.
- Probe tactfully to discover more information about the internal company dynamics and culture.
- Walk through the front door with a plan for negotiating a salary.
- Be prepared for anything: to relax with an employer or to address the company's qualms about you.

6

Motivation

Motivation

The word motivation is derived from "Motive" which is defined as an active form of desire craving or need which must be satisfied.

All motives are directed towards goal and the need and desires affect or change your behavior which becomes goal oriented. Motivation, therefore, is creating goal oriented behavior among employees in an organization.

Motivation management is a modern, practical approach that will be useful to management trainers and trainees. Also, it will be a good guide in solving motivation problems within an organization. In reality, it does not add significantly to the theories of Pavlov, Maslow, McClelland, Herzberg, and Vroom. It seems to borrow a little from each of their works on motivation.

Motivation is a continuous challenge among managers today. The problems and solutions to motivation problems can be complex to say the least. Tools and ideas are available to managers and leaders to help with motivation. Studying the timeless theories of Herzberg, McClelland, Vroom, Pavlov, and Maslow can provide ideas and solutions to motivation problems. Motivation management and the individual motivation profile are also useful tools in discovering how to motivate certain individuals. Improving motivation starts with employee selection and high organizational expectations.

Managers that utilize these tools and ideas can be successful motivators.

Characteristics of Motivation

1. Individuals differ in their motivation level.
2. Motivation changes time to time.
3. Motivation is complex.

Theories of Motivation

There are two major motivation theories based on how employees motivate and what motivates employees. These are two theories known as content theory and process theory. Content theory attempts to specify what sort of events or outcomes motivate behavior of employees. Process theory attempts to explain how different kinds of events or outcomes motivate behavior of employees. Both the theories are summarized as follow. In process theory performance always comes into picture. In process theory there is relation between cause and effects, for example even if you will study hard for 6 hours you may or may not get first division.

Content Theory

1. Maslow's hierarchy Theory of Needs.
2. Herzberg's Two Factor Theory.
3. Alderfer's ERG Theory.
4. McClelland Theory of Achievement.

Process Theory

1. Skinner's Reinforcement Theory.
2. Vroom's Expectancy Theory.
3. Adam's Equity Theory.
4. Lock's Goal Setting Theory.

Over the years, many psychologists have attempted to define and categorise what motivates people. This became particularly important after the Second World War as the Western nations attempted to rebuild their drained industrial economies, and during the '50s and '60s much was researched and written about Human Relations. It was recognised that people who worked in organisations were more than just numbers and, if properly managed, could not only produce more, but also contribute more.

What is motivation? What factors influence motivation and, therefore need to be addressed? How does a supervisor or manager motivate employees to do their best? Can it be done using the older, mid-twentieth century theories of Maslow, McClelland, Herzberg, Vroom, and Pavlov in today's business world? Or, should theories based on more modern research, which is more up to date, be used? The challenge of an organization's leaders and managers to motivate is extremely complex. They must find out what works for them in their situation in their respective organizations. We will look at the traditional theories from the early to mid-twentieth century. We will see how they can still be applied in business today. We will also analyze a more modern theory, which may be more applicable today. We will compare the two generations of theories. There is probably no "absolute" to this study, because both generations of theories have many parallels to each other. We will attempt to answer all of the preceding questions in the pages to follow.

Motivation can be defined in a variety of ways, depending on whom you ask. If you ask someone on the street, you may get a response like, "It's what drives us" or "Motivation is what makes us do the things we do." As far as a formal definition, motivation can be defined as "forces within an individual that account for the level, direction, and persistence of effort expended at work", according to Schermerhorn, et al. This is an excellent working definition for use in business. Now that we understand what motivation is, we can look at the factors that help managers to be able to motivate and then look at some of the theories on motivation.

A Brief Look at Motivation Theories

Pavlov did extensive studies on classical conditioning. Classical conditioning is "a form of learning through association that involves the manipulation of stimuli to influence behavior". More simply, within organizations, employees associate an action with a following action, and then they expect the following action each time the initial action appears. This is a natural reaction for some. Pavlov's theory is difficult to argue with and is applicable today and probably will be for a long time.

Maslow's Hierarchy Theory of Needs

Maslow developed a "hierarchy of needs" or an order of needs that need to be fulfilled in each person. If a manager embraces Maslow's hierarchy, he/she will motivate employees, keeping the order of needs in mind. The hierarchy of needs is shown below:

1. *Self actualization*—need to grow and use abilities to the fullest; highest need
2. *Esteem*—need for respect, prestige, and recognition from others as well as self-esteem and personal sense of competence
3. *Social*—need for love, affection, and belongingness in one's relationships with others
4. *Safety*—need for security, protection, and stability in the personal events of everyday life
5. *Physiological*—most basic of human needs; need for food, water, and sustenance.

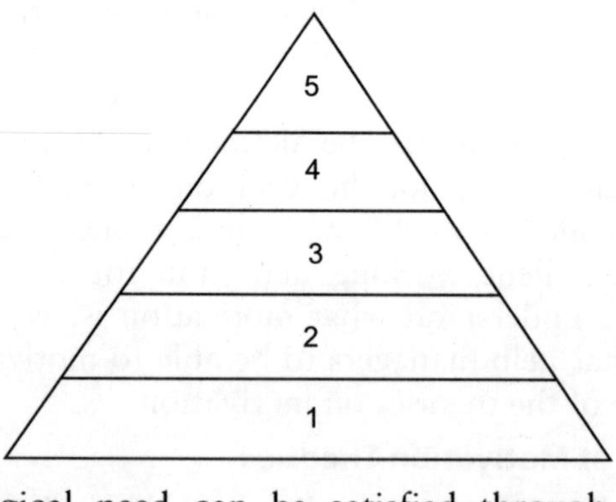

Physiological need can be satisfied through efforts and incentives as adequate wages and salary, good working conditions in order to provide comfort and avoid fatigue, bonus, fringe benefits, etc.

Safety and security needs met through steps with which includes job security, cost of living, increments, retirement benefits, life insurance and medical insurance, freedom to join unions, protection against automation, etc.

Social need includes love and affection. People find an opportunity in their work environment for establishing friendly interpersonal relationships. These can be satisfied by providing opportunity for employees to interact socially with each other in free environment. Creating team sprit by keeping work groups informal wherever possible with friendly and supportive with employees to discus matters relating to personal achievement and contribution and organization development.

Self-esteem needs involve feeling of satisfaction, achievement and recognition. The management can take following steps:

- Give recognition and encouragement for performance, contribution and delegation of additional authorities to subordinates.
- Design more challenging jobs and provide feedback on performance.
- Involve people in goal setting and decision-making.
- Organise adequate training and executive development programme to increase their competencies level.
- Provide some symbol for status and respect, job title, write-ups about achievements, citation, etc.

Self-actualization, need for growth and creativity which can be satisfied by the following steps:

- Provide autonomy to the employees. This will open the challenge of communications further and give the employees an opportunity to get involved.
- Autonomy will encourage and develop creativity among employees.
- Employees should be given an opportunity to share their own jobs.

Using this theory, managers can use the hierarchy to motivate people by satisfying the most important needs.

Herzberg Two Factor Theory

Herzberg Two Factor Theory is also known as "Theory X/ Theory Y" or "Motivation—Hygiene Theory". Frederick Herzberg studied and practised clinical psychology in Pittsburgh, where he researched the work-related motivations of thousands of employees. His findings were published in "The Motivation to Work" in 1959. He concluded that there were two types of motivation:

Douglas McGregor published "The Human Side of Enterprise" in 1960, in which he suggested that traditional management methods (which he called Theory X) might not be the only way to get people motivated. Instead, you could take a different approach (based on Theory Y) and achieve the same if not more.

Herzberg developed his two factor theory, taking a different approach from others. Herzberg argues that hygiene factors in the work setting are sources for job dissatisfaction. Also, he says that motivator factors in work tasks are sources for job satisfaction. His theories can be summarized by quote from him, "If you want people to do a good job, give them a good job to do." The theory of Herzberg may seem a little vague, but it is based on superb ideas. The two factor theory may be as useful, or more, than other theories of the time, because job context and content are major issues in the business world today.

Hygiene Factors that can demotivate if they are not present —such as supervision, interpersonal relations, physical working conditions, and salary. Hygiene Factors affect the level of dissatisfaction, but are rarely quoted as creators of job satisfaction.

Motivation Factors that will motivate if they are present—such as achievement, advancement, recognition and responsibility. Dissatisfaction isn't normally blamed on Motivation Factors, but they are cited as the cause of job satisfaction.

So, once you've satisfied the Hygiene factors, providing more of them won't generate much more motivation, but lack of the Motivation Factors won't of themselves demotivate. There are clear relationships to Maslow here, but Herzberg's ideas really shaped modern thinking about reward and recognition in major companies.

Theory X Assumptions:

- People inherently dislike work.
- People must be coerced or controlled to do work to achieve objectives.
- People prefer to be directed.

Theory Y Assumptions:

- People view work as being as natural as play and rest.
- People will exercise self-direction and control towards achieving objectives they are committed to.
- People learn to accept and seek responsibility.

Motivator Hygiene Factor Theory

Motivator factors increase job satisfaction:

- Achievement
- Recognition
- Work itself
- Responsibility
- Advancement
- Growth

Hygiene factors are those whose absence can create job dissatisfaction:

- Supervision
- Company policy
- Working conditions
- Salary
- Peer relationship
- Security

Theory Y is not a soft option. In fact, it can take as much management effort as Theory X, but the effects of a Theory Y approach will last longer. The Theory X manager is a dying breed (although it has to be said he's not yet extinct), and Theory Y lies behind most modern approaches to motivation. Nowadays the terminology is used as a polite way of referring to the old command-and-control approach to management: the trouble is the diehard Theory X manager won't pick up the subtle criticism!

Alderfer's ERG Theory

ERG theory is a fairly new addition to motivation literature; it has not been studied much. Preliminary evidence suggests, however, that ERG theory may be a more economical and powerful explanation of human motivation than either the needs hierarchy or manifest needs theory.

ERG theory developed by Alderfer extends and refines Maslow's needs hierarchy concept although there are several important differences between the two. The E, R & G stands for three basic needs categories. E stands for existence; R stands for relatedness; and G stands for growth.

Existence needs—roughly corresponds to the physiological and safety needs of Maslow's hierarchy.

Relatedness needs—involving the need to relate to others, are similar to social and esteem need.

Growth needs—are analogues to self-actualization need.

Like manifest needs, ERG theory suggests that more than one kind of need, for example Relatedness and Growth needs can motivate a person at the same time. A more important difference from Maslow's hierarchy is that ERG theory includes a frustration-regression components and satisfaction-progression component. The satisfaction progression process suggests that after satisfying one category of needs, a person progresses to the next level. On this point, the need hierarchy and ERG theory agree. The need hierarchy, however, assumed that the individual will remain at the next level until the needs at that level are satisfied. In contrast, ERG argues that a person who is frustrated in trying to satisfy a higher level of needs eventually will regress to the preceding level.

Suppose for instance a manager has satisfied her basic need at the relatedness level and now is trying to satisfy her growth need. For a variety of reasons, such as organization constraints (i.e. few challenging jobs) and the absence of opportunities to advance, she is unable to satisfy those needs. According to ERG theory, frustration of her growth need will cause the managers relatedness needs to once again become dominant as motivators.

Now, it has been confirmed that ERG is a content theory because after satisfaction of existence needs (physiological and safety needs of Maslow's hierarchy) it satisfies Relatedness needs (social and esteem need) and then satisfies Growth needs (self-actualization need). Apart from this there are few differences between ERG and Need hierarchy theory. Alderfer has given different classification of needs as ERG. Maslow's needs are hierarchical need but the Alderfer's needs are unidirectional.

McClelland Theory of Achievement

McClelland Theory of Achievement is also known as "Three needs theory". McClelland and his associates came up with a test to measure human needs. They came up with three needs: need for achievement, need for affiliation, and need for power. According to McClelland, these needs are acquired with time and life experience. McClelland urged managers to be able to identify these needs in others to help themselves understand how to motivate individuals. Different motivation approaches would be used depending upon which need is identified. McClelland's ideas are very good, according to this author, and they can be applied today and tomorrow.

McClelland suggests that three needs are important for us to understand motivation need for achievement. These three needs are summarized as follows:

Need for Achievement

- Need for Achievement
- Personal responsibility

- Feedback
- Moderate risk

Need for Power

- Influence
- Competitive

Need for Affiliation

- Acceptance and Friendship
- Cooperative

Skinner's Reinforcement Theory

Skinner's reinforcement theory is also known as "Behavioral modification theory" This theory attempts to specify that need behavioral modification is processed when behavior is undesirable (which doesn't define norms). It suggests that undesirable behavior should be modified and desirable behavior should be reinforced.

Vroom's Expectancy Theory

Vroom's expectancy theory argues that motivation is based on values and beliefs of individuals, or, how a person feels effort; performance and outcomes. He developed an equation to "calculate" motivation using three factors:

1. *Expectancy*—The probability that effort will be followed by personal accomplishment.
2. *Instrumentality*—The probability that performance will lead to outcomes.
3. *Valence*—The value of an individual of an outcome.

Vroom argues that a manager can use the equation M=E×I×V to predict whether a particular reward will motivate an individual. While the basis of Vroom's expectancy theory is very good, the equation seems a little awkward today.

An individual will act in a certain way based on the expectation that the act will be followed by a given outcome and on the attractiveness of that outcome to the individual.

Effort ——> Performance linkage (How hard will I have to work?)

Performance ——> Reward linkage (What is the reward?)

Attractiveness (How attractive is the reward?)

Suggestions for Motivating the Employees

- Recognize individual differences
- Match people to jobs
- Use goals
- Individualize rewards
- Link rewards to performance
- Check the system for equity
- Don't ignore money

Adam's Equity Theory

Adam's Equity Theory suggests that individuals compare their job inputs and outcomes with those of others and if the employee perceives inequity, he/she will act to correct the inequity: The following indicators play a vital role to justify the inequity:

- Lower productivity
- Reduced quality
- Increased absenteeism
- Voluntary resignation.

(J. Stacey Adams, 1965)

The equity theory assumes that the own social comparison of employees to their peers is the most important factor for motivation. The expectancy theory suggests that people are motivated to work toward rewards, bonuses and other goodies. In my opinion, only a combination of these two, with the expectancy theory following the equity theory in relevance is a valid approach. I do not believe in only the social aspects and mind-setting of employees although the social position and treatment is probably the required precursor before additional goodies and goals can create a vital effect on motivation.

Lock's Goal Setting Theory

Lock's Goal Setting Theory suggests that behavior is driven by goals and aspirations, such that specific and difficult goals lead to higher level of achievement. In other words Specific goals increase performance, and difficult goals, when accepted, result in higher performance than easy goals.

A Look at a More Recent Theory

Sheila Ritchie and Martin developed their motivation management theory in the late 1990's. The basic assumption is that "'the task of the manager is to find out what motivates people' and to make them 'smile more and carp less.'" From literature and their own observations, they identified twelve "motivational drivers." These include human needs for interesting work, achievement, self-development, variety, creativity, power, influence, social contact, money and tangible rewards, structure and rules, long-term relationships, and good working conditions. They then developed a motivational profile survey with thirty-three questions. After scoring, a unique pattern of the individual's motivational drivers is revealed that can be compared to the data of the original one thousand three hundred fifty-five respondents.

Knowing an individual's profile, a manager can then tailor a motivation method for that person. For instance, if a manager is considering giving an employee a raise and their profile shows that creativity and variety motivate this person, then the manager should reward accordingly, not with a raise. Ritchie and Martin claim that each of the twelve drivers is independent of the others. The motivation management theory of Ritchie and Martin would be classified as a content theory, which suggest that motivation results from the individual's attempts to satisfy needs. The order of the twelve drivers listed above reflects the profile scores of the original sample. This is to say that, among this group of managers, the needs for interesting work and achievement were most important (note: money came ninth in the original study).

Comparison between the Two Generations

Both generations of theory have strengths and weaknesses when compared to the other. We will examine these differences in the following paragraphs.

Out With the Old, In With the New

Ritchie and Martin's study is based on contemporary data that is more credible in today's business world, instead of data that is fifty to sixty years old. Motivation management can also serve as a tool for self-analysis and for individual or group motivation profiles. Ritchie and Martin also recognize a wide range of individual differences, rather than one universal approach. Maslow and Herzberg both argued that their respective theories applied to everyone. Lastly, it offers a guide for managers who are seeking to improve individual and group motivation. Ritchie and Martin advise managers to focus on the motivational profile of the person, regardless of occupational or cultural background.

Motivation Theories are Like Wine; They Get Better With Age

The factors of the older theories are based on evidence, and Ritchie and Martin's twelve drivers seem to be somewhat arbitrary. Sampling in the older theories was generally more diverse. Motivation management was based on a study of all managers of training programs. Also, there was no mention by the group of managers of the basic needs such as food, drink, sex, and security. Many parallels are apparent in the motivational factors of motivation management and it's predecessors. All of the factors seen in this modern theory have been seen before, thus any claim of originality would have to be considered somewhat suspect in the least.

Methods for Managers to Gauge Motivation Probability

Employee Selection

A manager's ability to motivate starts earlier than most people think with employee selection. The hiring of employees that are self-motivated is crucial to the success of any business. If an employee is motivated from within, then the "motivator" aspect of a manager's job is less difficult. As with many ideas, this "easier said than done". There is a colossal barrier to only hiring those that are self-motivated. With the legal restraints today in regard to discrimination, managers often give up trying to make "good" hiring decisions for fear of discriminating illegally. Therefore, most managers have become solely reliant on intuition during the hiring process. The trick seems to be to try to hire those that are motivated to do what is best for the organization without discriminating against those who may be motivated, but not to work, and those that have the skills necessary for a position but lack the motivation all together. It is this challenge that will puzzle today's managers and those of tomorrow.

Another method that managers can utilize to help them motivate their employees is incorporating high organizational expectations. Some leaders and managers build important productivity expectations into their organizational cultures. These expectations include a sense of responsibility, high productivity, and quality of output. These expectations are impressed upon new employees. These managers show this by having new employees watch "pace setters" to demonstrate that these expectations are taken very seriously throughout the organization.

By employing these two methods, managers, more than likely, will not need to motivate their employees as much or as often. This is not to say that motivation can be neglected at any point. Managers must continually motivate their employees, but this can be made easier by attempting to hire self-motivated employees and impressing high standards upon them and reinforcing the standards on a daily basis.

Six Theories of Motivation for Sound Leadership

Harnessing human motivation is a core competency of the transformational leader. Unlike managers who tend to rely on authority to make things happen inside organizations, the transformational leader harnesses the power inherent in human motivation.

I remember a few years ago sitting in a class on human motivation with a professor who forced us to read about every published theory on motivation published in the scholarly journals over the past 70 years. Finally, toward the end of the class one courageous (and desperate) student went ahead and asked him, "Of the many theories we have covered, which two or three are the most important to learn and to apply?"

The professor gave an ambiguously ambiguous answer which went, "They are all important since each one has been thoroughly researched." While a correct answer, it was also completely useless. This led to my search for a set of theories that one can learn and apply in the real world.

Within the world of psychology, there are two general schools of thought regarding motivation. The first school is called the behaviorist school. Those who hold this philosophy are not interested in black box of the human mind—they focus on observable behavior.

The contrasting school of thought are the motivational theories within the field of cognitive psychology. In this area there are many, many theories that take into account factors such as needs, beliefs, scripts, schemas, volition, attitudes, values, etc.

On the cognitive side of things, three models are worth knowing: needs, equity, and expectancy theories. Many have run across Maslow's Hierarchy of needs, but one especially important need theory is known McClelland's Learned Needs.

Needs Theory. McClelland felt that certain needs are not preprogrammed into the body via the genes, but learned from the environment. We learn to affiliate (or not affiliate) with people, how to exercise power, and how to be achievement oriented. Because these needs are learned, McClelland would teach need for achievement, something associated with success in various fields of endeavor. It's believed, for example, that need for achievement is one of the primary motive forces driving entrepreneurs to start a business.

Equity Theory. Adam lays the groundwork to understand why people perceive something as fair or unfair. This is a most serious issue for management, not to appear to have favorites and treat people the way they want to be treated.

Expectancy Theory. This approach focuses on the beliefs that influence effort and performance. For example, when if one believes that one's efforts result in a certain level of performance associated with a desired reward, likely one will take action. Of course, the exact opposite is also true. A low correlation between effort, performance and reward breeds inaction.

On the behavioral side, there are three behavioral theories worth understanding.

Classical Conditioning. Made famous by the Russian Nobel Laureate by the name of the E.I. Pavlov, it's not widely used within the world of business. But it goes a long way toward explaining the nature and power of advertising to influence our purchase behavior. The more widely known, widely used and widely applied behavioral theory is known as behavior modification.

Behavioral Modification. Also known as operant conditioning, many people have contributed to this theory, the best known being Harvard psychologist B.F. Skinner. To the behaviorist, behavior falls into two categories, it's either desired or undesired. Sometimes I think there's a third category called, "I don't care" behavior. For example, we might see someone walking down the street who throws a cigarette on the ground. But since it's a "I don't care", behavior, we do not act to modify that person's behavior.

When a behavior is undesired or desired, we need to take some type of action to apply a consequence. This consequence will cause a desired behavior to increase in frequency or an undesired behavior decrease in frequency. Behavior modification is especially attractive since it's an easy to apply, and one of the easiest to learn of the motivation theories.

Modeling. The third type of motivation theory is known as vicarious learning (modeling). Human beings learn of a tremendous amount from watching and observing others. The most obvious example is young children, were a boy or the young girl observes their father and mother and imitates that individual. So the old saying, "Monkey see, monkey do", rings true for humans.

The same process goes on in organizations. New employees don't know exactly how to act and so observe others to figure out what they need to do. In fact, the one person most watched in all organizations is one's boss.

Together the three behavioral theories and the three cognitive ones present a strong foundation for understanding what motivates most work behaviors. If you understand and master them, you can truly tap human potential.

Important Motivational Quotes

"Most salesmen try to take the horse and make him drink. The real job is to make the horse thirsty."

Motivation

Ask any person who is successful in whatever he or she is doing what motivates him/her, and very likely the answer will be "goals". Goal Setting is extremely important to motivation and success. So what motivates you? Why are you in college? If you are in college because that's what your parents want, you may find it difficult to motivate yourself. Sure, it's possible to succeed with someone else providing the motivation for you. ("If you graduate from college, I'll give you a car!" or worse "If you don't graduate from college, you won't get a car.") But motivation that comes from within really makes the difference.

Certainly, you need some intelligence, knowledge base, study skills, and time management skills, but if you don't have motivation, you won't get far. Think about this analogy. You have a car with a full tank of gas, a well-tuned engine, good set of tyres, quadraphonic CD system, and a sleek, polished exterior. There it sits. This car has incredible potential. (Have you heard that before?) However, until a driver sits behind the wheel, puts the key in the ignition, and cranks it up, the car doesn't function. You guessed it; the KEY is MOTIVATION.

Interest is an important motivator for a student. So is a desire to learn. When you link these two things together, you create success. Often success in an endeavor leads to more interest and a greater desire to learn, creating an upward spiral of motivation toward a goal you have established.

So be honest with yourself. Are you genuinely interested in being in college? Have you set realistic goals for yourself? How can you develop the internal motivation that really counts? When it comes to motivation, KNOWING is not as important as DOING.

Attach a Dream to Your Hero

Everyone has a hero, but few attach a dream to them. Achievers have a dream with a hero that represents the person they want to be.

People, who attach a dream to their hero, become achievers. People, who do not attach a dream to their hero, remain followers.

Opportunity is attracted to people with a dream. They are the first to be hired, first to be offered opportunity, and first to be promoted. Bigger the dream the faster doors open. People without a dream are last to be hired, last to be promoted, and first to be laid-off in a force reduction. For non-dreamers, doors remain closed. "WHY?" People with a dream act differently than non-dreamers, dreamers develop an attitude that radiates energy; they have a sense of purpose and meaning to their lives. Radiant energy is an attitude that bosses like and to which they offer opportunity. This is how the impossible becomes possible.

Priorities

There are three priorities, CHEAP, QUICK and GOOD. You can have any two.

- A good job quick—won't be cheap.
- A quick job cheap—won't be good.
- A good job cheap—won't be quick.

Note: A single priority increases efficiency. At the other end, if all three elements have equal priority the results are reversed, low quality, high cost, and difficult to finish. This is the result of rotating priorities, which means, no one knows what the goal is. Priority of the moment depends on current mood.

What is Your Leadership Style?

High Efficiency

- Do it.
- Do it then tell me what you did.
- Tell me what you are going to do and do it.
- Tell me what you want to do and wait for a decision.

- Don't do anything without my approval.
- Don't do anything until I tell you.

Seven Rules of Motivation

1. **Set a major goal, but follow a path.** The path has mini goals that go in many directions. When you learn to succeed at mini goals, you will be motivated to challenge grand goals.
2. **Finish what you start.** A half finished project is of no use to anyone. Quitting is a habit. Develop the habit of finishing self-motivated projects.
3. **Socialize with others of similar interest.** Mutual support is motivating. We will develop the attitudes of our five best friends. If they are losers, we will be a loser. If they are winners, we will be a winner. To be a cowboy we must associate with cowboys.
4. **Learn how to learn.** Dependency on others for knowledge supports the habit of procrastination. Man has the ability to learn without instructors. In fact, when we learn the art of self-education we will find, if not create, opportunity to find success beyond our wildest dreams.
5. **Harmonize natural talent with interest that motivates.** Natural talent creates motivation, motivation creates persistence and persistence gets the job done.
6. **Increase knowledge of subjects that inspires.** The more we know about a subject, the more we want to learn about it. A self-propelled upward spiral develops.
7. **Take risk.** Failure and bouncing back are elements of motivation. Failure is a learning tool. No one has ever succeeded at anything worthwhile without a string of failures.

Innovation in Motivational Theory

Employee motivation theory—team building activities, workshops, inspirational quotes, and the power of positive experience

Alignment of aims, purpose and values between staff, teams and organization is the most fundamental aspect of motivation. The better the alignment and personal association with organizational aims, the better the platform for motivation. Where people find it difficult to align and associate with the organizational aims, then most motivational ideas and activities will have a reduced level of success. Motivation is a complex area. It's different for each person. Motivational receptiveness and potential in everyone changes from day to day, from situation to situation. Get the alignment and values right, and motivational methods work better. Motivational methods of any sort will not work if people and organisation are not aligned. People are motivated towards something they can relate to and something they can believe in. Times have changed. People want more. You should view the following motivational methods and ideas as structures, activities and building blocks, to be used when you have a solid foundation in place. The foundation is a cohesive alignment of people's needs and values with the aims and purpose of the organization. More about people-organization alignment and motivation.

Motivational methods and theory—assuming people and organization are aligned

Motivational and inspirational quotes, poems, posters, motivational speakers and stories, team building games and activities, all develop employee motivation for sales and business staff in all kinds of organizations. Motivational and inspirational experiences improve employees' attitudes, confidence and performance. Good leadership demands good people, motivation skills and the use of inspirational techniques. Motivational methods are wide-ranging, from inspirational quotes and poems, to team building games and activities, as ice-breakers, warm-ups and exercises for conferences, workshops, meetings and events, which in themselves can often be helpful for staff motivation too. See the motivation principles and template for staff motivation questionnaires and surveys. Motivation is an essential part of life coaching processes and techniques too. Motivated people perform better—see McGregor's XY Theory for example. People playing games or competing in teams learn about each other, they communicate better and see each other in a new light. Mutual respect grows. See the Johari Window theory for example. People often enjoy events which include new non-work activities, especially when bosses and superiors take part in the same teams as their junior staff, which also helps cohesiveness and 'can-do' culture. Inspirational quotes, stories and poems all help motivation too. Powerful positive imagery stimulates visualisation in the conscious and sub-conscious brain, which encourages self-motivation, developmental behavior, confidence and belief. Playing games enables people to experience winning and achieving in a way that their normal work might not. People become motivated to achieve and do better when they have experienced the feelings of success and achievement, regardless of context. This is why fire-walking and outward-bound activities have such powerful motivational effect. All of these ideas, and more explained below, contribute to improving motivation, inspiration and performance. Here is the theory of how team building games, activities like juggling develop motivation, positive images in quotes and stories, inspirational posters, quotations, motivational speakers, team workshops and brainstorming, etc. all help to strengthen relationships, build understanding, increase motivation and improve performance.

How games and other inspirational references and activities help motivation and motivational training

Work and business-based training commonly concentrates on process, rules, theory, structure and logic, all of which tend to develop and use the left-side of the brain. However, modern successful organizations rely just as heavily on their people having well-developed 'soft' skills and attributes, such as self-motivation, confidence, initiative, empathy and creativity, which all tend to use the right-side of the brain. For more information about brain type and bias see the Benziger theory section, for example. Using games and activities like juggling helps to unleash right-side brain skills, because these activities necessarily draw on a person's intuitive, spatial and 'feeling' capabilities—found in the right-side of the brain.

Also, using activities and references that take people out of their normal work environment creates new opportunities for them to experience winning, achievement, team-working, learning and personal development, in ways that are often not possible in their usual work context. Experiencing these positive feelings is vital for the conscious and sub-conscious visualisation of success and achievement, essential for broadening people's horizons, raising their sights, setting new personal standards and goals, and increasing motivation. The use of role playing games and role play exercises is an especially effective motivational and visualisation technique, despite people's normal aversion to the practice. Inspirational references, stories, quotes and examples also help the life coaching process.

Ice-breakers and warm-ups for motivation

When a group or team of people assemble for a conference, or training course, there is always a feeling of uncertainty and discomfort. Even if people know each other, they feel uncomfortable in the new strange situation, because it is different. Mankind has evolved partly because of this awareness to potential threats and fear of the unknown. Games and team building activities relax people, so that they can fully concentrate on the main purpose of the day, whatever it is, rather than spending the morning still wondering what everyone else is thinking. See the stress theory section for examples. Activities and games are great levelers—they break down the barriers, and therefore help develop rapport and relationships.

Building confidence for motivation

Learning something new and completely different liberates the mind. Facing a challenge, meeting it and mastering it helps build confidence.

Motivational team building

When you break down barriers, misunderstandings, prejudices, insecurities, divisions, territories and hierarchies—you begin to build teams. Get a group of people in a room having fun with juggling balls or spinning plates and barriers are immediately removed. Teams unite and work together when they identify a common purpose—whether the aim is the tallest tower made out of newspapers, or a game of rounders on the park. Competition in teams or groups creates teams and ignites team effort.

Motivational coaching and training motivation

Learning to juggle or some other new activity demonstrates how we learn, and how to coach others. Breaking new tasks down into stages, providing clear instructions, demonstration, practice, time and space to make mistakes, doing it one stage at a time...all the essential training and coaching techniques can be shown, whether juggling is the vehicle or some other team-building idea, and the learning is clearer and more memorable because it is taken out of the work context, where previously people 'can't see the wood for the trees'. Games and activities provide a perfect vehicle for explaining the training and development process ('train the trainer' for example) to managers, team leaders and trainers.

Personal motivation styles and learning motivation

Everyone is different. Taking part in new games and activities outside of the work situation illustrates people's different strengths and working style preferences. Mutual respect develops when people see skills and attributes in others that they didn't know existed. Also, people work and learn in different ways.

Continual development and motivation

Learning and taking part in a completely new activity or game like juggling demonstrates that earning is ongoing. The lessons never finish, unless people decide to stop learning. Juggling the basic 'three ball cascade' pattern doesn't end there —it's just a start—as with all learning and development. Master juggler Enrico Rastelli practiced all the daylight hours juggling ten balls. Introducing people, staff or employees to new experiences opens their minds to new avenues of personal development, and emphasises the opportunity for continuous learning that is available to us all.

Improving empathy and communications for motivation

"Seek first to understand, and then to be understood" (Steven Covey). To communicate we must understand the other person. Empathy and intuitive skills are right-side brain. Conventional classroom training or distance learning do nothing to address this vital area. Juggling and playing spontaneous or creative games definitely promote development and awareness in the right-side of the brain, which we use when we communicate and understand others. Team activities and games promote communications and better mutual understanding—essential for good organizational performance.

Motivation and creativity

Creativity and initiative are crucial capabilities for modern organizational effectiveness. Juggling and other games activities dispel the notion that actions must be according to convention, and that response can only be to stimulus. Successful organizations have staff that initiate, create, innovate, and find new ways to do things better, without being told. Using mind and body together in a completely new way encourages pro-active thought and lateral thinking, which opens people's minds, and develops creative and initiative capabilities.

Motivation for problem-solving and decision-making

Problem-solving is integral to decision-making—see the problem-solving and decision-making section. Learning to juggle or taking part in new challenging stimulating activities uses the intuitive brain to solve the problem, the same part that's vital for creatively solving work problems. People who can solve problems creatively can make decisions—and organizations need their staff and employees to have these abilities.

Physical activity is motivational

Team building activities like juggling, construction exercises, or outdoor games, get the body moving, which is good for general health and for an energetic approach to work. A minute of juggling three balls is 200 throws, the equivalent of pumping over 20 kilos. Physical activity also provides significant stress relief, and stress management is part of every organization's duty of care towards its employees. People concentrate and work better when they have had some light exercise and physical stimulus. Physical activity energises people and reduces stress and tension.

Team building workshops are empowering and motivational

See the section on workshops. Workshops are good vehicles for team building games and activities, and also great for achieving team consensus, collective problem-solving, developing new direction and strategy, and to support the delegation and team development process.

Team building games and activities are motivational

Learning new things—even simple skills like plate-spinning —help to build confidence, promote team-working and unleash creativity. Taking part in workshops and Brainstorming sessions are empowering activities. Combine all three and it's even more effective for team building, development and motivation. See particularly the 'Hellespont Swim' case study and exercise.

If you think about it, all manner of left-side-brain conventional training and business skills can be integrated within an innovative, participative right-side-brain activity-based approach, to increase interest, participation, involvement, retention and motivation.

Saying thanks is hugely motivational

Saying thanks and giving praise are the most commonly overlooked and under-estimated ways of motivating people. And it's so easy. Saying thanks is best said naturally and from the heart, so if your intentions are right you will not go far wrong. When you look someone in the eye and thank them sincerely it means a lot. In front of other people even more so. The key words are the ones which say thanks and well done for doing a great job, especially where the words recognise each person's own special ability, quality, contribution, effort, whatever. People always appreciate sincere thanks, and they appreciate being valued as an individual even more. When you next have the chance to thank your team or an individual team-member, take the time to find out a special thing that each person has done and make a point of mentioning these things. Doing this, the praise tends to carry even greater meaning and motivational effect.

Motivational Quotes—Using Inspirational Quotations and Sayings is Motivational

Inspirational quotations, phrases and sayings are motivational when used in team building sessions, conferences, speeches and training courses. Inspirational quotes contribute to motivation because they provide examples and role models, these inspirational images stimulate motivational images and feelings for the brain to visualise. Powerful positive imagery found in motivational quotations and poems is genuinely motivational for people, especially in teams—it builds confidence and belief. Inspirational examples motivate people in the same way that the simple 'power of positive thinking', and 'accentuate the positive' techniques do—people imagine and visualise themselves behaving in the way described in the quotation, saying, story or poem. Visualization is a powerful motivational tool—quotes, stories and poems provide a very effective method for inspiring and motivating people through visualization, imagination and association.

Here are a few motivational quotes, relating to different situations and roles, for example; achievement, management, leadership, etc. When using quote for motivation it's important to choose material that's relevant and appropriate. Motivational posters showing inspirational quotes or poems can be effective for staff and employee motivation, and in establishing organizational values. There are more quotations about inspiration and achievement on the quotes section. These quotes all make effective motivational posters.

Motivational Quotes

"We cannot solve our problems with the same level of thinking that created them" (Albert Einstein).

"It is amazing what you can accomplish if you do not care who gets the credit" (President Harry S. Truman).

"In the midst of winter, I finally learned that within me there lay an invincible summer" (Albert Camus, 1913-60, French author & philosopher).

"If you're not part of the solution you must be part of the problem" (the commonly paraphrased version of the original quote: "What we're saying today is that you're either part of the solution, or you're part of the problem" by Eldridge Cleaver 1935-98, founder member and information minister of the Black Panthers, American political activist group, in a speech in 1968—thanks RVP).

"A dream is just a dream. A goal is a dream with a plan and a deadline" (Harvey Mackay—thanks Brad Hanson).

"I have learned that success is to be measured not so much by the position that one has reached in life as by the obstacles overcome while trying to succeed" (Booker T. Washington).

"Most people never run far enough on their first wind to find out they've got a second. Give your dreams all you've got and you'll be amazed at the energy that comes out of you" (William James, American Philosopher, 1842-1910—thanks Jean Stevens).

"Whatever you can do—or dream you can, begin it. Boldness has genius, power and magic in it" (Johann Wolfgang von Goethe, German writer, 1749-1832—thanks Yvonne Bent).

"A dwarf standing on the shoulders of a giant may see farther than the giant himself" (Didacus Stella, circa AD60).

"If I have seen further, it is by standing on the shoulders of giants" (Sir Isaac Newton, 1676).

"The most important thing in life is not to capitalise on your successes—any fool can do that. The really important thing is to profit from your mistakes" (William Bolitho, from *Twelve against the Gods*).

"Out of the night that covers me, Black as the pit from pole to pole, I thank whatever gods may be. For my unconquerable soul. In the fell clutch of circumstance, I have not winced nor cried aloud: Under the bludgeonings of chance my head is bloody but unbowed.... It matters not how strait the gait, how charged with punishments the scroll, I am the master of my fate: I am the captain of my soul" (W.E. Henley, 1849-1903, from *Invictus*).

"Management means helping people to get the best out of themselves, not organising things" (Lauren Appley).

"It's not the critic who counts, not the one who points out how the strong man stumbled or how the doer of deeds might have done them better. The credit belongs to the man who is actually in the arena; whose face is marred with the sweat and dust and blood; who strives valiantly; who errs and comes up short again and again; who knows the great enthusiasms, the great devotions and spends himself in a worthy cause and who, at best knows the triumph of high achievement and who at worst, if he fails, at least fails while daring greatly so that his place shall never be with those cold and timid souls who know neither victory nor defeat" (Theodore Roosevelt, 23 April 1923).

"The world is divided into people who do things, and people who get the credit. Try, if you can, to belong to the first class. There's far less competition" (Dwight Morrow, 1935).

"What does not kill us makes us stronger." (Attributed to Friedrich Nietzsche, probably based on his words: "Out of life's school of war: What does not destroy me, makes me stronger" from *The Twilight of the Idols*, 1899.)

"A life spent in making mistakes is not only more honourable but more useful than a life spent doing nothing" (George Bernard Shaw, 1856-1950).

"I praise loudly. I blame softly" (Catherine the Great, 1729-96).

More Motivational and Inspirational Quotes

Motivational ideas for sales managers for sales teams

(These principles are applicable to all job roles subject to the notes at the end of this item.)

Motivation of sales people commonly focuses on sales results, but nobody can actually 'do' a result. What matters in achieving results is people's attitude and activity and the areas of opportunity on which the attitude and activity is directed.

What sales people can do is to adopt a positive and creative attitude, and carry out more productive and efficient activity, directed on higher-yield strategic opportunities. By doing these things, sales people and sales teams will improve their results. However, the tendency remains for sales managers, sales supervisors and team leaders (typically under pressure from above from executives who should know better) to simply direct people to 'meet the target', or to 'increase sales', or worse still, to pressurise customers into accelerating decision-making, which might work in the short-term but is extremely unhelpful in the medium-term (when business brought forward leaves gaps in the next months' forecasts), and damages the long-term (when as a result of supplier-driven sales pressure, the customer relationship is undermined or ruined).

Instead think about what really motivates and excites people, and focus on offering these opportunities to sales people and sales teams, on an ongoing basis. Don't wait until you find yourself 25% behind target with only half of the year remaining, and with targets set to increase as well in the final quarter. People will not generally and sustainably improve their performance, or attitude when they are shouted at or given a kick up the backside. People will, on the other hand, generally improve their performance if empowered to develop their own strategic capability and responsibility within the organisation. Herzberg, Adams, Handy, Maslow, McGregor, and every other management and motivation expert confirmed all this long ago.

Sales teams generally comprise people who seek greater responsibility. They also seek recognition, achievement, self-development and advancement. So if we know these things, does it not make good sense to offer these opportunities to them, because we know that doing so will have a motivational effect on them, and also encourage them to work on opportunities that are likely to produce increasing returns on their efforts? Of course. So do it.

If you are managing a sales team, try (gently and progressively) exploring with the team how they'd like to develop their experience, responsibilities, roles, status, value, contribution, within the business. Include yourself in this. Usually far more ideas and activity come from focusing on how the people would like to develop their roles and value (in terms of the scale and sophistication of the business that they are responsible for), rather than confining sales people to a role that is imposed on them and which is unlikely to offer sustainable interest and stimulation.

All businesses have many opportunities for new strategic growth available. Yours will be no different. Most employees are capable of working at a far higher strategic level, developing ever greater returns on their own efforts. Performance improvement is generally found through enabling people and teams to discover and refine more productive and strategic opportunities, which will lead to more productive and motivating activities.

For example, reactive sales people are generally able to be proactive account managers; account managers are generally able to be major accounts developers; major accounts developers are generally able to be national accounts managers; national accounts mangers are generally able to be strategic partner and channel developers; strategic partner and channel developers are generally able to be new business sector/service developers, and so on.... Again include yourself in this.

If necessary (depending on your organizational culture and policies) seek approval from your own management/executives for you to embark on this sort of exploration of strategic growth. (If you are unable to gain approval there are many other organizations out there who need people to manage sales teams in this way....) Obviously, part of the approach (and your agreement with your people—the 'psychological contract') necessarily includes maintaining and meeting existing basic business performance target levels. This is especially so since strategic growth takes time, and your business still needs the normal day-to-day business handled properly. But people can generally do this, i.e. maintain and grow day-to-day performance while additionally developing new higher-level strategic areas, because genuinely motivated people are capable of dramatic achievements. The motivation and capacity to do will come quite naturally from the new responsibility and empowerment to operate at a higher level.

N.B. The principles described above generally apply to most other job roles. People are motivated by growth and extra responsibility, while at the same time the organization benefits from having its people focus on higher strategic aims and activities. Be aware, however, that people in different roles will be motivated by different things, and particularly will require different types of support and guidelines when being encouraged to work at a higher strategic level. For example, engineers require more detail and clarification of expectations and process than sales people typically do; administrators are likely to require more reassurance and support in approaching change than sales people typically do.

For sure you should encourage and enable people to develop their roles, but make sure you give appropriate explanation, management and support for the types of people concerned. It's Valentine's Day, and it's difficult to step into a retail outlet without noticing this glorification of Cupid's love. Although the very act of commercialising something like Valentine's Day is, in my opinion, deception of the most awful kind, it does bring to our consciousness a tiny glimpse of the love that could be. It's amazing what love can do. Actually, it's more amazing what people can do when they are in love. For one thing, people learn to forgive easily when they're in love. Little transgressions are often overlooked when love is at the heart of the relationship. It seems that love can also be lop-sided, or even one-sided. This was almost outrageously illustrated by Greg Behrendt and Liz Tuccillo in the book *He's Just Not That Into You*. Although I just wasn't that into the book enough to read it, I am led to believe that it shows how people can trick themselves into believing that everything's okay in a relationship when in fact it's not. Some people will convince themselves, using every excuse, that although they're being treated badly, there's a perfectly good reason for it. This level of self-sacrifice and skewed tolerance is bizarre.

I'm a big supporter of the "for better, for worse" commitment, but for goodness' sake, you have to draw the line somewhere. Interestingly, the same principles that I notice in this love game can be applied to you and your job. Before you overreact by saying that most jobs are no more than a dysfunctional relationship, I must remind you that this is actually the whole point of my story. Just like with people, in careers you are also attracted initially by the physical attributes of a job. It is not uncommon to lust after the outer image of a job before you really get to know the job's personality. The truth is that it's not your fault either. Most companies will try and make jobs sound attractive. All methods are used to lure you to the job. If images are used, they're mostly of attractive people smiling at you as if to say, "Hey, look how happy we are in this job." Others explain all the fancy benefits you will get.

One could argue that paging through the job classifieds is like a personal speed dating process. Ever heard of someone trying to make themselves unattractive on a date? No way. It's because this is where you get hooked. If you choose to take the first step and start a relationship, chances are you could end up married. Jobs are not too dissimilar. There is also a honeymoon phase where you're in a state of constant bliss, forgetting all the little irritations and ignoring the warning signs. But as this phase subsides, reality starts to bite—hard. Suddenly you are confronted with the real job—the struggle and slog of having to stay motivated despite the daily grind of unrewarded work.

What really counts is the fact that you are entering a relationship with a system. Jobs consist of thousands of intricate and complex interactions with people and other systems. Everyday you make deposits and withdrawals from this interaction. Just like in a romantic relationship, when you give more than you receive in a job you can become weary and disheartened. You begin to regard the job as a mere shell of some former attraction and it becomes unworthy of your love, that is, unless you learn to love. If we feel there is balance in a job we stay attracted to it. Any abusive relationship is doomed to failure. It's the ones where give and take are fair and balanced that seem to last longer. Let me admit that I, too, have been blinded by the physical attraction of a job. I, too, have experienced abusive jobs. So let's explore how you could possibly love your job.

For starters, get to know what is at the heart of the job. What is the underlying personality of the job? What does it demand and how does the job respond to you? Try to find meaning in what you do, and see if the job gives back to you. Without exploring this you could just discover the job is just not that into you. And soon the love will be lost. There is no doubt that in each and everyone of us there is at the very least a tiny desire to be looked after. I'm not really talking about a spoonfed, maternal pampering kind of caring. Although that does sound quite tempting. I'm talking about that occasional feeling that someone perhaps has our interests at heart. This is vital in the workplace, where it is almost certain that you are going to be dependent on others for your success. You will not notice it all the time, mainly because you are expected to pretty much get on with your work. But shucks! When this feeling is lost or deliberately broken, it can feel as if your whole world is in danger of collapsing.

That is, of course, if you really placed your trust in another person for the well-being of your career. Something happened this week that gave me such a good illustration of the different symptoms that blind trust can display in the workplace. It immediately showed up in a company that has been brought to its knees through a sheer tabloid-style exposé of its leadership. It's given me two perspectives. These are what I call superficial loyalty and counterfeit trust. They're slightly different in principle, but seem to have similar results.

When I come across an organisation that appears to have great success, I become interested in understanding what the seeds are for that achievement. It's often because managers and leaders heroically tackle the external world for the company, blazing trails and opening new opportunities. The charisma and magnetism that often come with leaders like this can easily cause you to follow in a gullible, almost naïve, manner.

It's not to say these leaders are wrong. It just means their amazing visionary talents can leave people in a state of constant nirvana-like belief. This positive energy can be so strong that thoughts of problems or difficulties are almost denied. You can probably get away with that for a while but at some point someone's got to do the dirty work. Business is like that, and your career will consist of times when things are more tough than easy. You have to learn to build some resilient tactics to remain productive. If you choose to remain blindly loyal to leaders, the results can be catastrophic when things go wrong.

Never hand over your destiny to someone else who may show a tendency for stubborn heroics. It also doesn't mean you have to question every move. I just believe that you have to keep your wits about you. The other more sinister trust breakdown is when it comes across in a counterfeit way. This is more menacing and can play horribly on your emotions. It's when your leaders and managers purposefully and sometimes forcefully buy your trust. The bottom line is that it's fake. It often occurs when you are feeling insecure and you reach out to someone who appears to have the answers. Leaders like this give a little here and there and lock you into a relationship that is built on falsehood.

Whether it's sharing information with you, or promises of a bigger salary, you begin to hand over your trust cheaply in return for the recognition and reward. Beware of this danger. Unless there is a genuine meaningful foundation, the relationship can be broken swiftly when things go wrong. So what do you do about it? Always stay in control of your thoughts, beliefs, behaviour and choices. Develop your own wisdom through exploring the truth. Understand your personality and what feeds your decision-making.

You also need to remember that visionary leaders are not the sole cause of trust and relationship breakdowns. Often, the combination of this and insecurity or plain old gullible belief is what leads to the ultimate breakdown. So, if you find yourself in a situation where your trust is tested, remain resilient. It's the strength inside that will allow you to bounce back. Not the heroics of an imaginative conqueror.

What are you willing to go through to become great? To have every major celebrity on the planet from Oprah Winfrey to Brad Pitt at our beck and call would be worth a little struggle. Our beloved international elder statesman Nelson Mandela not only enjoys this luxury, but moreover they phone him. The question that must be explored if you ever want to achieve this status is: Are you willing to spend the equivalent of 27 years in prison to have that level of power? Most of us aren't even willing to resist dessert to achieve the quintessential abdominal 6 pack.

Fortune magazine's UK October/November 2006 edition explored this subject. They studied some of history's greatest athletes, politicians and business people. A profound, old-fashioned discovery was made. Hardwork and brutal discipline across multiple streams of each person's life was essential. In the case of poker player Jennifer Harman, it wasn't enough to workhard at understanding the game, she discovered to be great it was essential to also be healthy and in shape to sustain her mental discipline.

Winston Churchill, one of the 20th century's greatest orators, practised his speeches compulsively. Kapil Dev, the greatest cricket player of all time, practised well beyond the normal brutal workouts. Of course, just thinking about hard work and discipline is uncomfortable. If becoming great requires something that we all hate, let's find a way to enjoy it.

It's pretty undisputable that sex sells, so why not sell this proposition to yourself in a sexy way. Fortune's research notes building mental models of your business (pictures of how all the elements fit together) and practising this over and over will expand your models and increase performance.

Whether you are in business or some other field, stretching your mental boundaries by doing and thinking about the task has been proven to work. It's unrealistic to expect everyone to achieve greatness; however, research shows that it can be achieved by those willing to work a little harder. As we go into the holiday season, challenge yourself to see practice across all areas of your life as sexy and you'll be surprised what power your version of 27 years in prison will produce!

Time waits for no man or woman. Whether we like it or not we are becoming older every minute of the day. Making the most of our potential with regard to this involves three critical elements: planning; having meaning and purpose; and just being. Why do we make New Year Resolutions in the first place? Simply because we would like our lives to be better, more fulfilled, more organised and more satisfying, or because we are trying to fulfil more of our innate potential. Sadly, however, it is well-known that many of these resolutions have been abandoned by the time February dawns. There are a few steps we can take to increase the chances that our resolutions will take.

One of these skills is intellectual, a second is emotional and the third is in the spiritual realm. Firstly, the intellectual skill. We need to understand that planning is the only control we can exercise over the future. Planning is a skill in itself that needs to be mastered. We need to have a goal and then have considered all the givens and the not-givens. So say, for example, we want to do something in the new year.

We would need to ask ourselves some basic questions:

1. **What is my goal?** Who and what is involved? (components); who needs to do what (functions); by when should it be done (time)? How should it be done, in what order (process); where and when should each task be done (conditions); how well does the task need to be done (standards)? With what or with whom do these tasks need to be performed? (resources). Is anyone's permission required to perform these tasks (authority); what is my reason for pursuing this goal? Finally, how will I reward myself for approximating and finally achieving the goal? Asking these questions as part of the goal-setting exercise will assist you in anticipating what may

befall you along the road to your destination. Pre-warned is prepared.

2. **Emotional competence.** Goals need to be aligned with what we attach meaning and purpose to. What we pursue needs to fit with what we believe in. When we are tired or distressed and our energy is low, it is very often only the fuel of passion which enables us to pick ourselves up and continue along our chosen road. Goals are often not accomplished because our motivation to achieve them in the first place is fraught with error. If we are pursuing a particular goal to please others, or because we think we should, the resolution is fragile from the beginning. So questions to ask in order to align the goals with our internal motivation would be: Why do I want to achieve this goal? What value that I believe in does it address? How will it make my life better? In which way will it bring me closer to who I am, what I believe in or what I strive to be? What may I have to give up if I achieve this goal? How will people who care about me react to my pursing this goal? How will those who do not care about me react?

   Who will support me, who will sabotage me, who will struggle with the new me? What am I afraid of? What can I do or to whom can I go when I run out of energy, faith, or determination? Remember your emotions tell you what you want and need. They are a messenger that conveys to you whether you are happy or distressed at what life has given you. So learning to read these emotions, interpreting them and managing them is critical in ensuring your resilience and stability along the rocky road to success.

3. **The spiritual competence**. The adage reads "adapt or die". What this means is that life is constantly changing and moving around us. In fact, we ourselves are constantly having to change, and adapt in order to survive. One of those fundamental changes is that

> we age. As we age or needs change, our perceptions alter, and we need to become more aware of maintaining our abilities, playing to our strengths and, or working with those that lessen.

For myself, this has been the greatest lesson. As a young person (20-35), I found the skill of planning essential in my path of career success. I would write down my goals, I would prioritise them and most of the time whether they were personal, family or professional I would look back a year later to have accomplished 80 per cent of the goals set. These goals focused around earning money, getting another degree, losing weight, exercising and or being promoted at work. In my later years (35-45) meaning became fundamental to my decisions. Why was I doing this? Why was I here? How did this fit with who I was, or had become, or hoped to become? Did it work for or against me, in my striving to be truer to myself, and fulfil more of my unique potential? Where could I go, or what could I do, so that I could be a better version of me?

Over the last couple of years I encountered a rude shock when trying to implement my age-old habit of being pro-active and planning for the year to come. I had no desire to do so. Nothing seemed to beckon me. Nothing seemed quite important enough to pursue. This was most uncomfortable for an achiever and a habitual pursuer of goals.

Over time I have come to understand that there are horses for courses. And that even skills like planning have a time and space. Now I am learning to look, to listen, to explore, to understand and simply to be with what is presented to me. It is then that I can decide how to be, and how to respond optimally. I no longer try to control the future. I simply do the best that I am able to, with each day, that I am given as a gift. I am kinder and less judgmental. I am less ego driven and not as ambitious. I practice more humility and try to be more understanding. So you see. Plan while you can. Align those plans with what gives you meaning and purpose. And then simply do the best with what you have. Ultimately it's not all about getting more of what you want, but about being happy with and wanting what you have.

The year is winding to a close and South Africa is holding its breath in the hope that this year's summer-holiday death toll will be lower than it has been in previous years. Homicide and road accidents continue to feature in the top-10 causes of death each year, which makes the role of the paramedic—the crucial first link in the critically injured patient's "chain of survival"—all the more crucial. "We need to pay tribute to the selfless men and women who staff ambulances and emergency response cars around the country," says Michael Emery, executive marketing manager of ER24, one of South Africa's leading Emergency Medical Care Networks. "At the same time we realise that good people are always required in the profession and we would like to share some information about becoming a paramedic with those young people leaving school at the end of the year who would like to enter a profession where they can really make a difference."

A paramedic is a trained medical professional whose responsibility is to render advanced life support to critically ill or injured patients in the pre-hospital emergency environment. As such, the paramedic forms an integral part of the Emergency Care Team's treatment of a patient. There are three levels of emergency practitioners: Basic, Intermediate and Advanced. Basic Life Support practitioners save many lives every year by applying life-saving skills like CPR and airway maintenance. Intermediate Life Support practitioners perform electrical defibrillation and set up intravenous lines, but only Advanced Life Support practitioners who are trained to perform relatively invasive field care are called paramedics.

A good paramedic needs to be calm, patient, responsible and enjoy working with people. They should be good at problem-solving and time-management. Organisational skills are also very important. Paramedics often have to perform their duties under stressful conditions, and in difficult and potentially dangerous situations. They need to be mentally and physically fit, as well as be able to make split-second decisions and remain calm under pressure. While the career may be a demanding one, the rewards will always far outweigh the daily trials and tribulations. Most commonly, paramedics respond to medical emergencies out in the field for the purpose of stabilising the victim's condition so that he or she can be transported to medical facilities. Working as a paramedic can also mean being on standby at large events like sports meetings. In addition to their medical duties, which can include insertion of endotracheal tubes, initiation of IV lines, administration of various medications and interpretation of electrocardiograms at the scene of an emergency, a paramedic will also be required to manage the incident scene and to liaise with provincial services, such as traffic, metro police and firefighters. Paramedics are also responsible for managing a team of medics, patient care and transportation, community interaction, training and administrative functions. As far as entry to the profession is concerned, the National Diploma in emergency care (NDip EMC) is currently being phased out and replaced with a four-year degree programme, the BTech EMC, which, as per the SAQA NQF, constitutes a professional degree.

You may be the greatest "schmoozer" a company has ever seen, but without being able to deliver on the deal, your networking talents are wasted in the corporate world. Debbie Goodman, MD of Jack Hammer Executive Headhunters, says her clients generally want to hire people with excellent track records, qualifications and networks. "But even if you have one of the strongest networks in the industry, if you can't close a business deal, your desirability is diminished," she says. An extensive contact network is valuable, as the ability to open doors is vital in any competitive market. Far more attractive, however, is an individual who brings in business and closes deals.

"Companies are looking for people with good social skills, but they place more significance on making sure the sale is closed—a professional with these abilities is undoubtedly of greatest value to an organisation," Goodman says. "In some companies, internal schmoozing still has a role to play in an employee's progression to the top—'drinking with the boys' or playing golf with top management goes without saying in order to be considered a 'team player'. "These days, however, in the majority of organisations your progression is more directly linked to your performance off the green." Goodman says obviously the necessity to "schmooze" will feature as part of everyone's career path at some stage, whether it be helping superiors look good on their way to the top or publicising their own job well done. Yet she cautions that employees often need to bide their time and should expect to pay their dues when climbing the corporate ladder, rather than expecting to be able to rise to the top by relying largely on social skills. "We advise people to strike a balance—to get ahead in their career it helps to be popular, but bringing in the business will earn the respect of their colleagues and pave their way to the top."

The Ethics and the Social Responsibility of Management

Each of us has our own set of values and beliefs that we have evolved over the course of our lives through our education, experiences and upbringing. We all have our own ideas of what is right and what is wrong and these ideas can vary between individuals and cultures.

As a manager you bring with you your own concept of what is right and what is wrong. Every decision that you make, for better or for worse, is the application of these values to the question at hand. This is made more difficult by the pressures of organisational life. There are the pressures of productivity, competition, bosses.... Sometimes managers make decisions which conflict with their own or society's values because of what they see as the pressures of the business world.

But what is the right thing to do when it comes to social responsibility? This is one of the most crucial questions that managers will face in the next decade. Is it a manager's job just to maximise profits? Or should managers be concerned with using their organisation to carry out other social responsibilities such as controlling pollution, employing disadvantaged groups or supporting education?

Managers need to provide the right organisational climate to ensure that their employees can see that by working towards the organisational goals they are also achieving some of their own goals. These goals could be such things as financial rewards or personal rewards such as the respect of their colleagues or job satisfaction or a combination of any number of things that the employee considers to be important. It is no good giving someone a pay rise if they are dissatisfied with the job and they do not see money as a very important factor in their working life. Yvonne McLaughlin suggests that there is an equation which gives a good model of the basic requirements and how they relate to each other in order to achieve the best staff performance in your organisation.

Performance = Ability × Effort × Organisational support

The performance of your organisation's staff is an equation of their ability to do the job (what they can do) multiplied by the effort that they are actually willing to put into the job multiplied by the amount that the organisation helps them to achieve their tasks.

7

Training and Development

The objective of training and development is to enable employee to acquire the knowledge, skills, abilities and attitudes necessary to enable them to improve their performance. Staff training and development should focus on the department's objectives and goals and staff's competencies in achieving them. A strategic approach has the following characteristics:

- Commitment to training and developing people;
- Regular analysis of operational requirements and staff competencies;
- Linking training and development to departmental goals and objectives;
- Skilled training personnel;
- Regular evaluation;
- A continuous learning culture;
- Joint responsibility between managers and staff for identifying and meeting training needs; and
- A variety of training and development methods for different circumstances and learning styles.

Key Components

Training

Departments manage their own training function and have varying levels of responsibility to do this effectively:

- Management formulates departmental training

policies and draws up training and development plans to support departmental missions, objectives and values.

- Managers identify competencies and training needs, implement training activities and provide coaching and supervision to ensure staff development occurs.
- Staff takes responsibility to make the most of the opportunities provided to maximise their potential. Various types of training are provided in the civil service:

  Induction: To familiarize new recruits with job requirements and procedures, departmental objectives and performance standards; and the values and norms of the department.

  Management Development: To equip managers with the knowledge and skills required and to widen their perspective.

  Vocational: To provide staff with the professional or technical knowledge and skills required for work.

  Language and Communication: To meet operational needs (e.g. Thai, Vietnamese) and to prepare for the future (Putonghua and written Chinese).

  Computer: To provide staff with basic computers skills.

Development

The purpose of career development is to identify and develop the potential within staff, to build existing skill levels, and to prepare staff to take on greater responsibility during their career.

Career development has to balance the needs and aspirations of the individual with the needs of the service—where these conflict, the needs of the service should prevail.

Posting: Postings for staff should take account of the previous experience of the individual and his future needs and potential. Staff can either be developed to have a broad experience across a number of areas or they can focus on a particular area and develop in-depth experience. Determining the most appropriate way to develop staff is a balance between the needs of the organisation and the aspirations of the individual. Future posting aspirations should be discussed with staff on the understanding that in the final analysis the needs of the civil service are paramount.

Acting Appointment: There are three kinds of acting appointments:

- Acting "with a view"—whereby staff are posted to the acting rank to assess their suitability for substantive promotion.
- Acting "with a singling out effect"—whereby staff who do not merit immediate promotion or an acting appointment with a view to substantive promotion but who are nevertheless assessed to have better potential than other officers to undertake the more demanding duties in the higher rank, are placed in the higher rank to assess their suitability for substantive promotion.
- Acting for administrative convenience—whereby staff are placed in a higher rank to cover the absence of the normal post holder, e.g. through sickness, long holiday or maternity leave. Staff acting for administrative convenience revert to their substantive rank on the return of the substantive post holder.

Apart from acting for administrative convenience which is more ad hoc, the other two types of acting provide opportunities for staff to be exposed to more onerous duties and responsibilities, thereby testing their ability.

Secondment: Secondment from departments for attachments in policy branches in the Government Secretariat are good ways to expose staff to a different working environment which places greater emphasis on policy formulation and resource control. Apart from secretariat attachments, secondments and exchange schemes with overseas and private sector counterparts can be arranged to broaden staff's exposure.

As a brief review of terms, training involves an expert working with learners to transfer to them certain areas of knowledge or skills to improve in their current jobs. Development is a broad, ongoing multi-faceted set of activities (training activities among them) to bring someone or an organisation up to another threshold of performance, often to perform some job or new role in the future.

Reasons for Employee Training and Development

Training and development can be initiated for a variety of reasons for an employee or group of employees, for example:

(a) When a performance appraisal indicates performance improvement is needed.

(b) To "benchmark" the status of improvement so far in a performance improvement effort.

(c) As part of an overall professional development program.

(d) As part of succession planning to help an employee be eligible for a planned change in role in the organisation.

(e) To "pilot", or test, the operation of a new performance management system.

(f) To train about a specific topic.

Topics of Employee Training

1. *Communications*: The increasing diversity of today's workforce brings a wide variety of languages and customs.
2. *Computer skills*: Computer skills are becoming a necessity for conducting administrative and office tasks.
3. *Customer service*: Increased competition in today's global marketplace makes it critical that employees understand and meet the needs of customers.
4. *Diversity*: Diversity training usually includes explanation about how people have different perspectives and views, and includes techniques to value diversity.

5. *Ethics*: Today's society has increasing expectations about corporate social responsibility. Also, today's diverse workforce brings a wide variety of values and morals to the workplace.
6. *Human relations*: The increased stresses of today's workplace can include misunderstandings and conflict. Training can make people to get along in the workplace.
7. *Quality initiatives*: Initiatives such as Total Quality Management, Quality Circles, benchmarking, etc. require basic training about quality concepts, guidelines and standards for quality, etc.
8. *Safety*: Safety training is critical where working with heavy equipment, hazardous chemicals, repetitive activities, etc. but can also be useful with practical advice for avoiding assaults, etc.
9. *Sexual harassment*: Sexual harassment training usually includes careful description of the organisation's policies about sexual harassment, especially about what are inappropriate behaviors.

General Benefits from Employee Training and Development

There are numerous sources of on-line information about training and development. Several of these sites (they're listed later on in this library) suggest reasons for supervisors to conduct training among employees. These reasons include:

1. Increased job satisfaction and morale among employees.
2. Increased employee motivation.
3. Increased efficiencies in processes, resulting in financial gain.
4. Increased capacity to adopt new technologies and methods.
5. Increased innovation in strategies and products.
6. Reduced employee turnover.
7. Enhanced company image, e.g. conducting ethics training (not a good reason for ethics training!).

8. Risk management, e.g. training about sexual harassment, diversity training.

Basic Requirements of Learners in Training and Development

To Learn, You Must Be Willing to Grow, to Experience

Learning often involves new skills, developing new behaviors. After many years of classroom education, it's easy for us to take a course where all we must do is attend each meeting, take notes and pass tests—and call this learning. One can complete a Masters in Business Administration (MBA), but unless they're willing to actually apply new information, they'll most likely end up with an office full of unreferenced textbooks and a head full of data, but little knowledge and wisdom. For the learning process to succeed, the individual must be willing to take risks. Stick your neck out, including by telling the instructor when you're confused or disappointed in the course. Don't wait until the course is over when nothing can be done about it.

Growth Involves the Entire Learner

If learning is to be more than collecting new information, then we must involve ourselves completely in our learning experiences. Unfortunately, too many development programs still operate from the assumption that the learner can somehow separate personal development from professional development. So, we end up getting a great deal of information about finance and sales, but little help with stress and time management. Then, after schooling, when we enter the hectic world of management, we struggle to keep perspective and we're plagued with self-doubts. True learning involves looking at every aspect of our lives, not just what's in our heads. So include courses, e.g. in Stress Management and Emotional Intelligence, in your training and development plans.

Growth Requires Seeking Ongoing Feedback

Many of us don't know what we need to learn—we don't know what we don't know. Therefore, feedback from others is critical to understanding ourselves and our jobs. Feedback is useful in more ways than telling us what we don't know. Feedback also deepens and enriches what we do know.

Research indicates that adults learn new information and methods best when they (a) actually apply the information and methods, and (b) exchange feedback around those experiences. However, we're often reluctant to seek advice and impressions from others, particularly fellow workers. We're sometimes reluctant to share feedback with others, as well. The Giving and Receiving Feedback might be useful to you.

The courage to overcome our reluctance and fears is often the first step toward achieving true meaning in our lives and our jobs.

Trust Your Instincts to Learn

Learning doesn't come only from other people telling you what you need to know and how you need to learn it! The highly motivated, self-directed learner can make a "classroom of life". Everything becomes an experience from which to learn. You can design your own learning experiences! Think about what you want to learn, how you might learn it and how you'll know if you've learned it. You can get a great deal from this Free Management Library. For example, take half an hour a week to review materials in the library. You'll get a strong (free) sense about management. Glance at topics in the Personal Development topic, including, for example:

Self-Assessments (numerous self-assessments)

Goals—Setting Personal Goals

Changing Your Behavior

Learner's Basic Requirements for Effective Learning

Learning Style Inventory

Mind power

Student Skills, include:

—Reading Skills

—Tips for Studying More Effectively

—Tips to Do Better on Tests.

Basic Requirements of Supervisors with Employees in Training and Development

Include Learners in Training and Development Planning

The learner will get the most out of the plan if he or she feels strong ownership in the plan. Ownership comes from taking part in developing the plan. Also, professional development rarely includes only gaining knowledge and skills about a job role. Professional development often includes self-development as well, e.g. admitting one's limits and capabilities. Learners are often the best experts at realizing their own needs for self-development. Therefore, learners should be involved in as much as possible in developing the plan.

If Available, Have Human Resources Representative Play Major Role

A trained human resources professional can be a major benefit in employee development. The representative usually has a good understanding of the dynamics of training and development. The representative often has strong working knowledge of the relevant policies and procedures related to training and development. In addition, the representative can be an impartial confidant for the learner.

Provide Ongoing Feedback and Support

Even if things seem to be going fine, be sure to stop in and visit the learner on a regular basis. Some learners may not feel comfortable asking for help. Supervisors should provide any feedback, that is, timely and useful information for the learner. Provide ongoing affirmation and support.

When Assessing Results of Employee's Learning, Maximize Feedback About Performance

Consider getting feedback from the learner's peers and subordinates about the learner's needs and progress to meet those needs. A 360-degree performance review is a powerful practice when carried out with clarity and discretion. When first carried out, it may be wise to get the help of an outside professional.

Budget Necessary Funds for Resources that Learner Will Need

Funds may be required, e.g. for course tuition and materials, self-study materials, videos, training fees, labor to attend courses, etc.

Supervisor and Learner should Set Aside Regular Times for Meetings

Scheduling meetings beforehand makes it much more likely that regular, ongoing feedback will occur between the supervisor and learner.

Suggestions to Enrich any Training and Development Plans

Planning—Some Considerations When Developing the Plan

Be Sure to Document a Training and Development Plan (Goals, Methods and Evaluation)

Carefully consider using some form of training and development plan, even if thinking about informal means of training and development. Sketching out a plan with goals, intended methods and evaluation, will at least give you a sense of what you want and how you'll recognize if you've gotten it or not. Don't expect perfection in the plan or the learner. Start simple, but start. Then update the plan as you go along.

Don't Worry About Whether Your Plan is Perfect or not—The Plan is Guide, not Law

The key is to get started. Start simple, but start. Do the best that you can for now. There is no perfect plan. You're doing the plan according to your nature and needs. Also, it's not important to stick to the plan for the sake of the plan. Deviations from the plan are to be expected. It's important that deviations are recognized and explained.

Remember that Development is a Process

Often, the ongoing reflection and discussions between supervisor and learner are far more important than results produced by learners during the training and development process. Appreciate this interaction as much as reaching any objectives in the plan.

Goals—Selecting Training and Development Goals

Select 2-4 Goals to Get Started

Each of these goals will be associated with, e.g. 2-4, learning objectives that when reached by the learner will result in the learner reaching the overall training goal. (More about learning objectives later in a basic framework for developing a training and development plan.)

Determine the Goals Yourself—Don't Adopt Them from Another Program, Writer, etc.

It's very tempting to get a copy of a formal training program's goals and make them your own. It's very tempting to read a writer's suggestions about what a leader should be and adopt those suggestions as requirements in your program. Almost everyone wants to have more character, be charismatic, be more visionary, work well with groups, be more communicative, support followers, etc.

But you may very well have already have met those goals! Because writer's suggestions sound very virtuous, e.g. to have more character, does not mean that you don't already have a great deal of character that already incorporates the values needed for strong and effective leadership in your organization.

Therefore, give careful thought to your training and development goals. Ultimately, you and your supervisor are the best judges of what you should aim to learn.

Set Realistic Expectations

As explained in previous information about Training Analysis, learning goals should be established based on needed areas of knowledge and skills. These needs are established by referencing relevant strategic goals, competencies lists, job descriptions, job analysis, tasks analysis, etc. Be sure these goals are realistic.

There is a vast amount of management literature today, much of it asserting the need for continued change among organizations and employees. Often, we're expected to achieve total quality and total integrity. We're encouraged to transform ourselves and our organizations. These expectations can serve as powerful visions to provide direction and purpose. However, as these expectations become strong requirements in the workplace, they must be carefully considered and planned. Otherwise, they can spawn a great deal of despair and cynicism. Consequently, be realistic about training and development plans. Particularly regarding development efforts such as leadership development, it can be very seductive to have goals such as "total integrity". If you want "total integrity" as a goal, know what behaviors will depict total integrity and then identify those behaviors in your training and development plan.

Don't Forget the Most Important Sources of Suggestions: Supervisors and Subordinates

When selecting training and development goals, ask your supervisor for feedback. For example, if you're planning a leadership development program for yourself, ask your supervisor for suggestions about how you could improve. He or she may be the best person to give you ideas for goals and methods. He or she has had to develop leadership skills and also has watched you over the years. Also, don't forget to ask your subordinates for suggestions. They often have impressions about you that you'll never find out about, unless you ask for them.

Integrate Results Expected from the Learner with Goals in the Performance Plan

Include the training and development goals in the performance review planning and discussions. This affords ongoing tracking and discussion to ensure that training and development results are actually carried over into the results in the workplace. If the supervisor and employee have been conducting the employee performance management process and perceived a "performance gap", then the performance review process already includes the goals needed by the training and development plan. "Growth gap" and "opportunity gap" training goals should also be included in the performance review process as career development goals to ensure ongoing tracking and discussion. However, be very careful about evaluating the employee on whether they achieved career goals or not. Many variables can occur which hamper the employee from achieving career goals. Instead, focus performance evaluations on achievement of performance standards.

Methods—Remember Basic Principles about Adult Learning

Adults Learn Best by Applying Information to Current, Real-World Needs

Therefore, select training and development methods that include the learner's actually applying new information and methods in the workplace to a real-life problem. It's often difficult for learners to translate discussion about simulated situations (e.g. case studies) back to the workplace. On-the-job training can be very powerful when complemented with new information and methods, and time for reflection.

Adults Learn Best by Exchanging Feedback About Experiences

Learners benefit a great deal from ongoing feedback around their experiences when applying new information and materials. Ideally, training and development experiences afford learners the opportunity to describe the results of applying new information and methods, what they thought would happen, what actually happened and why, and what the learner gained from the experience.

Methods—Some Basic Mistakes to Avoid

After 12 to 16 years of classroom education, we tend to fall pray to several common myths about training and development. The following advice is geared to help learners avoid those myths:

1. *Don't mistake data and information for knowledge and wisdom.* Too often, when we want to learn something, we take a course, carefully analyze the material and consider ourselves as having learned the information. Yet how much of the material from our courses have we really practiced? Paulo Freire, who is probably responsible for educating more human beings than anyone in history, asserts that "without practice, there is no knowledge".
2. *Don't mistake entertainment for enlightenment.* Go to your library, look at the hundreds, maybe thousands of books there. How many did you really need? How much of the authors' advice did you

actually follow? How many books met the strong promise you felt when you first read the title?

3. *Don't mistake analysis for learning.* Assignments over the years ask us to "analyze the content and then write a paper". Yet, Eastern philosophies that have existed thousands of years before ours, remind us of the role of intuition, and of the role of reflection on our experiences (on our practices). Use more than your brain, use your intuition and your heart.
4. *Don't mistake education to occur only in classrooms.* Yet research indicates that adults learn best when they apply information to meet current, real needs in their lives, that is, when they ground their theories in practice. And they learn best when exchanging ongoing feedback around these practices.

General Suggestions to Build More Learning into the Plan

1. *For every learning method, answer "How will this learning effect the real world?"* Have your supervisor or best friend hold you accountable to answer that question. It may be the most important question in your plan and its answer may leave you feeling the most fulfilled when the plan has been implemented.
2. *Include learning activities that go well beyond the safety of reading and writing papers.* Take some risks. Have your spouse or close friends suggest what you most need to learn and how. Ultimately, ensure that you're not engaged in extended arguments about "How many angels will fit on the head of a pin—come the New Millennium?"
3. *Take advantage of real-life learning opportunities in the workplace.* Your life and job afford you numerous opportunities from which to learn. For example, if you're designing a plan to develop leadership skills, then select learning methods that involve leading efforts in your community. Volunteer to a local nonprofit or professional organization.

4. *Practice principles of unconventional educators, such as Paulo Freire and Myles Horton.* Freire and Horton taught people to read, not just for the sake of learning, but to meet real and current needs in the lives of their learners. Horton, who didn't write any scholarly papers in his life, started the Highlander Folk School. The school had no classrooms, no expert lecturers. Yet, Martin Luther King said that Highlander probably had more to do with addressing desegregation than he did. In another case, after leaving Highlander, a young black learner refused to go to the back of the bus—Rosa Parks.

General Considerations to Build More Learning into Our Lives

Many of us give far more attention to the learning we glean from our classrooms than we do from the rest of our lives. Many of us come to realize this situation only after we've graduated. Again, some suggestions:

1. *Write down ten most important things you've learned—How did you learn them*? It's ironic that, considering the thousands of exercises we've been assigned in our lives, this exercise is never among them! Yet it's probably one of the most important. Next to each thing you learned, note what you did to learn it. Do you know? Did it occur in a classroom? What theory spawned that learning?
2. *Once a week, write down a key learning experience—What did you learn*? You will learn far more from your real-world experiences (or practices), including from your intimate relationships with others, than you will from all of the classrooms and all of the books in the world!
3. *Involve yourself in community service—Great "Classroom" in life*! These services are powerful "practices" that soon spawn rich, deep learning in our lives!
4. *For one minute, stare at yourself in the mirror: Ask "How do I feel about myself?"* Update your training

and development plan to address any concerns you have about the person staring back at you in the mirror. As with any successful therapy or managing or teaching, you must first start with yourself.

Summary of Above Suggestions to Enrich Training and Development

Some Basic Requirements of Learners

Learners must be willing to grow, to experience growth involves the entire learner, growth requires seeking ongoing feedback.

Some Basic Requirements of Supervisors

Include learners in development of training and development plan. If available, have human resources representative play major role. Provide ongoing feedback and support when assessing results of learning, maximize feedback about performance budget necessary funds for resources learner will need. Set aside regular times for supervisor and learner to meeting.

Developing the Training and Development Plan

Document a training and development plan (Goals, Methods and Evaluation). Don't worry about whether your plan is perfect or not—The plan is guide, not law, remember that development is a process.

Selecting Training and Development Goals

Select 2-4 goals to get started. Determine the goals yourself—Don't adopt them from another program. Set realistic expectations.

Don't forget the most important sources of suggestions: supervisors and subordinates integrate results expected from the learner with goals in the performance plan.

Basic Principles About Adult Learning When Selecting Methods

Adults learn best by applying information to current, real-world needs. Adults learn best by exchanging feedback about experiences.

Basic Mistakes to Avoid When Selecting Methods

Don't mistake data and information for Knowledge and Wisdom.

Don't mistake Entertainment to be Enlightenment.

Don't mistake Analysis to be Learning.

Don't mistake Education to occur only in Classrooms.

Basic Considerations to Build More Learning into the Training and Development Plan

For every method in your plan, ask "How will this learning effect the real world?"

Go well beyond the safety of reading and writing papers. Take advantage of real-life learning opportunities in the workplace. Consider principles of unconventional educators, such as Paulo Freire and Myles Horton.

Basic Considerations to Build More Learning into Our Lives

Write down ten most important things you've learned—How did you learn them? Once a week, write down the key experiences over past week and what you learned. Involve yourself in community service—great "Classroom" in life! Finally, take five minutes to stare in the mirror. Ask "How do I feel about myself?"

Strong Value of Self-directed Learning in the Workplace: How Supervisors and Learners Gain Leaps in Learning

What is Self-directed Learning?

Self-directed training includes the learner initiating the learning, making the decisions about what training and development experiences will occur, and how. The learner selects and carries out his own learning goals, objectives, methods and means to verify that the goals were met.

Probably, the most important skill for today's rapidly changing workforce is skills in self-reflection. The highly motivated, self-directed learner with skills in self-reflection can approach the workplace as a continual classroom from which to learn.

Supervisors and employees who work together to accomplish formal, self-directed learning in the workplace also accomplish continuous learning for continued productivity and learning.

Most Learning is Informal and Self-directed in Nature

We buy a book and think about the writer's viewpoint. We attend a presentation given at a local school. We take some time at the end of the day to think about our day and what we learned from it. These are all informal forms of self-directed learning.

Self-directed learning becomes even more powerful when it's systematic, that is, when we decide:

1. What areas of knowledge and skills we need to gain in order to get something done (our learning needs and goals).
2. How we will gain the areas of knowledge and skills (our learning objectives and activities).
3. How we will know that we've gained the areas of knowledge and skills (learning evaluation).

Self-directed Learning is Ideal for the Workplace

Self-directed learning programs hold numerous advantages over traditional forms of classroom instruction for employees in the workplace, whether they be leaders, managers, or individual contributors. Bouchard [*Self-directed Learning in Organizational Settings* (working paper), Concordia University, Montreal, Canada] explains, "Over the years, it has become increasingly clear that traditional approaches to program design and delivery in the workplace and in associative organizations present some important weaknesses. Problem areas include: coping with the short life span of useful knowledge; passing down acquired competencies to succeeding cohorts; accommodating the demands of productivity while providing for a continuity of learning; [and] enabling learners to pursue activities that correspond to their learning styles and needs." After many years of reflection about learning, eminent psychologist, Carl Rogers, founder of self-directed therapy, asserted that "anything that can be taught to another is relatively inconsequential, and has little or no significant influence on behavior." He adds, "The only learning which significantly influences behavior is self-discovered, self-appropriated learning."

Self-directed learning programs:

1. Are more effective in development because learning accommodates employees' learning styles and objectives.
2. Save substantial training costs because learners learn to help themselves and each other with practical and timely materials.
3. Achieve increased employee effectiveness in their jobs as they learn to learn from their own work experiences and actually apply their learning in their places of work.

How Supervisors can Help Employees Learn in the Workplace

The supervisor's attitude and knowledge about learning has a tremendous impact on the development of employees. A Re-examination, cites numerous suggestions (from Lowry) in order to better enable self-directed learning in the workplace. Some of those suggestions are listed below, and are wonderful ways for supervisors and learners to turn the workplace into a classroom:

1. Help the learner identify the starting point for a learning project and discern relevant [ways] of examination and reporting.
2. Encourage adult learners to view knowledge and truth as contextual...and that they can act on their world individually or collectively to transform it.
3. Create a partnership with the learner by negotiating a learning contract for goals, strategies and evaluation criteria.
4. Be a manager of the learning experience rather than an information provider.
5. Teach inquiry skills, decision-making, personal development, and self-evaluation of work.

6. Help learners develop positive attitudes and feelings of independence relative to learning.
7. Recognize learners' personality types and learning styles.
8. Use techniques such as field experience and problem-solving that take advantage of adults' rich experience base.
9. Encourage critical thinking skills by incorporating... such activities as seminars.
10. Create an atmosphere of openness and trust to promote better performance.
11. Behave ethically, which includes not recommending a self-directed learning approach if it is not congruent with the learner's needs.
12. Obtain the necessary tools to assess learner's current performance and to evaluate their expected performance.
13. Provide opportunities for self-directed learners to reflect on what they're learning.
14. Promote learning networks, study circles, and learning exchanges (self-managed teams of self-directed learners).
15. Provide staff training on self-directed learning and broaden the opportunities for its implementation.

Fisher adds that "Self-directed learning is more than a form of education. It is a component in human development.

Tools to "Celebrate a New Hire"

Part of HR's job is to educate managers on the importance of making new hires feel welcomed and important. Managers and employees need to take a larger role in "closing the sale" and owning the process of assimilating the new hires because their talent will improve the teams chance of meeting it's goals. Managers should consider using one or more of the following "celebration tools" to raise the enthusiasm of and for the new hire:

1. A phone call from the CEO/GM welcoming them to the organization.
2. An invitation by the CEO/GM to visit their office on their first day (or the CEO stopping by their work space).
3. A letter from the CEO/GM welcoming them to the organization.
4. Cake and candles on the first morning to celebrate their joining the "family"/team.
5. A new hire luncheon on the first day to meet the team.
6. Welcome banner for their cubical signed by the CEO and all.
7. Take a Team Picture on the first day and have it signed by all.
8. Give them a Tee Shirt signed by all.
9. Place a Notice/Ad in the Local Paper welcoming them to let everyone know of your new team member (like consulting/law firms do).
10. Give them a Plaque—Celebrating their First day.
11. Give them a "2 for dinner" certificate to tell their spouse or friend about their new job.
12. Place a welcome note/picture on your corporate Web site.
13. Put new hires pictures in our local ads or in regular corporate advertising.
14. Send their spouse/kids first day welcome gifts, corporate products or cards to make them feel they are part of the team and to build support for the new company.
15. Have other spouses call and welcome their spouses.
16. Have a new employee lunch for spouses during their first month.
17. Have a "No forms/video/manuals" policy during the first day/week. Consider sending them to their home

to read prior to starting or let it wait until at least week two.

18. Give them a "new hire" pin/hat to let all know they deserve special help. The pin/hat also entitles them to ask "dumb questions".
19. Give them a "pre-dated" five year pin to show them we expect them to be part of the team for a long time.
20. Give them a "meet everyone card" that requires (rewards) them for getting the initials of all key team members on the card during the first__days.
21. Give them a "new hire" reserved parking spot to celebrate their first week.
22. Give them a License Plate Cover for their car announcing their new company.

Time to Productivity Tools

Many workers encounter delays and frustrations in getting "the tools and training they need to start off running in their new job. By increasing the effectiveness of orientation programs delays can be minimized and workers can begin producing days or weeks earlier than under traditional programs. Most of these TTP tools need to be used before the new employee starts:

23. Change the managers and teams performance appraisal and reward systems to include time to productivity for new hires.
24. Prior to starting get the new hire their E-mail address, password, telephone #, ID card, corporate credit card, a departmental org chart/telephone directory, etc.
25. Provide them a Glossary of acronyms, buzzwords and on-line FAQ's so they don't have to ask uncomfortable questions about these buzz words (they are afraid to ask because it might make them seem like a dumb hire). Knowing these words might also decrease the number of errors on the job.

26. Assign them a departmental "mentor" to assist them during the first month in getting answers they need. An alternative is a orientation team to own the process.
27. Give them a copy of our mission/vision statement, our departments short-term plan, and org chart prior to the first day.
28. Give them telephone directory (updated with their name in it if possible).
29. Ask them who they would like to meet during their first week and have the meetings already scheduled.
30. Have their business cards mailed to their house before their first day.
31. Give them a "Help Source" Card with the names/ E-mail addresses of people with a reputation as "helping types".
32. Do a survey of your past "new hires" and identify their problems, frustrations and things they would liked to have "More of/Less of". Do the same at exit interviews to see if poor Orientation played a part.
33. Develop a "new hire" network of new hires and recent hires so a recent hire can act as a Big Brother/ Sister for a brand new hire.
34. Develop a set of success measures and metrics so that the process can be continually improved and those that helped in orientation can be rewarded. Include training, MIS and operations to ensure all details are measured.
35. Pre-assess the training needs of the candidate and schedule the required development before the candidate starts. Give the new hire the tools they need as fast as possible in order to succeed.
36. Pre-schedule a series of one on one meetings with the new hire to identify their frustrations and problems before they get out of hand.

Anticipating and Answering their Questions

Under traditional orientation programs most questions are asked by the candidate while they are in HR and generally they are asked only on the first day. Through focus groups and surveys possible questions can be anticipated and answered before the candidate garners the courage to actually ask the question. By expanding the time for questions, providing assimilation help over several weeks and making it easier to get answers you will improve a new hires productivity and lower a new hires frustration level.

37. Assign a "Welcome coordinator" or concierge that they can call before they start their job.
38. Give them access to the company Intranet or call center so they can learn about the firm and it's benefits before they start.
39. Give them "Silly/Dumb" question "coupons" to give to people. The coupons can help ease their fear of asking "dumb" questions.
40. Identify questions specific to their particular job through interviews with previous hires in their job class.
41. Designate the recruiter as the HR person responsible for helping the candidate get answers to most of their questions before they start as well as after their beginning date.

Tools to Make them Part of the Team

Helping the manager understand what the worker expects (why they accepted the position) and how to best manage them is almost as important as helping the worker understand the firm's culture and the team's expectations. By helping managers understand the need to develop an early strategy on how to assimilate, manage and develop the new hire, HR can make a significant strategic contribution.

42. Plan an hour of uninterrupted time with the manager on their first day.

43. Pre-schedule a series of "no cancel" meetings with the boss and key team members during the first month.
44. Give the new hire $25 certificates to give to the top 5 mentors that help them the most during their first week/month.
45. Get the manager to ask them for a "What they dislike list"—and then develop a what they want "More or Less of" list and then manage to it.
46. Ask them about their Dream job and how they can best be managed. Periodically manage toward it.
47. Develop an individual "Challenge" plan for the first three months to ensure that the employee is continually challenged in their job.
48. Develop an individual "Growth/Development" plan for the first three months to ensure they are developing at an acceptable rate.
49. Assigned a recent hire from the team as a mentor to ease the transition.
50. Have the CEO/GM do the orientation presentation to show the new hires how important they are to the organization.
51. Give them five "free lunch coupons" to use on co-workers so that they will rapidly get to know them and the local restaurants as well.
52. Expand the recruiters job description to including staying in touch with "their hires" and using their knowledge to help managers understand and manage their new employees.
53. Give them a "Rouges" gallery (pictures of the whole team) on the intranet (or hard copy) of all team members so it will be easier for them to put names with the faces they meet.

Additional Assimilation/Orientation Tools

54. Don't let the "intern"/HR Benefits person do the orientation! Dump the dull video's and take out the

boring stuff (Have a comedian do it if necessary like they do in comedy traffic school)!

55. Do a frustration (barriers to productivity) survey among the new hires at the end of the first, third and sixth month. Manage to the results.
56. Benchmark other firms best practices (Corning, 3COM, HP, etc.).
57. Use orientation as a intelligence gathering process. Find out all you can at time of hire. Ask them who at their old firm is good and ready to leave, what are their best practices, etc. Ask them why they took the job and why they rejected other firms. Feed that information back to the recruiters to help improve our recruiting process and to managers so we can improve on how we manage our new hires.
58. Extend orientation to at least a week (to as much as six weeks) so that you don't initially overwhelm them with information. Stop doing it in one day.
59. Give them a list of the "best" restaurants, schools, childcare, etc. in the neighborhood to help them feel comfortable with their new neighborhood.
60. If they have relocated, consider getting the spouses and kids of your current employees to help orient them to the "cool things" in the community.
61. Develop a New Hire electronic chat room/list server/ Web page to help them help each other. Consider forming an affinity group and pay for their lunches.
62. Do a post-orientation survey and ask them what they want more of and less of from orientation. Ask them to write down any new ideas or solutions they have on how to improve orientation and use them.
63. Consider varying the length and type of orientation depending on the job/importance of the hire.
64. Develop the capability to do orientation "remotely", globally and Just in Time.

Quick Guide to Employee Orientation—Help for Managers and HR

We would not be understating the case if we said that orienting employees to their workplaces and their jobs is one of the most neglected functions in government. Countless horror stories exist about how a new employee has received a ten minute talk with the manager, and directed to his or her office position, with no further guidance or instruction. Not only is this exceedingly stressful for the employee, but it virtually guarantees a very long period of unproductiveness for the employee.

In this month's PSM Supplement we present an overview of the orientation process, and a checklist that you can use when orienting new staff. As you read the article, keep in mind that orientation is also important for existing employees if (a) they have never received proper orientation or (b) there have been many changes in the organization and it's purpose and function.

Purposes of Orientation

Orientation isn't a nicety! It is used for the following purposes:

1. *To Reduce Start-up Costs*

Proper orientation can help the employee get "up to speed" much more quickly, thereby reducing the costs associated with learning the job.

2. *To Reduce Anxiety*

Any employee, when put into a new, strange situation, will experience anxiety that can impede his or her ability to learn to do the job. Proper orientation helps to reduce anxiety that results from entering into an unknown situation, and helps provide guidelines for behavior and conduct, so the employee doesn't have to experience the stress of guessing.

3. *To Reduce Employee Turnover*

Employee turnover increases as employees feel they are not valued, or are put in positions where they can't possibly do their jobs. Orientation shows that the organization values the employee, and help provide tools necessary for succeeding in the job.

4. *To Save Time for Supervisor and Co-Workers*

Simply put, the better the initial orientation, the less likely supervisors and co-workers will have to spend time teaching the employee.

5. *To Develop Realistic Job Expectations, Positive Attitudes and Job Satisfaction*

It is important that employees learn early on what is expected of them, and what to expect from others, in addition to learning about the values and attitudes of the organization. While people can learn from experience, they will make many mistakes that are unnecessary and potentially damaging.

Two Kinds of Orientation

There are two related kinds of orientation. The first we will call Overview Orientation, and deals with the basic information an employee will need to understand the broader system he or she works in. Overview Orientation includes helping employees understand:

- Government in general, the department and the branch,
- Important policies and general procedures (non-job specific),
- Information about compensation and benefits,
- Safety and accident prevention issues,
- Employee and union issues (rights, responsibilities), and
- Physical facilities.

Often, Overview Orientation can be conducted by the personnel department with a little help from the branch manager or immediate supervisor, since much of the content is generic in nature.

The second kind of orientation is called Job-Specific Orientation, and is the process that is used to help employees understand:

- Function of the organization, and how the employee fits in,
- Job responsibilities, expectations, and duties,
- Policies, procedures, rules and regulations,
- Layout of workplace, and
- Introduction to co-workers and other people in the broader organization.

Job specific orientation is best conducted by the immediate supervisor, and/or manager, since much of the content will be specific to the individual. Often the orientation process will be ongoing, with supervisors and co-workers supplying coaching.

Orientation Tips

1. Orientation should begin with the most important information (basic job survival).
2. Orientation should emphasize people as well as procedures and things. Employees should have a chance to get to know people and their approaches and styles in both social and work settings.
3. Buddy an employee to a more experienced person, but make sure the more experienced person wants to buddy up, and has the inter-personal skills. This provides ongoing support.
4. Introduce employees to both information and people in a controlled way. A new employee can't absorb everything at once, so don't waste your time. Space out introductions.

Conclusion

Orientation (or lack of it) will make a significant difference in how quickly an employee can become more productive, and also has long-term effects for the organization. To help you in the orientation process, we have included a checklist for the Job-Specific Orientation. Note that any complete program will include other elements...those that would be included in the Overview Orientation.

8

Job Characteristic Model

Job Description and Specification

Job specification is a written statement of qualifications, traits, physical and mental characteristics that an individual must possess to perform the job duties and discharge responsibilities effectively.

Job descriptions describe the job and not the individual who fills the job. They are the result of job analysis within a given organization and are essential to the selection and evaluation of employees. Job advertisements or postings are based on the job description. The character of the organization is the basis for the description of positions. Information about the organization might include:

1. Name of Company
2. Main Product(s) and/or Service(s)
3. Location
4. Number of Employees
5. Company Structure
6. Names of Officers
7. Hours of Work

Job Specification

The first step in the program of job specification is to prepare a list of all jobs in the company and where they are located. The second step is to secure and write up information about each of the jobs in a company. Usually, this information includes:

1. Physical specifications.
2. Mental specifications.
3. Emotional and social specifications.
4. Behavioral specifications.

Physical Specifications: Physical specifications include the physical qualifications or physical capacities which vary from job to job. Physical qualifications or capacities include physical features like height, weight, chest, vision, hearing, ability to lift weight, ability to carry weight, health, age, capacity to use or operate machines, tools, equipment, etc.

Mental Specifications: Mental specifications include ability to perform, arithmetical calculation, to interpret data, information blue prints, to read electrical circuits, ability to plan, reading abilities, scientific abilities, judgment, ability to concentrate, ability to handle variable factors, general intelligence, memory, etc.

Emotional and Social Specifications: Emotional and social specifications are more important for the post of managers, supervisors, foremen, etc. They include emotional stability, flexibility, and social adaptability in human relationship, personal appearance including dress, posture, poise, features and voice required by the job.

Behavioral Specifications: Behavioral specifications play an important role in selecting the candidates for higher level jobs in the organizational hierarchy. This specification seeks to describe the acts of managers rather than the traits that cause the acts. These specifications include judgments, research, creativity, teaching ability, maturity (capable of accepting responsibility) trial of conciliation, self-reliance (self-starter sticks to own decisions), dominance (giving orders in a personal way), etc.

Employee Specifications

Job specifications information must be converted into employee specification information in order to know what kind of person is needed to fill a job. Employee specification is like a brand name which spells that the candidate with a particular employee specification generally possesses the qualities specified under job specification, for example, the employee with the educational qualification of MBA generally knows the concepts, managerial skills like decision-making, inter-personal, leadership, etc. However, the validity of this assumption can be tested through selection procedure. Employee specification is useful to find out the suitability of particular class of candidates to a particular job. Thus, employee specification is useful to find out prospective employees (target group) whereas job specification is useful to select the right candidate for a job. Employee specification information includes the following:

1. Job Grade: Middle Management.
2. Job Title: Credit Manager.
3. Physical and Health: Normal health, able to visit factories, fields—able to walk extensively.
4. Energy Level and Temperature: High ability to adjust to increasing temperature.
5. Appearance, Dress: Neat-suitable to traveling.
6. Mental Abilities: Alertness, ability to read and perceive accurately.
7. Special Abilities: Flexibility, adaptability.
8. Special knowledge or Skills: Must know local language skills of conciliation, appreciation.
9. Skill in Operating Special Equipment: Driving two wheelers and light vehicles.
10. Degree of Personal Traits.
11. Maturity: Must be capable of accepting responsibility to recover.
12. Self-Reliance: Stick to own appraising decisions.
13. Dominance: Must dominate the field officers and branch managers.
14. Creativeness: Creative thinking in developing new schemes of advances and recovery.

15. Particular Skills: Calculating, analytical, interpretation, appraising, etc.
16. Others.
    - Age
    - Sex
    - Educational Qualifications
    - Experience
    - Physical specifications: Height, weight, etc.
    - Social background
    - Family background
    - Extra-curricular activities
    - Hobbies.

Some items of employee specification information are target for criticism. It is criticized that the privacy of the employee may be affected if the information like social background and family background is asked and taken into consideration to judge whether a candidate possesses certain traits, behavioral specifications and social specifications. However, the organization may adapt the counseling technique to solicit such information rather than using application blank. And the organizations should give the benefit of doubt to the candidate in judging the behavioral and social specifications basing on sex, family and social background of the candidate. However, job analysis once applied is of great use of performing various functions of HRM.

Various contents of a job specification can be prescribed in three terms:

(1) Essential qualities which a person must possess;
(2) Desirable qualities which a person may possess; and
(3) Contra-indicators which are likely to become a handicap to successful job performance.

Based on job description and job specification, employing organizations insert advertisements in newspaper, other publications, internet, etc. in order to minimize the size of the advertisements, most of the organizations prefer to include various contents of the job description and job specification only briefly; the details of such contents may be mentioned in the application forms to be filled-in by the prospective candidate or may be communicated to the candidate at the time of interview. In cases where candidates are selected not for specific jobs but for a pool of jobs like IAS, PCS, etc. in government service; management trainees in business organizations; probationary officers in commercial banks/ financial institutions, etc.; positions existing in various ministries/departments, business functions (production, marketing, finance, human resource, etc.) are notified.

If you look at the content of a job specification, you will find that various qualities that a job incumbent should possess may be divided into two broad categories: technical qualities and behavioral qualities. Technical qualities consist of knowledge and skills related to 'how a job should be performed'. Knowledge refers to the possession of information, facts, and techniques of a particular job. Skills refer to the proficiency required to use the knowledge to perform the job. Generally technical qualities are job specific, that is, technical qualities which are relevant to a particular job will not be relevant to another job if both jobs differ significantly. Behavioral qualities are not job-specific but are of universal nature and are applicable in most of the jobs.

Job Analysis

Job analysis is the systematic assembly of all the facts about a job. The purpose is to study the individual elements and duties. All information related to the salary and benefits, working hours and conditions, typical tasks and responsibilities is required for the job analysis. The results of job analysis are job description and job specification and it is the systematic assembly of all the facts about a job. The purpose is to study the individual elements and duties. All information related to the salary and benefits, working hours and conditions, typical tasks and responsibilities is required for the job analysis.

The Job; not the person is an important concept of job analysis. The analysis is conducted of the Job, not the person.

While job analysis data may be collected from incumbents through interviews or questionnaires, the product of the analysis is a description or specifications of the job, not a description of the person.

Purpose of Job Analysis

The purpose of job analysis is to establish and document the 'job relatedness' of employment procedures such as training, selection, compensation, and performance appraisal.

Determining Training Needs

Job analysis can be used in training/"needs assessment" to identify or develop:

- Training content,
- Assessment tests to measure effectiveness of training,
- Equipment to be used in delivering the training, and
- Methods of training (i.e. small group, computer-based, video, classroom...).

Compensation

Job analysis can be used in compensation to identify or determine:

- Skill levels,
- Compensable job factors,
- Work environment (e.g. hazards; attention; physical effort),
- Responsibilities (e.g. fiscal; supervisory), and
- Required level of education (indirectly related to salary level).

Selection Procedures

Job analysis can be used in selection procedures to identify or develop:

- Job duties that should be included in advertisements of vacant positions;
- Appropriate salary level for the position to help determine what salary should be offered to a candidate;

- Minimum requirements (education and/or experience) for screening applicants;
- Interview questions;
- Selection tests/instruments (e.g. written tests; oral tests; job simulations);
- Applicant appraisal/evaluation forms; and
- Orientation materials for applicants/new hires.

Performance Review

Job analysis can be used in performance review to identify or develop:

- Goals and objectives;
- Performance standards;
- Evaluation criteria;
- Length of probationary periods; and
- Duties to be evaluated.

Methods of Job Analysis

Several methods exist that may be used individually or in combination. These include:

- Review of job classification systems;
- Incumbent interviews;
- Supervisor interviews;
- Expert panels;
- Structured questionnaires;
- Task inventories;
- Check lists;
- Open-ended questionnaires;
- Observation; and
- Incumbent work logs.

A typical method of Job Analysis would be to give the incumbent a simple questionnaire to identify job duties, responsibilities, equipment used, work relationships, and work environment. The completed questionnaire would then be used to assist the *Job Analyst* who would then conduct an interview of the incumbent(s). A draft of the identified job duties, responsibilities, equipment, relationships, and work environment would be reviewed with the supervisor for accuracy. The Job Analyst would then prepare a job description and/or job specifications. The method that you may use in Job Analysis will depend on practical concerns such as type of job, number of jobs, number of incumbents, and location of jobs.

What Aspects of a Job are Analyzed?

Job analysis should collect information on the following areas:

- **Duties and Tasks.** The basic unit of a job is the performance of specific tasks and duties. Information to be collected about these items may include: frequency, duration, effort, skill, complexity, equipment, standards, etc.
- **Environment.** This may have a significant impact on the physical requirements to be able to perform a job. The work environment may include unpleasant conditions such as offensive odors and temperature extremes. There may also be definite risks to the incumbent such as noxious fumes, radioactive substances, hostile and aggressive people, and dangerous explosives.
- **Tools and Equipment.** Some duties and tasks are performed using specific equipment and tools. Equipment may include protective clothing. These items need to be specified in a Job Analysis.
- **Relationships.** Supervision given and received. Relationships with internal or external people.
- **Requirements.** The knowledge, skills, and abilities (KSA's) required to perform the job. While an incumbent may have higher KSA's than those required for the job, a Job analysis typically only states the minimum requirements to perform the job.

Job analysis is a systematic approach to defining the job role, description, requirements, responsibilities, evaluation, etc.

It helps in finding out required level of education, skills, knowledge, training, etc. for the job position. It also depicts the job worth, i.e. measurable effectiveness of the job and contribution of job to the organization. Thus, it effectively contributes to setting up the compensation package for the job position.

Importance of Job Analysis

Job analysis helps in analyzing the resources and establishing the strategies to accomplish the business goals and strategic objectives. It forms the basis for demand-supply analysis, recruitments, compensation management, and training need assessment and performance appraisal.

Components of Job Analysis

Job analysis is a systematic procedure to analyze the requirements for the job role and job profile. Job analysis can be further categorized into following sub-components.

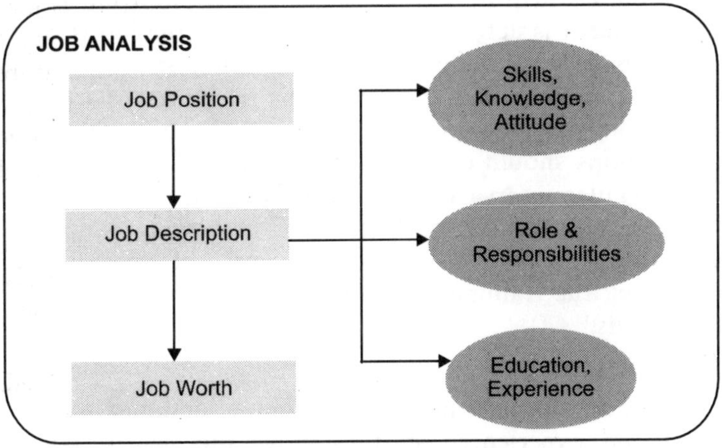

Job Position

Job position refers to the designation of the job and employee in the organization. Job position forms an important part of the compensation strategy as it determines the level of the job in the organization. For example, management level employees receive greater pay scale than non-managerial employees. The non-monetary benefits offered to two different levels in the organization also vary.

Job Description

Job description refers the requirements an organization looks for a particular job position. It states the key skill requirements, the level of experience needed, level of education required, etc. It also describes the roles and responsibilities attached with the job position. The roles and responsibilities are key determinant factors in estimating the level of experience, education, skill, etc. required for the job. It also helps in benchmarking the performance standards.

Job Worth

Job worth refers to estimating the job worthiness, i.e. how much the job contributes to the organization. It is also known as job evaluation. Job description is used to analyze the job worthiness. It is also known as job evaluation. Roles and responsibilities help in determining the outcome from the job profile. Once it is determined that how much the job is worth, it becomes easy to define the compensation strategy for the position. Therefore, job analysis forms an integral part in the formulation of compensation strategy of an organization. Organizations should conduct the job analysis in a systematic way at regular intervals. Job analysis can be used for setting up the compensation packages, for reviewing employees' performance with the standard level of performance, determining the training needs for employees who are lacking certain skills.

Job Evaluation

Job evaluation is a practical technique, designed to enable trained and experienced staff to judge the size of one job relative to others. It does not directly determine pay levels, but will establish the basis for an internal ranking of jobs.

The two most common methods of job evaluation that have been used are first, whole job ranking, where jobs are taken as a whole and ranked against each other. The second method is one of awarding points for various aspects of the job. In the points system various aspects or parts of the job such as education and experience required to perform the job are assessed and a points value awarded—the higher the educational requirements of the job the higher the points scored. The most well-known points scheme was introduced by Hay management consultants in 1951. This scheme evaluates job responsibilities in the light of three major factors—know-how, problem solving and accountability.

Some Principles of Job Evaluation

- Clearly defined and identifiable jobs must exist. These jobs will be accurately described in an agreed job description.
- All jobs in an organization will be evaluated using an agreed job evaluation scheme.
- Job evaluators will need to gain a thorough understanding of the job.
- Job evaluation is concerned with jobs, not people. It is not the person that is being evaluated.
- The job is assessed as if it were being carried out in a fully competent and acceptable manner.
- Job evaluation is based on judgement and is not scientific. However, if applied correctly it can enable objective judgements to be made.
- It is possible to make a judgement about a job's contribution relative to other jobs in an organization.
- The real test of the evaluation results is their acceptability to all participants.
- Job evaluation can aid organizational problem-solving as it highlights duplication of tasks and gaps between jobs and functions.

Job Evaluation—The Future

As organizations constantly evolve and new organizations emerge there will be challenges to existing principles of job evaluation. Whether existing job evaluation techniques and accompanying schemes remain relevant in a faster moving and constantly changing world, where new jobs and roles are invented on a regular basis, remains to be seen. The formal points system, used by so many organizations is often already seen to be inflexible. Sticking rigidly to an existing scheme may impose barriers to change. Constantly updating and writing new jobs together with the time that has to be spent administering the job evaluation schemes may become too cumbersome and time consuming for the benefits that are derived.

Does this mean that we will see existing schemes abandoned or left to fall into disrepute? Will providers of job evaluation schemes examine and, where necessary, modify them to ensure they are up to date and relevant? Simply sticking rigidly to what is already in place may not be enough to ensure their survival.

Job Evaluation—More

Job evaluation is essentially one part of a tripartite subject, which is collectively referred to as Job Study (other names exist). The three parts are Job analysis; Job Evaluation—the information collected is evaluated using a numerical scale or ranking and rating methodology; and Merit Rating—BSI definition (32542).

BSI definition—32529—"Any method ranking the relative worth of jobs which can then be used as a basis for a remuneration system".

It is essentially a comparative process.

Job evaluation evaluates selected job factors, which are regarded as important for the effective performance of the job, according to one of several alternative methods. The resulting numerical gradings can form the basis of an equitable structure of job gradings. The job grades may or may not be used for status or payment purposes.

Explanation: Job evaluation is concerned with measuring the demands the job places on its holder. Most factors that contribute to this job pressure, e.g. physical strength required, knowledge of mathematics required, are assessed and the result is a numerical estimate of the total job pressure. When evaluations are carried out on all hourly paid personnel the techniques used include establishing relative wage rates for different tasks. It is possible to use it for all grades of personnel, even senior management.

Illustration: The Time Span of Discretion is an interesting and unusual method of job evaluation developed by Elliot Jaques for the Glacier Metal Company. In this method the job pressure is assessed according to the length of time over which managers decisions commit the company. A machine operative, for example, is at any moment committing the company only for the period needed to make one product unit or component. The manager who buys the machine is committing the company for ten years.

What is "Job Design"?

Job design refers to the way that a set of tasks, or an entire job, is organized. Job design helps to determine:

- What tasks are done,
- How the tasks are done,
- How many tasks are done, and
- In what order the tasks are done.

It takes into account all factors which affect the work, and organizes the content and tasks so that the whole job is less likely to be a risk to the employee. Job design involves administrative areas such as:

- Job rotation,
- Job enlargement,
- Task/machine pacing,
- Work breaks, and
- Working hours.

A well-designed job will encourage a variety of 'good' body positions, have reasonable strength requirements, require a reasonable amount of mental activity, and help foster feelings of achievement and self-esteem.

How can job design help with the organization of work?

Job design principles can address problems such as:

- work overload,

- work underload,
- repetitiveness,
- limited control over work,
- isolation,
- shiftwork,
- delays in filling vacant positions,
- excessive working hours, and
- limited understanding of the whole job process.

Job design is sometimes considered as a way to help deal with stress in the workplace.

Is there a difference between job design and workplace design?

Job design and workplace design are often used interchangeably because both contribute to keep the physical requirements of a job reasonable. Job design refers to administrative changes that can help improve working conditions.

In comparison, workplace design concentrates on dealing with the workstation, the tools, and the body position that all influence the way a person does his or her work. Good workplace design reduces static positions, repetitive motions and awkward body positions.

What are features of "good" job design?

Good job design accommodates employees' mental and physical characteristics by paying attention to:

- Muscular energy such as work/rest schedules or pace of work, and
- Mental energy such as boring versus extremely difficult tasks.

Good job design:

- Allows for employee input. Employees should have the option to vary activities according to personal needs, work habits, and the circumstances in the workplace.
- Gives employees a sense of accomplishment.

- Includes training so employees know what tasks to do and how to do them properly.
- Provides good work/rest schedules.
- Allows for an adjustment period for physically demanding jobs.
- Provides feedback to the employees about their performance.
- Minimizes energy expenditure and force requirements.
- Balances static and dynamic work.

Job design is an ongoing process. The goal is to make adjustments as conditions or tasks change within the workplace.

What are common approaches to job design?

Achieving good job design involves administrative practices that determine what the employee does, for how long, where, and when as well as giving the employees choice where ever possible. In job design, you may choose to examine the various tasks of an individual job or the design of a group of jobs.

Approaches to job design include:

Job Enlargement: Job enlargement changes the jobs to include more and/or different tasks. Job enlargement should add interest to the work but may or may not give employees more responsibility.

Job Rotation: Job rotation moves employees from one task to another. It distributes the group tasks among a number of employees.

Job Enrichment: Job enrichment allows employees to assume more responsibility, accountability, and independence when learning new tasks or to allow for greater participation and new opportunities.

Job Engineering (Work Design): Work design allows employees to see how the work methods, layout and handling procedures link together as well as the interaction between people and machines.

What are the overall goals of job design?

Goals can be in many different areas and include:

Task Variety. To alleviate boredom, avoid both excessive static body positions and repetitive movements. Design jobs to have a variety of tasks that require changes in body position, muscles used, and mental activities.

Two methods are job enlargement and job rotation. For example, if an employee normally assembles parts, the job may be enlarged to include new tasks such as work planning, inspection/quality control, or maintenance. Alternatively, the tasks may include working in the same department, but changing tasks every hour. For example, in a laundry facility employees can rotate between various stations (sorting, washer, dryer, iron, etc.) as long as it provides for a change in physical or mental expenditure.

Work Breaks/Rest Breaks. Rest breaks help alleviate the problems of unavoidable repetitive movements or static body positions. More frequent but shorter breaks (sometimes called "micro breaks") are sometimes preferable to fewer long breaks.

During rest breaks, encourage employees to change body position and to exercise. It is important that employees stretch and use different muscle groups. If the employee has been very active, a rest break should include a stationary activity or stretching.

Allowance for an Adjustment Period. When work demands physical effort, have an adjustment period for new employees and for all employees after holidays, layoffs, or illnesses. Allow time to become accustomed to the physical demands of work by gradually "getting in shape". Employees who work in extreme hot or cold conditions also need time to acclimatize.

Provide Training. Training in correct work procedures and equipment operation is needed so that employees understand what is expected of them and how to work safely. Training should be organized, consistent and ongoing. It may occur in a classroom or on the job.

Vary Mental Activities. Tasks should be coordinated so that they are balanced during the day for the individual employee as well as balanced among a group of employees. You may want to allow the employee some degree of choice as to what types of mental tasks they want to do and when. This choice will allow the employee to do tasks when best suited to their 'alertness' patterns during the day. Some people may prefer routine tasks in the morning (such as checklists or filling in forms) and save tasks such as problem solving until the afternoon, or vice versa.

Can I use job design for teams?

Yes. Since most tasks are not done in isolation, job design is very often used for a group of employees. In some cases, teams can be created that have an overall responsibility for larger task or set of tasks. It is up to the team to decide how the job will be accomplished, which individual will do what tasks, and when. In most cases, team members will have many skills which allow them to change jobs from time to time. As with job design for individuals, additional opportunities such as inspection/quality control, maintenance, and related tasks such as ordering supplies are often assigned to the team in addition to their regular tasks.

What steps should I take when carrying out a job design project?

Although there are many ways to carry out job design, the following stages are essential:

Do an assessment of current work practices. Is job design needed or feasible? Discuss the process with the employees and supervisors involved and be clear about the process, or any changes or training that will be involved.

Do a task analysis. Examine the job and determine exactly what the tasks are. Consider what equipment and workstation features are important for completing the tasks. Identify problem areas.

Design the job. Identify the methods for doing the work, work/rest schedules, training requirements, equipment needed and workplace changes. Coordinate the different tasks so each one varies mental activities and body position. Be careful not to under or overload the job.

Implement the new job design gradually. You may want to start on a small scale or with a pilot project. Train employees in the new procedures and use of equipment. Allow for an adjustment period and time to gain experience with the new job design.

Re-evaluate job design on a continual basis. Make any necessary adjustments.

You may also want to establish a committee to represent the various groups involved. Job design should involve employees, unions, the health and safety committee and managers during the entire process. Participation of all parties increases communication and understanding.

Be clear that purpose of the job design is to strengthen the operations and its workforce, not to eliminate jobs or sets of skills.

Factors Affecting Job Design

Job design is affected by organizational, environmental and behavioral factors. A properly designed job will make it more productive and satisfying. If a job fails on this count, it must be redesigned based on the feedback. The various factors affecting job design are the following:

Organizational Factors

Organizational factors include characteristics of task, work flow, ergonomics and work practices.

Characteristics of Task: Job design requires the assembly of a number of tasks into a job or a group of jobs. An individual may carry out one main task which consists of a number of inter-related elements or functions. On the other hand, task functions may be spilt between a team, working closely together or strung along an assembly line. In more complex jobs, individuals may carry out a variety of connected tasks, each with a number of functions, or these tasks may be allocated to a group of workers or divided between them. Complexity in a job may be a reflection of the number and variety of tasks to be carried out, or the range and scope of the decisions that have to be made, or the difficulty of predicting the outcome of decisions.

The internal structure of each task, consists of three elements; Planning, Executing and Controlling. A completely integrated job will include all these elements for each of the tasks involved. The workers or group of workers having been given objectives in terms of output, quality and cost targets, decide on how the work is to be done, assemble the resources, perform the work and monitor output, quality and cost standards. Responsibility in a job is measured by the amount of authority, some one to put to do all these things. The ideal design is to integrate all the three elements.

Work Flow: The flow of work in an organization is strongly influenced by the nature of the product or service. The product or service usually suggests the sequence and balance between jobs, if the work is to be done efficiently. After the sequence of jobs is determined, the balance between the jobs is established.

Ergonomics: Ergonomics is concerned with designing and shaping jobs to fit the physical abilities and characteristics of individuals so that, they perform the jobs effectively. Ergonomics helps employees to design jobs in such a way that workers' physical abilities and job demands are balanced. It does not alter the nature of job tasks, but alters the location of tools, switches and other facilities, keeping in view that handling the job is the primary consideration.

Work Practices: Work practices are set ways of performing work. These methods may arise from tradition or the collective wishes of employees. Work practices were till now, determined by time and motion study which established the standard time needed to complete the given job. The study required repeated observations. The accuracy of the readings depended on competence of the work study engineer. Deviations from the normal work-cycle caused distortions in measurements, was biased towards existing work practices with little effort at method's improvement and could be carried out only when, production was under way.

A new technique has now emerged which, if introduced, could drastically alter the work practices. Called the MOST (Maynard Operating Sequence Technique), the technique uses a standard formula to list the motion sequence ascribed in index values.

Environmental Factors

Environmental factors affect the job design. These factors that have a bearing on job design are employees abilities and availability and social and culture expectations.

Employee Abilities and Availability: Efficiency consideration must be balanced against the abilities and availability of the people to do the work.

When Henry Ford made use of the assembly line, for example, he was aware that most potential workers lacked any automobile making experience. So, jobs were designed to be simple and required little training. Therefore, considerable thought must be given, as to who will actually do the work.

Social and Cultural Expectations: During the earlier days, securing a job was the primary consideration. The worker was prepared to work on any job and under any working conditions. Now, it is not the same. Literacy, knowledge and awareness of workers have improved considerably. So also, their expectations from the job. Hence, jobs be designed to meet the expectations of workers.

When designing jobs for international operations, uniform designs are almost certain to neglect national and cultural differences. Hours of work holidays, vacations, rest breaks, religious beliefs, management styles and worker sophistication and attitudes are just some of the predictable differences that can affect the design of jobs across international borders. Failure to consider these social expectations can create social dissatisfaction, low motivation, hard to fill job openings and a low quality of work life, especially, when foreign nationals are involved in the home country or overseas.

Behavioral Factors: Behavioral factors include feedback, autonomy, use of abilities and variety.

Job Characteristics Model

The job characteristics model has been developed on the basis of research designed to determine what kind of job features are satisfying and motivating to individuals. The model's five characteristics may be seen as the polar opposites of the qualities of jobs designed under a scientific management approach. The five characteristics are skill variety—the degree to which the job requires a variety of different activities so the worker can use a number of different skills and talents; task identity—the degree to which the job requires completion of a whole and identifiable piece of work; task significance—the degree to which the job has a substantial impact on the lives or work of other people; autonomy—the degree to which the job provides substantial freedom, independence and discretion to the individual in scheduling the work and in determining the procedures to be used in carrying it out; and feedback—the degree to which carrying out the work activities required by the job results in the individual obtaining direct and clear information about the effectiveness of his or her performance.

Job enlargement is doing different tasks and not just the same thing all the time. It may involve taking on more duties and adds variety to a person's job. Horizontal loading is often used which is giving people more jobs to do that require the same level of skill.

Job rotation is the movement between different jobs. One day a person may be working in one part of the factory and the next day they may work in a different part. This avoids the employee becoming bored as with job rotation they are doing different jobs all the time and learning new skills. Multi skilling is when people have many skills so they are able to carry out many different jobs. Multi skilling benefits the employer as if they are short of staff in one area, they can move people across.

Job enlargement means increasing the scope of a job through extending the range of its job duties and responsibilities. This contradicts the principles of specialisation and the division of labour whereby work is divided into small units, each of which is performed repetitively by an individual worker. Some motivational theories suggest that the boredom and alienation caused by the division of labour can actually cause efficiency to fall. Thus, job enlargement seeks to motivate workers through reversing the process of specialisation. A typical approach might be to replace assembly lines with modular work; instead of an employee repeating the same step on each product, they perform several tasks on a single item. In order for employees to be provided with job enlargement they will need to be retrained in new fields which can prove to be a lengthy process. However, results have shown that this process can see its effects diminish after a period of time, as even the enlarged job role become the mundane, this in turn can lead to similar levels of demotivation and job dissatisfaction at the expense of increased training levels and costs. The continual enlargement of a job over time is also known as 'job creep', which leads to an unmanageable workload.

Job enrichment is an attempt to motivate employees by giving them the opportunity to use the range of their abilities. It is an idea that was developed by the American psychologist Frederick Herzberg in the 1950s. It can be contrasted to job enlargement which simply increases the number of tasks without changing the challenge. As such job enrichment has been described as 'vertical loading' of a job, while job enlargement is 'horizontal loading'. An enriched job should ideally contain:

- A range of tasks and challenges of varying difficulties.
- A complete unit of work—a meaningful task.
- Feedback, encouragement and communication.

Techniques of Job Characteristic Model

Job enrichment, as a managerial activity includes a three steps technique.

1. Turn employees' effort into performance:
   - Ensuring that objectives are well-defined and understood by everyone. The overall corporate mission statement should be communicated to all. Individual's goals should also be clear. Each employee

should know exactly how he/she fits into the overall process and be aware of how important their contributions are to the organization and its customers.

- Providing adequate resources for each employee to perform well. This includes support functions like information technology, communication technology, and personnel training and development.
- Creating a supportive corporate culture. This includes peer support networks, supportive management, and removing elements that foster mistrust and politicking.
- Free flow of information. Eliminate secrecy.
- Provide enough freedom to facilitate job excellence. Encourage and reward employee initiative. Flextime or compressed hours could be offered.
- Provide adequate recognition, appreciation, and other motivators.
- Provide skill improvement opportunities. This could include paid education at universities or on the job training.
- Provide job variety. This can be done by job sharing or job rotation programmes.
- It may be necessary to re-engineer the job process. This could involve redesigning the physical facility, redesign processes, change technologies, simplification of procedures, elimination of repetitiveness, redesigning authority structures.

2. Link employees performance directly to reward:
    - Clear definition of the reward is a must.
    - Explanation of the link between performance and reward is important.
    - Make sure the employee gets the right reward if performs well.
    - If reward is not given, explanation is needed.

3. Make sure the employee wants the reward. How to find out?

- Ask them.
- Use surveys (checklist, listing, questions).

Job Enrichment

"You know that retaining experienced employees is a key factor in our continued success, yet I see us losing more and more of our long-standing account managers. Our survey shows they are bored with their jobs. I want a quick motivational training program for all employees starting in a week. Let's make sure this doesn't continue to happen!"

"We want to make sure we hang on to our top performing service representatives. I want you to put together an hour presentation showing them the options for advancement in our company. We can't afford to lose these people to the competition."

As with so many similar requests, analysis will most likely show that a training solution would not be very effective for either of the above scenarios. If the root causes of the scenarios are truly related to boredom and lack of preparation for advancement, job enrichment could be an excellent non-training intervention.

Job enrichment is a type of job redesign intended to reverse the effects of tasks that are repetitive requiring little autonomy. Some of these effects are boredom, lack of flexibility, and employee dissatisfaction (Leach & Wall, 2004). The underlying principle is to expand the scope of the job with a greater variety of tasks, vertical in nature, that require self-sufficiency. Since the goal is to give the individual exposure to tasks normally reserved for differently focused or higher positions, merely adding more of the same responsibilities related to an employee's current position is not considered job enrichment.

The basis for job enrichment practices is the work done by Frederick Herzberg in the 1950's and 60's, which was further refined in 1975 by Hackman and Oldham using what they called the Job Characteristics Model. This model assumes that if five core job characteristics are present, three psychological states critical to motivation are produced, resulting in positive outcomes (Kotila, 2001). Figure 1 illustrates this model.

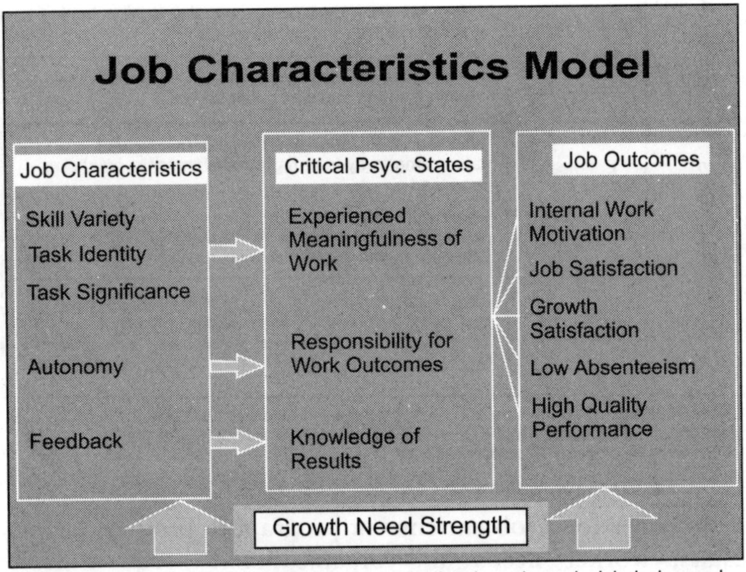

Note: From Drez, J. (1999). Chapter seven motivation through needs, job design, and satisfaction, slide 20. Retrieved February 14, 2004, from http://www.siu.edu/departments/cola/psych/psyc323/chat07/index.htm.

Fig. 1: Job Characteristics Model

Job enrichment can only be truly successful if planning includes support for all phases of the initiative. Ohio State University Extension began a job enrichment program in 1992 and surveyed the participants five years later. The results, broken down into 3 sub-buckets of data beyond the main grouping of advantages/disadvantages as shown in Fig. 2, indicate the University had not fully considered the planning and administrative aspects of the program (Fourman and Jones, 1997). While the benefits are seemingly obvious, programs fail not because of a lack of benefits, but rather due to implementation problems. These problems can include a perception of too great a cost, lack of long-term commitment of resources, and potential job classification changes (Cunningham and Eberle, 1990).

ADVANTAGES	Renewal	reduction in boredom, making new contacts, thinking about new career options, change in viewpoint.
	Exploration	trying new skills, developing new relationships, testing management & administrative skills.
	Specialization	re-education, in-depth exploration, using special skills, meeting a need that was under-served.
DISADVANTAGES	Balance	time allocation, tough decisions about workload, taking time away from regular assignments, balancing workload.
	Clarity	lack of information needed to be successful, lack of clear plans and goals, guidance in using time.
	Orientation	lack of structured introduction to special assignment, not being taught new responsibilities, difficulty in learning new networks, lack of instruction, sink or swim approach.

Note: The data represented are from "Job Enrichment in Extension" by Louis S. Fourman and Jo Jones, 1997, *Journal of Extension*, *35*, Retrieved February 14, 2004, from http://www.joe.org/joe/1997october/iw1.html

Fig. 2: Ohio State University Extension Job Enrichment Survey Results

In order for a job enrichment program to produce positive results, worker needs and organizational needs must be analyzed and acted upon. According to Cunningham and Eberle (1990), before an enrichment program is begun, the following questions should be asked:

1. Do employees need jobs that involve responsibility, variety, feedback, challenge, accountability, significance, and opportunities to learn?
2. What techniques can be implemented without changing the job classification plan?
3. What techniques would require changes in the job classification plan?

When asked about the successes of a Training Generalist job enrichment program begun in 2002, Karen Keenan, Learning Manager with Bank of America, stated the accomplishments were, "greater than expected". The Training Generalist program has resulted in three successful participants to date. According to Ms. Keenan, positive results can be directly tied to a program that addressed the strategic goal of greater resource flexibility without adding to staff, as well as to proper planning, guidance, and feedback for the participants. Having a voluntary program contributed as well, attracting a high caliber of individuals eager to expand their skills and be positioned for advancement. To date, all three Training Generalists have experienced promotions and additional recognition while affording Ms. Keenan's team financial results and workload flexibility it could not have otherwise achieved.

A job enrichment program can be a very effective intervention in some situations where a Performance Technician is faced with a request for motivational training. Ralph Brown (2004) summed it up very nicely:

"Job enrichment doesn't work for everyone. Some people are very resistant to more responsibility or to opportunities for personal growth, but...researchers report that some people they expected to resist, seized the opportunity. Enriching jobs is a particularly effective way to develop employees provided the jobs are truly enriched, not just more work for them to do."

Motivating Employee in Today's System:

- Compressed work weeks.
- Flexible Time.
- Job Sharing.
- Tele-commuting.

Suggestions for Motivating Employees:

- Recognize individual differences.
- Match people to jobs.
- Use goals.
- Ensure that goals are perceived as attainable.
- Individualize rewards.
- Link rewards to performance.
- Check the system for equity.
- Don't ignore money.

REFERENCES

Brown, R. "Design Jobs that motivate and develop people." Retrieved February 14, 2004. http://www.media-associates.co.nz/fjobdesign.html.

Cunningham, J.B., & Eberle, T. (1990). "A guide to job enrichment and redesign." Retrieved February 10, 2004. http://faculty.washington.edu/~janegf/jeguide.pdf.

Drez, J. (1999). "Chapter seven motivation through needs, job design, and satisfaction," slide 20. Retrieved February 14, 2004. http://www.siu.edu/departments/cola/psych/psyc323/chat07/index.htm.

Fourman, L.S. and Jones, J. (1997, October). "Job enrichment in extension." *Journal of Extension*, 35, Number 5, Retrieved. http://www.joe.org/joe/1997october/iw1.html.

Kotila, O. (2001). "Job enrichment." Retrieved February 8, 2004. http://academic.emporia.edu/smithwil/001fmg456/eja/kotila456.html.

Leach, D. and Wall, T. (n.d.). "What is Job design." Retrieved February 10, 2004. http://www.shef.ac.uk/~iwp/publications/whatis/ job_design.pdf.

Literature

Feder, B.J. 2000, "F.I. Herzberg, 76, Professor And Management Consultant", *New York Times*, Feb. 1, 2000, p. C26. Available from: ProQuest Historical Newspapers The New York Times (1851-2003). [28 October 2006].

Hackman, J.R. and Oldham, G.R. 1976, "Motivation through the design of work: Test of a Theory", *Organizational Behavior and Human Performance*, [Online], vol. 16, no. 2, pp. 250-79. Available from: Science Direct [1 November 2006].

Mione, P. 2006, "Job Enrichment", Online paper.

9

Employee Satisfaction

Total Quality Management (TQM) as a philosophy of modern management has evolved over the years to become more and more encompassing through the integration of various processes and activities. Failures in TQM implementation can be attributed to a wide variety of reasons, including:

- The failure to sustain quality effects and change the culture of work.
- The failure to translate TQM principles into tangible outcomes and lack of measurement for improvement purposes.
- The failure to understand that quality is a long-term process and that it needs resourcing for long-term results.

Quality has to be seen in totality, as an all encompassing philosophy. Total Quality recognizes contribution from all employees and ensures that people are aligned towards the same ultimate goal, that of meeting customer satisfaction. This can only be achieved if the following are encouraged within the organization:

- Customer satisfaction is the goal of everyone in the company.
- Everyone shares the same objectives.
- Everyone sees him or herself as a link in the entire production process.

- Each person treats the next person in the chain as an internal customer who must be given the same standard of quality as the external customer.

This paper briefly discusses on benchmarking customer satisfaction for best practice. It is generally accepted that the art of benchmarking originated in Japan. If one looks at the Japanese approach in modern competitiveness, benchmarking is practiced in various ways. One of the most commonly used approaches and perhaps the most effective is an application of a principle called Shukko, or the loaning of employees to other firms. This has lead to three types of benefits; transfer of technology, acquiring of specific knowledge and developing performance of managers.

What is Benchmarking?

It is important to distinguish between the meaning of a benchmark and the art of benchmarking or its practice on a continuous basis.

A benchmark can be defined as follows:

- Anything taken or used as a point of reference or comparison.
- Something that serves as a standard by which others may be served.
- Anything or something that is comparatively measurable.
- A physiological or biological reference value against which performance is compared.

Benchmarking is used in the following ways:

- As an enabler for achieving and maintaining high levels of competitiveness.
- As a measurement of business performance against the best of the best through a continuous effort of constantly reviewing processes, practices and methods.
- As a process which can be characterized by a standard and variables.

- As a continuous process of measuring our product, services and business practices against the toughest competitors and those companies recognized as industry leaders.
- To emulate the best by continuously implementing change and measuring performance.

Why Benchmarking?

Benchmarking is needed to be applied for the following reasons:

Benchmarking is a good strategic planning method and as such avoids stretch objectives and set credible, easy to reach target. It exposes the organization to state-of-art practices and by instigating a continuous learning process, can help in the cultivation of a culture based on change and continuous improvement. It is extremely a good vehicle for people education, involvement and empowerment and in optimizing their creative potential in the area of innovativeness.

The Link between TQM and Benchmarking

It has already been argued that TQM implementation is a two-legged journey. Besides creating a climate of continuous improvement intrenally, companies can embark on optimizing their internal and external operations using benchmarking. If one accepts that a definition of TQM is to meet customer requirement both internally and externally, this can often be achieved using performance teams. Indeed, it is through a bottom-up approach of people involvement empowerment that problems are solved and performance is enhanced.

On the other hand, benchmarking is about establishing companies' objectives using practices of best in class. Benchmarking is a top-down effect. This effect needs to communicate the objectives properly and relies on employees performing with the view of meeting those objectives. It is only by taking the two effects that companies can start to aspire to best in class position.

Benchmarking Customer Satisfaction

1. **Customer retention—a key to profitability.** Customer

retension is normally the direct result of a high level of customer satisfaction. In theory, if customer needs are satisfied, there is no reason for his/her royalty to change unless the product or service offered is becoming obsolete or poor in value. Research has demonstrated the importance of the delivery of a service or product being sold. Some researchers, in analysing delivery, have gone to the extent of suggesting that the service encounter—the moment when the transaction takes place—is the service itself. These ideas have been extremely important; they have helped change managers' thinking about service and its delivery. Intuitively, it seems reasonable that there should be a positive realtionship between well-served customer and companies' profitability, the improvement of customer satisfaction is certainly a business virtue to which many aspire. Talking to analyse the relationship between service, customer satisfaction and profitability, the key to profitability is to be found in customer retention. This is measured in terms of the number of customers present at both the beginning and end of a period, divided by the number of those present at the beginning. The premise is that the longer customers stay in a company, the more profitable they become. Of course there are positive and negative reasons for this argument, like, the cost of acquiring new customers is high, regular customers cost less to serve, long-term customers are often willing to pay a premium for service, and many more.

Evidence suggests that customer retention is a pathway to much higher levels of profitability and success. The best providers of service are those that are able to respond most quickly to complaints. This means giving more empowerment to front-line providers of service.

2. Retaining customer loyalty. Sustaining customer satisfaction and retaining customer loyalty depends on a number of factors. Building a highly loyal customer base cannot be done as an add-on. It must be integrated to a company's basic business strategy. Loyalty leaders are successful because they have designed their entire business systems around customer loyalty. They recognize the fact that customer loyalty is earned by consistently delivering superior value. High customer loyalty means that profit margins can be higher as the cost of acquiring customers is reduced. Competing on the basis of loyalty requires the understanding of the relationships between customer retention and the rest of the business and being able to quantify the linkage between loyalty and profits. This involves the rethinking of four important aspects of the business—customers, product or service offerings, employees and measurement systems. To get the full benefit of a loyalty based system, all these facets must be understood and attended to simultaneously. When all areas are aligned, they reinforce each other and the results are outstanding.

3. **The right customer.** Customers are obviously an essential ingredient of a loyalty based system. The success depends on their retention for a long time. Companies should target the right customers—not necessarily the easiest to attract or most profitable in the short time, but those likely to do business with customer over time. Finding loyal customers require taking a look at the customer segments to which a company can deliver superior value. A homogeneous customer segment improves the economics of serving the segment and the resources can be targeted on likely segments. Pricing should be used to filter out customers unlikely to be loyal as opposed to being used to attract new customers. Customers who are inherently disloyal are unproductive and should be discarded.

4. **Lifetime product and services.** Once a company has identified the customer it should keep, it has to go about the business of keeping them. That means satisfying the customers' evolving needs. Companies that fail to use their knowledge of customers to develop the product, or service those customers, will leave the door open for another company to lure them away. Continually catering to core customer segments' needs has been found to be easier than having to search for a new customer segment.

5. **Loyal employees.** The longer employees stay with the company, the more familiar they become with the business, the more they learn, and the more valuable they can be. Those employees who deal directly with customers day after day have

a powerful effect on customer loyalty. Long-term employees can serve customers better than newcomers can; after all, a customer's contact with the company is through employees and not the top executives. It is with the employees that the customer builds a bond of trust and expectations and when those people leave, the bond is broken.

6. Measure of loyalty. Even the best designed loyalty based system will deteriorate unless an effective measurement system is established. Measures establish the feedback loops that are the foundation of organizational learning. Only through effective learning can an organization consistently deliver value in an ever-changing world. The first step in developing effective measures is to understand the cause and effect relationship in the system. The primary mission of a loyalty based company is to deliver superior value to customers. Success or failure in this mission can be clearly measured by customers loyalty. Customer loyalty has three second order effects:

1. Revenue grows as a result of repeat purchases and referrals;
2. Costs decline as a result of lower acquisition expenses and from the efficiencies of serving experienced customers; and
3. Employee retention increases because of job pride and satisfaction. This in turn creates a loop that reinforces customer loyalty and further reduces costs as hiring and training costs shrink and productivity rises.

As costs go down and revenues rise, profit increases. Unless managers measure and monitor all these economic relationships, they will default to their short-term profit-oriented accounting system which focuses only on the second and third order effects. This only leads to decisions that will reduce value and loyalty.

How does the Benchmarking Process Work?

In the specific context of customer service, how does the benchmarking process work? The first point to note is that the customer service is perceptual. Whatever one's hard internal measures of service might say about service performance, the perceptions are the reality. Productivity measures, however useful, do not actually reflect the things that the customer values. The approach to service benchmarking follows a four-stage process:

1. Identify the key components of customer service as perceived by the customer.
2. Establish the relative importance of those service components to customers.
3. Identify the company position on the key service components relative to the competition.
4. Analyze the data to see if service performance matches customers' service needs.

Example of Best Practice—A Software Experience

The quality process should be market driven. As implies it should focus all processes around the customer in order to develop world-class solutions to support customer requirements. All activities should be driven by three market driven quality goals—customer satisfaction, empowered employees and excellence or efficiency in all activities. Supporting these goals there should be a prioritized strategy that begins with management commitment and leadership. The vision should be defined and directed by the top management. However, one must always remember that to have the program successful the approach has to be bottom-up. Hence, the second priority should be to empower employees to use their own creativity and customer knowledge to do whatever it takes to satisfy their customers needs while being ethical and profitable. Lastly, the priority should be to ensure that the customer becomes the unrelenting focus of each employee. The market driven quality depends on the initiatives like; defining of market needs, reducing cycle time, employee involvement and measurement. The objectives of the strategy should be:

- To transform the company into a market driven solution-oriented enterprise.
- To keep the company on top in terms of client or customer satisfaction so that else will follow.

- See market driven quality as a matter of survival in a global market where customers expect more and competitors provide more everyday, not as a yardstick to measure company's standing with customers and competitors.

To ensure that your market driven quality system works, all business units of your company should be assessed on using various criteria based upon core values and concepts. These criteria could be:

- Market driven quality principles,
- Leadership,
- Continuous improvement and innovation,
- Full involvement and empowerment,
- Cycle-time reduction,
- Design quality and problem prevention,
- Long-range outlook,
- Management by fact,
- Partnership development, and
- Public responsibility.

The customer focus and satisfaction criteria should examine the company relationships with customers and its knowledge of customer requirements and key quality factors which determine marketplace competitiveness. The company should also examine the methods of determining customer satisfaction, current trends and level of satisfaction, and those relative to competitors.

How to Retain an Employee?

After you have invested considerable time and money recruiting and training your employees, you must now determine how to make sure those valuable employees are productive and get them to remain loyal to your firm. Retention of employees is essential to maintain client relationships and keep recruiting and training costs in line. Losing an experienced employee almost always results in significant costs to your firm. The keys to employee satisfaction and retention are founded on strong leadership and sound management practices. If you can master these arts, you should have happy, loyal employees and clients, resulting in growth, profits and personal gratification. This article will discuss key factors in motivating and retaining good people.

Operating Systems: The foundation of an efficient and effective workplace is the structure, discipline and consistency provided by well-conceived systematic operating methods. World-class companies like Disney, McDonalds and Ritz Carleton all have well-defined operating methods. A policies and procedures (P&P) manual is critical to ensure that employees understand what is expected of them and know how they should handle the myriad of duties and responsibilities in the day-to-day operation of the office. The P&P manual spells out how you would like things done in your office and your expectations for the behavior of your employees. As your operation grows larger, the system becomes more important because your ability to oversee and communicate directly and frequently with each employee becomes more difficult. Written operating systems are absolutely essential when you expand to more than one office location. Creating an Intranet is also a good idea for large operations. To fully understand the importance of operating systems, I suggest that you read *The E-Myth Revisited* by Michael Gerber.

Employment Agreement: Legal agreements are a necessary evil to ensure that there is a meeting of the minds as to exactly what the parties agree to when they enter into a relationship such as that of employer and employee. As the employer, it is appropriate for you to establish standard terms and conditions under which you are willing to employ your workers. The agreement should specify the term, termination, duties, responsibilities and compensation. At Peoples Income Tax, we incorporate our policies and procedures manual into the agreement by reference and provide each employee with a copy, for which they sign a receipt. We also attach detailed job description to the agreement as an exhibit. Confidentiality and non-solicitation provisions are essential. A non-compete provision is often used; but to be enforceable, it must be reasonable in scope, distance and duration. Other standard legal provisions must also be included. Sample employment agreements are included in Peoples' P&P manual. Make sure each employee you hire fully understands the terms of the agreement, including the restrictive covenants that survive termination of employment. If employees understand up-front exactly what is expected of them and you make it clear that the clients and customers belong to the company, they are less likely to shirk their responsibilities or try to steal your clients if they leave. For legal advice, be sure to consult with a qualified attorney who is familiar with the laws in your state and locality.

Training: Pre-work training should include a review of your policies and procedures, with special emphasis on the most important subjects. (Each employee should receive a personal copy of your P&P Manual to read before coming to the training class.) In addition to training in your policies and procedures, customer service and marketing should be covered at length. Special emphasis should be placed on your corporate culture. New employees need more training than priors, but all employees should receive training each year. New employees should also have several days of on-the-job training with the office manager or experienced employees before beginning their position; and they should not be left on their own in the office until they are experienced enough to feel confident. Many of the frustrations employees feel on the job—as well as most errors and client problems—are due to inadequate training. Comprehensive training will make your life as a manager much easier, and your employees and clients will be happier.

Tools to do the Job: Employee costs constitute the greatest expense in any service business. Not giving your employees adequate tools to do the job is penny wise and pound foolish. Computers need not be state-of-the-art, but they do need to be fast and reliable enough to minimize down time and reduce employee and client frustration. If your office is not operating with a Local Area Network (LAN), you should set one up without delay. A LAN manages printer sharing and centralizes client files for easy computer cross-checking, e-filing, and report writing. Copiers should be reliable and fast, with automatic feed, and ample supplies always on hand. A fax is no longer a costly luxury for most offices, but a necessity. Internet access is almost as important as the phone for effective communication and is becoming more essential for research. Don't forget to provide the little things, like reliable staplers, staple removers, scissors, pens, post-its, business card holders, etc. An appointment book, a Rolodex (or software address book), and reference books and resources should also be provided. Comfortable, functional office furniture and adequate shelving and storage are also essential. Don't forget aids for employees with special needs, such as under-desk computer drawers and keyboard & mouse cushions. At Peoples Income Tax, we use checklists of office furnishings, equipment and supplies used to take inventory and request missing or shortage items. Attention to detail and providing adequate tools to do the job will eliminate a key source of employee frustration and increase employee productivity and satisfaction.

Office Atmosphere: How your employees feel about their jobs is greatly influenced by your office atmosphere. Extravagance is not necessary, but the office should be attractively decorated and a pleasant place to work. Little things like a fresh coat of paint and a wallpaper border make a big difference. A stereo (with ceiling speakers) tuned to a soft neutral music enhances the office atmosphere and creates an illusion of privacy. Don't neglect the back room and the restroom. We pay as much attention to decorating and appointing our restrooms as we do our client reception areas. We also provide a microwave and refrigerator for the back room of every office and, space permitting, a table and chairs where our associates can eat. The impression you make on your employees is just as important as the image you project to your clients. Keeping the office clean and uncluttered requires the cooperation of all employees, and you should insist that every employee pitches into help. However, you should regularly hire contractors for heavy cleaning (e.g. carpet, windows and restroom). Your employees' attitudes are affected by their physical work environment; make sure it is positive!

Support: Your employees will appreciate having adequate support. They need someone readily available to help when they have questions or encounter problems. Support can be provided on-site by an office manager or veteran employee or by telephone or e-mail when on-site help is not available. Having adequate help to properly serve all clients in the office is also essential for employee morale. The important point is that your people should not feel like they are out there on their own with no one to turn to when they need help. If they feel this way, they might as well go into business on their own.

Corporate Culture: World-class companies always have in common World-class cultures. Leaders of such businesses recognize that their companies exist to satisfy a social need. Profits are not the goal, but are a byproduct of meeting the needs of customers and employees. Businesses also have a responsibility to give back to the communities in which they operate. Most employees also have a need to make meaningful contributions to society through their work. They also like to take pride in their work and deliver quality products and services. And they need to continue to learn and grow professionally. A good corporate culture enables employees to combine their strengths to meet these mutual needs as part of a dynamic team.

Your company's culture starts with your company's mission and values, which should be well thought-out and articulated in writing. A mission statement and set of guiding principles is typically developed by the company's owner or CEO to reflect his or her business philosophy. Input should also be solicited from key employees. When hiring new employees, it is essential to confirm their understanding of and agreement with your company philosophy. Your values must not merely be lip service, but should be internalized and practiced daily by all employees. As the owner or CEO, you must set the standard for your people.

Compensation: A performance-based compensation plan should be designed to encourage your employees to behave in ways that will result in attainment of the goals of your company, while also meeting your employees' personal objectives. Company goals usually include growth, profitability, quality service, efficiency, effectiveness, and image and reputation. To attract desirable employees, your base pay and earnings potential should be competitive within your industry (equal to or better than your main competitors for employees). The pay plan must be objective and fair to all employees. Rewards should be commensurate with contributions. The behaviors and attitude your pay plan should encourage include honesty, professional pride, continuing professional education, loyalty, thoroughness, accuracy, efficiency, teamwork, salesmanship, courtesy, concern for clients, self-direction, frugality and long-term thinking. Peoples' compensation plan, devised with these factors in mind, includes a competitive guaranteed wage as a draw against commissions for individual and office production. Additional commissions are paid for experience, helping to generate office revenue growth, and attaining and maintaining professional. Establishing a sound compensation plan is one of the most important projects you will undertake. Once the plan is established, it is difficult to make radical changes. Your compensation plan is an essential element of your ability to compete effectively.

Benefits: Providing whatever benefits you can, puts you in a better competitive position to attract and retain seasonal employees. A profit sharing plan could be adopted for all employees to share in the profit pool in proportion to their annual earnings relative to total earnings of all employees. The profit pool could be some percentage (e.g. 10-20% as determined by management) of the increase in pretax profits over the prior year. Peoples Income Tax has a Fidelity 401k plan through its membership with the U.S. Chamber of Commerce that permits all year-round and seasonal employees to participate, and the company makes 3 per cent contributions.

Some of Peoples' seasonal tax associates who work part-time during the off-season providing client service and teaching an income tax school work enough hours to qualify for the company's group health insurance plan. Group life and disability insurance and other benefits can be obtained through professional associations. Even if the employee pays the full premium, group rates tend to be lower than individual coverage. Group discounts for products and services are often extended to employees through professional associations and company membership in the local Chamber of Commerce. Peoples Income Tax, as a small employer, was able to become a member of the Virginia Credit Union, making all of Peoples' employees eligible for the benefits of credit union membership. Peoples' also provides paid time off for its associates to volunteer for company approved charitable activities such as providing free tax service for welfare-to-work program participants and residents of homeless and battered women shelters. Be creative. Little perks, like buying pizza for the staff of the office on the busiest days of the work week, help to make your employees appreciate their jobs. Be creative!

Recognition: Numerous studies and surveys have documented the fact that money is not always the primary motivator for most employees. Recognize your people frequently for their good work and they will repeat the performance frequently. Praise must be sincere and should be distributed equitably, if warranted. When possible, praise people publicly in meetings or employee newsletters. Be sure to give people credit and rewards for good ideas they come up with that benefit the company. Reinforce the right behaviors. Avoid saying "Great but". Look for key measures to recognize employees, such as production, client retention rate, etc. Come up with contests to recognize your employees, such as the most referrals for another service you offer, or the most new clients brought in. Give recognition certificates, plaques and prizes and other than money, such as tickets for movie rental or sports events, or gift certificates for merchandise or dinner. Giving something tangible makes a more lasting impression. Praising your best performers (the top 10-20%) will raise the bar for your weaker people. The goal is to encourage behaviors that build your business and recognize your people for practicing those behaviors as often as possible.

Communication: Lack of effective communication from management is usually the greatest cause for employee dissatisfaction and premature departure. The best managers listen to and communicate frequently with all employees; and they make it easy for employees to tell them about problems and concerns. Communication should include training, group and individual meetings and, most important, daily discussions between you and your employees. The larger your organization becomes, the more difficult it is to keep in touch with all of your employees, especially if you have multiple offices. Yet, as the manager, you must make the time to regularly talk with everyone. E-mail is a good communication vehicle, but the phone is more personal; and neither can replace face-to-face meetings. Publishing employee newsletters is a good way for larger organizations to enhance communication. An Intranet can also be an effective internal communication vehicle. Keep communication simple, provide adequate information and provide examples for clarity. Show your trust in your people and make them feel included by sharing with them financial and other company inside information. Management can make much better decisions by getting input from front-line employees. If your people know that their voices are heard and they feel like they are part of the decision-making process, they will be much happier, loyal and more likely to support new ideas and programs.

Empowerment: Engage your employees in decision-making; give them the authority to act in the best interests of the company. Provide training in resolving client problems and then trust them to make the right decisions. Give your people some time to think and plan by building in some slack through adequate staffing and by providing clerical support. Don't criticize employee' mistakes; instead celebrate honest mistakes. Recognize that making decisions naturally results in making mistakes because no one is perfect. If you criticize honest mistakes, your people will stop making decisions. Failure is also OK, because it is a normal part of the road to success. Nothing is more gratifying than to see your people develop the skills and confidence to act independently and to make sound decisions that are in the best interests of the company and your clients.

Leadership: Much has been written about leadership and you should take the time whenever the opportunity arises to read ideas on how to be a more effective leader. Here are ten basic keys: (1) Integrity: always tell the truth and always keep your promise, even if it hurts to do so. (2) Trust: You must first demonstrate your trust in people by making yourself vulnerable before you can expect them to place their trust in you. (3) Respect: If you really don't care about your people they will sense your lack of concern and will not have respect for you. (4) Fairness: Treat all employees fairly and equally (including family members) regardless of your personal feelings. (5) Vision: To be a true leader, you must have an unfaltering vision, be able to communicate it to your people, and get them to understand and share in your excitement for the vision. (6) Optimism: You must always be positive and confident that the company will succeed; but you should also be realistic. (7) Decisive: A leader must make decisions and stick with them as long as they make sense. Consensus is not always better than an individual decision, particularly in a crisis situation. Remember, the buck stops with you! Trust your intuition. Intuition draws upon your experience, stored knowledge and information you may not even realize you have in your head. (8) Example: You must practice what you preach or you will have little credibility. (9) Teamwork: Insist on mutual respect, courtesy and cooperation among your people. This fundamental attitude was crucial in shaping our nation and is also essential to build your company. (10) Authority: Remember that authority is not vested in your position as the boss. Authority resides with the people who report to you and they have the power grant it to you or not.

Having Fun: People like to work in an environment that is enjoyable; they can get burned out if the work environment is totally serious and strictly business. Great companies like Southwest Airlines have come up with creative ways for employees to have fun. I think every manager should read the bestseller book, *NUTS!*, By Southwest chairman, Herb

Kelleher. If you're not naturally good at getting people to have fun, designate a key employee to assume this role. A friend, Hugh Goldthorpe, who is a top executive with Owens and Minor of Richmond, Virginia, has adopted (and had printed on his business cards) his official job title as Head Cheerleader.

Summary: Motivating and keeping employees requires effective management practices and strong leadership skills. A good operating system and adequate training are essential. Your people need the proper tools and support to do the job. A performance-based compensation plan should be designed very carefully to ensure that your employees are encouraged to help build the business and are rewarded for their contributions, and provide as many extra benefits as possible. A positive corporate culture and a pleasant work environment are more important than money to most good employees. Recognition and communication are among your key responsibilities as a manager. Screening new employment prospects to ensure they fit in and buy into your culture will prevent future problems. Employment agreements are a must and should be reviewed by and explained to new hires. A valuable project is to identify the 2-3 greatest frustrations of your employees and your clients and devise ways to eliminate these irritations. Employees should be trusted, included and empowered to make decisions and act autonomously. They also need to be part of a harmonious team working for the mutual benefit of the clients, the company and themselves. And they would enjoy being at a fun place to work! Ultimately, your management and leadership skills and efforts will determine your success in providing an atmosphere where your employees will be motivated to be effective and will remain loyal to your company.

Five Recruiting and Hiring Tips

These five tips will help you in recruiting and hiring a candidate who will become a successful, contributing superior employee.

1. Hire for Today's Need and Tomorrow's Vision. Remember that you're hiring for the future. While a new employee has to make economic sense for today's tasks, the best hires are people who position you to profit as your business moves into the future. New people should provide the skills you need in the future, not just match the job demands you see today. Be clear about your strategic direction for the future, and then hire the talent to help you achieve it.

2. Understand the Job. Finding the right people to hire is much easier when you first analyze the job you want to fill. Ask yourself what kinds of people do the best in this job? If you're lucky enough to have a top performer already in the job, learn from them.

Observe their behavior, ask them questions and talk with their peers to get a clear understanding what characteristics make them effective in their job.

3. Be Legal. The Equal Employment Opportunity Commission (EEOC) is the federal agency responsible for enforcing Title VII (Civil Rights Act), Title I, Title V (Americans with Disabilities), Equal Pay Act, and the Age Discrimination in Employment Act. If an interviewee feels he has been denied a job because of discrimination, he can file a lawsuit with the EEOC.

If the claimant ultimately wins the lawsuit, remedies may include, among other things, compensatory damages, back wages, reinstatement and possibly punitive damages. Make sure your hiring process is legal.

4. Be Practical. Don't count on your conversational skills to choose between candidates. At a basic level, your standardized hiring process should include criteria-based screening of an adequate number of candidates, a background check, standardized assessments and structured interviews.

Many assessment and interview tools are available, all of which will provide much more reliable results than the traditional interview. The more important the position, the more rigorous the hiring process should be.

5. Hiring Top Talent Means More Profit. The right person will make contributions to your company's productivity and profitability that far exceed salary cost. But the wrong person can cost you plenty.

Grime's Top Ten Tips to Attract, Retain and Motivate Employees

1. Pay employees fairly and well, then get them to forget about money.

2. Treat each and every employee with respect. Show them that you care about them as persons, not just as workers.

3. Praise accomplishments and attempts:

- Both large and small
- Verbally and in writing
- At least four times more than you criticize
- Promptly (as soon as observed)
- Publicly...and in private
- Sincerely

4. Clearly communicate goals, responsibilities and expectations. NEVER criticize in public—redirect in private.

5. Recognize performance appropriately and consistently:

- Reward outstanding performance (e.g. with promotions and opportunities).
- Do not tolerate sustained poor performance—coach and train or remove!

6. Involve employees in plans and decisions, especially those that affect them. Solicit their ideas and opinions. Encourage initiative.

7. Create opportunities for employees to learn and grow. Link the goals of the organization with the goals of each individual in it.

8. Actively listen to employees concerns—both work related and personal.

9. Share information promptly, openly and clearly. Tell the truth...with compassion.

10. Celebrate successes and milestones reached—organizational and personal. Create an organizational culture that is open, trusting and fun.

ABSENCE MANAGEMENT

Absence management is a key issue for any organization. In a small business, the absence of a vital employee can have far-reaching effects. At the other end of the scale, reducing absenteeism in a large company by even 1 per cent improves profitability and impacts positively on future success.

Managing ABSENCE provides a flexible service, individually designed to meet a company's needs and work within parameters tailored to match that company's requirements.

The absence management service instigates a proactive response from day one of an employee's absence. A managing ABSENCE Occupational Health Nurse will provide support, implement a program of rehabilitation, and advise the employee on accessing appropriate healthcare services.

At each stage of this process, the employee's line manager will be provided with detailed and confidential reports via e-mail. Ultimately senior management within the company will be able to access all the collated information within a secure, web-based format. This will provide an invaluable tool for identifying employee absence trends; accessing employee absence/attendance data; and providing a record of information relating to health implications of accidents or other processes in the workplace.

As well as providing vital support to the employee, managing ABSENCE assists the management of a company in negotiating the potential minefields of new disability legislation, issues of confidentiality, and individual freedom laws.

The benefits of using an absence management service are enormous: absence issues are managed fairly and with reference to an organization's own policies; confrontation within the organization is avoided; potential problems are identified and managed proactively by a support system which encompasses management and employees.

Managing ABSENCE is a Preventative Healthcare Company, providing a full range of occupational health services. These include pre-employment services, long-term absence management, health surveillance and health promotion programs. Absence management is vital for the provision of employee and management support which safeguards the health, safety and welfare of an organization:

- Employee Benefits
- Careers
- Compensation
- Employee Development
- Hiring and Recruiting
- Workforce Management
- Workplace Health and Safety

Employee Benefits

Make sure you offer your employees a comprehensive benefits plan, which can include health insurance, disability insurance, life insurance, retirement plans, flexible compensation, and time off from work:

- Benefits Compliance
- Dependent Care Plans
- Employee Assistance Plans (EAP)
- Employee Ownership
- Insurance Benefits
- Retirement Benefits
- Time Off

Dependent Care Plans

Many employers establish dependent care plans that help to fund childcare expenses and healthcare. Learn about the tax advantages of these plans and the guidelines set by the IRS.

Employee Assistance Plans (EAP)

Employee assistance plans are another distinguishing factor in a competitive job market. Investigate commuter programs, tuition reimbursement, and other perks to beef up your benefits package.

Employee Ownership

Stock purchase plans are a popular benefit option at companies of all sizes. Find out about how closely held companies and public enterprises structure their programs and learn the tax implications of ESOPs and ESPPs.

- Employee Stock Options Plans (ESOPs)
- Employee Stock Purchase Plans (ESPPs).

Retirement Benefits

Long-term and even short-term employees look at what retirement benefits their employer offers. Learn more about the legal requirements and options for sponsoring 401(k), pension, and Social Security plans:

- 401(k)
- Pension
- Social Security Planning
- Estate Planning
- IRAs

Time Off

Establishing a set policy regarding employee time off ensures a fair and consistent approach to employee requests. Find out how to factor in such situations as bereavement, illness, reserve duty, jury duty.

REFERENCES

"Recruitment and Selection Right Job for the Right Man at the Right Time: An HR Myth." www.hrprofessor.com

"HR Management Get Productive Employees! Web-based & Easy to Use. Fast Implementation." www.successfactors.com/hcm

"Hire Right the First Time Web-based Assessment & Interview Immediate Results, Completely Legal". www.peoplekeys.com

10

Employee Benefits and Compensation

In a sluggish economy, compensation system gets a new focus by rewarding star performers more than the rest of the pack. Employee benefits typically refers to retirement plans, health life insurance, life insurance, disability insurance, vacation, employee stock ownership plans, etc. Benefits are increasingly expensive for businesses to provide to employees, so the range and options of benefits are changing rapidly to include, for example, flexible benefit plans. Benefits are forms of value, other than payment, that are provided to the employee in return for their contribution to the organization, that is, for doing their job. Some benefits, such as unemployment and worker's compensation, are federally required.

Compensation: A performance-based compensation plan should be designed to encourage your employees to behave in ways that will result in attainment of the goals of your Company, while also meeting your employees' personal objectives. Company goals usually include growth, profitability, quality service, efficiency, effectiveness, image and reputation. To attract desirable employees, your base pay and earnings potential should be competitive within your industry (equal to or better than your main competitors for employees). The pay plan must be objective and fair to all employees. Rewards should be commensurate with contributions. The behaviors and attitude your pay plan should encourage include honesty, professional pride, continuing professional education, loyalty, thoroughness, accuracy, efficiency, teamwork, salesmanship, courtesy, concern for clients, self-direction, frugality and long-term thinking. Peoples' compensation plan, devised with these factors in mind, includes a competitive guaranteed wage as a draw against commissions for individual and office production. Additional commissions are paid for experience, helping to generate office revenue growth, and attaining and maintaining professional. Establishing a sound compensation plan is one of the most important projects you will undertake. Once the plan is established, it is difficult to make radical changes. Your compensation plan is an essential element of your ability to compete effectively.

Worker's compensation is really a worker's right, rather than a benefit. Compensation includes topics in regard to wage and/or salary programs and structures, for example, salary ranges for job descriptions, merit-based programs, bonus-based programs, commission-based programs, etc.

Benefits: Providing whatever benefits you can put in a better competitive position to attract and retain seasonal employees. A profit sharing plan could be adopted for all employees to share in the profit pool in proportion to their annual earnings relative to total earnings of all employees. The profit pool could be some percentage (e.g. 10-20% as determined by management) of the increase in pretax profits over the prior year. Peoples Income Tax has a Fidelity 401k plan through its membership with the U.S. Chamber of Commerce that permits all year-round and seasonal employees to participate, and the company makes 3 per cent contributions.

Some of Peoples' seasonal tax associates who work part-time during the off-season providing client service and teaching an income tax school work enough hours to qualify for the company's group health insurance plan. Group life and disability insurance and other benefits can be obtained through professional associations. Even if the employee pays the full premium, group rates tend to be lower than individual coverage. Group discounts for products and services are often extended to employees through professional associations and company membership in the local Chamber of Commerce.

Peoples Income Tax, as a small employer, was able to become a member of the Virginia Credit Union, making all of Peoples' employees eligible for the benefits of credit union membership. Peoples' also provides paid time off for its associates to volunteer for company approved charitable activities such as providing free tax service for welfare-to-work program participants and residents of homeless and battered women shelters. Be creative. Little perks, like buying pizza for the staff of the office on the busiest days of the work week, help to make your employees appreciate their jobs. Be creative!

Prominent examples of benefits are insurance (medical, life, dental, disability, unemployment and worker's compensation), vacation pay, holiday pay, and maternity leave, contribution to retirement (pension pay), profit sharing, stock options, and bonuses. (Some people would consider profit sharing, stock options and bonuses as forms of compensation.)

You might think of benefits as being tangible or intangible. The benefits listed previously are tangible benefits. Intangible benefits are less direct, for example, appreciation from a boss, likelihood for promotion, nice office, etc. People sometimes talk of fringe benefits, usually referring to tangible benefits, but sometimes meaning both kinds of benefits.

You might also think of benefits as company-paid and employee-paid. While the company usually pays for most types of benefits (holiday pay, vacation pay, etc.), some benefits, such as medical insurance, are often paid, at least in part, by employees because of the high costs of medical insurance.

Major Benefits and Compensation

Higher Education Assistance Policy

The policy will provide assistance to all eligible employees to pursue higher education (Full Time/Part Time) and thus help them enhance their performance and professional abilities.

Certification Incentive

This is to motivate and provide incentive to the employees to acquire latest skill sets.

Flexible Benefits Plan

This gives the employees the freedom to choose their own salary structure based on their requirements.

Variable Pay

The variable component is directly linked to the company performance as well as individual performance.

Special Skills Bonus

Many companies have a process of identifying critical skills and calibrating employees with those skills on competency framework. Based on the competency levels, these employees are rewarded a quarterly incentive plan.

Longevity Bonus

In order to retain key domain knowledge in a particular account and maintain continuity for the client's benefit, growing company has introduced this bonus in key accounts. This bonus is based on the duration spent on a particular account and is payable quarterly.

Compensation Benchmarking

Good companies carry out Benchmarking exercise for compensation practices with the key competitors and necessary adjustments are carried out.

Hospitalization Policy

The employee, on joining of the company is entitled for coverage of Hospitalization policy provided he/she submits the data required for coverage at the time of joining. Coverage entitles the employee to a "Cash less" transaction up to the eligible limits, at any of the covered Hospitals.

Accident Insurance Policy

The employee is entitled for coverage under Group Term Life insurance policy. The employee is covered under the policy as long as he is in the service of the company.

In case of Accidental Permanent/Partial Disability and Permanent Total Disability. The employee is covered under the policy as long as he is in the service of the company.

Master Health Check-up

This provides Medical Check up for employees above 40 years of age so that they can remain fit for the exigencies of the job.

Compensation and Benefits Manager

Job Description and Activities

Amid a fast evolving compensation and benefits environment, specially competition for skilled labor is heightening. The cost of employee benefits continues to mount. New rules and compliance standards are proliferating. A compensation and benefits manager has responsibility for developing, implementing and administering the organization's rewards and benefit policies. This will include salaries and bonuses plus employee benefits, such as pensions. Life assurance, profit-sharing, company cars and medical insurance packages may also be an area of responsibility, as can arranging relocation and expatriate packages. The terminology used to describe this area of work can vary; job titles may also include compensation and rewards manager and remuneration manager.

Within very large organizations there may be specialist managers who deal with only one aspect of compensation and benefits work, such as the company pension scheme, payroll or the salary structure. For those staff working across all areas of this specialism, typical duties include:

- Monitoring the organization's salary structure and benefits provision to ensure a balance between control of costs and attracting and retaining staff;
- Researching and analysing salary rates and benefits offered by other employers in the same sector;
- Undertaking job evaluations to ensure that the differences in pay between those doing different jobs within the organization are fair and are perceived to be so;
- Making recommendations on changes to pension and insurance schemes;

- Identifying and determining the causes of personnel problems and developing recommendations for improvement;
- Developing and implementing new benefit packages, ensuring that these are current and competitive and in line with legal requirements;
- Negotiating with union representatives on issues relating to pay and benefits;
- Managing the payroll system;
- Developing and maintaining personnel record systems in accordance with current legislation.

Compensation—Fringe Benefits

Corporate executives often receive extraordinary fringe benefits that are not provided to other corporate employees. Any property or service that an executive receives in lieu of or in addition to regular taxable wages is a fringe benefit that may be subject to taxation. A fringe benefit provided in connection with the performance of services, regardless of its form, must be treated as compensation includible in income.

Although it is clear that fringe benefits are taxable, employers may not treat them as wages for income and employment tax purposes. Employers may classify a taxable fringe benefit under expense accounts other than compensation, resulting in a failure to subject the fringe benefit to income and employment taxes.

Because the tax treatment of fringe benefits can vary depending on the facts and circumstances under which they are provided, it may be helpful to follow a 3-Step analysis when examining a particular item an employer gives or makes available to an executive:

- First, identify the particular fringe benefit and start with the assumption that its value will be taxable as compensation to the employee.
- Second, check to see if there are any statutory provisions that exclude the fringe benefit from the executive's gross income.

- Third, value any portion of the benefit that is not excludable for inclusion in the executive's gross income. Fringe benefits are generally valued at the amount the employee would have to pay for the benefit in an arm's length transaction.

Some of the most common fringes provided to executives:

- Athletic Skyboxes/Cultural Entertainment Suites
- Awards/Bonuses
- Club Memberships
- Home Loans/Personal Loan
- Spousal/Dependent Life Insurance
- Relocation Expenses
- Non-commercial Air Travel
- Employer-paid Vacations
- Spousal or Dependent Travel
- Qualified Retirement Planning
- Corporate Credit Card—Many companies provide corporate credit cards to executives and other employees. The difference between the rank and file credit card accounts and those maintained for executives is generally the method of reimbursement. Top level executives are permitted to use the card at will. A monthly statement may be mailed directly to the corporation and the account may be paid in full without the submission of a business expense report. Lower level executives are generally required to submit an expense report and are reimbursed for business related expenses. Personal expenses paid on behalf of executives are taxable fringe benefits that should be included in wages.
- Transportation—If an employer provides a car or other road vehicle for an executive's use, the amount excludable as a working condition fringe benefit is the amount that would be allowable as a deductible business expense if the executive paid for its use.

- Wealth Management—As part of their employment agreement or as a separate written or oral agreement, many executives are provided either a sum of money for financial planning or the services of the accounting firm used by the company.

The Workmen's Compensation Act 1923

The Workmen's Compensation Act, aims to provide workmen and/or their dependents some relief in case of accidents arising out of and in the course of employment and causing either death or disablement of workmen. It provides for payment by certain classes of employers to their workmen compensation for injury by accident.

Who is a Workman

Workman means any person (other than a person whose employment is of a casual nature and who is employed otherwise than for the purposes of the employer's trade or business) who is a railway servant as defined in Section 3 of the Indian Railways Act, 1890 not permanently employed in any administrative, district or sub-divisional office of a railway and not employed in any such capacity as is specified in Schedule II, or employed in any such capacity as is specified in Schedule II, whether the contract of employment was made before or after the passing of this Act and whether such contract is expressed or implied, oral or in writing. The provisions of the Act have been extended to cooks employed in hotels, restaurants using power, liquefied petroleum gas or any other mechanical device in the process of cooking.

Employees Entitled to Compensation

Every employee (including those employed through a contractor but excluding casual employees), who is engaged for the purposes of employer's business and who suffers an injury in any accident arising out of and in the course of his employment, shall be entitled for compensation under the Act. Employer's liability for compensation (Accidents). The employer of any establishment covered under this Act, is required to compensate an employee: Who has suffered an accident arising out of and in the course of his employment, resulting into: (i) death, (ii) permanent total disablement, (iii) permanent partial disablement, or (iv) temporary disablement whether total or partial, or Who has contracted an occupational disease.

However the Employer shall not be Liable. In respect of any injury which does not result in the total or partial disablement of the workmen for a period exceeding three days; In respect of any injury not resulting in death, caused by an accident which is directly attributable to the workmen having been at the time thereof under the influence of drugs, or the willful disobedience of the workman to an order expressly given, or to a rule expressly framed, for the purpose of securing the safety of workmen, or the willful removal or disregard by the workmen of any safeguard or other device which he knew to have been provided for the purpose of securing the safety of workmen. The burden of proving intentional disobedience on the part of the employee shall lie upon the employer. When the employee has contacted a disease which is not directly attributable to a specific injury caused by the accident or to the occupation; or when the employee has filed a suit for damages against the employer or any other person, in a Civil Court.

Contracting Out

Any contract or agreement which makes the workman give up or reduce his right to compensation from the employer is null and void insofar as it aims at reducing or removing the liability of the employer to pay compensation under the Act.

What is Disablement

Disablement is the loss of the earning capacity resulting from injury caused to a workman by an accident. Disablement's can be classified as (a) Total, and (b) Partial. It can further be classified into (i) Permanent, and (ii) Temporary. Disablement, whether permanent or temporary is said to be total when it incapacitates a worker for all work he was capable of doing at the time of the accident resulting in such disablement.

Total disablement is considered to be permanent if a workman, as a result of an accident, suffers from the injury specified in Part I of Schedule I or suffers from such combination of injuries specified in Part II of Schedule I as would be the loss of earning capacity when totaled to one hundred per cent or more. Disablement is said to be permanent/partial when it reduces for all times, the earning capacity of a workman in every employment, which he was capable of undertaking at the time of the accident. Every injury specified in Part II of Schedule I is deemed to result in permanent partial disablement.

Temporary disablement reduces the earning capacity of a workman in the employment in which he was engaged at the time of the accident.

Accident Arising Out of and in the Course of Employment

An accident arising out of employment implies a casual connection between the injury and the accident and the work done in the course of employment. Employment should be the distinctive and the proximate cause of the injury. The three tests for determining whether an accident arose out of employment are: At the time of injury workman must have been engaged in the business of the employer and must not be doing something for his personal benefit; That accident occurred at the place where he as performing his duties; and Injury must have resulted from some risk incidental to the duties of the service, or inherent in the nature condition of employment.

The general principles that are evolved are: There must be a casual connection between the injury and the accident and the work done in the course of employment; The onus is upon the applicant to show that it was the work and the resulting strain which contributed to or aggravated the injury; It is not necessary that the workman must be actually working at the time of his death or that death must occur while he was working or had just ceased to work; and Where the evidence is balanced, if the evidence shows a greater probability which satisfies a reasonable man that the work contributed to the causing of the personal injury it would be enough for the workman to succeed. But where the accident involved a risk common to all humanity and did not involve any peculiar or exceptional danger resulting from the nature of the employment or where the accident was the result of an added peril to which the workman by his own conduct exposed himself, which peril was not involved in the normal performance of the duties of his employment, then the employer will not be liable.

Compensation in Case of Occupational Diseases

Workers employed in certain types of occupations are exposed to the risk of contracting certain diseases, which are peculiar and inherent to those occupations. A worker contracting an occupational disease is deemed to have suffered an accident out of and in the course of employment and the employer is liable to pay compensation for the same. Occupational diseases have been categorised in Parts A, B and C of Schedule III. The employer is liable to pay compensation:

When a workman contracts any disease specified in Part B, while in service for a continuous period of six months under one employer (Period of service under any other employer in the same kind of employment shall not be included). When a workman contracts any disease specified in Part C, while he has been in continuous service for a specified period, whether under one or more employers (Proportionate compensation is payable by all the employers, if the workman had been in service under more than one employer).

If an employee has after the cessation of that service contracted any disease specified in the said Part B or Part C, as an occupational disease peculiar to the employment and that such disease arose out of the employment, the contracting of the disease shall be deemed to be an injury by accident within the meaning of the Act.

Calculation of Compensation

The amount of compensation payable by the employer shall be calculated as follows:

(a) In case of death—50% of the monthly wages X Relevant Factor or Rs. 50,000, whichever is more, and Rs. 1000 for funeral expenses.

(b) In case of total permanent disablement specified under Schedule I—60% of the monthly wages X Relevant Factor or Rs. 60,000, whichever is more.

(c) In case of partial permanent disablement specified under Schedule I—Such percentage of the compensation payable in case (b) above as is the percentage of the loss in earning capacity (specified in Schedule I).

(d) In case of partial permanent disablement not specified under Schedule I—Such percentage of the compensation payable in case (b) above, as is proportionate to the loss of earning capacity (as assessed by a qualified medical practitioner).

(e) In case of temporary disablement (whether total or partial). A half-monthly installment equal to 25% of the monthly wages, for the period of disablement or 5 years, whichever is shorter.

When Compensation to be Deposited with Commissioner?

The amount of compensation is not payable to the workman directly. It is generally deposited along with the prescribed statement, with the Commissioner who will then pay it to the workman. Any payment made to the workman or his dependents, directly, in the following cases will not be deemed to be a payment of compensation: in case of death of the employee; in case of lump sum compensation payable to a woman or a minor or a person of unsound mind or whose entitlement to the compensation is in dispute or a person under a legal disability. Besides, compensation of Rs. 10 or more may be deposited with the Commissioner on behalf of the person entitled thereto. The receipt of deposit with the Commissioner shall be a sufficient proof of discharge of the employer's liability.

Amounts Permissible to be Paid to the Workman/Dependents Directly

Following amounts may be paid directly to the workman or his dependents. In case of death of the workman, any advance on account of compensation upto [an amount equal to three months' wages of such workman] may be paid to any dependent. In case of lump sum compensation payable to an adult male worker not suffering from any legal disability. In case of half-monthly payments payable to any workman.

Registration of Agreements of Compensation

Where the amount payable as compensation has been settled by agreement a memorandum thereof shall be sent by the employer to the Commissioner, who shall, on being satisfied about its genuineness, record the memorandum in a registered manner.

However, where it appears to the Commissioner that the agreement ought not to be registered by reason of the inadequacy of the sum or amount, or by reason that the agreement has been obtained by fraud or undue influence or other improper means he may refuse to record the agreement and may make such order including an order as to any sum already paid under the agreement as he thinks just in the circumstances.

An agreement for payment of compensation which has been registered shall be enforceable under this act notwithstanding anything contained in the Indian Contract Act, or any other law for the time being in force.

Effect of Failure to Register Agreement

When a memorandum of any agreement is not sent to the Commissioner for registration, the employer shall be liable to pay the full amount of compensation, which he is liable to pay under the provisions of this Act.

Filing of Claims

A claim for the compensation shall be made before the Commissioner. No claim for compensation shall be entertained by the Commissioner unless the notice of accident has been given by the workman in the prescribed manner, except in the following circumstances:

In case of death of workman resulting from an accident which occurred on the premises of the employer, or at any place where the workman at the time of the accident was working died on such premises or such place or in the vicinity of such premises or place;

In case the employer has knowledge of the accident from any other source, at or about the time of its occurrence; in case the failure to give notice or prefer the claim, was due to sufficient cause.

Limitation

Workman, to the Commissioner, may file the claim for accident compensation in the prescribed form, within 2 years from the occurrence of the accident or from the date of death. The claim must be preceded by (i) a notice of accident, and (ii) the claimant-employee must present himself for medical examination if so required by the employer.

Attachment and Assignment of Compensation

No compensation payable under this Act, whether in lumpsum on half-monthly payments, can be attached, charged or passed on to any person other than workman by operation of law, nor can it be setoff against any other claim.

Duties of Employers

To pay compensation for an accident suffered by an employee, in accordance with the Act.

To submit a statement to the Commissioner (within 30 days of receiving the notice) in the prescribed form, giving the circumstances attending the death of a workman as result of an accident and indicating whether he is liable to deposit any compensation for the same.

To submit accident report to the Commissioner in the prescribed form within 7 days of the accident, which results in death of a workman or a serious bodily injury to a workman.

To maintain a notice book in the prescribed from at a place where it is readily accessible to the workman.

To submit an annual return of accidents specifying the number of injuries for which compensation has been paid during the year, the amount of such compensation and other prescribed particulars.

To send a notice of the accident in the prescribed form, to the Commissioner and the employer, within such time as soon as it is practicable for him. The notice is precondition for the admission of the claim for compensation.

To present himself for medical examination, if required by the employer.

Appeal/Bar to Civil Remedy

An appeal against and order of the Commissioner lies to the High Court, within 60 days of the order. The employer is required to deposit the compensation before filing the appeal.

No right to compensation in respect of any injury shall exist under this act if he has instituted in Civil Court a suit for damages in respect of the injury against the employer or any other person; and no suit for damages shall be maintainable by a workmen in any Court of law in respect of any injury—if he has instituted a claim to compensation in respect of the injury before a Commissioner; or if an agreement has come to between the workman and his employer providing for the payment of compensation in respect of the injury in accordance with the provisions of this Act.

11

Employee Relations and Grievances

Employee Relations: The purpose of staff relations is to ensure effective communication between management and staff, to secure maximum cooperation from staff, and to motivate staff to give their best by ensuring that they feel fairly treated, understand the overall direction and values of the Civil Service and those of their departments, and how decisions that affect them have been reached.

The principles that govern staff relations are that, where possible:

- management should communicate regularly and openly with staff;
- staff should be consulted on matters that affect them;
- problems and disputes should be resolved through discussion and consultation;
- the government should uphold the resolutions of the International Labour Organization conventions; and
- management should devise and encourage activities that contribute to staff's well-being.

Key Components of Employee Relations

Securing Staff Commitment

The public judges service by personal experience. This is largely determined by the staff who handle individual cases—

often front-line staff. Staff commitment is thus crucial to providing the quality of service that the public expects.

Front-line staff have difficult jobs to do and should be fully trained to answer questions, to know the rules they must administer, and to be taught how to deal with unusual cases as well as the inevitable difficult customer. In short they need to know how to be positive, helpful and courteous—everyday.

Managers are responsible for ensuring that programmes are in place for this purpose. They must also lead by example, so that the principles of good service cascade through all levels of the department.

Consultation

At the central level, there are four staff consultative councils: the Senior Civil Service Council, the Model Scale I Staff Consultative Council, the Police Force Council and the Disciplined Services Consultative Council. It is Government's policy that staff should be consulted on all significant changes to terms and conditions of service.

At the departmental level, Departmental Consultative Committees provide a consultative channel between management and staff representatives, mainly on departmental matters.

Managers should listen to their staff, and encourage them to air their views or make suggestions. In addition to formal channels, this can be achieved through opinion surveys, suggestion schemes, working groups, and other informal discussions.

Communication

Communication is a two-way process, for releasing staff's ideas, energy and ambitions. Through communication, management helps staff understand the mission, objectives and values of the department, and staff can let management know their ideas and aspirations for giving their best. To achieve effective communication, managers normally consider the following:

- The message they intend to send;

- Who they need to communicate with;
- The most effective form of communicating this particular message;
- How the audience would be likely to receive the message.

Formal communication channels include the consultative machinery, meetings, briefings, newsletters and circulars. Informal channels include recreational and sports activities, and day-to-day contact.

Recognition

Recognition of individual or group achievements and efforts will help promote the right attitude to work, and bring out the best in staff. Apart from pay increase, promotion and job extension, recognition is a good way to motivate staff. The following formal schemes help to motivate staff:

- Commendation/Appreciation Letters
- Long Service Travel Awards
- Long and Meritorious Service Award
- Retirement Souvenirs
- Honours and Awards
- Staff Suggestions Scheme
- Staff Motivation Scheme

Informal schemes include competitions, prizes, and articles in newsletters.

Resolving Disputes

Disputes between management and staff should be avoided if possible by prompt and constructive discussion between the two sides. Disputes are resolved at the departmental level as far as possible. Where they cannot be resolved by the department, or where they relate to issues of service-wide implications such as pay and conditions of service, the relevant policy branch and the Civil Service Branch would be involved.

Addressing Grievances

The government operates an open and fair system to deal with complaints and appeals from staff. Departments normally designate senior officers to handle staff complaints. Procedures for staff to lodge complaints are widely published and made known to staff on their first reporting for duty and are re-circulated at regular intervals.

Complaints should be expeditiously dealt with. In particular, the government is committed to providing a working environment which is free from sexual harassment for its staff. Detailed guidelines on the handling of complaints of this nature have been promulgated.

Employee Welfare

As a good employer, the government considers it important to provide welfare and recreational facilities to staff in maintaining staff morale, enhancing their loyalty and esprit de corps. The following are schemes/facilities that help to achieve this:

- Staff Welfare Fund
- Staff Relief Fund
- Staff Recreation Room
- Staff Recreation Club
- Holiday Bungalows

There are also rules and guidelines to help staff in distress. In the unfortunate event that staff encounter misfortune, they can approach their supervisor or departmental secretary to see what help can be given.

Grievance: A disagreement between an employee and supervisor on the terms or conditions of employment. The causes for a grievance may include, but are not limited to, complaints concerning wages, hours of work, working conditions, performance evaluations, job assignments, or the interpretation or application of a rule, regulation or policy.

Grievance Cell

Grievance Cell is also popularly known as Ombuds Cell. This cell or department is controlled by ombudsman. Now a days every good company has his own ombudsman in ombuds cell to take proper care of his employees. We should treat our employees as we generally treat with the loyal customer. We shouldn't forget that "one dissatisfied employee can break at least 20 loyal employees". Employees are human capital and they are associate of the company. Every employee is the face value of the company and if he/she will not be happy with the company then he/she can never make happy to any customer rather there are chances he/she can break loyal customer. One more important thing we delay in making decision due to personal busy schedule or more involvement with other project. We should tackle it and solve it on priority and with full justice as per the human resource policy of the company. It is important to note it happens some time suppose two loyal managers have involved in a issue to take one good executive. If this good executive is already reporting to a manager but the he/she is not happy with this manager and wants to switch over to any of the two good managers. Here ombudsman should fire that executive and we can never let three of them to fight for a good executive.

Grievance Policy

The company is committed to provide an ethical and friendly work environment that requires supervisors and officials at all levels to treat employees fairly and consistently in all matters related to their employment and to make personnel decisions consistent with the labor laws. Employees have the right to express concerns/grievances through informal and formal avenues without interference, coercion, intimidation, harassment or retaliation.

This policy applies to all employees, and offers different levels of recourse (informal and formal) for regular employees and other employees:

1. The informal problem-solving procedure has been established to resolve work-related problems as quickly as possible and is available to all university employees, regardless of classification, hours worked, or length of appointment. Employees are encouraged to pursue the resolution of work-related concerns through the informal problem-solving procedure prior to seeking recourse through the formal grievance procedure.

2. The formal grievance procedure has been established to resolve those work-related issues that could not be resolved through the informal problem-solving procedure. The formal procedure is only available to employees in regular positions at the university with the exception of probationary status employees.

Discrimination Complaints on the basis of race, caste, colour, religion, national origin, sex, age, disability, or veteran status. Please consult with the Manager, Human Resources/Affirmative Action if you have a question as to which policy applies to the grievance.

General Provisions

- Each individual is encouraged to become familiar with his or her responsibilities and this grievance and appeals process. The company grievance and appeals policy and procedures will be communicated to each new employee, both orally and in writing, during new employee orientation.
- If an employee feels that she/he has been dealt with in an unfair way, she/he is encouraged to proceed first through the informal problem-solving procedure prior to seeking recourse through the formal grievance procedure.
- The formal grievance procedure must be initiated within twenty (20) working days of the action or inaction for which the employee feels aggrieved.
- The burden of proof to show that the action taken against the employee is in violation of university policy or state or federal law or regulation rests with the grievant.

Dispute Solving Procedures

Informal Problem-solving Procedures

Whenever possible, employees are encouraged to pursue the resolution of work-related concerns through open discussion with the party(s) involved. Such discussions should be held early to prevent problems from escalating. Each department supervisor is responsible for establishing a mutual understanding with employees of the need to resolve problems objectively and without fear of retaliation. Most work-related problems can and should be resolved informally within the department. If an employee has a work-related problem, the company strongly encourages him/her to schedule a meeting with the person to whom he/she reports, and make a good faith-effort toward resolution.

If the work-related problem is not resolved through informal open discussions with the immediate supervisor, either party may then request a confidential review by the Director, Human Resources/Affirmative Action Officer or the next supervisor in line. The Manager, Human Resources/ Affirmative Action or the next supervisor in line will attempt to promote resolution of the complaint.

This concludes the informal problem-solving process.

Formal Grievance Procedures

If resolution has not been obtained through the informal problem-solving process, a regular employee may proceed with the formal grievance procedure.

Step 1: Written Grievance

Within twenty (20) working days of the occurrence of the action or inaction for which the employee feels aggrieved, the employee should file a written, signed grievance with the Director, Human Resources/Affirmative Action. The written grievance should contain the following information: name and address of grievant; nature and date of action or inaction; name(s) of person(s) responsible for the action or inaction; requested relief or corrective action, and any background information that the grievant believes to be relevant. If the Director, Human Resources/Affirmative Action is the immediate supervisor named in the grievance, the appropriate vice president will designate another administrator to assume all grievance responsibilities normally assigned to the Director.

The Manager, Human Resources/Affirmative Action will either forward a copy of the grievance to the employee's immediate supervisor or notify the employee in writing that the complaint does not warrant action under this policy.

If the grievance is forwarded to the immediate supervisor, the supervisor will respond in writing to the employee within five (5) working days of receipt and provide a copy of the response to the Manager, Human Resources/Affirmative Action.

If the grievant is notified that the complaint does not warrant action under this policy, he/she has five (5) working days to appeal the decision by the Manager, Human Resources/Affirmative Action. The appeal must be in writing. If the grievant appeals, the Manager, Human Resources/ Affirmative Action will forward the complaint to the Chair of the Staff Grievance Committee, who shall convene a review panel (three members of the Staff Grievance Committee) to consider the appeal. The review panel will notify the grievant within ten (10) working days of its decision. The decision of the review panel is final.

Staff Grievance Committee

The President shall appoint the Staff Grievance Committee, which shall consist of twenty (20) staff members [ten (10) from the Non-Exempt Subcommittee and ten (10) from the Exempt Subcommittee]. The Staff Grievance Committee will elect a Chair, and members of the Committee will serve two (2) year terms. Members may be reappointed at the Directors discretion.

Step 2: Appeal of Immediate Supervisor's Response

If the employee is not satisfied with the supervisor's written decision, the employee may, within five (5) working days of receipt of the decision, notify the Manager, Human Resources/ Affirmative Action of his/her desire to file an appeal of the supervisor's decision with the appropriate department head. The Manager, Human Resources/Affirmative Action will then forward a copy of the written grievance to the department head with a request for review. (If the employee reports directly to the department head, the copy shall be forwarded to the appropriate Director.) The department head (or Director) has the option of meeting with the grievant and supervisor, either separately or together, before responding in writing. Either party may decline to attend the meeting. If a meeting is agreed upon, the department head has the option of contacting the Manager, Human Resources/Affirmative Action to be present at the meeting for procedural advice only.

The department head (or Director) has five (5) working days from receipt of the written request for review to provide the employee with a written decision that affirms, amends, or reverses the supervisor's decision. A copy of the decision will be sent to the employee's supervisor and to the Manager, Human Resources/Affirmative Action.

Step 3: Request for Hearing

If the grievance is not resolved in Step 2, the employee may, within five (5) working days of receipt of the department head's (vice president's) decision, file a signed, written request for a hearing with the Manager, Human Resources/Affirmative Action.

Upon receipt of the written request for a hearing, the Manager, Human Resources/Affirmative Action will immediately begin the process of appointing a Hearing Panel. The Hearing Panel will consist of five (5) panelists selected from the Staff Grievance Committee. The membership of the panel will be provided to the employee and the supervisor within five (5) working days and may be challenged by either party in writing to the Manager, Human Resources/Affirmative Action. Both parties may challenge the selection of a prospective hearing panel member one time without a statement of reasonable cause; however, neither party may select or recommend a member of the Hearing Panel. Any additional challenges by either party must include a statement of reasonable cause. Rulings on challenges with a reasonable cause statement will be made by the Manager, Human Resources/Affirmative Action.

The Hearing Panel will elect its Chair.

The hearing will be conducted within twenty (20) working days, or as soon as practicable, after receipt of the employee's written request. The Manager, Human Resources/Affirmative Action will send a notice confirming the date, time, and place of the hearing to the employee, supervisor, and members of the Hearing Panel no later than five (5) working days prior to the hearing, together with copies of documents relevant to the grievance.

The Hearing Panel may request that an attorney from the Office of General Counsel sit as an advisor to the panel during the hearing. The attorney would be available to answer procedural questions and to assist in maintaining the decorum of the proceeding. The attorney will not be present during deliberation.

Grievance Hearing Procedures

The hearing procedures specified below are intended to serve as a broad outline for ensuring a fair and impartial hearing. However, the Hearing Panel Chair may approve departure from these procedures, if, in the opinion of the Chair, all parties have been treated fairly. The Hearing Panel Chair will be responsible for maintaining decorum.

Advisors: Parties will have the right to an advisor of their choice; however, neither party may proceed through their advisor. Any party who chooses to bring an advisor to the hearing must provide the name of the advisor to the Manager, Human Resources/Affirmative Action at least five (5) working days prior to the hearing date. Any advisor not listed will not be allowed to attend. If the grievant's advisor is an attorney, then an attorney from the Office of General Counsel must also be present at the hearing.

Record of Hearing: The hearing, but not the deliberations, will be electronically recorded so that there is an official record of what occurred. The Manager, Human Resources/ Affirmative Action will have responsibility for recording the hearing and no other recording will be allowed. Either party may obtain a copy of the tapes at the requesting party's expense. The request must be made in writing to the Manager, Human Resources/Affirmative Action. The tapes of the hearing will be kept by the Manager, Human Resources/Affirmative Action for at least three years after the resolution of the appeal.

Documents and Witnesses: The issues before the Hearing Panel will be limited to those raised by the written grievance. Both parties shall provide the Manager, Human Resources/ Affirmative Action with all documents to be used and relied on at the hearing and names of potential witnesses no later than five (5) working days prior to the hearing date. No new information will be accepted after this date, except in compelling circumstances as determined by the Manager, Human Resources/Affirmative Action or the Chair of the Hearing Panel. In such event, the hearing will be delayed until all interested parties have had a fair opportunity to consider the new information and prepare a response, if necessary. There will be a simultaneous exchange of this information between the parties, which will be facilitated by the Manager, Human Resources/Affirmative Action within two (2) working days of the hearing date.

It is the responsibility of the grievant and the supervisor to notify their respective witnesses as to the date and time of the hearing. It is not the responsibility of the Manager, Human Resources/Affirmative Action to contact witnesses and ascertain whether such witnesses consent to provide information at the hearing.

Retaliation against any employee for participating or not participating in a grievance hearing is strictly prohibited. Retaliation by a employee will be handled as a separate disciplinary action under this policy.

Opening Statement and Closing Statement: At the hearing, all parties will be afforded a reasonable opportunity for oral opening and closing arguments. The amount of time allowed for opening and closing statements may be limited by the Hearing Panel. The complainant will make the first opening statement. The respondent will then make an opening statement. After all witnesses are presented, the complainant will make a closing statement, which will be followed by the respondent's closing statement.

Witnesses: Only listed witnesses will be allowed to address the Hearing Panel. If information is made available to the Hearing Panel during the course of the hearing that the Hearing Panel deems necessary for the resolution of the hearing, the Panel is vested with the authority to request testimony from additional witnesses or request additional documentation. The Hearing Panel can only hear testimony from additional witnesses and can only review additional documents if it allows both parties additional time to prepare a response.

Witnesses will not be present during the questioning of any party or any other witness. The number of witnesses and the length of testimony may be limited by the Hearing Panel. The Hearing Panel may also decline to hear from a witness if the testimony is determined to be repetitive, irrelevant, or for other good reason.

After opening statements, the complainant will present witnesses. After the complainant has questioned each witness, the respondent will be given an opportunity to question each witness.

After the complainant has presented all witnesses, the respondent then has an opportunity to present witnesses. The respondent may question these witnesses, and then the complainant will have an opportunity to question the respondent's witnesses.

The Hearing Panel may ask questions of a witness at any time.

After all parties and the Hearing Panel have concluded questioning the witness, the witness will be reminded that all testimony is confidential and will be excused from the room.

Since this is an administrative hearing, legal rules of evidence will not apply.

Disruptive Behavior: Disruptive behavior by any participant, as determined by the Hearing Panel, will not be tolerated and will be grounds for expulsion from the hearing.

Hearing Panel Outcomes and Recommendation Transmittal: After the hearing is concluded, the Hearing Panel will convene in closed session to deliberate its findings and arrive at majority decision. Within five (5) working days after the date of the hearing, the Panel will prepare and submit a report containing fact findings and recommendation(s) to the Manager, Human Resources/Affirmative Action, who will forward the report to the appropriate Cabinet-level supervisor or vice president. (If the vice president was involved in Step 2, the findings will be forwarded to the vice president who is not in the employee's appeal chain. For example, if the Provost and Director for Administrative Affairs is the department head in Step 2, the Director, Human Resources/Affirmative Action will forward the fact findings and recommendations to the vice president for Administration and Finance and vice versa.)

Step 4: Administrative Actions

Within five (5) working days from the receipt of the Hearing Panel's report, the appropriate Cabinet-level supervisor/Director will take action on the recommendation(s). The Cabinet-level supervisor/vice president may accept or reject the recommendation(s) of the panel, or may return the case to the panel with instructions to conduct further deliberations or answer specific questions. If the case requires further deliberation, the Manager, Human Resources/ Affirmative Action will establish new time schedules and communicate them to all members of the panel. The Cabinet-level supervisor/vice president will make a decision and forward it to the Manager, Human Resources/Affirmative Action, who will notify the employee and the supervisor by mailing copies of the decision by certified mail.

Grievance Appeals

Both the employee and the supervisor have the right to appeal to the President. Appeals must be received in the Director office not later than ten (10) working days after the person appealing has been notified of the action taken by the Cabinet-level Supervisor/Director. If either party has requested an interview or is requested to appear for an interview by the Director, then both parties must be informed. The intent of the Director review is not to hear new evidence. The intent of this review is to ensure that the hearing and recommendations of the Hearing Panel were not arbitrary, capricious, or discriminatory, did not violate the rights of the parties and did not violate the concepts of fair play to both parties. The President shall respond in writing to the appeal within fifteen (15) working days from the date of receipt. The copy of the response will be forwarded to the Manager, Human Resources/Affirmative Action for inclusion in the hearing file. The decision of the Director is final.

12
Absenteeism Control

Absenteeism means absent (excluding entitled leaves + OD)—should be counted as absenteeism. If individual remains absent beyond 3 times in period of 12 months without intimation, then he is called as habitual absent case. Normally, 6-8% absenteeism is found in all industry. If it is beyond consecutively, then the matter is serious.

There are many kinds of absence. Some, such as annual vacation, are generally considered beneficial for both the organization and the employee. Since they are usually scheduled, their effect on the organization can be fairly easily absorbed; the same can be said of statutory holidays. Other absences, such as those caused by illness and family-related demands, are generally unavoidable, as are those due to inclement weather.

Absenteeism, a term used to refer to absences that are avoidable, habitual and unscheduled, is a source of irritation to employers and co-workers. Such absences are disruptive to proper work scheduling and output, and costly to an organization and the economy as a whole. Although absenteeism is widely acknowledged to be a problem, it is not easy to quantify. The dividing line between avoidable and unavoidable is difficult to draw, and absenteeism generally masquerades as legitimate absence. The Labour Force Survey (LFS) can provide measures of time lost because of personal reasons—that is, illness or disability, and personal or family responsibilities. However, within these categories, it is impossible to determine if an absence is avoidable or unscheduled. LFS data on absences for personal reasons can, however, be analyzed to identify patterns or trends that indicate the effect of absenteeism.

Frequent absence from the workplace may be indicative of poor morale or of sick building syndrome. However, many employers have implemented absence policies which make no distinction between absences for genuine illness and absence for inappropriate reasons. One of these policies is the calculation of the Bradford factor, which only takes the total number and frequency of absences into account, not the kind of absence. As a result, many employees feel obliged to come to work while ill, and transmit communicable diseases to their co-workers. This leads to even greater absenteeism and reduced productivity among other workers who try to work while ill. Workforces often do excuse absenteeism caused by medical reasons if the worker supplies a doctor's note or other form of documentation. Sometimes, however, in the workforce, people choose not to show up for work and do not call in advance, which most businesses find to be unprofessional and inconsiderate. This is called a *no call, no show.*

Absent does not only mean not being at work. Absent also means:

Arriving late (or poor timekeeping, if you like. It is still absent as long as the employee is not at work).

Leaving early (again, if you like, poor timekeeping. It is still absent if he is not at work).

Extended tea or lunch breaks—the employee is not at the workstation, and therefore absent.

Attending to private business during working hours—the employee is at work, but is not attending to his/her duties in terms of the employment contract—and is therefore absent.

Extended toilet breaks—same as extended lunch or tea breaks.

Feigned illness—thus giving rise to unnecessary visits to the on-site clinic, or take time off to "visit the doctor"—which they never do, because they don't need a medical certificate for less than 2 days off.

Undue length of time in fetching or carrying (tools from the tool room, for example, or drawings from the drawing office, etc.).

Other unexplained absences from the workstation or from the premises.

There are a number of remedies—a large number, in fact—that can be used to combat this scourge.

Deal with Absenteeism

A policy that provides guidance within an organization about how to manage the state of chronic absence from work is very important. Absenteeism is usually addressed through progressively stricter disciplinary measures that can result in the termination of the individual's employment. This is generally governed by the organization's attendance policy.

Absenteeism is a minor problem that can snowball into a much larger problem. However, there are ways to deal with it:

(1) Keep track of absences. Take note when an employee doesn't show up, and see if there is a pattern, i.e. if an employee calls out sick on Fridays or days with good weather.

(2) Establish a firm policy, and make sure that employees are aware of it. Make employees call and speak to someone when they call out sick, not just leave a message. Ask employees to bring doctors' certification if the level of absenteeism becomes excessive.

(3) Always give employees a "return-to-work" interview. The interview should make the employee feel that his or her work is valuable and that consequently, his or her presence was missed in the office. The supervisor should use the interview as an opportunity to explore reasons for the employee's absence and to express any doubts or concerns about the employee's attendance.

Calculation of Absenteeism of Cost

You can calculate any organization's annual cost of absenteeism.... Calculation about Annual Cost of Absenteeism per year in May & Baker.

________ × ________ = ________

(# work days lost per year) (cost per work day) (annual cost)

There are 180 employees working in May & Baker Pharmaceuticals Ltd. On an average one employee remains three times absent in a year. Employee's average salary is 170 per day.

Total employees = 180

Average work days lost per year = 180 (employees) × 3 (days in year) = 540 days

Average salary per employee = 170

Annual cost of absenteeism per year = 540 days × 170 (salary per day) = Rs. 91800

Guidelines for Absenteeism Control

There are two types of absenteeism, each of which requires a different type of approach:

1. Innocent Absenteeism. Innocent absenteeism refers to employees who are absent for reasons beyond their control; like sickness and injury. Innocent absenteeism is not culpable which means that it is blameless. In a labor relations context this means that it cannot be remedied or treated by disciplinary measures.

2. Culpable Absenteeism. Culpable absenteeism refers to employees who are absent without authorization for reasons which are within their control. For instance, an employee who is on sick leave even though he/she is not sick, and it can be proven that the employee was not sick, is guilty of culpable absenteeism. To be culpable is to be blameworthy. In a labor relations context this means that progressive discipline can be applied.

For the large majority of employees, absenteeism is legitimate, innocent absenteeism which occurs infrequently. Procedures for disciplinary action apply only to culpable absenteeism. Many organizations take the view that through the process of individual absentee counseling and treatment, the majority of employees will overcome their problems and return to an acceptable level of regular attendance.

Identifying Excessive Absenteeism

Attendance records should be reviewed regularly to be sure that an employee's sick-leave days are excessive compared to other employees. If a supervisor suspects that an employee is excessively absent, this can be confirmed through reviewing the attendance records.

If all indications show that an employee is excessively absent, the next step is to gather as much information as possible in order to get a clearer picture of the situation. The employees' files should be reviewed and the employee's immediate supervisor should document all available information on the particular employee's history.

Individual Communication

After all available information has been gathered, the administrator or supervisor should individually meet with each employee who has been identified as having higher than average or questionable (or pattern) absences. This first meeting should be used to bring concerns regarding attendance to the employee's attention. It is also an opportunity to discuss with the employee, in some depth, the causes of his or her attendance problem and possible steps he or she can take to remedy or control the absences. Listen carefully to the employee's responses.

The tone of the meeting should not be adversarial, but a major purpose of the interview is to let the employee know that management treats attendance as a very important component of overall work performance. Keep your comments non-threatening and work-oriented. Stick to the facts (i.e. patters, profiles, rates, etc.). The employee should be given a copy of their attendance report with absences highlighted for discussion.

This interview will give you the opportunity to explore in depth with the employee the reasons for his or her absence. Gather facts—do not make any assumptions. Provide support and counseling and offer guidance as the occasion demands to assist the employee to deal with the specific cause of the absence.

Often, after the initial meeting employees reduce their absenteeism. The meeting shows that you are concerned and that absenteeism is taken seriously. The employee's attendance should be closely monitored until it has been reduced to acceptable levels. Appropriate counseling should take place as is thought necessary. If a marked improvement has been shown, commend the employee. The meeting should be documented and a copy placed in the employee's file.

Proof of Illness

Sometimes it is helpful in counseling employees with excessive innocent or culpable absenteeism to inquire or verify the nature and reasons of their absence.

The extent to which an employer may inquire into the nature of and reasons for an employee's absence from the workplace is a delicate issue. The concepts of an employee's privacy and an employer's need for information affecting the workplace often come into conflict. Seldom is the conflict more difficult to resolve than where personal medical information is involved.

Unions will often strongly object to any efforts by management to inquire more deeply into the nature of an employee's illness. You will need to consider the restraints of any language in collective agreements in relation to this issue.

Generally speaking, however, the following "rules of thumb" can be derived from the existing jurisprudence:

1. There is a prevailing right to privacy on the part of an employee unless the employer can demonstrate that its legitimate business interests necessitate some intrusion into the employee's personal affairs.
2. When such intrusion is justified it should be strictly limited to the degree of intrusion necessitated by the employer's interests.
3. An employee has a duty to notify his employer of an intended absence, the cause of the absence and its expected duration. This information is required by the employer to meet its legitimate concerns to have

at its disposal facts which will enable it to schedule work and organize its operation.

4. An absent employee has an obligation to provide his employer with information regarding any change to his condition or circumstances relating to it which may affect the employer's needs as described in item #3 above. As such, the interests of the employer in having this information outweighs the individual employee's right to privacy.
5. An employer rule requiring proof for every absence is unreasonable if an absenteeism problem does not exist.
6. A mere assertion by the person claiming to be sick is not satisfactory proof.
7. The obligation to prove sickness, where the employer requires proof, rests with the employee.
8. An employer is entitled upon reasonable and probable grounds to refuse to accept a physician's certificate until it contains sufficient information to satisfy the employer's reservations (i.e. seen by physician, some indication of return to work, etc.). Non-production of a required medical certificate could result in loss of pay until the certificate is produced.
9. Where a medical certificate is rejected by an employer (as in #8 above) the employer must state the grounds for rejection and must point out to the employee what it requires to satisfy the onus of proof.
10. An employer may require an employee to prove fitness for work where it has reasonable grounds to do so. In a healthcare setting, the nature of the employer's business gives it a reasonably irresistible interest in this personal information for the purpose of assessing fitness.
11. Where any unusual circumstances raise reasonable suspicion that an employee might have committed an abuse of an income protection program, an employer

> may require an employee to explain such circumstances. For example, an employer may require responses as to whether the illness confined an employee to his/her bed or home; whether an employee engaged in any outside activity and the reasons for the activity.

In summary, any intrusion into the employee's privacy must be shown to be reasonable, based on the individual circumstances and in relation to the operation of the employer's business. If income protection abuse is suspected the extent to which such intrusion is "reasonable" would be far greater than in the case where it is not. If you are not clear on whether an inquiry is legally justified it is advisable to consult your superior.

After the Initial Interview

If after the initial interview, enough time and counseling efforts, as appropriate, have passed and the employee's absenteeism has not improved, it may be necessary to take further action. Further action must be handled with extreme caution—a mistake in approach, timing or severity can be crippling from both an administration and labor relation's point of view.

Determining whether counseling or disciplinary action is appropriate, depends on whether the employee's absences are innocent or culpable. If the employee's absenteeism is made up of both innocent and culpable absences, then each type must be dealt with as a separate issue. In a labor relation's context innocent absenteeism and culpable absenteeism are mutually exclusive. One in no way affects the other.

Counseling Innocent Absenteeism

Innocent absenteeism is not blameworthy and therefore disciplinary action is not justified. It is obviously unfair to punish someone for conduct which is beyond his/her control. Absenteeism, no matter what the cause, imposes losses on the employer who is also not at fault. The damage suffered by the employer must be weighed against the employee's right to be sick. There is a point at which the employer's right to expect the employee to attend regularly and fulfill the employment contract will outweigh the employee's right to be sick. At such a point the termination of the employee may be justified, as will be discussed.

The procedure an employer may take for innocent absenteeism is as follows:

1. Initial counseling(s)
2. Written counseling(s)
3. Reduction(s) of hours and/or job reclassification
4. Discharge.

Initial Counseling

Presuming you have communicated attendance expectations generally and have already identified an employee as a problem, you will have met with him or her as part of your attendance program and you should now continue to monitor the effect of these efforts on his or her attendance.

If the absences are intermittent, meet with the employee each time he/she returns to work. If absence is prolonged, keep in touch with the employee regularly and stay updated on the status of his/her condition. (Indicate your willingness to assist.)

You may require the employee to provide you with regular medical assessments. This will enable you to judge whether or not there is any likelihood of the employee providing regular attendance in future. Regular medical assessments will also give you an idea of what steps the employee is taking to seek medical or other assistance. Formal meetings in which verbal warnings are given should be given as appropriate and documented. If no improvement occurs written warning may be necessary.

Written Counseling

If the absences persist, you should meet with the employee formally and provide him/her with a letter of concern. If the absenteeism still continues to persist then the employee should be given a second letter of concern during another formal meeting. This letter would be stronger worded in that it would warn the employee that unless attendance improves, termination may be necessary.

Reduction(s) of hours and or job reclassification

In between the first and second letters the employee may be given the option to reduce his/her hours to better fit his/her personal circumstances. This option must be voluntarily accepted by the employee and cannot be offered as an ultimatum, as a reduction in hours is a reduction in pay and therefore can be looked upon as discipline.

If the nature of the illness or injury is such that the employee is unable to fulfill the requirements of his/her job, but could for example, benefit from modified work, counsel the employee to bid on jobs of such type if they become available. (N.B. It is inadvisable to "build" a job around an employee's incapacitates particularly in a unionized environment. The onus should be on the employee to apply for an existing position within his/her capabilities.)

Discharge

Only when all the previously noted needs and conditions have been met and everything has been done to accommodate the employee, can termination be considered. An Arbitrator would consider the following in ruling on an innocent absenteeism dismissal case:

1. Has the employee done everything possible to regain their health and return to work?
2. Has the employer provided every assistance possible? (i.e. counseling, support, time off.)
3. Has the employer informed the employee of the unworkable situation resulting from their sickness?
4. Has the employer attempted to accommodate the employee by offering a more suitable position (if available) or a reduction of hours?
5. Has enough time elapsed to allow for every possible chance of recovery?
6. Has the employer treated the employee prejudicially in any way?

As is evident, a great deal of time and effort must elapse before dismissal can take place.

These points would be used to substantiate or disprove the following two fold test:

1. The absences must be shown to be clearly excessive.
2. It must be proven that the employee will be unable to attend work on a regular basis in the future.

Corrective Action for Culpable Absenteeism

As already indicated, culpable absenteeism consists of absences where it can be demonstrated that the employee is not actually ill and is able to improve his/her attendance.

Presuming you have communicated attendance expectations generally, have identified the employee as a problem, have met with him/her as part of your attendance program, made your concerns on his specific absenteeism known and have offered counseling as appropriate, with no improvement despite your positive efforts, disciplinary procedures may be appropriate.

The procedures for corrective/progressive discipline for culpable absenteeism are generally the same as for other progressive discipline problems. The discipline should not be prejudicial in any way. The general procedure is as follows:

1. Initial Warning(s) (Verbal warning)
2. Written Warning(s)
3. Suspension(s)
4. Discharge.

Verbal Warning

Formally meet with the employee and explain that income protection is to be used only when an employee is legitimately ill. Advise the employee that his/her attendance record must improve and be maintained at an improved level or further disciplinary action will result. Offer any counseling or guidance as is appropriate. Give further verbal warnings as required. Review the employee's income protection records at regular intervals. Where a marked improvement has been shown, commend the employee. Where there is no improvement, a written warning should be issued.

Written Warning

Interview the employee again. Show him/her the statistics and point out that there has been no noticeable (or sufficient) improvement. Listen to the employee to see if there is a valid reason and offer any assistance you can. If no satisfactory explanation is given, advise the employee that he/she will be given a written warning. Be specific in your discussion with him/her and in the counseling memorandum as to the type of action to be taken and when it will be taken if the record does not improve. As soon as possible after this meeting provide the employee personally with the written warning and place a copy of his/her file. The written warning should identify any noticeable pattern.

If the amount and/or pattern continues, the next step in progressive discipline may be a second, stronger written warning. Your decision to provide a second written warning as an alternative to proceeding to a higher level of discipline (i.e. suspension) will depend on a number of factors. Such factors are, the severity of the problem, the credibility of the employee's explanations, the employee's general work performance and length of service.

Suspension

If the problem of culpable absenteeism persists, following the next interview period and immediately following an absence, the employee should be interviewed and advised that he/she is to be suspended. The length of the suspension will depend again on the severity of the problem, the credibility of the employee's explanation, the employee's general work performance and length of service. Subsequent suspensions are optional depending on the above condition.

Dismissal

Dismissal only after consultation with the appropriate superiors should be considered when all of the above conditions and procedures have been met. The employee, upon displaying no satisfactory improvement, would be dismissed on the grounds of his/her unwillingness to correct his/her absence record.

Combating Absenteeism

For Supervisors/Managers. Recently, I was asked by a manager how he should deal with the fact that on any given day 10 per cent of his employees are absent from work. I informed the manager that the problem of employee absenteeism is a problem best resolved by taking the following four positive interventions versus taking a negative or punitive approach.

Change Management Style. We are all aware of the fact that when employees call in ill, it does not mean they are truly too physically ill to work. One reason, outside of illness, that employees are absent is stress, and the number one reason employees are stressed has to do with their relationship with their manager/supervisor. Management styles that are too authoritarian tend to promote high levels of absenteeism among employees. Authoritarian managers are managers who have poor listening skills, set unreachable goals, have poor communication skills, and are inflexible. In other words, they yell too much, blame others for problems, and make others feel that it must be their way or the "highway". Authoritarian managers tend to produce high absenteeism rates. By identifying managers who use an authoritarian style, and providing them with management training, you will be taking a positive step not only toward reducing absenteeism, but also reducing turnover, job burnout, and employee health problems such as backaches and headaches.

Change Working Conditions. The employees in your company probably work in a well-lighted climate controlled building. The working conditions I am referring to relate to co-worker relationships. Not only does relationship stress occur between the employee and manager, but it also exists between employees. Frequently I hear employees say they did not go to work because they are fearful of or angry with another employee. These employees usually report they just could not deal with "so and so" today, so they called in ill. Companies that adopted policies and values that promote employee respect and professionalism, and promote an internal conflict resolution procedure, are companies that reduce employee stress. A reduction in employee stress reduces employee absenteeism.

Provide Incentives. Giving employees incentives for reduced absenteeism is not the same as rewarding or giving employees bonuses for reduced absenteeism. An incentive provides an employee with a boost to their motivation to avoid unnecessary absenteeism. It simply helps the employee decide to go to work versus staying home and watching Jerry Springer. The types of incentive programs used by companies are numerous. Some companies allow employees to cash-in unused sick days at the end of every quarter, others give an employee two hours of bonus pay for every month of perfect attendance; and still others provide employees with a buffet lunch, a certificate of achievement, or even a scratch-off card concealing prizes. The type of incentive program that your company uses should be one created especially for your company. You can create an incentive program tailored to your unique company by allowing employees to help you develop the incentive program. For example, your employees may not care about receiving a Rs. 100/- saving bond for perfect attendance, but they might respond very well to being able to leave one hour early on Friday if they have perfect attendance all week. The duration of the incentive program is also very important. Once again allow your employees to help guide you to determine the length of time between incentives. Some companies find that they can simply reward employees with perfect attendance once a year, while others decide once a month is best, and still others decide once a week works best. The general rule of thumb is to reward workers more frequently, the younger they are and the more difficult the work is to perform. Also, it is best to start with small incentives and work up to larger ones, if necessary.

Develop an Attendance Policy. Every company should have an attendance policy. An attendance policy allows a manager to intervene with an employee who is frequently absent. Besides stress as a primary reason for employee absenteeism, other causes relate to alcoholism, domestic violence, and family problems. If you confront an employee about his or her frequent absenteeism, and they inform you it is due to personal problems, consider referring the employee to an Employee Assistance Program (EAP). If the employee's absenteeism relates to a medical problem or a family member with a medical problem, you may have to consider allowing the employee to use the benefits allowed to them under the American's with Disability Act (ADA) or the Family and Medical Leave Act (FMLA). Early identification of these employees will get them back to work as fast as possible. Lastly, make sure that you have an attorney review your attendance policy to make sure it does not violate any State or Federal labor laws. By incorporating the above four strategies into your company you will not only reduce absenteeism you will reduce employee burnout, turnover, poor morale, and workplace negativism.

For Employees Who are Frequently Absent

One of the most important steps you can take if you are frequently absent, is to keep your employer informed. Employees who are frequently absent without good cause are generally absent due to numerous frivolous reasons. Employees who are absent for good cause have legitimate reasons, e.g. sickness or family member illness, and the employee needs time off to resolve their personal problems. Most employers generally understand the need to be gone from work due to a legitimate reason; therefore, it is important to communicate clearly and accurately so your employer does not assume you are out for frivolous reasons.

As an employee you are allowed to take up to 12 weeks of unpaid leave under the federal Family and Medical Leave Act (FMLA). The 12 weeks of leave may be taken continuous or intermittently, thereby allowing the employee to work on a less than full-time schedule.

FMLA can be used for the care of a child after birth, adoption, or foster care placement.

FMLA is available to care for an immediate family member (spouse, child, parent) who has a serious health condition.

FMLA can be used for your own serious health concerns. It does not cover for the common cold, flu, ear aches, upset stomach, common headache, or routine dental care.

In order to be covered by FMLA you must be considered an "eligible" employee. An eligible employee must have 12 months (1,250 hours) of employment, and your employer must employ 50 or more employees within 75 miles of the worksite. Employees must provide 30 days of advance notice for foreseeable events. There are different exemptions present for both school teachers and state/local government employees.

If you are an eligible employee, your employer must maintain your benefits, allow you to return to the same or equivalent position, and not decrease your pay or benefits at the conclusion of 12 weeks. If you believe you are eligible for FMLA, inform your supervisor or HR department that you are requesting FMLA coverage. Your employer is required to provide you with written notice, within two business days, informing you if you are eligible or not.

New Approaches to Cutting Staff Absence

Developing positive workplace practices and new ways of working:

- organizations with the worst records have twice the absence rates of the best ones—there may be factors relating to the work involved, but it indicates that many firms have scope for improvement;
- men under 40 have half the absence rate of women of the same age;
- public sector employees report sick more often than those in the private sector;
- trade unionists report sick more often than non-union employees.

There is scope to draw some contentious conclusions from these findings—for example, there is greater job security in the public sector, a reason for not being so motivated to struggle in to work? Whatever the reasons, these differences highlight areas where, at least to some extent, individual's criteria for considering themselves unfit for work vary.

The Industrial Society report *Maximising Attendance* also highlights a divergence of opinion between what managers think are the top five causes of absence and what employees say themselves:

How Employees Report Absence	In Manager's Own Opinion
1. Cold/Flue	1. Cold/Flue
2. Stomach Upset/Food Poisoning	2. Stress/Emotional Problems/ Personal Problems
3. Headaches/Migraines	3. Monday Morning Blues/ Extending The Weekend
4. Back Problems	4. Low Morale/Boring Job
5. Stress/Emotional Problems/ Personal Problems	5. Childcare Problems/Family Sickness

If managers are correct as seeing the reason in the left hand column as often being "code" for some of the reasons they list, it pinpoints areas where employers could take positive action to reduce absenteeism.

Leaving aside surveillance, interrogation and other more draconian approaches, which no doubt some employers might favor, there are preventative measures which employers could take. For example:

- Family friendly policies, from flexible hours to workplace crèches to help employees cope with childcare problems;
- Providing more varied/interesting/responsible work to combat "low morale/boring job" syndrome;
- Compressed working week options to cater positively for those who may need longer weekends;
- Mentoring, counseling, fitness programmes, on-site massage, etc. to help people through stress, emotional

problems or personal problems, plus careful monitoring of workloads.

The Industrial Society suggests other steps organizations could take:

- having a clear policy on absence monitoring;
- training managers to manage attendance;
- training employees to recognize and manage signs of stress;
- improving employee motivation through training and development opportunities;
- using return-to-work interviews after illness and informal procedures to keep individuals informed and to resolve problems by consensus.

These approaches tackle absenteeism by seeking to reduce the number of absences.

An alternative approach is to alter the nature of absences, so that absence from the workplace does not mean that no work is done at all.

When people are absent—unless for an agreed appointment with the doctor or dentist—it is usually for a whole day at a time. But people who may not feel up to the commute journey and eight hours of continuous work may nonetheless feel able and willing to put in a few hours of work. This is particularly the case where the reported illness really belongs to the employee's child, rather than the employee.

Looked at this way, it can be said that traditional and inflexible work practices require people to be absent from work for longer than they need to be planned.

All across the country parents (usually it is mothers) call in sick when they are not, so that they can look after a sick child. They then crawl into work when they really are sick by way of compensating, or if they feel they can't be sick "again" so soon after the last absence. Unhealthy patterns emerge amongst parents: they routinely work when they should be recuperating, and share their diseases in the workplace.

Much simpler, more honest and more productive are work environments where employees feel free to tell their line managers and colleagues that their child is ill, and then work from home. (And it helps to be properly set up for this, with remote access, etc.).

A similar process could apply to people who are well enough to work intermittently at home, but for whom a day in the office could be very debilitating. This is especially helpful for people with chronic or intermittent conditions. A work regime which requires nine-to-five seven days a week can be intrinsically disabling for some people with chronic conditions or long-term illnesses, or who are recuperating from serious illness or injury. Flexible hours and home based working can allow people in this position to maximize their contribution, and to increase their wage-earning potential.

In the end, the solutions should be about focusing on what people can do, rather than on their non-attendance on the workplace.

13

Management Development

It could be argued that competition itself might very well be the best form of talent identification, with competition seeing the best or most talented athletes in India rise to the top in their chosen sport and you know that Indian icon such as Sachin Tendulkar, M.S. Dhoni, Sania Mirza to name a few. However, many athletes that do not succeed in the particular sport because they might be better suited to a different sport but never realise that. With this in mind and considering that without talent identification, talent development would be a waste of time and resources.

Management development is very important initiative and the right investment that not only gives brand image and recognition but also equip employee to make confident decision in day to day working performance. Ultimately management development training improves efficiency level of employees and generates more profits for the organization. There are seven miracle words in management development that we need to know broadly such as Mentoring, Coaching, Professional development, Job rotation, Executive education and Upward feedback.

Mentoring

There are many perspectives on the definition of mentoring, especially since the relatively recent popularity of personal and professional coaching. Traditionally, mentoring might have been described as the activities conducted by a person (the mentor) for another person (the mentee) in order to help that other person to do a job more effectively and/or to progress in their career. The mentor was probably someone who had "been there, done that" before. A mentor might use a variety of approaches, e.g. coaching, training, discussion, counseling, etc. Today, there seems to be much ongoing discussion and debate about the definitions and differences regarding coaching and mentoring.

Tips for Mentors

In an effort to be helpful, some mentors go too far. They offer to do things we believe are unwise. Here are some examples along with what we believe are preferable steps to take:

- Investing financially in mentee's business or life pursuits.

Occasionally, you may be invited by your mentee to buy something, invest in his/her business, pay his/her bills, or otherwise bring money into the relationship. Doing so in a formal mentoring partnership changes the relationship and causes a conflict of interest. In counseling this is called a "dual relationship". No longer can you be neutral and objective about the mentee's performance. He/She won't be as open with you about problems, concerns, and mistakes for fear you'll withdraw (or regret) your support. The mentee could even become inappropriately dependent upon you, something to avoid in all mentoring relationships.

Preferred response: I'm honored that you asked, and I have to say no. I'd like to keep our relationship strictly a mentoring partnership at this time. Once our formal partnership has ended, I'd be glad to entertain a discussion about options like that. How about if we identify some other sources for you....

- "Working" for your mentee.

This is a cousin of Example 1. In this case, your mentee "hires" you (with or without pay) to do an actual work task. Examples: write his/her resume, complete a scholarship application, inventory Web-based degree programs, interview his/her fellow employees about how the mentee is performing on the job. In each of these situations, you're doing the work the mentee should be doing (or paying someone else to do).

Preferred response: I appreciate your faith in my ability to do that task. However, this is a step I'd rather not take. I prefer working behind the scenes with you and helping you do this important task yourself. I'll be very glad to give you feedback as you go along.

- Playing personal counselor.

This one can happen before you even realize it, so discuss some boundaries when you're setting up the partnership. Effective mentors don't limit their helping to work-related issues. In fact, the best mentors help mentees with their total life issues and challenges. Yet, they pay attention to "the line". They resist giving critical personal advice and counseling especially when the mentee is experiencing big psychological challenges. These can include major marital or family difficulties, drug or alcohol misuse, depression, and other potentially complex and even life-threatening situations.

Preferred response: I'm glad you mentioned ____. I care very much about you and want to support you as you deal with this. As we discussed when we set up our relationship, we may run into something I'm not an expert on. I believe this is one of those situations. How about if we talk with _____ on this and come up with a way you can get the assistance you need?

If you're in a work setting, by all means get advice from your human resources or personnel experts anytime you believe your mentee is heading into difficult areas. If you're on your own, make an anonymous call to a local or national mental health hotline or consult another expert for some guidance.

When you're starting out as a mentor, you won't always be clear about where to set your boundaries. Whenever possible, check with your program coordinator or someone else you trust to develop limits that are right for you.

A sense of purpose and the ability to be purposeful are key to personal and organizational success. Mentoring can be a highly effective means of evoking purposefulness, and so generate high levels of motivation and corporate intent. Now it explores how mentoring can be used to uncover purpose, what the impact on the individual of increased purposefulness can be, and how individual and organizational purpose can be aligned to the benefit of both.

Increasingly, organizations need to be able to continuously reinvent themselves so as to stay aligned with and responsive to their customers and other stakeholders. Creating the necessary changes can involve a wide range of programs and initiatives such as culture change, process re-engineering, benchmarking, total quality management, values alignment, and so forth. What all these have in common is that, to be successful, they have to be accompanied by behavioral change by the organization's stakeholders and, in particular, by the organization's senior executives. Executive mentoring is an intervention designed to support such senior executives and other key staff in making the necessary behavior changes.

Executive Mentoring

Executive Mentoring is a specialist form of management development and education. It is particularly suited to senior executives who have risen above the scope of formal management development programs and require highly focused development and support tailored to the particular challenges facing them in their business.

Executive Mentoring stimulates and manages the individual growth necessary to deliver business performance beyond present levels and beliefs of what is possible. It does this by helping executives:

- build a solid personal foundation and demonstrate strong confidence in self and others;
- develop their personal vision and uncover their value priorities;
- think strategically and inspire shared vision, mission and values;
- determine appropriate goals, strategies, tactics and action plans;

- enhance their management and leadership skills;
- identify their personal winning strategies;
- uncover self sabotage, recognise repeating patterns and introduce change to interrupt habitual responses;
- elicit high commitment to personal change and development.

Purpose of Mentoring

Being mentored can, therefore, be a challenging and stretching experience, inviting executives to draw on and develop hidden personal resources and qualities. And it can be an exciting, stimulating journey of self-discovery and development which opens up new opportunities for personal fulfilment and achievement. In either case it involves a journey into the unknown and unfamiliar ways of being and doing; we may have to confront our fear of failure and, paradoxically, our fear of success; we may have to cast aside long held beliefs about who we are and what we are capable of; and we may have to resist strong pressure from family and colleagues to lapse back to our habitual ways. Thus, to create and then sustain change in the face of the many forces which may pull us back, a powerfully motivating context is necessary. That context is Purpose.

Purpose

Your purpose expresses who you are, who you are becoming, and what contribution you can make. You have a sense of purpose when your life has a direction and meaning which you have chosen. (Purpose differs from Vision which is about what you want to create and achieve. You choose a Vision but discover your Purpose.)

When our lives, at home and at work, are aligned with our purpose, then our lives are meaningful and we connect to deep wells of energy within ourselves.

A prime reason why a sense of purpose is important is that it provides the strong container or context through which we can manage our inner experience of change. But to create that change we must be able to express that purpose in the world, that is, to be purposeful.

Being Purposeful

You are being purposeful when you are fully living your purpose, that is when you are expressing your purpose in the moment rather than working towards achieving it in the future. Purposefulness can also be described as wilfulness (in its sense of 'full of Will') and has the following qualities:

- energy, dynamic power, intensity
- mastery, control, discipline
- concentration, attention, focus
- determination, decisiveness, resoluteness, promptness
- persistence, endurance, patience
- initiative, courage, daring
- organization, integration, synthesis (Assagioli, 1973).

Bringing Purpose into the present requires the ability to be present—or to have Presence. Put simply:

Purpose + Presence = Purposefulness

Presence is the ability to be with another person with such inner self-knowledge that the other person is able to ponder the depths of who he or she is with awareness and clarity. It is the single most important skill the mentor requires. Marianne Williamson describes presence rather more poetically: "We are all born to shine, as children do. We were born to make manifest the glory of god that is within us. It's not just in some of us; it's in everyone. And as we let our own light shine, we unconsciously give other people permission to do the same. As we are liberated from our own fear, our presence automatically liberates others" (Williamson, 1992). This is also an excellent description of the essence of mentoring.

Developing Purpose

The Mentoring for Change model provides a framework and methodology for mentoring. This model has four elements of the mentoring process—Freeing Up, Envisioning, Implementing, and Sustaining. Figure 1 shows the corresponding elements of mentoring on purpose—Satisfying Needs, Uncovering Purpose, Being Purposeful, and Realising Purpose.

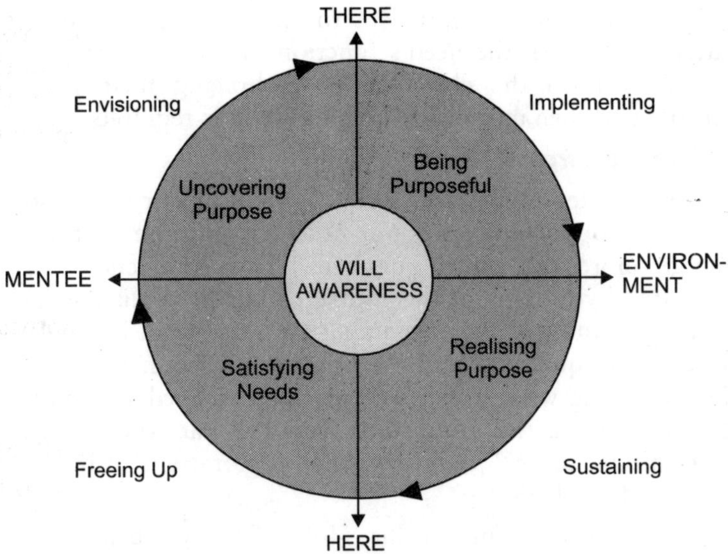

Fig. 1: Mentoring on Purpose

Satisfying Needs

Needs are those things which must be satisfied for us to have a solid foundation to our lives. For this reason, mentoring on purpose will often start in this quadrant of the model.

When we are driven by our needs (e.g. for appreciation, self-worth, security, love, success) it is difficult to express and live by our purpose because our energy and attention are devoted to getting our needs met. In developing a sense of our purpose, it is therefore important to determine whether our behavior is being driven by our needs. If it is, then we must find ways to get those needs satisfied once and for all so that their fulfilment no longer gets in the way of our purpose. So, for example, we may be a team-leader and have a strong need to belong. If we try to get our belonging needs met from the team when we are supposed to be challenging its members to new levels of performance, we are likely to fail both to provide the leadership the team requires and to get our own needs met. More appropriate ways of getting this need met must be found.

Sometimes, mere awareness that a need is being met in inappropriate ways is sufficient to enable people to drop the pattern. But often the need's function has been to protect the individual from the challenge of embracing their sense of purpose and then more wide ranging work is required.

Uncovering Purpose

As we release ourselves from the hold of our needs, so we create the opportunity for our sense of purpose to begin to emerge more fully into our lives. This emergence can be facilitated by looking at the course of our lives, distinguishing the themes and patterns, becoming aware of what is unfolding, noticing the qualities of those times when we have felt most alive, recalling what it was we especially enjoyed as a six year-old, considering the Tombstone Test ("What would you like your epitaph to be?"), and by other explorations of the wider context of our lives.

Steve Jobs, trying to lure John Sculley, then CEO of PepsiCo, to Apple famously and ultimately successfully evoked Sculley's sense of purpose by asking "Do you want to spend the rest of your life selling sugared water or do you want a chance to change the world?" (Sculley, 1988)

A more analytical approach to working with both Purpose and Needs is to work with value priorities. Values sit at the gateway between our inner and outer worlds. They describe what is fundamentally important, and hence meaningful to us and so are directly related to our sense of purpose and to our needs. Instrumentation, such as the VMI from Values Technology Inc. which can be used to uncover individual and organizational values and place them in a developmental framework of 125 global values (Figure 2), can be used to measure value priorities. This can be a particularly effective way to identify those values which are just emerging into our lives and which point us towards our unfolding purpose.

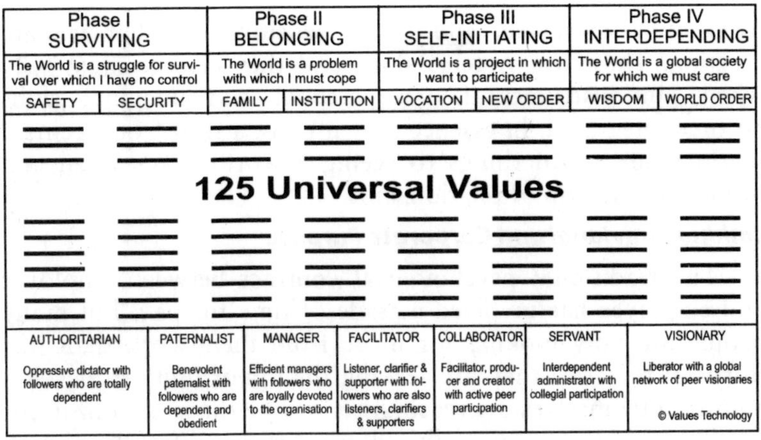

Fig. 2: VMI Values Measurement Framework

Being Purposeful

A sense of purpose does not necessarily lead to purposeful behaviour. Purpose is passive; purposefulness is active and emerges out of a process in which we express ourselves through what we do. Connecting our sense of purpose to the actions we take involves clarifying our values, developing our intention, deliberating on the possible ways of realising our purpose, choosing one or more, affirming the choice, formulating plans, and finally acting.

In being purposeful, we must mobilise our mind and our feelings. At the intellectual level our sense of purpose provides a powerful reason for making the changes; and at the emotional level our purposefulness provides the motive force to bring our purpose into existence.

Realising Purpose

Once we are taking purposeful action we must ensure that this is creating the outcomes we seek to achieve. To do this we have to learn to perceive clearly our impact on our environment (e.g. organization, family, team) and be able to sense the intricate web of connections in which we exist, and to see the whole as well as the parts.

We have to develop the ability to sustain our new behaviours and ways of being, to develop new habits, to learn from our experience, and to be sensitive to what we are creating. These are systems skills and they emerge most fully when our instrumental, interpersonal and imaginal skills become integrated. In essence they involve a shift from seeing a world made up of things to seeing a world that's open and primarily made up of relationships.

Linking Individual and Corporate Purpose

The traditional psychological contract between employer and employee has involved a trade of time for pay. But many people are now looking for more from their work than just financial rewards; they are seeking the opportunity to develop and fulfil themselves. Increasingly it will be those organizations which are able to satisfy this desire for more fulfilling work which will be able to attract and retain the best staff. Thus, the challenge that organizations face is how to provide their staff with the opportunity for more personally meaningful work whilst simultaneously enabling the organization to meet its goals.

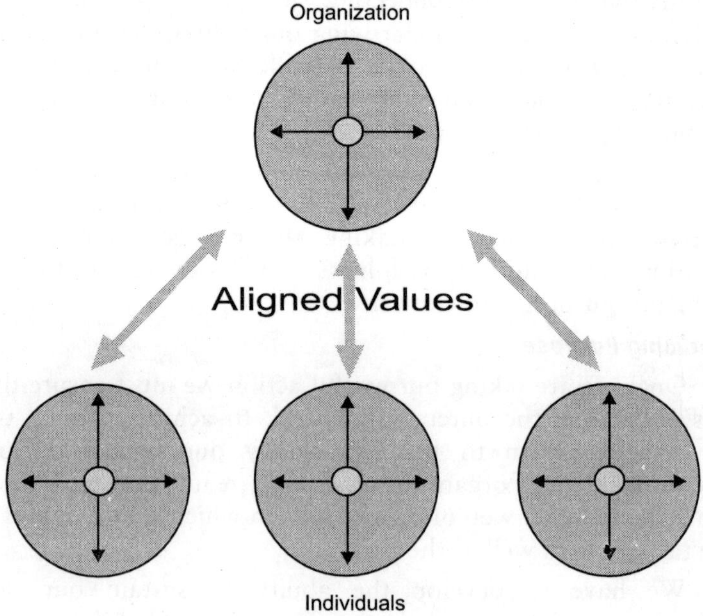

Fig. 3: Aligning Individual and Organization

In fact, organizations too can be described as having purpose, although it is more usually referred to as the organizational mission. An organization's mission expresses itself in a variety of ways—through the structures, polices processes, etc. of the organization—but predominantly it comes from the sense of purpose of the people who make up the organization. And just as individual purpose can be accessed through personal values, so organizational mission can be accessed through corporate values. It is values that provide the link between the individual's purpose and the organization's mission. This is not to say that the individual should have the same value priorities as the organization—though there does need to be a core of shared values—but that the stage of development of the individual's value system should match that of the organization.

Conclusion

Living our purpose consistently is a profound challenge. It requires high levels of self-awareness, a firm commitment, a strong sense of our own self-worth, a willingness to take risks, and the emotional discipline to travel outside our comfort zone. In essence it requires that we develop the skills of self-leadership. The role of the mentor in this is to help the mentee continually deepen their understanding of reality, develop their sense of self, learn to listen for what is emerging, and to encourage them to live their purpose.

Coaching

The field of personal and professional coaching has grown substantially over the past 10 years or so. This type of coaching usually involves working in a partnership between coach and clients to provide structure, guidance and support for clients to:

1. Take a complete look at their current state, including their assumptions and perceptions about their work, themselves and others;
2. Set relevant and realistic goals for themselves, based on their own nature and needs;

3. Take relevant and realistic actions toward reaching their goals; and
4. Learn by continuing to reflect on their actions and sharing feedback with others along the way.

Coaching can be especially useful to help individuals address complex problems and/or attain significant goals and do so in a highly individualized fashion. Today, there seems to be much ongoing discussion and debate about the definitions and differences regarding coaching and mentoring.

Coaching, implemented at an organizational level, can deliver dramatic results and drive significant financial impact to the bottom line. Today's values-based organizations employ coaching to build alignment, to develop their current and future leaders, and to ensure the success of corporate training programs. Coaching is about action and results! Coaching for Individuals gives people the boost they need to get from where they are to where they want to be. Thousands of people have hired a coach to: Kick a stalled career into high gear, Stay on top of mounting responsibilities, Take the next big step on the leadership path & Handle difficult and important relationships.

Seasoned business coaches provide personalized, consistently-focused coaching to help individuals reach their professional goals. They help individuals discover and leverage their strengths, recognize obstacles to success, and identify a course of action to help them maximize performance.

Coaching is a deliberate process utilizing focused conversations to create an environment for individual growth, purposeful action, and sustained improvement. Our 1 to 1 coaching services are customized for the each individual. Samples of the different types coaching follow; however, coaching is not limited to these categories.

Types of Coaching

Executive Coaching—Develops fast-trackers and high performing leaders. Often executives need an objective, neutral sounding board to discuss challenges, opportunities and their perspective. Our coaches allow executives and managers to step away from their day-to-day routine and effectively strategize on how they can reach beyond where they are currently.

Professional Development Coaching—It is similar to executive coaching and is offered at all levels within the organization.

Career Development/Transition Coaching—It is for individuals needing and/or wanting movement from their current position. Career coaching helps individuals to utilize their strengths, to see where they may have blind spots and to identify a course of action.

Organizational Coaching—From start to finish, our organizational coaching initiatives are designed for impact. The benefits extend from the individual to the entire organization, providing both with improved productivity and performance.

Organizational Coaching benefits include:

- Aligning individual performance with team and organizational objectives;
- Maximizing and leveraging strengths;
- Increasing and enhancing communication between managers, direct reports and teams;
- Helping individuals take ownership and responsibility for their behaviors and actions;
- Encouraging individuals to stretch beyond their assumed constraints.

Organizational Change—What is supporting your organizational change initiative? How do your leaders get help in addressing their challenges with the new direction of the organization? What is the cost to the organization of not moving effectively and efficiently through the change initiative?

Organizational Coaching provides a platform where individuals can discuss challenges, concerns and appropriate actions they need to take in a safe and objective environment. Coaches working in this arena help individuals achieve balance between their own needs and those of the overall organizational change objectives.

Example—One organization needed to retain key employees during the process of transforming its structure from a traditional hierarchical pyramid to a flat structure. With support from their coaches, the leaders found an environment for problem solving and venting without doing damage to key organizational relationships. Through the coaching, relationships between managers and their direct reports improved. Of the several key people who stayed with the company, one said "coaching was the glue that kept me in the organization".

Strategic Alignment—What keeps your senior leaders up at night? Who can they talk to about these things? Strategic Alignment coaching initiatives help leaders meet their strategic goals and expand those goals throughout the organization. The use of Impact Maps supports strategic objectives at all levels in the organization, and leaders are coached to understand how their individual contributions have a significant impact on the greater team.

Development of Leadership "Bench Strength"

This coaching is for high potential, fast-trackers who are vital to the organization. It provides the support they need to reach maximum effectiveness as quickly as possible.

Sales Leader Development—Our sales coaching offering is customized to support the efforts of sales leaders and sales teams. With its emphasis on sales productivity and highly leveraged activities, the laser focus of this coaching solution has a direct impact on helping individuals and organizations achieve revenue goals and other key sales performance objectives.

Leaders who utilize coaching skills have more effective teams, higher morale, and better bottom-line results than those who don't. These leaders have high levels of retention of key people, better customer service in their organizations, and higher productivity. And let's face it—people remember them and their impact.

How can leaders become more coach-like in their behaviors and actions? Coaching Essentials for Leaders focus on the development and practical application of core coaching skills and a coaching conversation model, enabling leaders to become more 'coach-like' with their colleagues and teams. Through personalized, one-on-one follow-up coaching sessions, leaders are encouraged to apply, evaluate and discuss the effectiveness of their new behaviors.

Conclusion

It is clear that talent identification is a diverse subject that is not easily summed up. There are many different views on what talent identification accomplishes and how it should be structured. While the resources needed to implement programs are similar to many countries in the 90's this does not mean that talent identification would not be worthwhile. By linking talent identification to the already existing school system, results can still be achieved in talent identification.

At the same time talent identification programs need to be scientifically based and assessment should be continuous rather than being done once only in order to maximise a country's or individual sport's return from its sporting resources.

Professional Development

The recommendations are as follows:

1. Let trainer lead—empower trainers to accomplish their jobs more effectively and to grow as professionals, put teachers in charge of training functions and/or planning. The moment you will provide more autonomy and authority to the company people, they will feel more responsible and accountable for that particular job. They will then put their best effort to get organizational desired result.
2. Make staff development serve wider goals—Part of more general vision of technology used in department which is part of larger vision of the company's overall mission. Managers from all departments must be computer savvy because they should be autonomous and independent in case of situational urgency.

3. Department's statements of vision and planning regarding technology need to be reviewed—and possibly revised—annually to account for technology development and change in direction and condition.
4. Presentation skills—Everyone should be active and participative in interactive training session so that they can communicate their views and innovative ideas to the organization before team members in crisp and communicative sentence confidently.
5. Must evaluate—Professional acumen and professional development should be evaluated time to time to assess success rate of professional development and this also helps in planning training module for future training. Beliefs and behaviors are part of a reciprocal process. There is need to examine and change both.
6. Fix particular date for training in a month so that you can work upon effectively. This will also help you to get training need analysis for those particular executives. Through this you can organize an effective training session.

Job Rotation

Job rotation is an approach to management development where an individual is moved through a schedule of assignments designed to give him or her a breadth of exposure to the entire operation. Job rotation moves employees from one task to another. It distributes the group tasks among a number of employees.

Job rotation is also practiced to allow qualified employees to gain more insights into the processes of a company, and to reduce boredom and increase job satisfaction through job variation. The term job rotation can also mean the scheduled exchange of persons in offices, especially in public offices, prior to the end of incumbency or the legislative period. This has been practiced by the German green party for some time but has been discontinued.

At the senior management levels, job rotation—frequently referred to as management rotation, is tightly linked with succession planning—developing a pool of people capable of stepping into an existing job. Here, the goal is to provide learning experiences which facilitate changes in thinking and perspective equivalent to the "horizon" of the level of the succession planning.

For lower management levels, job rotation has normally one of two purposes: promotability or skill enhancement. In many cases senior managers seem unwilling to risk instability in their units by moving qualified people from jobs where the lower level manager is being successful and reflecting positively on the actions of the senior manager. Many military forces use the job rotation strategy to allow the soldiers to develop a wider range of experiences, and an exposure to the different jobs of an occupation.

For the executive, job rotation takes on different perspectives. The executive is usually not simply going to another department. In some vertically integrated organizations, for example, where the supplier is actually part of same organization or subsidiary, job rotation might be to the supplier to see how the business operates from the supplier point of view. Learning how the organization is perceived from the outside broadens the executive's outlook on the process of the organization. Or the rotation might be to a foreign office to provide a global perspective.

For managers being developed for executive roles, rotation to different functions in the company is regularly carried out. This approach allows the manager to operate in diverse roles and understand the different issues that crop up. If someone is to be a corporate leader, they must have this type of training. A recent study indicated that the single most significant factor that leads to leader's achievement was the variety of experiences in different departments, business units, cities, and countries. An organized and helpful way to develop talent for the management or executive level of the organization is job rotation. It is the process of preparing employees at a lower level to replace someone at the next higher level. It is generally done for the designations that are crucial for the effective and efficient functioning of the organization.

Benefits of Job Rotation

Some of the major benefits of job rotation are:

- It provides the employees with opportunities to broaden the horizon of knowledge, skills, and abilities by working in different departments, business units, functions, and countries.
- Identification of Knowledge, skills, and attitudes (KSAs) required.
- It determines the areas where improvement is required.
- Assessment of the employees who have the potential and caliber for filling the position.

Job Rotation is a Big Motivator

The challenges of keeping a 21st century employee motivated at work are vast. Today, an organization has very few options at hand, thanks to the ever increasing competition.

Keeping an employee interested is not an easy job which is why employee retention is a major challenge that most HR teams face. This is where 'Job Rotation' helps. Job rotation has many advantages. One of them is that it keeps the employee interested in his work as he gets different job profiles and his work does not become monotonous.

One of the other major advantage of job rotation is that it gives an employee a chance to learn a lot more than he normally would. He becomes multi-skilled and this is an asset that is always helpful.

For example, if an employee falls sick or is on leave and can't report to work and if there is a shortage of staff on a particular day, then thanks to the practice of job rotation, an organization has enough skilled manpower to replace the employee temporarily and take up his job. Many organizations use job rotation as a tool to curb absenteeism. The reason being, if an employee gets something new to learn, he would be more willing to report to work.

Clearly, job rotation has a lot of advantages and one feels that every organization must have it. However, every silver cloud has a dark lining. In order to ensure that job rotation is done properly and efficiently, a proper policy must be in place.

This is because a lot of employees may initially resist for job rotation as they may be skeptical about it. This is why goal setting is very necessary in job rotation. This would help in convincing an employee that this policy would be for his own benefit and they would stand to gain a lot from it.

Job rotation ensures that an employee does not feel 'stressed' out from the job, as this is a major issue that HR teams face today. To develop a good job rotation program the organization must assess its needs and requirements. This kind of a program can be used either for promotion, sideward movements or succession planning. Whatever the need be, it should be clearly identified before making such a program so as to help the organization know in which direction it is moving.

Job rotation programs are known to help an organization develop management talent as well as it helps in improving its competitive advantage over its rivals. It is a known fact that for an organization to succeed it is of paramount importance to ensure that the top management is very skillful and is aware of the happenings in the industry.

With so much competition today, decisions made by the top management can change the fortunes of an organization drastically. Thus, whatever training and advantage that can be given to them is an added bonus.

One of the most difficult issues that an HR team faces would be the criteria on which job rotation should be done. The amount of experience, education, leadership assessment as well as management preference has to be kept in mind. This makes it very complex as a lot of details need to be looked into before selecting the right employee.

Employees with a good amount of experience generally are preferred as their experience would help them adapt to different situations in a better manner compared to a fresher who's just joined the organization. What further works in the favour of an old employee is the fact that he has been around for a longer time and thus is likely to feel cheated if a fresher was given a chance to learn something new before him?

Clearly, job rotation has its advantages but making a fair policy for the same is not easy. However, if the organization succeeds in doing this then it surely will have long-term benefits in the end, a fact that every organization needs to looks into.

Use Job Rotation to Reduce Training Costs

Sustaining employee interest in a single job is not easy, which is perhaps why retention poses such a big challenge for businesses today. People outgrow their jobs quickly and it may not be possible for employers to provide enough diversity within a vertical career framework to maintain employee interest in the job. This is where job rotation steps in to provide much needed variety and job enrichment from an employee's perspective. Job rotation programs serve a variety of purposes from simply staffing jobs, to providing orientation to new employees, preventing stagnation and job boredom, and giving employees the opportunity to explore alternative career paths.

Employees who participate in job rotation programs develop a wide range of skills, are more adaptable to changes in jobs and career, and in general are far more satisfied with their jobs when compared to workers who specialise in a single skill set or domain. Here are a few tips for you to make the most of a job rotation program in your organization.

To be effective, job rotation programs need to be carefully planned and organized. Most job rotation programs fail simply because not enough thought goes into implementing them, or because they are merely viewed as stop gap arrangements with no recognition of the added value it brings to employees.

Preparation is key to the success of any job rotation program. Carefully analyse the feasibility of setting up a program, work out the implementation issues, and set up realistic schedules for each position. Formulate clear policies regarding who will be eligible, whether it will be mandatory or voluntary, whether employees will be restricted to certain jobs or will be open to all job classifications.

Consider making job rotation a part and parcel of your training and career development initiatives. Not all jobs may be suitable for job rotation, but the large majority of jobs including technical, clerical, HR, administrative and managerial tasks can be handled by comparative non-experts with a little training. Alternatively, you can also link rotation with the individual career goals of employees and make it a part of a planned career development initiative. Involve the employee in planning job rotations so that there is a clear understanding of mutual expectations, and the road ahead.

Understand that job rotation is not a substitute for training. It must be supported by parallel developmental goals and initiatives, and skills that are not enhanced by job rotation need to be dealt with through separate training programs and management coaching. Decide who will benefit the most from participating in job rotation programs.

Some organizations tend to rotate employees faster in early-career stages and slow down in later-career stages. This practice is based on the assumption that employees who are at an early stage of their career are more open to job rotation than senior level executives.

People who are starting out in their careers typically are more eager to demonstrate their willingness to learn, to advance and to take on increasing responsibilities to enhance their skill development. They also have more to learn and benefit from rotation experiences, adding higher value to their career prospects. But job rotation can also be used to assist later career and plateaued employees, to mitigate the mind-numbing monotony of the plateauing process, and make the employees' work more interesting and stimulating.

Job rotations can be used as a developmental alternative to promotions. In times of economic recession or downsizing, it may not be always possible to reward employees with promotions and big hikes. In such a scenario, job rotations are a way of demonstrating that the company has faith in employees' abilities and wants to provide them with opportunities for career growth.

Adopt best practices to get the most out of your rotation programs. Pay utmost attention to the selection of jobs, partnering with employee goals and increasing awareness among staff about the value of job rotations as a developmental tool.

Job rotation offers a number of benefits for organizations. It is especially useful in helping employees cultivate valuable, organization specific skills, and prepares the ground for lateral transfers and promotions. A systematic, well-designed job rotation program can help reduce training costs, reduce turnover, and improve employee morale and productivity. It can also endow a company with greater flexibility, and help take the edge out of contingency staffing. But perhaps the greatest benefit that accrues to organizations through job rotation programs is its capacity to contribute to employee self-worth, motivation and job satisfaction.

How does Job Rotation Work?

A closer look at some Indian companies shows that job rotation is becoming an increasingly accepted practice. Consider LG Electronics India. In the past five years, close to half the Korean electronics major's 2,800 employees have switched functions within the organization at least twice. And what is an India-specific HR policy for LG is the norm worldwide for IBM. In fact, the IT giant has some high-profile job swaps to its credit.

Just last year (2007), then chief financial officer John Joyce switched functions and designation with Mark Loughridge, the senior vice-president, global services. And last year, two senior professionals, Somnath Sinha, the erstwhile head of global operations, and Ashish Kumar, erstwhile head, sales, moved to India.

At McDonald's too, cross-functional job rotations are encouraged, globally and in India. "It is a win-win situation—win for the organization, the team and the employee," says

Amit Jatia, joint venture partner and managing director, McDonald's, western India.

Job rotation is not an instinctive process. "There has to be a clear justification why you're hand picking certain employees to be transferred," states Yasho Vardhan Verma, director, human resources, LG Electronics India. "It works, provided it's done objectively." Companies should base all inter-functional transfers on a structured performance assessment, and pick the best performers to change jobs. The parameters of judging performance need to include not only functional skills but also core and leadership competencies. LG's appraisal forms, for instance, sport eight performance parameters, each of which is quantified. The higher the percentage scored in core skills and leadership parameters, the more likely the candidate is to be considered for rotation.

"People move—but only for the right reasons," points out Martin Appel, vice president, human resources IBM India. "The company needs to show them a proper and realistic career map." IBM, for instance, conducts annual interviews where it examines a potential next role for each employee after mapping his preferences.

Most companies agree that employees are more willing to accept job switches if there's a safety net below them—training programs, for instance, that help bridge the gap between unrelated functions such as HR and marketing. If the rotation is not planned well and not linked to career and succession plans, the company may end up losing a good employee.

Have Heirs Handy

Picking the best performer from a team means that team is less one asset. So a succession plan that identifies and develops worthy substitutes, from within the same team, is critical. In 2003, when LG carried out a large-scale job rotation exercise in its manufacturing and research and development division, the planning began a year earlier. The trigger was LG's need to decentralise the R&D and manufacturing function to the five business units.

"We didn't want to hire from outside," says Verma. Instead, LG shortlisted the best performers among product heads and trained in aspects such as costing and finance for over a year. "Simultaneously, we also identified the No. 2 performers to replace the product manufacturing heads," says Verma.

Prepare for Opposition

Not all employees are eager for change. That's especially true of younger, less experienced officers. "Job rotation did not work well when we tried moving newer employees," shares Jatia of McDonald's. LG officials, too, admit that job rotation didn't work with fresh management recruits, who were uncomfortable with the idea of being planted in various functions.

Also, unlike globally, Indians value vertical growth (moving designations in the same function) more than lateral growth. Timing is critical in such cases. Companies need to identify potential job swaps at the right time—when the employee has matured in a particular function and is mentally ready for a move.

Going by the experiences of Indian companies that means giving employees three years in a job before suggesting a switch. Handled well, job rotation brings several benefits. At LG, it has worked as an effective retention tool for top talent. "It's a great way to meet the aspirations of employees," points out Verma. While attrition level at LG is around 8 per cent, Verma claims there have been negligible drop-outs among the 1,200 employees who've switched functions. McDonald's, too, claims longer tenures (five to six years) among employees who rotate jobs. Job rotation can be a boost for good performers. "Work portfolios get re-organized, jobs get enriched and some fresh blood comes in.

Executive Education

The interest in executive education continues to grow across the globe. Employees and employers are recognizing the need to reinforce and reinvigorate their own leadership capacities and those of others within their organizations.

Companies and individuals are looking at the opportunities and making choices that will affect their growth potential throughout their life span. "Today, particularly, new entrants in the workforce are becoming portfolio workers. They are interested in building their own resume or portfolio. At the same time, companies are recognizing the need for more knowledgeable leaders. These intersecting interests are driving the creation of more opportunities and the need to carefully consider the options."

Smart Business talked with Mescon for more information on executive education and some of the things that employees and employers should consider.

What is driving the interest in executive education?

The world of business is moving at an incredibly fast pace. Companies are looking for better leaders who are equipped with the most up-to-date information and skills. Employees are looking at adding skill sets to be better able to compete in the changing marketplace. Education becomes a team retention tool that is very important to the employee and a plus for the organization. We like to say, 'learn today, lead tomorrow'.

What are some of the things that companies need to consider?

There are three main areas of education available. They are specific skill development, leadership development, and special tracks for high potential (HiPot) candidates. The special tracks for the HiPot managers are accelerated programs.

Companies need to determine what skills and qualities will best serve them and seek out the programs that will meet those needs. The key is the applicability of the knowledge.

How are these programs being delivered?

What we see evolving is a mix of the traditionally delivered onsite and the emerging online programs. There is still a place for, and many benefits of, an interactive person-to-person education.

Twenty-four hour access is an expectation of the younger generation. They are looking for programs that are convenient to them and not necessarily the organization. Location and variety of programs are also factors. Both forms of delivery have their benefits, and we are seeing them used effectively in tandem.

Who is paying the costs of these programs?

It is a combination of both the company and the employee. Pro-active companies are providing many opportunities. Smart employees will augment whatever is available from their company with things that complement and help build their own portfolio.

Employees need to control their own destiny. Most of the costs of many of the captive in-house MBA programs are paid for by the companies. Some companies pay only for credit courses and others pay for credit or noncredit. It may depend on their goals.

How important is credit over noncredit?

The individual needs to decide for themselves and in conversation with their employer the importance of degrees. Credit may be very important in some cases and in others not so important. It is up to the individuals to give the proper assessment and due diligence in determining what is best for them. Some programs have the option of credit or not. There is usually no difference in cost or content. A person may not be eligible for credit because he or she already has an MBA or may not have the prerequisite courses to obtain credit. Thus, more choice is available.

What do you see in the future for executive education?

There are unique alliances developing that reflect the changing expectations of corporate America. We are starting to see 'pay-for-performance' models. If XYZ Corporation doesn't receive what it expects from a contracted program, it doesn't pay for it. This puts the onus on the university to provide the program the company wants in a way that the participants fully grasp.

There is a profound amount of research that supports the fact that corporate entities that provide more education do better.

Upward Feedback

Upward feedback helps managers walk the talk and it is the management assessment tool.

By creating a customized management assessment tool, organizations can help managers replace outdated attitudes and behaviors with ones that foster empowerment.

Before an organization can create a higher level of employee commitment, managers need to understand how their behavior and attitudes affect workplace productivity. Upward feedback systems—in which managers are reviewed by subordinates, direct reports, peers, internal customers and their manager—can help clarify the changes that must be made in organizational culture and determine what additional training is needed.

Periodic assessments every six to twelve months give managers a way to measure their behavior, and as soon as something is measured, it generally begins to improve. This consistent feedback also helps to reduce anxiety about changing, while at the same time, it provides a systematic way to focus attention on the need to exert consistent pressure to continuously improve.

"When you introduce an employee involvement or empowerment program, you're building new expectations that employees will have about managers. These expectations that managers will change foster employee dissatisfaction over time if managers don't start to behave differently," said Sharon Scharringhausen, assistant vice president, human resources, of Heller Financial.

The discouragement employees will show as they come to believe that their company's empowerment program is just talk, will decrease morale and possibly even performance. On the other hand, well-implemented empowerment programs build the employee confidence necessary for employees to step out of their old order-taking roles and become creative problem solvers.

When Heller Financial in Chicago decided in the late 1980s to build a more empowering culture, it was facing an industry downturn in the competitive leveraged-funding market and was afraid of losing its strong results orientation. Heller needed to maintain its speedy response to its customers while encouraging its managers to become empowering and more participative.

The executive team, lead by human resources, developed a customized, management skills-assessment survey focusing on two aspects—building empowerment and maintaining a strong results orientation. The survey was launched at the general-manager level and was later expanded to include middle managers.

According to Jack Hart, vice president of human resources, when the program began in 1989, "The survey gave managers a tool to deal with the uncertainty that accompanies such a profound change by helping them figure out how to retain their results orientation and still be empowering."

In a similar fashion, Ball-InCon, a glass manufacturer in Muncie, Ind., is using a customized "walk your talk" executive assessment in an all-out effort to drive quality and empowerment deep into the corporate culture.

David Westerlund, vice president of human resources, said, "We are using the survey because we feel each executive must model the quality message by completely behaving in alignment with our new focus on quality and employee involvement. We give our executives feedback from their direct reports, other members of their staff, peers and their manager to allow us to measure their personal progress with our major culture shift to total quality."

Motorola, which won the Baldrige Award in 1988, recently introduced a customized Leadership Role Model Survey to determine if executive behavior aligns with the company's values and culture. Nancy Rus, vice president of organizational development at Motorola, interviewed the three people who make up the "Office of the President," as the first step in developing a 360° assessment that reflects Motorola's commitment to empowerment. The assessment was introduced in June 1992 at a Vice President's Institute managed by Debby King, vice president of Motorola University.

"Our plan is to reassess this group in nine to twelve months and to continue, every few months, to assess other executives and give them their data in small groups as a part of our effort to stimulate open communication, teamwork and networking among executives," said King.

Benchmark Results

In the past, the biggest obstacle to customized surveys was the amount of time required to develop the questions, create the survey forms, process the data, and print reports. Today, companies can purchase or lease software that allows them to automate the process and create useful graphic reports.

Trish Baker, manager of organizational consulting services at Acuson Corp., a medical instrumentation maker in Mountain View, Calif., started with a survey that gathered feedback from human resources' internal customers, then expanded the assessment to measure the effectiveness of quality programs and management training.

"A sophisticated computer software program made it easy for us to develop customized assessments that are directly related to our management training and quality programs," Baker said. "It has also made it possible for us to provide a speedy response to various work teams with specialized needs. Today, behavioral and skills assessments are part of our company's lifestyle."

Create the Right Questions

Developing the right questions for the assessment is fundamental to the long-term success of empowerment programs, because the questions behaviorally define your new employee-involvement culture.

One of the best ways to design the questionnaire is to pull together a series of cross-functional teams representing the different levels and different departments that will be included in the assessment process. Prior to the meeting, create the key values or skill dimensions around which the teams will develop and group questions. Work with a consultant or an internal committee to develop preliminary questions. Print the questions in large letters, each on a different brightly colored card, using a different color for each dimension. Also, prepare a typed copy of the questions that are on the posted cards as a handout for each participant. Arrange to meet in a room with a big blank wall on which the cards can be posted with "sticky take", so they can be easily moved around as the meeting progresses.

When the meeting begins, ask the group to come up with additional categories—these should be written on new colored cards and posted. Next, in small groups, brainstorm new questions for the additional dimensions and post these.

Finally, give each person a set of colored dots. The number of dots will match the number of questions or items desired for the survey. Ask each person to read all the colored cards and post dots on questions he or she thinks should be included in the survey.

This method will result in some clear visual messages—some cards will have few or no dots and other cards will have many. The group will be able to immediately drop some questions and identify overlapping dimensions (such as vision and strategy or empowerment and delegation). Through further discussion, the group can tighten up the questions. Later, the internal or external consultant can meticulously edit each question so it focuses on only one specific issue.

Each question, in its final form, must be so clear and easy to understand that all the people reading it will interpret it the same way. Above all else, each question must focus on only one behavior or skill.

When you print your assessment, organize by dimension. Some instruments switch back and forth between areas, and this design leaves many respondents confused. It is far better to group your questions by the particular value or dimension you want to measure.

At Amdahl, a mainframe computer company in Santa Clara, Calif., Patrick Wilson, director of development processes and systems, brought together a group of vice-presidents and middle managers from different departments, along with key human resources generalists and OD consultants, to develop a customized assessment. They used the color-card process, described above, to develop the core of Amdahl's management profile for first-level and middle managers.

Wilson is now preparing to take this process to manufacturing to develop additional items that are pertinent to that group, and then Linda Thompson, director of organization and employee development, will take the process to the field.

"By the end of 1993, we'll have customized surveys for each different business area that we plan to repeat annually," said Thompson.

Assess Regularly to Ensure Change

Following the initial survey and assessment process, managers can be referred to training programs to help them learn the skills and attitude changes required to create an empowered workforce. Knowing that they will be reassessed increases managers' motivation to practice and implement their new skills. Regular re-assessments will also help human resources to evaluate the effectiveness of various training programs in stimulating managers to change.

Over time, customized assessments prove whether or not the changes in managerial behavior necessary to support employee empowerment are taking place. And, because these management assessments provide a bottom-up performance feedback, managers hear directly from employees whether or not their behavior is empowering.

Develop "Best in Class" Norms

Your survey will have the most impact if a "Best in Class" benchmark is developed for your managers. This can be done, after the first assessment of a significant number of managers, by comparing their assessment results with their actual performance ratings.

A relatively straightforward way of comparing is to download the results from all the managers' assessments into a statistical software package, ideally the same software used to generate the assessments. Examine the correlation of managers' performance ratings with the performance reported on the management assessment by the various respondent groups (managers, direct reports, peers, internal customers). Check the correlations with the overall management assessment and with each item of the assessment. Once you identify which items are highly correlated with the performance evaluation, you will have an accurate view of the behaviors and skills that actually play a role in evaluating performance. At this point, you can decide whether it is appropriate to revise the performance management system or the assessment questions.

Next, use a basic survey software package to separate those managers with performance ratings that put them in the top 25 per cent. Then, on each of your managers' assessment reports, print a graphic that indicates the average assessment scores of managers rating in the top 25 per cent. This practice adds motivational value to your assessment process and clearly shows managers what they need to do to succeed in the company's culture.

Find Out What's Really Happening

Customized management assessments can uncover paradoxes and contradictions in company culture that more traditional surveys overlook. One company's customized assessment found that a significant number of middle managers ranked in the top 25 per cent when their performance was rated by their managers. However, the same managers were perceived through their direct reports and by other staff members to be over-controlling, overly concerned about mistakes, and involved in far too many day-to-day details.

The assessment pointed out an interesting contradiction inherent in the company's culture: To be perceived by senior management as a strong performer, middle managers had to micro-manage—even though the company had embarked two years before on an intensive program of employee involvement, empowerment and self-managed work teams. Clearly, senior management had never truly adapted to empowerment and was communicating that to middle management via top-down performance reviews.

Managers Key to Quality Work

Employee creativity and talent need to be both unleashed and harnessed by managers. This is a delicate task that is not easily taught, but can be helped along by periodic management assessments. Customized management assessments help companies develop their own unique method of empowerment, finely tuned to their unique culture, their industry, their business environment and their employees.

Managers Blind to Their Own Attitudes

Leaders exert a profound impact on the degree of empowerment employees feel. How a manager delegates tasks, makes decisions and provides feedback can either foster or destroy employee empowerment.

Executives and managers often inadvertently derail the very programs they verbally support. It is a typical human error to think that because we say we're "empowering employees", for example, that we actually are. Getting the empowerment rhetoric down is not enough; managers must walk their talk and realize that employee involvement is not a skill taught to employees but an attitude that must permeate their behavior.

Numerous personality studies suggest that 60 to 70 per cent of the population dislike and fear change—especially change that touches them on a deep, personal level. A manager asked to move his or her office may be annoyed, but a manager asked to change fundamental attitudes toward employees will be much more threatened.

14

Performance Management

Performance management is a very important Human Resource Management function. Its objective is to improve overall productivity and effectiveness by maximizing individual performance and potential. Performance management is concerned with.

- improving individual and collective performance;
- communicating management's expectations to supervisors and staff;
- improving communication between senior management, supervisors and staff;
- assisting staff to enhance their career prospects through recognizing and rewarding effective performance;
- identifying and resolving cases of underperformance; and
- providing important links to other Human Resource Management functions, such as training.

Key Components of Performance Management

Motivation

Motivation is in many ways the key to the success of Human Resource Management development. Managers should aim to increase performance through self-motivation, rather than having to use external motivation (i.e. the imposition of rules and continual improvements to conditions of service) to bring about higher standards of performance. The civil service has many formal programs to enhance motivation, and these are discussed in the "staff relations" section of this booklet. However, even more important is the motivational impact that supervisors have on their staff.

Principle. The basic principle underpinning motivation is that if staff are managed effectively, they will seek to give of their best voluntarily without the need for control through rules and sanctions—they will eventually be self-managing.

Procedures. Some of the most effective ways for managers to motivate staff include giving praise; recognition; and positive feedback; passing on feedback from more senior managers; and letting other staff know which staff have been responsible for praiseworthy work and/or effort. Too often, staff experience 'management by mistake', where most of the feedback received is corrective or punitive for mistakes they are perceived to have made.

If staff feel that their decisions are generally supported, and when genuine mistakes are made they will be guided in the right direction, they will be more positive, confident and prepared to take on responsibility and decision-making.

When staff are shown clear expectations, valued, trusted, encouraged and motivated, then they will be more likely to give of their best.

Performance Appraisal

Performance appraisal assesses an individual's performance against previously agreed work objectives. It serves two functions. First, it enables management to evaluate an individual's performance in the current job to identify strengths and overcome weaknesses. Second, it provides information to assist management plan postings, transfers and promotions. In so doing, management is able to compare performance and potential between officers of the same rank.

Principles. The basic principles governing performance appraisal are—

- Heads of Department/Heads of Grade have the flexibility to design their own appraisal system within the framework of these principles;

- Performance appraisal should be regarded as a multi-purpose management tool. Outcomes from staff appraisal should guide other Human Resource Management functions;
- It is joint responsibility of the individual and the supervisor;
- It is a continuous and ongoing process;
- It should relate individual performance to departmental objectives;
- Checks and balances should be built into the system to ensure fairness and objectivity; and
- Outstanding performance at one rank does not necessarily indicate suitability for promotion to a higher rank.

Procedure. Except for officers on probation, performance appraisal is normally carried out once a year. Different grades/departments may have their own performance appraisal form which enshrines the principles set out in the preceding paragraph.

At the beginning of the reporting cycle, the appraisee should agree with the appraising officer on the main objectives or responsibilities over the reporting period. The list of objectives or responsibilities should be reviewed between the appraisee and the appraising officer during the reporting cycle to see if changes are necessary. At the end of the reporting cycle, the appraising officer will write his assessment. He will pass his assessment to the countersigning officer for the latter's views.

To provide feedback to the appraisee, the appraising officer and the countersigning officer decide between them who should interview the appraisee to discuss with him/her the performance during the reporting period. The interviewing officer should show the entire report to the appraisee before the interview. A summary of the discussion at the interview and the points made by the appraisee should be recorded in the appraisal form. After the interview, the appraisal form is passed to the grade manager for his assessment.

Promotion

Promotion denotes that an individual has the competencies, i.e. the skills, abilities, knowledge and attitudes, required to perform effectively at the next higher rank. The competencies reflect the knowledge and skills exhibited in observable behaviour in the relevant areas of work. Promotion provides motivation to perform well and is an important part of performance management.

Principles. The principle of merit, or the best person for the job is key to promotion. Ability, potential and experience are taken into account in the assessment. The process of assessment should be fair and transparent. It is kept separate from the day to day management of performance and from the annual performance appraisal. The former should be a continuous process, while the latter can be used to assist in determining suitability for promotion.

Promotion Procedures. Heads of Department/Heads of Grade have flexibility to invite certain officers to apply for promotion, or allow officers to opt out of promotion.

As a general rule promotion boards are convened to:

- increase transparency and impartiality; and
- provide an opportunity to consider eligible officers' potential and organizational succession planning.

Where necessary and appropriate, promotion interviews are held to assist in assessment to supplement information provided in staff reports. This will apply to situations where staff reports are insufficient and questionable in terms of fairness or consistency. The promotion boards should be aware of potential unfairness if some staff are interviewed and others are not.

It is good management practice to provide promotion feedback to the staff who were considered but were not selected after a promotion exercise, to enhance communication. Departments respond to enquiries from staff arising from promotion exercises. They are encouraged to take a proactive approach in giving promotion feedback to staff after the relevant exercise has taken place.

Guidance and Supervision

Day-to-day guidance and supervision is necessary to provide direction and feedback to staff. It reinforces the annual performance appraisal, helps groom officers for promotion, and assists staff who are not performing well.

Principles. Guidance and supervision reinforces behaviour that contributes to good performance and discourages behaviour that blocks progress. Feedback should be:

- frequent—staff should not have to wait until formal performance review or appraisal for feedback;
- balanced—it should focus on good and bad performance;
- immediate—immediate feedback has much more impact than feedback given several weeks or months later;
- specific—staff should be in no doubt what actions feedback covers; and
- constructive—feedback should focus on overcoming difficulties or reinforcing successful behaviour.

Procedure. Guidance and supervision is offered on a day-to-day basis as needed.

Addressing Poor Performance

- counseling—staff should be told the areas where they need to improve and how this should be achieved; and
- appraisal—if staff do not respond to counseling their poor performance will be indicated in their annual appraisal.

If no improvement is shown after counseling and appraisal, there is a formal process of dealing with non-performance involving written warning, stoppage of increment and retirement in the public interest.

Human Resource Management Performance Measures

Effective monitoring depends on having the right performance measures in place. Human Resource Management performance measures should therefore relate to all aspects of Human Resource Management.

Management information will not always be statistically quantifiable and measurable data, but it should be as objective as possible and based on observable quantifiable measures wherever possible.

Targets and Indicators

Departments can set targets for Human Resource Management performance. This would normally be done in consultation with the policy branch, and likely to be only for a few selected aspects. Departments should also monitor developments in other areas of interest to them, using such measures as indicators.

Civil Service Branch is consulting departments in preparing a list of Human Resource Management performance measures which can be used by departments to help them monitor and improve their own Human Resource Management practices. Some of the information collected will be required by Civil Service Branch to assist in fulfilling its responsibility to monitor Human Resource Management across the civil service and develop appropriate policy which is based on accurate, up-to-date information.

Examples of Performance Measures

Manpower Planning:

- turnover by rank/grade and reason
- growth of ranks
- existence of a manpower plan
- existence of a succession plan
- staff leaving during probation

Training and Development:

- training need analysis
- number of training days per staff per year
- existence of a training plan
- number of career development interviews conducted

Staff Relations:

- days lost through industrial action
- number of staff complaints
- number of suggestions by staff
- number of meetings held

Performance Appraisal Application

Basic Purposes

Effective performance appraisal systems contain two basic systems operating in conjunction: an *evaluation system* and a *feedback system*.

The main aim of the evaluation system is to identify the performance gap (if any). This gap is the shortfall that occurs when performance does not meet the standard set by the organization as acceptable.

The main aim of the feedback system is to inform the employee about the quality of his or her performance. (However, the information flow is not exclusively one way. The appraiser also receives feedback from the employee about job problems, etc.)

One of the best ways to appreciate the purposes of performance appraisal is to look at it from the different viewpoints of the main stakeholders: the employee and the organization.

Employee Viewpoint

From the employee viewpoint, the purpose of performance appraisal is four-fold:

(1) Tell me what you want me to do

(2) Tell me how well I have done it

(3) Help me improve my performance

(4) Reward me for doing well

Organizational Viewpoint

From the organization's viewpoint, one of the most important reasons for having a system of performance appraisal is to establish and uphold the *principle of accountability*.

For decades it has been known to researchers that one of the chief causes of organizational failure is "non-alignment of responsibility and accountability". Non-alignment occurs where employees are given responsibilities and duties, but are not held accountable for the way in which those responsibilities and duties are performed. What typically happens is that several individuals or work units appear to have overlapping roles.

The overlap allows—indeed actively encourages—each individual or business unit to "pass the buck" to the others. Ultimately, in the severely non-aligned system, no one is accountable for anything. In this event, the principle of accountability breaks down completely. Organizational failure is the only possible outcome.

In cases where the non-alignment is not so severe, the organization may continue to function, albeit inefficiently. Like a poorly made or badly tuned engine, the non-aligned organization may run, but it will be sluggish, costly and unreliable. One of the principal aims of performance appraisal is to make people accountable. The objective is to align responsibility and accountability at every organizational level.

Appraisal Methods

In a landmark study, Locher & Teel (1977) found that the three most common appraisal methods in general use are rating scales (56%), essay methods (25%) and results-oriented or MBO methods (13%). For a description of each, follow the button links on the left.

Certain techniques in performance appraisal have been thoroughly investigated, and some have been found to yield better results than others.

Encourage Discussion

Research studies show that employees are likely to feel more satisfied with their appraisal result if they have the chance to talk freely and discuss their performance. It is also more likely that such employees will be better able to meet future performance goals (Nemeroff & Wexley, 1979).

Employees are also more likely to feel that the appraisal process is fair if they are given a chance to talk about their performance. This is especially so when they are permitted to challenge and appeal against their evaluation (Greenberg, 1986).

Constructive Intention

It is very important that employees recognize that negative appraisal feedback is provided with a constructive intention, i.e. to help them overcome present difficulties and to improve their future performance. Employees will be less anxious about criticism, and more likely to find it useful, when they believe that the appraiser's intentions are helpful and constructive (Fedor et al., 1989).

In contrast, other studies (Baron, 1988) have reported that "destructive criticism"—which is vague, ill-informed, unfair or harshly presented—will lead to problems such as anger, resentment, tension and workplace conflict, as well as increased resistance to improvement, denial of problems, and poorer performance.

Set Performance Goals

It has been shown in numerous studies that goal-setting is an important element in employee motivation. Goals can stimulate employee effort, focus attention, increase persistence, and encourage employees to find new and better ways to work (Locke et al., 1981).

The usefulness of goals as a stimulus to human motivation is one of the best supported theories in management. It is also quite clear that goals which are "...specific, difficult and accepted by employees will lead to higher levels of performance than easy, vague goals (such as do your best) or no goals at all" (Harris & DiSimone, 1994).

Appraiser Credibility

It is important that the appraiser (usually the employee's supervisor) be well-informed and credible. Appraisers should feel comfortable with the techniques of appraisal, and should be knowledgeable about the employee's job and performance.

When these conditions exist, employees are more likely to view the appraisal process as accurate and fair. They also express more acceptance of the appraiser's feedback and a greater willingness to change (Bannister, 1986).

Rating Scales

The rating scale method offers a high degree of structure for appraisals. Each employee trait or characteristic is rated on a bipolar scale that usually has several points ranging from "poor" to "excellent" (or some similar arrangement).

The traits assessed on these scales include employee attributes such as cooperation, communications ability, initiative, punctuality and technical (work skills) competence. The nature and scope of the traits selected for inclusion is limited only by the imagination of the scale's designer, or by the organization's need to know.

The one major provision in selecting traits is that they should be in some way relevant to the appraisee's job. The traits selected by some organizations have been unwise and have resulted in legal action on the grounds of discrimination.

Advantages

The greatest advantage of rating scales is that they are structured and standardized. This allows ratings to be easily compared and contrasted—even for entire workforces.

Each employee is subjected to the same basic appraisal process and rating criteria, with the same range of responses. This encourages equality in treatment for all appraisees and imposes standard measures of performance across all parts of the organization.

Rating scale methods are easy to use and understand. The concept of the rating scale makes obvious sense; both appraisers and appraisees have an intuitive appreciation for the simple and efficient logic of the bipolar scale. The result is widespread acceptance and popularity for this approach.

Disadvantages

Trait Relevance

Are the selected rating-scale traits clearly relevant to the jobs of all the appraisees? It is inevitable that with a standardized and fixed system of appraisal that certain traits will have a greater relevance in some jobs than in others.

For example, the trait "initiative" might not be very important in a job that is tightly defined and rigidly structured. In such cases, a low appraisal rating for initiative may not mean that an employee lacks initiative. Rather, it may reflect that fact that an employee has few opportunities to use and display that particular trait. The relevance of rating scales is therefore said to be context-sensitive. Job and workplace circumstances must be taken into account.

Systemic Disadvantage

Rating scales, and the traits they purport to measure, generally attempt to encapsulate all the relevant indicators of employee performance. There is an assumption that all the true and best indicators of performance are included, and all false and irrelevant indicators are excluded.

This is an assumption very difficult to prove in practice. It is possible that an employee's performance may depend on factors that have not been included in the selected traits. Such employees may end up with ratings that do not truly or fairly reflect their effort or value to the organization. Employees in this class are systemically disadvantaged by the rating scale method.

Perceptual Errors

This includes various well-known problems of selective perception (such as the horns and halos effect) as well as problems of perceived meaning.

Selective perception is the human tendency to make private and highly subjective assessments of what a person is "really like", and then seek evidence to support that view (while ignoring or downplaying evidence that might contradict it).

This is a common and normal psychological phenomenon. All human beings are affected by it. In other words, we see in others what we want to see in them.

An example is the supervisor who believes that an employee is inherently good (halo effect) and so ignores evidence that might suggest otherwise. Instead of correcting the slackening employee, the supervisor covers for them and may even offer excuses for their declining performance.

On the other hand, a supervisor may have formed the impression that an employee is bad (horns effect). The supervisor becomes unreasonably harsh in his assessment of the employee, and always ready to criticize and undermine them.

The horns and halo effect is rarely seen in its extreme and obvious forms. But in its more subtle manifestations, it can be a significant threat to the effectiveness and credibility of performance appraisal.

Perceived Meaning

Problems of perceived meaning occur when appraisers do not share the same opinion about the meaning of the selected traits and the language used on the rating scales.

For example, to one appraiser, an employee may demonstrate the trait of initiative by reporting work problems to a supervisor. To another appraiser, this might suggest an excessive dependence on supervisory assistance—and thus a lack of initiative.

As well, the language and terms used to construct a scale—such as "Performance exceeds expectations" or "Below average skill"—may mean different things to different appraisers.

Rating Errors

The problem here is not so much errors in perception as errors in appraiser judgment and motive. Unlike perceptual errors, these errors may be (at times) deliberate.

The most common rating error is central tendency. Busy appraisers, or those wary of confrontations and repercussions, may be tempted to dole out too many passive, middle-of-the-road ratings (e.g. "satisfactory" or "adequate"), regardless of the actual performance of a subordinate. Thus, the spread of ratings tends to clump excessively around the middle of the scale.

This problem is worsened in organizations where the appraisal process does not enjoy strong management support, or where the appraisers do not feel confident with the task of appraisal.

Essay Method

In the essay method approach, the appraiser prepares a written statement about the employee being appraised.

The statement usually concentrates on describing specific strengths and weaknesses in job performance. It also suggests courses of action to remedy the identified problem areas.

The statement may be written and edited by the appraiser alone, or it be composed in collaboration with the appraisee.

Advantages

The essay method is far less structured and confining than the rating scale method. It permits the appraiser to examine almost any relevant issue or attribute of performance. This contrasts sharply with methods where the appraisal criteria are rigidly defined.

Appraisers may place whatever degree of emphasis on issues or attributes that they feel appropriate. Thus the process is open-ended and very flexible. The appraiser is not locked into an appraisal system the limits expression or assumes that employee traits can be neatly dissected and scaled.

Disadvantages

Essay methods are time-consuming and difficult to administer. Appraisers often find the essay technique more demanding than methods such as rating scales. The technique's greatest advantage—freedom of expression—is also its greatest handicap. The varying writing skills of appraisers can upset and distort the whole process. The process is subjective and, in consequence, it is difficult to compare and contrast the results of individuals or to draw any broad conclusions about organizational needs.

Results Method: (MBO Method)

The use of management objectives was first widely advocated in the 1950s by the noted management theorist Peter Drucker.

MBO (management by objectives) methods of performance appraisal are results-oriented. That is, they seek to measure employee performance by examining the extent to which predetermined work objectives have been met.

Usually the objectives are established jointly by the supervisor and subordinate. An example of an objective for a sales manager might be: Increase the gross monthly sales volume to $250,000 by 30 June.

Once an objective is agreed, the employee is usually expected to self-audit; that is, to identify the skills needed to achieve the objective. Typically they do not rely on others to locate and specify their strengths and weaknesses. They are expected to monitor their own development and progress.

Advantages

The MBO approach overcomes some of the problems that arise as a result of assuming that the employee traits needed for job success can be reliably identified and measured.

Instead of assuming traits, the MBO method concentrates on actual outcomes.

If the employee meets or exceeds the set objectives, then he or she has demonstrated an acceptable level of job performance. Employees are judged according to real outcomes, and not on their potential for success, or on someone's subjective opinion of their abilities.

The guiding principle of the MBO approach is that direct results can be observed, whereas the traits and attributes of employees (which may or may not contribute to performance) must be guessed at or inferred.

The MBO method recognizes the fact that it is difficult to neatly dissect all the complex and varied elements that go to make up employee performance.

MBO advocates claim that the performance of employees cannot be broken up into so many constituent parts—as one might take apart an engine to study it. But put all the parts together and the performance may be directly observed and measured.

Disadvantages

MBO methods of performance appraisal can give employees a satisfying sense of autonomy and achievement. But on the downside, they can lead to unrealistic expectations about what can and cannot be reasonably accomplished.

Supervisors and subordinates must have very good "reality checking" skills to use MBO appraisal methods. They will need these skills during the initial stage of objective setting, and for the purposes of self-auditing and self-monitoring.

Unfortunately, research studies have shown repeatedly that human beings tend to lack the skills needed to do their own "reality checking". Nor are these skills easily conveyed by training. Reality itself is an intensely personal experience, prone to all forms of perceptual bias.

One of the strengths of the MBO method is the clarity of purpose that flows from a set of well-articulated objectives. But this can be a source of weakness also. It has become very apparent that the modern organization must be flexible to survive. Objectives, by their very nature, tend to impose a certain rigidity.

Of course, the obvious answer is to make the objectives more fluid and yielding. But the penalty for fluidity is loss of clarity. Variable objectives may cause employee confusion. It is also possible that fluid objectives may be distorted to disguise or justify failures in performance.

Benefits of Appraisal

Perhaps the most significant benefit of appraisal is that, in the rush and bustle of daily working life, it offers a rare chance for a supervisor and subordinate to have "time out" for a one-on-one discussion of important work issues that might not otherwise be addressed.

Almost universally, where performance appraisal is conducted properly, both supervisors and subordinates have reported the experience as beneficial and positive.

Appraisal offers a valuable opportunity to focus on work activities and goals, to identify and correct existing problems, and to encourage better future performance. Thus the performance of the whole organization is enhanced.

For many employees, an "official" appraisal interview may be the only time they get to have exclusive, uninterrupted access to their supervisor. One employee of a large organization said after his first formal performance appraisal, "In twenty years of work, that's the first time anyone has ever bothered to sit down and tell me how I'm doing."

The value of this intense and purposeful interaction between a supervisor and subordinate should not be underestimated.

Motivation and Satisfaction

Performance appraisal can have a profound effect on levels of employee motivation and satisfaction—for better as well as for worse.

Performance appraisal provides employees with recognition for their work efforts. The power of social recognition as an incentive has been long noted. In fact, there is evidence that human beings will even prefer negative recognition in preference to no recognition at all.

If nothing else, the existence of an appraisal program indicates to an employee that the organization is genuinely interested in their individual performance and development. This alone can have a positive influence on the individual's sense of worth, commitment and belonging.

The strength and prevalence of this natural human desire for individual recognition should not be overlooked. Absenteeism and turnover rates in some organizations might be greatly reduced if more attention were paid to it. Regular performance appraisal, at least, is a good start.

Training and Development

Performance appraisal offers an excellent opportunity—perhaps the best that will ever occur—for a supervisor and subordinate to recognize and agree upon individual training and development needs.

During the discussion of an employee's work performance, the presence or absence of work skills can become very obvious—even to those who habitually reject the idea of training for them!

Performance appraisal can make the need for training more pressing and relevant by linking it clearly to performance outcomes and future career aspirations.

From the point of view of the organization as a whole, consolidated appraisal data can form a picture of the overall demand for training. This data may be analyzed by variables such as sex, department, etc. In this respect, performance appraisal can provide a regular and efficient training needs audit for the entire organization.

Recruitment and Induction

Appraisal data can be used to monitor the success of the organization's recruitment and induction practices. For example, how well are the employees performing who were hired in the past two years?

Appraisal data can also be used to monitor the effectiveness of changes in recruitment strategies. By following the yearly data related to new hires (and given sufficient numbers on which to base the analysis) it is possible to assess whether the general quality of the workforce is improving, staying steady, or declining.

Employee Evaluation

Though often understated or even denied, evaluation is a legitimate and major objective of performance appraisal.

But the need to evaluate (i.e. to judge) is also an ongoing source of tension, since evaluative and developmental priorities appear to frequently clash. Yet at its most basic level, performance appraisal is the process of examining and evaluating the performance of an individual.

Though organizations have a clear right—some would say a duty—to conduct such evaluations of performance, many still recoil from the idea. To them, the explicit process of judgment can be dehumanizing and demoralizing and a source of anxiety and distress to employees.

It has been said by some that appraisal cannot serve the needs of evaluation and development at the same time; it must be one or the other.

But there may be an acceptable middle ground, where the need to evaluate employees objectively, and the need to encourage and develop them, can be balanced.

Reward Issues

Some interesting insights into what can go seriously wrong in a system of reward-linked performance appraisal is found in the work of Deets & Tyler (1986).

The Xerox Experience

The Reprographic Business Group of the Xerox Corporation operated a very traditional system of performance appraisal based on rating scale methods. The rating outcomes were linked to pay outcomes. In fact, the results had direct effects on merit pay rises—everyone at Xerox knew that and expected it.

The Xerox system included all the common features of rating scale systems. The appraisal interviews were held annually and conducted by the employee's immediate supervisor.

Accomplishments of the preceding year were recorded and performance levels were judged according to various predefined criteria. The system included some elements of essay appraisal, since appraisers were required to write brief supporting statements for each rated criterion.

The Xerox system also called for a summary rating; an ultimate digit, from a low of 1 (for unsatisfactory) to a high of

5 (exceptional). The summary rating attempted to encapsulate the whole year's performance in a single number.

The significance of that final number was immense. It literally determined the size of the employee's annual pay rise. The higher the rating, the bigger the rise. For Xerox employees, the thing that really mattered about appraisal was getting the biggest possible final number.

Analysis of ratings over time showed that more than 95 per cent of employees were either 3s, 4s or 5s; that is, the spread of ratings heavily favored the higher end of the scale. Almost every employee, according to the appraisal system, was performing at or above the average.

The lower end of the scale, the ratings of "below average" and "unsatisfactory" was very rarely used. The effect of this distortion was that any employee who scored less than a 4 ("exceeds expected performance level") began to feel like a failure!

The appraisal process became a sort of ratings lottery; the aim of the game was to get the highest possible score and win the jackpot. The process became fixated on that all-important final digit.

This situation placed tremendous pressure on appraisees and appraisers alike. The appraisers had the unenviable task of deciding the winners from the losers. No wonder most of them preferred to hand out an abundance of overly-generous ratings!

Xerox eventually replaced this system with an MBO/essay form of appraisal. They abandoned rating scale methods completely.

That may have been an over-reaction, since the fault did not lie with the method itself so much as with its intimate—and ultimately inflexible linkage—to the annual pay rise. When reward outcomes are so closely linked to the size of a rating on a five point scale, the difference of one point either way can become very important and provocative.

The Xerox rating system might have worked if the direct causal relationship between the summary rating and merit pay outcomes had been eliminated or at least softened.

The Case for Linkage

The question of whether appraisal results should be allowed to directly influence decisions about pay increases (and other reward outcomes such as promotion) has been hotly contested. It is still one of the most contentious issues in human resources management.

One of the main reasons for separating appraisal results from reward decisions is the belief that a too-close link would create an overly-threatening and potentially punitive system.

Employees, apprehensive at the prospect of being judged, would have the added anxiety of knowing that the result will directly impact their pay packet and career outcomes.

Pressure

This kind of appraisal pressure results in a win/lose mentality of the sort that developed at Xerox. Rather than the appraisee being willing to openly discuss their performance, they become anxious and defensive. Naturally, the typical appraisee is not eager to admit to anything that might impair their chances of a pay rise or other reward.

There is a deep irony in the fact that many organizations, while having excellent systems of appraisal, allow their merit pay and promotion decisions to be made by inferior means. Often the matter is left to the discretion of one or two supervisors or managers, with a cursory review being made by the HR department.

There is also the work of Bannister & Balkin (1990), which has reported that "discussions of pay at the time of performance appraisal" increases employee acceptance of appraisal and their satisfaction with the process. This undermines the arguments for separation.

As well, there is evidence that incongruity between appraisal results and later pay and promotion outcomes is a source of employee discontent and de-motivation.

Pay increases and promotions send powerful messages to employees. If these messages don't match up with the appraisal results, employees are quick to dismiss the whole process as a farce. Efforts have been made to convince employees otherwise, but the "bottom line" for many is who got the extra money or who got the new job.

Management Trick?

The separation of appraisal results and reward outcomes is, at best, a contrived situation. At worst, it may convey the impression that appraisal is some sort of deception, a trick by management, designed to give an appearance of openness and fairness while "real issues" like pay and promotions are decided in secret.

Nor is the practice of putting a six-month buffer between appraisals and pay reviews an effective method of avoiding the issue. Far better to define and clarify the relationship between appraisal, performance and reward outcomes.

The view of the separatists, which insists that appraisal results and reward outcomes should be insulated from each other, may be an over-reaction to the potential abuses.

There is evidence that appraisees appreciate the existence of a link between appraisal and reward results. To many, the existence of such a link is intuitively sensible.

From the perspective of the organization, the inclusion of carefully collected appraisal data in pay and promotion matters may contribute to better quality decisions. It should also help ensure a greater degree of congruity between appraisal results and subsequent reward outcomes.

Even so, many advocates of separation will be reluctant to concede the possibility of any form of constructive linkage between appraisal and rewards.

This is a shame, because the potential of performance appraisal encompasses more than employee development. Admittedly there are risks in linking reward outcomes; but there are also risks, and a potential for harm, in contriving to deny that any linkage exists.

At the very least, an organization wishing to form the mildest of reward links might consider a frank discussion of reward criteria during the appraisal interview.

Those organizations that are determined to keep their appraisal and reward issues separated might ask themselves whether performance appraisal is really the tool they need. Perhaps what they actually desire is some form of developmental appraisal.

Conflict and Confrontation in Appraisal

Invariably the needs arise during a performance appraisal to provide an employee with less than flattering feedback.

The skill and sensitivity used to handle these often difficult sessions is critical. If the appraisee accepts the negative feedback and resolves to improve, all is well. But if the result is an angry or hurt employee, then the process of correction has failed. The performance of an employee in such cases is unlikely to improve and may deteriorate even further.

Self-Auditing

According to Krein (1990), appraisers should not confront employees directly with criticism. Rather, they should aim to let the evidence of poor performance emerge "naturally" during the course of the appraisal interview. This is done by way of open-ended questioning techniques that encourage the employee to identify their own performance problems.

Instead of blunt statements or accusations, the appraisers should encourage an employee to talk freely about their own impressions of their performance. For example, consider the case of employee who has had too many absent days. The appraiser, in accusatory mode, might say:

> Your attendance record is unacceptable. You'll have to improve it.

A better way to handle this might be to say:

> Your attendance record shows that you had 7 days off work in 6 months. What can you tell me about this?

The technique is to calmly present the evidence (resisting the temptation to label it as good or bad) and then invite the employee to comment. In many cases, with just a gentle nudge from the appraiser here and there, an employee with problems will admit that weaknesses do exist.

This is much more likely when an employee does not feel accused of anything, nor forced to make admissions that they do not wish to make.

If an appraiser can get an employee to the stage of voluntary admission, half the battle is won. The technique described by Krein is a type of self-auditing, since it encourages the employee to confront themselves with their own work and performance issues.

The technique is useful because it is more likely to promote discussion and agreement on the need for change. Confrontation techniques that rely on "charge and counter-charge" tend to promote adversarialism—and that leads to denial and resentment.

Ownership of Problems

Perhaps the most powerful aspect of the self-auditing process is that employees are more willing generally to accept personal "ownership" of problems that have been self-identified. This sense of ownership provides an effective basis for stimulating change and development. (Some would argue that it provides the only basis.)

Nevertheless there are individuals who will not admit to anything that appears to reflect poorly on them. With ego defenses on full-alert, they will resist the process of self-auditing very strongly. In such cases, appraisers may have no choice but to confront the poor performer directly and firmly with the evidence they have.

Sometimes the shock of direct confrontation will result in the employee admitting that they do need to make improvements. But sometimes it will just make their denial of the problem worse.

In providing any feedback—especially negative feedback—appraisers should be willing and able to support their opinions with specific and clear examples. Vague generalizations should be avoided.

The focus should be on job-related behaviors and attitudes. If a specific observation cannot be supported by clear evidence, or touches on issues that are not job-related, it may be best to exclude all mention of it.

Appraisers must carefully scrutinize their own perceptions, motives and prejudices.

Common Mistakes in Appraisal

Where performance appraisal fails to work as well as it should, lack of support from the top levels of management is often cited as a major contributing reason.

Opposition may be based on political motives, or more simply, on ignorance or disbelief in the effectiveness of the appraisal process.

It is crucial that top management believe in the value of appraisal and express their visible commitment to it. Top managers are powerful role models for other managers and employees.

Those attempting to introduce performance appraisal, or even to reform an existing system, must be acutely aware of the importance of political issues and symbolism in the success of such projects.

Fear of Failure

There is a stubborn suspicion among many appraisers that a poor appraisal result tends to reflect badly upon them also, since they are usually the employee's supervisor. Many appraisers have a vested interest in making their subordinates "look good" on paper.

When this problem exists (and it can be found in many organizations), it may point to a problem in the organization culture. The cause may be a culture that is intolerant of failure. In other words, appraisers may fear the possibility of repercussions—both for themselves and the appraisee.

Longenecker (1989) argues that accuracy in performance appraisal is impossible to achieve, since people play social and political games, and they protect their own interests. "No savvy manager...", says Longenecker, "...is going to use the appraisal process to shoot himself or herself in the foot".

No matter what safeguards are in place, "...when you turn managers loose in the real world, they consciously fudge the numbers." What Longenecker is saying is that appraisers will, for all sorts of reasons, deliberately distort the evaluations that they give to employees.

Indeed, surveys have shown that not only do many managers admit to a little fudging, they actually defend it as a tactic necessary for effective management.

The fudging motives of appraisers have, at times, a certain plausibility. For instance, a supervisor who has given an overly generous appraisal to a marginal performer might claim that their 'legitimate' motive was the hope of encouraging a better performance.

On the other hand, fudging motives can be a lot less admirable and sometimes devious: the appraiser who fudges to avoid the possibility of an unpleasant confrontation, the appraiser who fudges to hide employee difficulties from senior managers, the appraiser who fudges in order to punish or reward employees.

Judgement Aversion

Many people have a natural reluctance to "play judge" and create a permanent record which may affect an employee's future career. This is the case especially where there may be a need to make negative appraisal remarks.

Training in the techniques of constructive evaluation (such as self-auditing) may help. Appraisers need to recognize that problems left unchecked could ultimately cause more harm to an employee's career than early detection and correction.

Organizations might consider the confidential archiving of appraisal records more than, say, three years old.

Feedback-Seeking

Larson (1989) has described a social game played by poor performers. Many supervisors will recognize the game at once and may have been its victims.

The game is called feedback-seeking. It occurs where a poor performing employee regularly seeks informal praise from his or her supervisor at inappropriate moments.

Often the feedback-seeker will get the praise they want, since they choose the time and place to ask for it. In effect, they "ambush" the supervisor by seeking feedback at moments when the supervisor is unable or unprepared to give them a full and proper answer, or in settings that are inappropriate for a frank assessment.

The supervisor may feel "put on the spot", but will often provide a few encouraging words of support. The game seems innocent enough until appraisal time comes around. Then the supervisor will find that the employee recalls, with perfect clarity, every casual word of praise ever spoken!

This places the supervisor in a difficult bind. Either the supervisor lied when giving the praise, or least, misled the employee into thinking that their performance was acceptable (in fact, this is the argument that feedback-seekers will often make).

The aim of the game is that the feedback-seeker wants to deflect responsibility for their own poor performance. They also seek to bolster their appraisal rating by bringing in all the "evidence" of casual praise. Very often the feedback seeker will succeed in making the supervisor feel at least partly responsible. As a result, their appraisal result may be upgraded.

Was the supervisor partly responsible? Not really. The truth of the matter is that they have been "blackmailed" by a subtle social game. But like most social games, the play depends on the unconscious participation of both sides. Making supervisors aware of the game is usually sufficient to stop it. They must learn to say, when asked for casual praise, "I can't talk about it now...but see me in my office later".

This puts the supervisor back in control of the appraisal process.

Appraiser Preparation

The bane of any performance appraisal system is the appraiser who wants to "play it by ear". Such attitudes should be actively discouraged by stressing the importance and technical challenge of good performance appraisal. Perhaps drawing their attention to the contents of this website, for example, may help them to see the critical issues that must be considered.

Employee Participation

Employees should participate with their supervisors in the creation of their own performance goals and development plans. Mutual agreement is a key to success. A plan wherein the employee feels some degree of ownership is more likely to be accepted than one that is imposed. This does not mean that employees do not desire guidance from their supervisor; indeed they very much do.

Performance Management

One of the most common mistakes in the practice of performance appraisal is to perceive appraisal as an isolated event rather than an ongoing process.

Employees generally require more feedback, and more frequently, than can be provided in an annual appraisal. While it may not be necessary to conduct full appraisal sessions more than once or twice a year, performance management should be viewed as an ongoing process.

Frequent mini-appraisals and feedback sessions will help ensure that employees receive the ongoing guidance, support and encouragement they need.

Of course, many supervisors complain they don't have the time to provide this sort of ongoing feedback. This is hardly likely. What supervisors really mean when they say this is that the supervision and development of subordinates is not as high a priority as certain other tasks.

In this case, the organization may need to review the priorities and values that it has instilled in its supervisory ranks. After all, supervisors who haven't got time to monitor and facilitate the performance of their subordinates are like chefs who haven't got time to cook, or dentists who are too busy to look at teeth. It just doesn't make sense.

If appraisal is viewed as an isolated event, it is only natural that supervisors will come to view their responsibilities in the same way. Just as worrying, employees may come to see their own effort and commitment levels as something that needs a bit of a polish up in the month or two preceding appraisals.

Bias Effects

Gabris & Mitchell have reported a disruptive bias in performance appraisal known as the Matthew Effect.

It is named after the Matthew of biblical fame who wrote, "To him who has shall be given, and he shall have abundance: but from him who does not have, even that which he has shall be taken away."

In performance appraisal the Matthew Effect is said to occur where employees tend to keep receiving the same appraisal results, year in and year out. That is, their appraisal results tend to become self-fulfilling: if they have done well, they will continue to do well; if they have done poorly, they will continue to do poorly.

The Matthew Effect suggests that no matter how hard an employee strives, their past appraisal records will prejudice their future attempts to improve.

There is other research to support the theory that poor performers might not be given a fair chance to improve. A study of supervisors in nearly 40 different organizations found that subordinates tend to be divided into two groups: in-groupers and out-groupers.

This study, by Heneman, Greenberger & Anonyou (1989) reported that in-groupers are subordinates who seem to be favored by their supervisors. In their relationship with the boss, they enjoy "a high degree of trust, interaction, support and rewards".

On the other hand, out-groupers don't do as well. They appear to be permanently out of favor and are likely to bear the brunt of supervisory distrust and criticism. The effect is therefore similar to the horns and halo effect; supervisors tend to judge employees as either good or bad, and then seek evidence that supports that opinion.

It was found that when an in-grouper did poorly on a task, supervisors tended to overlook the failure or attribute to causes such as bad luck or bad timing; when they did well, their success was attributed to effort and ability.

But when an out-grouper performed well, it was rarely attributed to their effort or ability. And when an out-grouper performed poorly, there was little hesitation it citing the cause as laziness or incompetence.

It is not clear how supervisors make the distinction between in-groupers and out-groupers. Whatever the criteria, it is clearly not objective, equitable or reliable.

This bias must inevitably lead to a distortion of the appraisal process. It must also be a source of frustration for those employees who are discriminated against.

Frustration

The extent of this frustration was explored by Gabris & Mitchell. They studied an organization with a quarterly performance appraisal system. The workforce was divided into two groups: those who had been given high appraisal results consistently, and those who had low results consistently.

When the groups were asked if the appraisal system was fair and equitable, 63 per cent of the high performers agreed, compared to only 5 per cent of the lower performers.

The groups were asked if their supervisors listened to them. Of the high performers, 69 per cent said yes, while among the low performers, 95 per cent said no.

Finally, when asked if their supervisors were supportive, nearly half of the high performers agreed that they were, while none (nil, zilch, zero!) of the low performers agreed.

Of course, not everyone who gets a poor appraisal result is a victim of supervisory bias. Nor are all supervisors prone to making the same degree of in-group and out-group distinction. The effects discussed here are tendencies, not immutable effects.

But to some extent, it appears that certain employees may be unfairly advantaged, while others are disadvantaged, by bias effects in the judgments of supervisors.

It is a cardinal principle of performance appraisal that employees should have the chance to improve their appraisal results—especially if their past results have not been so good. It is a very serious flaw in the process of appraisal if this principle is denied in practice.

There are reasonable steps which can be taken to limit the effects of supervisory bias.

Awareness Training

The first line of defense lies in raising awareness of the problem. Supervisors need to be informed of the types of subtle bias that can interfere with their performance as appraisers. They need to understand that the in-group/out-group bias, for instance, reduces the morale and motivation of their subordinates.

Developing Poor Performers

Incentives, financial or non-financial, may be offered to encourage supervisors to make special efforts to help poor performers improve. Supervisory appraisals, for example, might stress the importance of working with poor performers to upgrade their performance. The possibilities are extensive.

Counseling, Transfer, Termination

There is always the possibility that an employee who receives poor appraisal results is, in fact, a chronic poor performer. No employer is obliged to tolerate poor performance forever. Consistently poor appraisal results will indicate a need for counseling, transfer or termination. The exact remedy will depend on the circumstances.

Sales and Support Performance Appraisal

Feedback for Sales and Customer Support

The ANPAS SAF is an appraisal instrument designed for evaluating employees in selling and customer support roles. It defines competency in this field as resting upon seven core attributes:

- Product and Market Knowledge
- Pro-activism
- Persuasive Communication
- Resilience
- Personal Presentation and Organization
- Closing Skills
- Internal Relations

Briefly these attributes are (each is described more fully in the SAF itself):

Product and Market Knowledge

Understanding and awareness of products and services offered, not only by the employee's own organization but also by competitors. Includes knowledge of customers and their needs.

Pro-activism

The ability and motivation to actively develop and maximize selling opportunities, rather then waiting passively for sales to "happen". Includes cross-selling, value-adding, referrals and repeat sales.

Persuasive Communication

The ability to generate credibility and trust by way of attentive, empathic and honest communication with customers and prospects.

Resilience

The determination to keep going in the face of setbacks, criticism, and rejection, even from tough and demanding customers. The willingness to go "the extra mile" to satisfy a customer and conclude a sale.

Personal Presentation and Organization

Refers to personal presentation, dress and grooming, as well as personal organization and manner, including issues such as attitude, non-verbal behavior, level of preparation and punctuality.

Closing Skills

The ability to negotiate, facilitate and encourage the conclusion of a sale (e.g. "asking for the order"), and overcoming the last elements of uncertainty or objection that might stand in the way.

Internal Relations

Builds and maintains effective working relations with internal staff, including both sales and non-sales staff. Shares information and market intelligence.

How the SAF is Used

The SAF generates a Sales Appraisal Score that ranges from a low of 0 to a high of 28 points. Ratings at the higher levels are associated with strong performance. Most sales and support employees fall in the competent range from 10 to 19 points.

SAF is useful for identifying the different performance levels of sales and customer support employees and encouraging higher levels of achievement. As well, the feedback given in the SAF can assist sales and customer support employees to analyze their own performance and seek to improve skills in areas that may be lacking.

Management Appraisal

Feedback for Supervisors and Managers

The MAF is a specialized rating instrument designed for the evaluation of managerial and supervisory leadership performance. It is based on the ANPAS Leadership Scale, which defines leadership competency as resting on eight key attributes:

- Resilience
- Delegation
- Credibility
- Strategic Skills
- Operational Skills
- Decision Skills

- Adaptability
- Persuasiveness.

Briefly these attributes are:

Resilience

Refers to mental and emotional 'toughness', ability to cope with pressure, criticism, setbacks, risks, etc. Willingness to take on difficult tasks and unpleasant responsibilities.

Delegation

Refers to willingness to encourage subordinates and others to take on responsibilities, providing emotional and psychological support, consulting and listening, sharing information, recognizing the contributions of others.

Credibility

Refers to the ability to inspire trust and respect by being forthright, honest, not prone to over-commitment, leading by example, showing consistency in speech and actions, behavior and attitudes.

Strategic Skills

Refers to the ability to think ahead, to remember the big picture even while immersed in short-term problems, to be able make long-term plans, to perceive emerging threats and opportunities and to identify what matters most.

Operational Skills

Refers to the ability to run day-to-day operations, using personnel and resources to best effect, and responding quickly to unexpected problems and opportunities, being able to manage on-time and on-budget.

Decision Skills

Refers to the ability to make appropriate well-informed decisions in a timely manner, balancing competing needs, dealing with complexity and confusion, and being decisive but not impulsive.

Adaptability

Refers to willingness and openness to change, and the ability to learn and adapt in fluid situations, turning past mistakes to good use, knowing when to abandon an established plan or goal for a better one.

Persuasiveness

Refers to the ability to motivate, persuade and galvanize others to a course of action, even where arduous or unpleasant; and encouraging others to co-operate and perceive their common interest or goal.

How the MAF is Used

While managers and supervisors may require extra skills from time to time, the eight key attributes are essential, at least to a moderate extent. If any of the attributes is seriously lacking, success in workplace leadership roles is unlikely to be achieved.

The ANPAS MAF generates a Management Appraisal Score that ranges from a low of 0 to a high of 32 points. Performance at the higher levels is associated with strong levels of leadership. Most managers and supervisors fall in the competent band from 12 to 20 points.

The MAF is useful for identifying the different performance levels of managers and supervisors. In turn, this can be used to identify employees who are, for example, suitable for promotion or in need of training or intervention. As well, the feedback given in the MAF can assist managers and supervisors to analyse their own performance and seek to improve skills in areas that may be lacking.

Painless Performance Appraisals

Performance appraisal—do these two little words give you shivers or smiles?

Many managers dread performance appraisals and will go to great lengths to avoid them. Yet in reality it can be one of the most positive and valuable activities that a manager performs. Years ago, Peter Drucker said that the best managers help their people do two main things: set goals and achieve them.

Why should we spend time on Performance Appraisals?

Performance appraisals serve three main purposes for the employer—to assess employee performance, to determine the role of the employee in the future, and to further employee development. More specifically, performance appraisals will assist a manager to:

- Ensure that employees are aligned with departmental and organizational goals;
- Measure and assess individual performance against standards and goals;
- Monitor productivity;
- Identify weaknesses and strengths that may have not ordinarily surfaced;
- Increase and improve communications resulting in getting to know the employee better;
- Provide administrative data for promotion, pay adjustment and training assignments;
- Send the message that you are not too busy to spend time with an employee and that you care about their performance.

Employees gain much from a thorough performance appraisal and can:

- Learn what behaviors and attitudes they need to improve or modify;
- Discuss the status of projects and goals; ensure that they are on the right track;
- Discuss their future.

Jointly, both parties have the opportunity to:

- Mutually identify and establish standards of performance that are challenging;
- Develop and build trust levels, confidence and respect;
- Listen meaningfully to each other and understand each other's roles;
- Provide feedback.

It is the process of appraisal that is vital to employee development and productivity. This process relies on good communications between the employer and employee to be successful.

Performance Appraisal Meetings

How Often should We Meet?

Performance appraisals should be governed by the organization's calendar, not the clock. Assuming that goals and objectives are set jointly at the beginning of the year, each quarter is an excellent time to formally review progress made against those goals. Moreover, managers should look for opportunities to coach their employees everyday.

How do I Prepare for a Meeting?

Before meeting with the employee, review all documentation. Ask the employee to prepare a summary of his or her own performance and review thoroughly. Seek out feedback from other managers or customers. Look for any commendations or letters you may have received about the employee during the year. Review notes from previous meetings. Plan the meeting in advance. Do not miss pre-arranged performance meetings. Both parties should give the meeting the highest priority possible.

Keep a file or a written log of employees' performance. Why a log? We all have imperfect memories. When managers do not prepare for appraisal meetings until the very end of the year, there is tendency to focus on the negative. A December retrospective is likely to lose track of many examples of positive performance from the previous eleven months.

Review the goals to ensure that they are attainable, challenging and still relevant. Clearly described goals where both parties input increases commitment in achieving these goals.

Where should We Meet?

An appropriate and quiet room is required. The most commonly used location, a manager's office, may not always be the best place as it is not neutral ground and telephone interruptions may ensue. A conference room or meeting room is often best.

The setting should relax employees, not add to their anxiety. Consider meeting in the employee's office if it has a door, or borrowing a colleague's office. Meeting somewhere other than your office also makes it easier to end the meeting.

Assessment: How to Give and Take?

The employee's assessment of his or her own performance is the first area of discussion. It is important to ensure that the employee is heard. In effective coaching, a manager will reflect and summarize the employee's views before moving to their own evaluation. A crucial manager responsibility is assessing and giving timely feedback to employees on their performance. Feedback that is given as soon as possible has proven to be the most effective in addressing the error or replicating the success. Examples of incidents in your documentation can be shared with the employee.

Assessing performance in some jobs where there are specific outputs, which can be counted and quantified directly, is ideal. For many jobs, however, measurement is a challenge. Employers must rely on the observations and judgements of managers to appraise performance. While established organizational performance measures will in most cases form the core of the appraisal, non-performance behaviours need to be considered and discussed in assessing the overall contribution of the employee. These include measures such as tardiness, absenteeism and turnover.

Why do I Worry So Much About the Appraisal Meeting?

Two of the most common fears that managers have about performance appraisals are confrontations and surprises. This is usually a result of a lack of communication between the manager and employee. Unfortunately, many managers avoid delivering performance reviews for fear of confrontation.

"No surprises" is a key element to any evaluation process. Employees want to know how they are performing. They want to be treated with respect and as partners throughout the performance cycle. To support this and ensure that there are no surprises, continuous assessment, and feedback is vital in communication and will lessen the likelihood of a confrontation.

Surprises beget confrontations. Communication prevents them. By means of periodic discussions throughout the year, fear and anxiety are reduced because the employee is well aware of any problems or concern areas. Otherwise the performance meeting could take on enormous proportions especially if it impacts salary. With all the tension in the room, how can it be a successful interchange?

How do I Communicate?

Deliver the appraisal in simple language. This isn't a meeting to renegotiate the objectives or the standards for performance that were set at the beginning of the year.

As you prepare for the review meeting, focus. People rarely hear everything, particularly when they are ill at ease or under stress. If you want the employee to hear a core message, make it clear to yourself first.

State the facts and be honest. Often, managers feel a need to hide the bad news. They are afraid to hurt the employee's feelings, they fear an argument, or they just do not feel comfortable discussing the individual's shortcomings. If the employee has not performed as well as expected or hoped, this is not necessarily a poor reflection on the manager. If someone's performance has been below standards, managers owe it to the employee, the organization, and themselves to inform the employee.

How do I End the Meeting on a Positive Note?

Encouragement. At the conclusion of the performance appraisal meeting, which also marks the end of one performance appraisal cycle and the beginning of the next, your job is to encourage. Motivate the employee to continue doing that, which makes a contribution or positive behaviours, and offer suggestions in areas where there is room for growth. Even if the employee's appraisal has not been as high as he/she expected, reinforce positive results and provide support in professional development. Look for small "wins".

Discussing the employee's professional development plan is an excellent opportunity to express support by letting the employee know that you are willing to invest time and the organization's training dollars in the employee's growth in the company. The performance management process is actually the organization's best retention tool. Let them know that you believe in them and their ability to improve. Your willingness to work with and invest in them is a wonderful turnaround tool to effect an attitude adjustment.

Why is the Process so Important?

The late Mason Haire is often quoted for the truism: "that which gets measured gets done". Managers will begin to see how they can use the process to obtain greater productivity and retention from their employees. Managers are held accountable for business results, as well as for retention of their people. But it is the process of having effective communications, clarifying expectations and encouraging professional development that provides the most value for both parties. Conducting an effective, thoughtful and skilled performance appraisal should be part of every management toolkit and not an HR paperwork program or once per year average-merit raise excuse.

Sources

"Performance Appraisals with More Gain, Less Pain," Harvard Management Communication Letter, March 2003.

Penguin Human Resources Consulting.

Tim Connor, Connor Resource Group, February 22, 1999.

"Employee Development", Human Resources Management in Canada, Prentice-Hall Canada.

Seven Ways to Improve Performance Appraisals

Well-designed appraisal systems can strengthen good relationships between supervisors and employees.

Performance appraisal interviews are the discussions everyone loves to hate. Supervisors resist doing appraisals because they take too long, are poorly designed or just because the supervisor feels uncomfortable giving feedback to employees. When done poorly, appraisals don't provide the information employees need to improve their performance, and both they and the organization suffer.

The Americans with Disabilities Act and the Civil Rights Act have increased the risks of having a poor appraisal system. Now is a good time to take another look at your system. If it's not working, the seven guidelines that follow should help you develop a system that supervisors and employees will understand and use—they might even like it, but don't count on it.

1. A Collaborative Approach

If both supervisors and employees help develop the appraisal system, they are likely to endorse it. To manage such a consensus approach, a consultant or senior human resource professional can guide a group of no more than 25 supervisors and employees through the following steps:

Step 1: Group members first discuss the goals they want to achieve and the problems they want to avoid with a new appraisal system. When they are finished, the group's leader will have a list of the desired benefits and concerns. Based on the factors the group identifies, they can then write the general sections of the appraisal form.

Step 2: The group must then identify the dimensions of performance they want to evaluate. This begins with brainstorming a list of possibilities—perhaps as many as 50. The list is trimmed to include only those performance dimensions that are directly observable, behavioral and job-related. Subjective personal traits such as maturity, personality and attitude are eliminated.

Working in small groups, participants prepare written definitions of the final performance dimensions. These definitions are then included on the appraisal form as organizational performance standards.

Step 3: In the final step, the group prepares guidelines for implementation of the new system. These guidelines must support the objectives and reflect the concerns identified in the first step. For example, the need for feedback, employee development and planning future goals are balanced with the desire for a less bureaucratic process. These factors are incorporated as the group decides which objectives to stress, how often to complete the forms, who will receive copies and how formal the process will be.

The collaborative approach has several advantages. First, the appraisal system is likely to be accepted and endorsed by both supervisors and employees since it was created by their peers. Second, the actual appraisal form will probably be more meaningful and appropriate since it directly reflects the objectives of their peers. In addition, performance dimensions are tailored to the organization and are clearly defined in appropriate terms. The policies and procedures take into account organizational objectives and concerns.

The primary disadvantage is that the group may develop a poor system that does not represent the wishes of the entire organization. However, a competent leader can ensure that the system is high-quality by carefully guiding the group.

In large organizations, it is best to work with several groups, each drawn from a different department. All groups will likely raise similar objectives and propose similar sections for the appraisal form. There is usually considerable overlap; however, each department may define performance dimensions differently. This leads to an organization-wide appraisal form with the same basic sections and policies, but with slight variations in performance dimensions.

2. Clear Objectives

Formal performance appraisal systems invariably support two objectives that compete with one another during the appraisal process. The first is to provide feedback to employees so they can develop themselves and improve their performance. The second is to document performance and to communicate and support administrative decisions about salary increases, promotions, transfers and so on.

A key to more effective appraisal systems is to focus on only one of these objectives at a time in separate interviews. Supervisors can conduct interviews to improve employee performance as often as necessary for the benefit of employees, supervisors and the organization as a whole. In addition to these interviews, supervisors can conduct annual salary reviews to sum up the year's performance and discuss administrative decisions based on that performance.

3. Focus on Observable Behavior

Although the discussion between supervisor and employee is the most important step in the appraisal process, supervisors are seldom trained to handle these discussions. The key to effective interviews is for employees to understand and use the feedback to develop themselves and improve their performance. Employees can't do that if the feedback from their supervisors isn't clear.

Useful feedback is behavioral, not personal. It is specific, directly observable and clearly job-related. Only two topics meet these criteria—results and performance.

Supervisors and employees are aware of the results employees achieve. Records will show whether employees are above or below sales quotas, whether the software they write meets user needs and so on. If supervisors see employees working, they can also observe how employees perform specific job responsibilities. Employees may supervise staff poorly, they may communicate well, follow safety policies or argue with co-workers and customers.

These observed behaviors can be discussed, and supervisors and employees can make plans to improve both performance and results.

4. Avoid Personal Feedback

Almost all appraisal forms contain a section on "employee strengths and weaknesses", in which supervisors comment on the personal aptitudes and qualities that contribute to or interfere with an employee's job performance. In addition, many forms ask supervisors to rate employees on personal traits such as maturity, attitude and personality.

Many problems arise when supervisors give employees this type of feedback. Employees often become defensive when they receive general, personal comments like, "you rate only 3 on a 5-point scale of maturity", or "you have poor interpersonal skill". Employees often disagree with the supervisor's ratings because the characteristic being evaluated is not directly observed.

Supervisors do not see initiative, attitude, maturity or even job knowledge and interpersonal skill; but instead they see a large number of individual behaviors from which they infer these traits and aptitudes. Supervisors who evaluate their employees in these vague, subjective terms may find themselves in court defending their performance appraisals against charges of EEO violations and discrimination against women and minorities.

5. Listen First, Talk Later

Many supervisors dislike appraisal interviews because they feel like a punitive parent sitting in judgment of their employees. An obvious way to avoid this top-down style is to encourage employees to talk about their own performance before giving feedback. Most employees are aware of what they do well at work (positive feedback), and what they want or need to do better (areas of improvement). Supervisors can always add positive feedback not already raised by the employee and areas for improvement later in the interview.

To ensure that employees are prepared to talk about their own performance, supervisors can schedule the performance appraisal interview ahead of time. They can ask employees to prepare for the meeting by considering their performance and results and by setting work goals and developmental plans.

6. Be Positive First, Negative Later

To keep performance appraisal interviews constructive and to minimize employees' defensiveness, supervisors can begin with the positive points employees raise about their performance and results. When asked to discuss their own performance (instead of being graded on a score card), employees often raise not only the positives but also their own weaknesses, and they often have ideas for how they can improve their performance.

7. Probe First, Prescribe Later

One final step is essential to make the performance appraisal interview as effective as possible. The discussion must conclude with specific plans to develop the employee and improve his or her performance and results.

Supervisors can help employees do a better job only by analyzing the employees' personal aptitudes, skills and qualities; as well as their knowledge, attitude, motivation, work methods, the work environment (including the quality of leadership, direction and feedback from the supervisor), and even personal problems outside work. The only way to improve employee performance and results is to deal with these causes.

The best source of this information is the employee. Supervisors record results and observe performance, but they can only make intelligent guesses about the causes. Employees can tell supervisors with certainty that they lack skill and need a course, that they are weak in product knowledge, that they are relying on work methods five years out of date, that they are bored with the job, that the supervisor is not giving them enough direction and feedback or that they are facing a personal crisis at home. In short, to help employees develop themselves and improve their performance and results, supervisors must learn from them. The secret is to ask questions.

The fact is, most people are aware of what they do well at work and what they need to improve. If given the opportunity, they will constructively criticize their own performance and make plans for improvement.

15

Employee Retention

How to Attract, Motivate & Retain Good Employees?

Today, we are faced with a greater challenge than ever before. It's not the changing vehicle technology, insurer relationships, or even equipment and products we use, but it is the immediate need for quality people to enter our industry so that we have the human resources to repair vehicles.

Does this opening sum up what we are facing in the automotive service industry? Most will agree that this is a critical concern for today and beyond. However, this statement was made at a national industry meeting in 1988!

The problem is we have a tendency to talk about it, complain about it, and sometimes worry about it, but in the end, we do very little about it. At times we may even feel that there is nothing we can do. But in reality, there is a great deal we can all do to improve this picture. It is our problem, and it is also our responsibility to fix it.

We are not Alone

Does it help that these problems of personnel shortages and such are not just limited to our industry? Just about every skilled trade faces the same crisis. We are in a heated competition with other industries to attract new people to automotive service. But many still don't realize it.

There are staggering statistics about the number of technicians who leave our industry each year. The following statistics are based on the collision repair industry. In 2004, the I-CAR Education Foundation Survey found:

9.1 per cent (17,895) of technicians left the industry.

15.3 per cent (30,289) of technicians changed employers.

The average age of a technician was 37.8.

Less than 1 per cent of technicians are female.

It is pretty disconcerting to see more than 17,000 technicians out of 197,965 leave our industry entirely.

Where Do New Employees Come From?

Most of our new hires come from "raiding" the competition. In fact, we should get a national award for recycling! In some areas of the country, it is like musical chairs every month or quarter. Certainly another concern is that we are all pulling from the same pool, which is almost exclusively male. There is no truth to the opinion that it requires a male to perform the repairs on vehicles today. Even in the collision or heavy mechanical industries, brute strength is not a requirement. More than 95 per cent of work done on a vehicle can be performed by any trained person—male or female.

Another important consideration is that all the vocational schools combined in the United States produce approximately 6,300 students to enter our industry on an annual basis. The vocational system only filled about 37 per cent of the openings created by people leaving the industry. To attract and recruit new employees, you must become actively involved in your vocational system if there is one. If you don't, who will?

Perception...Reality?

I have taught a number of seminars on this very subject and always ask the audience with a show of hands how many have children. I ask them to keep their hands up while I continue to ask, "How many of you have children who are entering the industry?" In almost all cases, the number of remaining hands dwindles to only a few.

There is no easy solution to this. But for our industry to survive, we must be able to continue the family-owned business entity and pass on both technical and management skills.

Attracting Good Candidates

To attract good candidates, your company's presentation must also be considered. Presentation refers to how your business looks, runs and feels to an outsider. Do you have the appearance of a state-of-the-art mechanical or collision repair facility? Or does the dust, grease and clutter present a stereotypical picture of our industry?

Another important component in attracting good candidates is to always be looking. Don't wait until a crisis forces you to hire the first person who can fog up a mirror. Evaluate your workforce monthly and determine its strengths and weaknesses.

Career or Temp Job?

Part of motivating and retaining good employees is distinguishing between whether a position you have is a career or a temporary job. If you don't know which it is, it will certainly be unclear to your employee as well.

Many studies show the No. 1 reason employees leave a position is that they didn't feel they knew what was expected of them. There is a saying I use often—I call it the "Law of Communication":

> If you don't tell someone what you want, it's likely it won't be what you expect.
>
> If you don't write down what you want, it's likely no one will remember the same.
>
> If you don't train for what you want, it's likely no one will know how.
>
> If you don't have incentives tied in, it's likely no one will have time to do it.

Richard Flint has a good definition of communication: "If both participants do not understand the same thing...it is not communication." Simply put, do you provide a clear path for candidates/new hires to understand their role and expectations within your company? Most do it by verbal communication and believe that is sufficient. As the Law of Communication says, you will not get the results you expect consistently.

For technicians in the collision industry, there is a national mentorship program available through Mentor@Work that I highly recommend. The key difference between a mentorship program and an apprenticeship program is that the latter is usually managed by an association or governmental body. The mentorship program is an internal program designed for your business.

A good mentorship program outlines the technical skills and tasks needed for each position of the collision or mechanical repair industries. It also trains and manages the mentors and their relationship to apprentices. This is a key component since many previous mentorships failed because the skills needed to manage, train and coach an apprentice were not skills our best techs possessed (or were even interested in obtaining).

Human Resource Management

In addition to a mentorship, the need for implementing more human resource management procedures into the business is often found during my visits to shops worldwide. Many shop owners and managers today are simply "promoted" technicians. They have not received adequate training on business or human resource management except through the "School of Hard Knocks". This can certainly be an expensive method.

It is important to manage your people. Managers should be trained in important human resources areas. One that is critical is employee evaluations and appraisals. How often do you evaluate your employees formally? I have seen many business owners evaluate employees only when they are about to "fire" them.

Pay Systems and Benefits

Benefits are also a vital consideration in attracting and retaining good people into our industry, but many shop owners/managers think it is strictly the paycheck. Research done many times over has proven this otherwise. Benefits also have become an extremely critical concern for businesses, especially in regard to health care costs.

When asked, almost all staff members who left the repairer ranks say the reason they left was for a better work environment and benefits.

There are a number of programs out there that can put money back into the employee's pockets, which have minimal costs to you as the employer. They include:

Pre-tax cafeteria plans for medical and child care expenses.

Medical discount plans (not health insurance but discounted services).

All of these can reduce costs to the employees, which translates to more disposable income.

The tool reimbursement programs actually reduce the company's expenses as well. I suggest you research tool reimbursement programs. There is a good informational web site at www.toolreimbursement.net that provides a clear understanding of how it can be beneficial, both in costs and retaining good employees.

ASA offers two benefit providers—Pro-Check National and Solutions Now!—that provide tool reimbursement programs. Both companies provide ASA members with special pricing on their tool expense reimbursement programs.

One important and underutilized benefit is training. We have analyzed facilities worldwide, and too often the commitment to training is more of a verbal one. Companies say they "train their employees", but when their training is reviewed it is not supported with actual expenses. In other words, I often see less than .5 per cent of sales budgeted for employee training.

Employee performance evaluations, pay plan, incentive system, training and benefits combine to attract, motivate and retain employees. Along with clear communication and a good company presentation, this will certainly improve your market area and organization. What's stopping you?

Eight Steps Retention Tips

1. Determine what motivates your individual employees. For most employees, money is not the key issue; relationships, fulfillment and recognition are.

2. Notice how much recognition an employee needs. Some employees can go years without praise, whereas others will leave after six months.

3. Understand that many employees are motivated by their social network at work. Encourage activities that make your employees feel like valued members of a team.

4. Realize that incentives don't have to be huge. A surprise gift certificate for the local ice cream parlor in the weekly paycheck will generate positive feelings.

5. Make benefits more accessible. If your company reimburses tuition for college courses, have a college administrator come to your company so employees can find out about classes and programs.

6. Consider telecommuting, job sharing and other flexible working arrangements.

7. Offer profit sharing incentives to encourage longevity.

8. Create clear career paths at the company.

Ten Ways to Attract and Retain Great Employees

Today, more and more organizations are changing the way they view and pay their employees. The move is away from the traditional "cost-of-doing-business" concept. Successful businesses are developing creative programs to guide employees to focus on improving business performance and rewarding them for their contributions. Unfortunately, many businesses and employees are still not ready to make the change.

In today's business environment, clearly the long-term winners will be companies that provide a flexible and challenging work environment, along with employee recognition and rewards. Organizations have to be willing to share their successes. If employees are asked to share the risks, then they have to share the rewards.

What do Employees Really Want?

In our work as consultants we often discuss what owners and employees think are the key motivating factors. Most business owners initially think money is the key issue. However, many employees state that they are looking for challenges, recognition, and empowerment.

Despite the current softness in the economy and the rise in the unemployment rate, the shortage of skilled insurance workers is still restraining growth for many agencies. Given this environment, what can a firm do to retain and attract the best and brightest employees, while challenging them to achieve the business' goals?

First, recognize that money, by itself, will not do it. High performing employees are searching for something more than just a high salary. The typical employee compensation plan should include a total package of rewards, recognition and environment. Some of the elements are "satisfiers" that allow a firm to attract and retain employees such as benefits, flex-time and training. Other elements of compensation are "motivators" such as bonuses, incentives, challenge and opportunity. A well-designed plan will have long-term and short-term compensation components.

The key to attracting and retaining the best people to the firm is the use of a "total compensation" approach. A firm that takes the time to carefully customize a "total compensation" package will transform individual employees into high performing, and committed employees.

There are three basic ingredients to the total compensation package that every agency must have:

(1) **Challenging Work.** The old system of directing and monitoring every task that an employee performs is out. Employees with multiple skills and authority are in. For example, a major retailer has a one-paragraph employee handbook that states: "Rule #1: Use your judgment in all situations. There will be no additional rules." To truly perform at this level requires enormous trust in the employees.

However, if a business is able to perform at this level it will reach incredible heights.

Provide additional opportunities for learning and skill development to spice work up. Encourage the staff to take classes to get licensed and for courses to earn the necessary CEUs. But, an expansion of training could provide more flexibility through a higher skilled workforce. Send the employees to Dale Carnegie, Microsoft software training, business skills seminars, team building sessions or a sales class.

(2) **Work Environment.** Today's workforce is looking for flexibility on the job and balance in their life. Management needs to evaluate ways to realistically provide this sought after flexibility in work. For example, tradition has it that the employees' work in an office with established work hours. Could the firm allow for variations, such as 4-day workweeks, working at home two days a week or job sharing? Flexible work hours are becoming a common tool to attract and retain good employees.

(3) **Recognition and Rewards.** Non-cash recognition awards are a very effective way to reinforce the agency's values. They can be a low-cost, high-impact element of the total compensation package. For example, employees who provide outstanding or innovative customer service receive special awards. One way is for employees to be nominated by customers or their peers.

Management needs to think about the types of awards that make sense for employees. Here are some examples:

- Provide a day off with pay.
- Provide tickets for sports, music or cultural events.
- Take out an advertisement in the local newspaper thanking your employees for their contributions.
- Provide a donation in an employee's name to the charity of his or her choice.
- Pay for tutoring for the winner's child.
- Have the winner's car detailed during work.
- Pay for the winner's house to be cleaned.

- Pay for an evening out for the winner and their spouse—dinner and babysitting.

Once the basic ingredients are established, the firm can then look into advanced tools to attract and retain employees. The following are some of the approaches that owners should also consider:

(4) **Profit sharing.** Although money is not always king, it still has a lot of clout. Firms that establish a bonus plan based on the business profitability will have employees that strive to increase sales and cut expenses. Profit sharing can be based on the profitability of the overall business or by profit centers such as commercial lines versus personal lines versus life and health. The pool of bonus money can then be distributed to the staff based on management's discretion.

A variation of profit sharing is to reduce the employees' base compensation while providing quarterly bonuses based on a department's performance. A plan that tracks employee performance will then allow them to see a direct correlation between their effort and their compensation.

(5/6) **Phantom Stock and Stock Appreciation Rights.** Stock Appreciation Rights (SARs) and phantom stock are both specialized deferred compensation techniques designed to provide an employee with the economic benefits of stock ownership without the employee actually owning any company stock. When an owner cannot or will not change the existing ownership structure, SARs and phantom stock are often used, to provide an employee with some sort of incentive compensation based on the actual business performance.

A SAR is simply a grant to an employee which gives that person a right, at some specific time in the future, to receive a cash award equal to the appreciation in value of a certain number of shares of company stock. In concept, SARs are similar to stock options, but different in several points. Stock options require the employee to purchase the company's stock at the grant price. However, SARs do not require a cash outlay from the employee. The employee only receives the appreciation in value of the stock.

Phantom stock on the other hand can be viewed as units of value, which directly correspond to an equivalent number of shares of company stock. These phantom stock units are then granted to an employee for a specific period of time. When the maturity period is reached, the employee is then compensated directly in cash, based on the value of the phantom stock. Unlike SARs, the amount of compensation with phantom stock usually includes the underlying value of the stock as well as any appreciation above the grant price. Another difference is that SARs are typically paid out when the employee chooses to exercise the SAR, while phantom stock typically has a fixed award date.

(7) **Deferred Compensation.** Deferred compensation is a method for producers to build long-term value for their efforts directly related to their books of business. We recommend using deferred compensation instead of ownership in the producer's book of business. The plan is often phased in over time until the producer is fully vested in the plan.

The agency benefits by having a system that encourages the producers to build their books as well as remain with the firm. It must be noted that a deferred compensation plan (as well as SARs and phantom stock) creates a contingent liability for the firm, which does negatively affect agency value. However, deferred comp is also "consideration," which helps uphold the covenant not-to-compete in a producer contract.

(8) **Split-dollar Life Policies.** A split-dollar plan is a way to provide life insurance for an employee or their spouse at a reduced cost to that individual. The premium for the insurance is shared by the employee and his or her employer (thus the name "split-dollar").

It is an effective way to retain key employees while the business is reimbursed for every dollar it advances. From the employer's perspective, split-dollar is an inexpensive method of buying life insurance for any personal or business needs of select employees. It enhances employee loyalty by providing substantial insurance benefits. Some split-dollar policies can provide funds which may be used for additional employee benefits in the future (deferred compensation, salary continuation, stock redemption, or retirement income).

From the employee's perspective, split-dollar can help replace needed family income that would be lost at the employee's death or help pay any estate taxes. If the employee owns the policy and collaterally assigns the policy to the employer, the employer can borrow against the cash value to the extent allowed by the collateral assignment form.

(9) **ESOPs.** Employee Stock Ownership Plans (ESOPs) are a way for business owners to sell shares in the company or to provide an additional benefit to all qualified company employees. These plans were initially created as a win-win for business owners and employees. ESOP contributions are tax deductible as are dividends if they are paid to employees directly, on their behalf to the ESOP or applied to the loan payments of a leveraged plan. Because the ESOP is funded with pre-tax dollars, the company's tax savings may increase even further.

The selling shareholder can also defer the capital gains on stock sold to an ESOP as long as the ESOP owns 30 per cent or more of the company's stock and the seller rolls over the sale proceeds into qualified replacement property (stocks or bonds of domestic companies). Employees pay no tax on the contributions until they are entitled to receive the stock when they leave the company or retire. At this point, the company generally buys back the stock through a buyback provision in the ESOP.

ESOPs are expensive to set up and maintain. Businesses need to be a certain size before it makes financial sense. We recommend that agency owners do their homework before seriously considering this option.

(10) **Stock Equity.** Stock ownership usually conjures up visions of importance and respect. Producers and employees feel that having the word "Owner" on their business card will improve sales and stature. Often the employees only understand the benefits of stock ownership and the drawbacks are ignored or not understood.

Agency owners are often unclear themselves whether or not they should offer stock to an employee. They usually first think about it either when a current employee is about to walk out the door and may not come back. Owners might often feel that they are forced to offer stock in order to entice a new producer to join the firm or to retain the employee, such as a producer with a book of business.

We recommend that owners think long and hard before offering stock to an employee. The decision whether or not to make an employee an owner needs to be based on a review of many factors. The right decision can propel the agency forward for many years to come. The wrong decision can mire the firm in unimportant muck.

A Final Thought

A good principle to follow is that if you want outstanding results, you need to be prepared to pay outstanding rewards. Implementation of a "total compensation" plan will motivate employees to improve not only their own performance but the performance of the firm as well.

Employee Recruiting and Retention

These training resources will help your organization hire and retain the quality people needed for organizational success.

Recruitment

Hiring the right person for the job can be easy—if you know how. Effective interviewing takes skill and knowledge. Selection decisions shouldn't be left to a hunch or a gut feeling. A variety of interviewing training programs are included in this recruitment and retention directory.

Retention

Retaining your employees, especially your high-performing employees, can be challenging in this fast-paced employment world. Help your organization retain seasoned employees through communicating support and appreciation with the help of these training programs and resources.

When your new employee starts the job, it takes him/her a while to adjust to new surroundings, new rules and new expectations. Begin your successful retention efforts with a proper orientation. New employee orientation efforts can help new team members feel more at home and let them know what others expect of them.

Attracting and Retaining Talent

We have observed a rapidly-growing trend by leadership in every industry to attract and retain good people who are capable of creating and maintaining a very competitive, creative, and cutting-edge culture.

After two decades of corporate downsizing, middle-management layoffs, merger-mania, and hostile take-overs, companies in every industry are waking up to the reality that they must make the management and motivation of their employees their number one strategic priority—or risk falling behind the competition!

Organizations are investing more time, energy, talent and dollars in this area than ever before—and with good cause. Obviously, without a responsive, top-notch workforce, it is impossible for management to fully execute and sustain a strategic plan. Without your people enthusiastically supporting your goals, your plan is likely to remain just that: a plan, and not a reality. Those who decline to invest in those areas mentioned above are certainly destined to pay even higher costs in the future. Today's workers are an entirely new breed: more demanding, more diverse, more technically astute, and less likely than workers of a generation ago to believe that the employer has their best interests at heart. They obviously want fair compensation. They know what they're worth and they're going to get it somewhere. However, that isn't all they want. Today's employees expect more than a job and a paycheck:

- they expect meaningful work;
- they expect to be challenged;
- they want to see the "big picture" and know where they fit in;
- they require expectations and guidance;
- they want to contribute;

- they demand feedback;
- they crave ongoing training (education).

These are just a few of the many demanding expectations you must meet if you want to attain the services of today's applicants.

In response to client requests, AchieveMax® has created a 20-point checklist of Productive Culture Requirements.

First, leadership and middle-management define, discuss, and then rate their organization on each element of the checklist. After arriving at average scores, they brainstorm to identify areas of immediate concern and develop action plans to address each area.

Several clients have admitted that they were quite surprised at many of the areas identified for improvement and even more surprised at some of their actual scores. Plans are now being made to ask front-line employees to rate the elements.

This feedback will not only provide targeted feedback for future action plans but will also send a message to employees of concern and action on behalf of leadership. This is just one of several steps your organization can take in attracting and retaining talent.

Employee Engagement Survey Program

The Employee Engagement Survey Program measures your company's retention health to provide a clear picture of strengths and opportunities for development. The program has two main components:

1. Employee Engagement Survey. Program participants complete this on-line survey, which measures organizational systems, climate/culture factors, and managerial behaviors that impact retention, including:

- Organizational systems
- Group/departmental factors
- Management practices
- Overall employee satisfaction

- The likelihood employees will leave your company within the next twelve months.

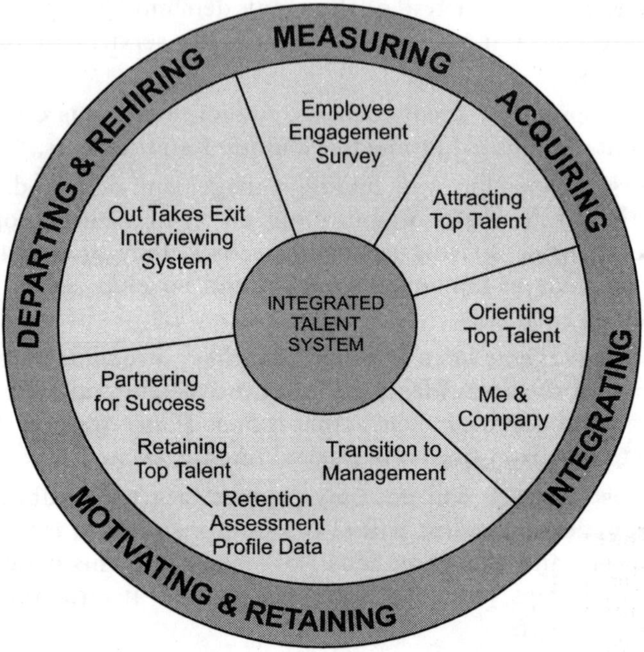

2. Retention Profile Report. ITS analyzes the survey results to produce a report that identifies your organization's attrition vulnerabilities and strengths and provides general and specific recommendations for improving employee retention.

Demographic information gathered in the survey is used to focus recommendations on those employee populations most in need of intervention. Reported findings and recommendations address:

- Current state of retention health
- Key retention risk factors
- Status of existing organizational systems
- Recommended strategies for improvement.

Supplementary Program Components can be used to enhance the analysis, findings and recommendations presented in the Retention Profile Report:

- Focus Groups for specific departments or populations to explore why those employees stay with or leave the company; early warning signals that have been observed; and retention best practices currently in use.
- An Organizational Systems Review to assess the strengths and potential vulnerabilities of existing systems for: recruitment and hiring, orientation and assimilation, performance management, learning and professional growth, career development, quality of work/life balance, and compensation and benefits.
- Review and analysis of exit interview data, gathered either with the Out Takes™ Exit Interviewing Service or via your organization's existing HR processes.

Out Takes Exit Interviewing System

The Out Takes Exit Interviewing System provides continuous tracking of the root causes of unwanted attrition at your company, to reveal attrition trends and the reasons behind them, and to help direct organizational efforts to increase employee commitment.

The Out Takes Exit Interviewing System has three primary components as well as an optional Re-recruiting Protocol:

1. **Out Takes On-line Exit Interview.** As part of your organization's exit process, departing employees complete this on-line survey anywhere from three to nine months following their departure. This standardized interview collects valuable data about employee demographics, job conditions and organizational systems, the departing employee's manager, your organization's culture, and the new employer. ITS can customize the standard interview content to meet your unique organizational requirements.

2. **Data Collection and Compilation.** Out Takes data collection is managed by the ITS service bureau. Depending on the level of detail needed to meet your diagnostic needs, ITS can compile your data by division/department, level of responsibility, length of tenure, and/or other demographic specifications most relevant to your retention goals.
3. **Out Takes Retention Reports.** The ITS service bureau generates Out Takes reports whenever you need them—monthly, quarterly, annually, or as required. Out Takes reports include:
   - A summary of the most critical retention factors impacting your organization.
   - Survey results organized by retention factor, with overall and item-level results for each factor.
   - The top reasons why departed employees have left your organization.
   - New employer data.
   - Analysis and recommendations from our Senior Retention Consultants on changes or enhancements to existing organizational systems or management practices.

Out Takes Re-recruiting Protocol

An increasing number of employees who have voluntarily terminated their employment are discovering that the grass isn't always greener on the other side. The Out Takes Re-recruiting Protocol allows you to augment your existing recruiting efforts by targeting these potential "boomerangers" for re-recruitment into your organization.

Linked to the Out Takes on-line exit interview, the Re-recruiting Protocol asks former employees if they are interested in returning to your company. If they are interested, the on-line re-recruiting process collects relevant data on the former employee's work history and current contact information; asks the former employee specific questions on their skill set and their interest in specific positions or career paths; and identifies what it would take for them to return to the organization.

Cost of Employee Turnover

The following is a comprehensive checklist of items to include when calculating the cost of turnover in any organization. To determine the costs, have the hourly and weekly cost of fully loaded payroll costs (i.e. salary plus benefits) of the vacant position, the management staff, the recruitment staff and others as outlined below.

It should be noted that the costs of time and lost productivity are no less important or real than the costs associated with paying cash to vendors for services such as advertising or temporary staff. These are all very real costs to the employer.

These calculations will easily reach 150 per cent of the employees annual compensation figure. The cost will be significantly higher (200% to 250% of annual compensation) for managerial and sales positions.

To put this into perspective, let's assume the average salary of employees in a given company is $50,000 per year. Taking the cost of turnover at 150 per cent of salary, the cost of turnover is then $75,000 per employee who leaves the company. For the mid-sized company of 1,000 employees who has a 10 per cent annual rate of turnover, the annual cost of turnover is $7.5 million!

Do you know any CEO who would not want to add $7.5 million to their revenue? And, by the way, most of that figure would be carried over to the profit line as well. What about the company with 10,000 employees? The cost of turnover equals $75 million!

Here is the list:

Costs Due to a Person Leaving

1. Calculate the cost of the person(s) who fills in while the position is vacant. This can be either the cost of a temporary or the cost of existing employees performing the vacant job as well as their own. Include the cost at overtime rates.

2. Calculate the cost of lost productivity at a minimum of 50 per cent of the person's compensation and benefits cost for each week the position is vacant, even if there are people performing the work. Calculate the lost productivity at 100 per cent if the position is completely vacant for any period of time.

3. Calculate the cost of conducting an exit interview to include the time of the person conducting the interview, the time of the person leaving, the administrative costs of stopping payroll, benefit deductions, benefit enrollments, COBRA notification and administration, and the cost of the various forms needed to process a resigning employee.

4. Calculate the cost of the manager who has to understand what work remains, and how to cover that work until a replacement is found. Calculate the cost of the manager who conducts their own version of the employee exit interview.

5. Calculate the cost of training your company has invested in this employee who is leaving. Include internal training, external programs and external academic education. Include licenses or certifications the company has helped the employee obtain to do their job effectively.

6. Calculate the impact on departmental productivity because the person is leaving. Who will pick up the work, whose work will suffer, what departmental deadlines will not be met or delivered late. Calculate the cost of department staff discussing their reactions to the vacancy.

7. Calculate the cost of severance and benefits continuation provided to employees who are leaving that are eligible for coverage under these programs.

8. Calculate the cost of lost knowledge, skills and contacts that the person who is leaving is taking with them out of your door. Use a formula of 50 per cent of the person's annual salary for one year of service, increasing each year of service by 10 per cent.

9. Calculate the cost impact of unemployment insurance premiums as well as the time spent to prepare for an unemployment hearing, or the cost paid to a third party to handle the unemployment claim process on your behalf.

10. Calculate the cost of loosing customers that the employee is going to take with them, or the amount it will cost you to retain the customers of the sales person, or customer service representative who leaves.

11. Subtract the cost of the person who is leaving for the amount of time the position is vacant.

Recruitment Costs

1. The cost of advertisements (from a $200.00 classified to a $5,000.00 or more display advertisement); agency costs at 20-30 per cent of annual compensation; employee referral costs of $500.00-$2,000.00 or more; internet posting costs of $300.00-$500.00 per listing.

2. The cost of the internal recruiter's time to understand the position requirements, develop and implement a sourcing strategy, review candidates backgrounds, prepare for interviews, conduct interviews, prepare candidate assessments, conduct reference checks, make the employment offer and notify unsuccessful candidates. This can range from a minimum of 30 hours to over 100 hours per position.

3. Calculate the cost of a recruiter's assistant who will spend 20 or more hours in basic level review of resumes, developing candidate interview schedules and making any travel arrangements for out of town candidates.

4. The cost of the hiring department (immediate supervisor, next level manager, peers and other people on the selection list) time to review and explain position requirements, review candidates background, conduct interviews, discuss their assessments and select a finalist. Also include their time to do their own sourcing of candidates from networks, contacts and other referrals. This can take upwards of 100 hours of total time.

5. Calculate the administrative cost of handling, processing and responding to the average number of resumes considered for each opening at $1.50 per resume.

6. Calculate the number of hours spent by the internal recruiter interviewing internal candidates along with the cost of

those internal candidates to be away from their jobs while interviewing.

7. Calculate the cost of drug screens, educational and criminal background checks and other reference checks, especially if these tasks are outsourced. Don't forget to calculate the number of times these are done per open position as some companies conduct this process for the final 2 or 3 candidates.

8. Calculate the cost of the various candidate pre-employment tests to help assess candidates' skills, abilities, aptitude, attitude, values and behaviors.

Training Costs

1. Calculate the cost of orientation in terms of the new person's salary and the cost of the person who conducts the orientation. Also include the cost of orientation materials.

2. Calculate the cost of departmental training as the actual development and delivery cost plus the cost of the salary of the new employee. Note that the cost will be significantly higher for some positions such as sales representatives and call center agents who require 4-6 weeks or more of classroom training.

3. Calculate the cost of the person(s) who conduct the training.

4. Calculate the cost of various training materials needed including company or product manuals, computer or other technology equipment used in the delivery of training.

5. Calculate the cost of supervisory time spent in assigning, explaining and reviewing work assignments and output. This represents lost productivity of the supervisor. Consider the amount of time spent at seven hours per week for at least eight weeks.

Lost Productivity Costs

As the new employee is learning the new job, the company policies and practices, etc. they are not fully productive. Use the following guidelines to calculate the cost of this lost productivity:

1. Upon completion of whatever training is provided, the employee is contributing at a 25 per cent productivity level for the first 2-4 weeks. The cost therefore is 75 per cent of the new employees full salary during that time period.
2. During weeks 5-12, the employee is contributing at a 50 per cent productivity level. The cost is therefore 50 per cent of full salary during that time period.
3. During weeks 13-20, the employee is contributing at a 75 per cent productivity level. The cost is therefore 25 per cent of full salary during that time period.
4. Calculate the cost of coworkers and supervisory lost productivity due to their time spent on bringing the new employee "up to speed".
5. Calculate the cost of mistakes the new employee makes during this elongated indoctrination period.
6. Calculate the cost of lost department productivity caused by a departing member of management who is no longer available to guide and direct the remaining staff.
7. Calculate the impact cost on the completion or delivery of a critical project where the departing employee is a key participant.
8. Calculate the cost of reduced productivity of a manager or director who looses a key staff member, such as an assistant, who handled a great deal of routine, administrative tasks that the manager will now have to handle.

New Hire Costs

1. Calculate the cost of bring the new person on board including the cost to put the person on the payroll, establish computer and security passwords and identification cards, business cards, internal and external publicity announcements, telephone hookups, cost of establishing email accounts, costs of establishing credit card accounts, or leasing other equipment such as cell phones, automobiles, pagers.

2. Calculate the cost of a manager's time spent developing trust and building confidence in the new employee's work.

Lost Sales Costs

1. For sales staff, divide the budgeted revenue per sales territory into weekly amounts and multiply that amount for each week the territory is vacant, including training time. Also use the lost productivity calculations above to calculate the lost sales until the sales representative is fully productive. Can also be used for telemarketing and inside sales representatives.

2. For non-sales staff, calculate the revenue per employee by dividing total company revenue by the average number of employees in a given year. Whether an employee contributes directly or indirectly to the generation of revenue, their purpose is to provide some defined set of responsibilities that are necessary to the generation of revenue. Calculate the lost revenue by multiplying the number of weeks the position is vacant by the average weekly revenue per employee.

Reducing Employee Turnover

With today's baby boomer generation beginning to retire from the labor market, many companies are finding it increasingly difficult to retain employees. Turnover is becoming a serious problem in today's corporate environment. The employment culture is changing as well. It is now relatively common to change jobs every few years, rather than grow with one company throughout the employment life as was once commonplace. In addition, employees are increasingly demanding a balance between work and family life.

Turnover costs for many organizations are very high and can significantly affect the financial performance of an organization. Direct costs include recruitment, selection, and training of new people. Much time and expense go into this process. Indirect costs include such things as increased workloads and overtime expenses for coworkers, as well as reduced productivity associated with low employee morale. Estimated costs vary from organization to organization, some as low as a few hundred dollars to as high as four times the annual salary of the employee.

It has been estimated that, on average, it costs a company one-third of a new hire's annual salary to replace an employee. Therefore, at minimum wage, the cost to replace an employee is estimated at $3,700.

There are many potential causes for turnover. Area economic conditions and labor market conditions affect general turnover rates and can be very difficult to manage. However, certain causes associated with turnover in any specific job or organization can be managed. These include such things as non-competitive compensation, high stress, working conditions, monotony, poor supervision, poor fit between the employee and the job, inadequate training, poor communications, and organization practices.

For a company to develop a retention strategy, several steps must be taken. First, they must assess the current situation and measure the turnover rate in their company. Turnover is calculated simply by dividing the number of annual terminations by the average number of employees in the workforce. The average employee turnover rate is 14.4 per cent annually, according to the Bureau of National Affairs. How does your company compare?

A company must also measure the cost of turnover, develop retention strategies, and plan for some expected turnover and a changing workforce culture. Employers must recognize that quality of work life is becoming more and more important to employees.

What initial steps can be taken to reduce turnover? First, hire the right people and continue to develop their careers. Does your company have an ongoing career development program, tuition reimbursement, or skills training program? An investment in upgrading the workforce is one of the best investments a company can make when looking at long-term growth. Hiring the people that are a good "fit" with the culture of the organization—meaning that their values, principles, and goals clearly match those of the company—and then training as necessary will go a long way toward ensuring employee loyalty and retention.

Second, most companies with low turnover rates are very employee oriented. They solicit input and involvement from all employees and maintain a true "open-door" policy that avoids closed-door meetings. Employees are given an opportunity for advancement and are not micro-managed. Intrinsic rewards are critical. Employees must believe they have a voice and are recognized for their contribution. Remember that "trust" and "loyalty" are a two-way street. Does your company's culture encourage open communication and employee input?

Third, develop an overall strategic compensation package that includes not only base and variable pay scales, but long-term incentive compensation, bonus and gain-sharing plans, benefit plans to address the health and welfare issues of the employees, and non-cash rewards and perks as well. To be competitive in today's labor market, most companies find it necessary to offer a standard benefit package, including health, dental, and life insurance, vacation and leave policies, and investment and retirement plans. But what more could be done that would be cost effective toward creating an employee-oriented work environment?

Creativity in compensation and benefits can make quite a difference to the welfare of the employee. A company should assess overall employee needs when addressing retention issues.

If employee welfare is a genuine concern, what about child care? How much employee absenteeism is attributable to not having a dependable babysitter? Although the costs and liabilities involved in providing onsite day care can be prohibitive, perhaps a company could subsidize childcare in some manner. Sometimes, just negotiating rates for your employees with area childcare providers could be very helpful. Maybe some kind of a company match would be possible. Household chore assistance is another possibility that is being used by some companies.

Consider other options—such as alternative work schedules or flextime, or perhaps preventative healthcare and wellness programs such as fitness center memberships—as possible cost-effective benefits. Don't forget that perks or non-cash rewards to recognize exceptional performance can be critical. Service recognition, event tickets, trips, and public recognition can send strong messages to the public regarding company culture and values. Simply examine the issues and needs of your employees and try to develop creative programs to address these needs.

Although many costs associated with these suggestions may seem prohibitive, as well they may be, the company must evaluate the costs of current turnover, analyze the reasons for the individual organization, and develop strategies that in the long-term are less costly than continued turnover. Some of these suggestions may not be so costly in comparison.

Just a word of caution: Be fair and consistent in establishing compensation. Promote from within if possible. Attempt to avoid bringing new people on board at a higher rate than current employees. Policies to prevent discussion of wages simply do not work. Furthermore, such policies are in complete opposition of "open-door" communications.

Although many companies use contract employees to address fluctuations in business, working side by side with someone who is making twice the rate of pay without any commitment or loyalty to the company can be a real morale killer. Avoid this if at all possible!

If your company follows these steps and shows a genuine concern for the well-being of your employees, you may not have to pay the highest wages in town to have the lowest employee turnover rate.

Fighting Employee Turnover Costs

Nothing can be more frustrating to a small business owner or manager than the constant aggravation of employee turnover. High or low employee turnover can be detrimental to your company. Learn what you need to know to calculate and curtail the revolving employee exit door in your business.

Employee turnover can vary as a result of the industry and location of your business. For instance, the food service industry typically experiences turnover of 100-300%. The stress of employee turnover is much greater on smaller businesses than larger corporations. Before you can take effective measures to reduce turnover, you first need to find the price your business pays in lost employees.

Calculating Employee Turnover Cost

A general approach to calculate employee turnover cost is to use 50% to 200% of an employee's annual salary.

Another more accurate method has been developed by PricewaterhouseCoopers Saratoga Institute.

This calculation uses the cost of hiring and training new staff. We will adjust some variables to match the needs of small business.

Total employee turnover cost = Costs of hiring new employees + Costs of training new employees

Costs of Hiring New Employees

The cost to your business when hiring new employees includes the following six factors plus 10% for incidentals such as background screening:

- Advertising
- Bonus signing
- Relocation pay
- Time for interviewing
- Travel expenses
- Pre-employee assessments.

Costs of Training New Employees

- Training materials
- Technology
- Employee benefit set up
- Time for trainers.

Tips for Reducing Employee Turnover

Hire the Right Demographic: Is your small business properly recruiting the right age group? Match your company profile with your target hiring group. If you can't offer career advancement to your workforce, then avoid hiring young career oriented staff. Consider hiring older employees who are less concerned with advancement.

Understand Employee Motivation: Retaining staff requires learning what's important to your employees. Look to the external motivators like recognition and rewards. Remember the internal motivators of purpose and passion.

Read Between the Lines: The real cause of employee turnover usually won't be found in your typical exit interview. Departing employees will provide the usual response of leaving for more pay or a better job. Inquire for deeper meaning. Was it a lack of support? Was the commission structure unreasonable? Take the time to get to the bottom of the turnover.

These three tips to reduce turnover are a good start to understanding your employee loss issue. Be critical and always look inward. You may be the source of the turnover. Make certain your management style is the way you would want to be managed. High turnover can be a signal your business is in trouble. Low turnover can also be a negative.

The Price of Low Employee Turnover

You aren't immune to the costs of employee turnover because your turn rate is low. Low turnover can be a bad sign. Over 40 per cent of distressed businesses have very low employee turnover, according to a study by Getzler & Company, Inc.

Employee turnover costs impact your bottom line and the culture of your business. "The organizations that achieve the most dramatic reductions in turnover and maintain those lower levels are usually the ones where the top executive or owner makes it a priority" says F. Leigh Branham, author of "Keeping the People Who Keep You in Business: 24 Ways to Hang on to Your Most Valuable Talent." Addressing the issue rests on your shoulders.

Ten Ways to Show Appreciation to Employees and Co-workers

From Food to Favors for Employee and Co-worker Appreciation

You can tell your colleagues, co-workers and employees how much you value them and their contribution any day of the year. Trust me. No occasion is necessary. In fact, small surprises and tokens of your appreciation spread throughout the year help the people in your work life feel valued all year long.

Looking for ideas about how to praise and thank co-workers and employees? Here are ten ways to show your appreciation to employees and co-workers:

- Praise something your co-worker has done well. Identify the specific actions that you found admirable.
- Say "thank you". Show your appreciation for their hard work and contributions. And, don't forget to say "please" often as well. Social niceties do belong at work. A more gracious, polite workplace is appreciated by all.
- Ask your coworkers about their family, their hobby, their weekend or a special event they attended.
- Your genuine interest—as opposed to being nosey—causes people to feel valued and cared about.
- Offer staff members flexible scheduling for the holidays, if feasible. If work coverage is critical, post a calendar so people can balance their time off with that of their co-workers.
- Know your co-worker's interests well enough to present a small gift occasionally. An appreciated gift, and the gesture of providing it, will light up your co-worker's day.
- If you can afford to, give staff money. End of the year bonuses, attendance bonuses, quarterly bonuses and gift certificates say "thank you" quite nicely. TechSmith staff received a percentage of their annual salary for their end of year bonus.
- Almost everyone appreciates food. Take co-workers or staff to lunch for a birthday, a special occasion or for no reason at all. Let your guest pick the restaurant.

- Create a fun tradition for a seasonal holiday. ReCellular employees draw names for their Secret Santa gift exchange. Alison Doyle, About's Guide to Job Searching, also works in Career Services at Skidmore College where they do a "gift grab" at their holiday party.

LuAnn Johnson who works in Human Resources at the Schaller Anderson Mercy Care Plan says, "We celebrate Treat Tuesday, every Tuesday between Thanks giving and Christmas. We match up departments or people who don't normally work together as a unit and assign a day to provide gooey, healthy or scrumptious treats for the other groups. It's a great mixer, an opportunity to show off our culinary skills and a morale builder—to say nothing of the sugar high!"

- Bring in bagels, doughnuts or another treat for staff and co-workers. Offerings such as cookies or cupcakes, that you've baked personally, are a huge hit. (Have you tried baking cupcakes in ice cream cones? People love them.) Another hit? Bring chocolate-chocolate anything.
- Last, but not least, provide opportunity. People want chances for training and cross-training. They want to participate on a special committee where their talents are noticed. They like to attend professional association meetings and represent your organization at civic and philanthropic events.

These are my top ten ways to show appreciation to employees and coworkers. Stretch your imagination. There are hundreds of other employee and co-worker appreciation ideas just waiting to be found. They'll bring you success in employee motivation, employee recognition and in building a positive, productive workplace.

Managing Employee Emotion—Individual Reaction to Performance Feedback Messages Relating to Pay or Bonuses

Understanding self-esteem is critical in determining individual reactions to performance feedback messages.

Performance feedback messages employees receive from managers or supervisors are among the most important types of organizational communication. But what supervisors say about pay or bonuses may affect employees more than what is said in a performance review. Such feedback is designed to motivate future performance as well as recognize and reward employees for productive past behavior. However, different people rarely react in the same way to the same messages, partly because of differences in self-esteem. Understanding self-esteem is critical in determining individual reactions to performance feedback messages. Self-esteem is clearly linked to a variety of job-related behaviors, including performance, job satisfaction and interpersonal skills. Consider, for example, the following illustrations:

- Bill Porter was given significant responsibilities in an important project late last year. Traditionally, employees working on such projects have received generous bonuses when the project was completed. However, a recession and supplier problems affected some of the project outcomes. While everyone did receive a bonus, it was smaller than bonuses others had received previously. Since then, Bill has been quite depressed and has mentioned to co-workers that he felt he really let the project team down. He has confided to several close friends that he just doesn't think he has the skills and ability that are needed in his job. Yesterday, Bill told his boss that he was thinking of quitting since "he wasn't doing much good around here anyway".
- Three years ago, Julie Kandel spent 18 months completely overhauling her company's computer network system. After many 12-hour days and 60-hour weeks, she completed the job on time and under budget. Julie's manager expressed a great deal of appreciation for her performance and told her it was the best work he had seen anyone do. However, at the same annual review, Julie was recommended for what she considered a "normal" raise. Unknown to

> Julie, the department's budget, which included the merit pay pool, had been reduced. During the year since her last merit review, Julie has worked on two similar, though smaller, projects and has done a mediocre job at best. She has become reluctant to take on new responsibilities. Her manager has complained that Julie seems "really unmotivated".

Both examples involve an employee's negative reaction to a feedback message about pay.

Self-esteem affects performance

Employees with low self-esteem are particularly vulnerable to the negative feedback that occurs when their expectations about pay are not met, making it difficult for them to sustain acceptable levels of performance. Research indicates that employees with low self-esteem are generally less productive, less creative and less motivated than employees with higher self-esteem.

In addition, individuals with low self-esteem are not as skilled as those with high self-esteem in interpersonal relations or conflict resolution. Indeed, they may often try to raise their own chronically low self-esteem by creating conflict, abusing sick or personal leave policies, or directing their anger at managers or peers. Furthermore, when given a negative feedback message, individuals with low self-esteem tend to react in much more dysfunctional ways than do individuals with higher self-esteem.

Differences in self-esteem are also associated with differences in "reactance"—the ways individuals respond to situations that initially appear to be uncontrollable—and "attribution"—the ways people assign causality.

Whenever people are confronted with a performance or task situation that is viewed as unacceptable, they make some attempt to regain control over the event in order to perform as others desire or expect. Research by Joel Brockner at Columbia University, has shown that individuals with low self-esteem exhibit less of this reactance than do individuals with high self-esteem.

Therefore, employees with high self-esteem make significant efforts to improve performance and gain control over outcomes. Employees with low self-esteem do not exhibit a significant change in effort or improvement in performance; in fact, decrease in both may occur. These employees may be viewed as chronically poor performers or lacking sufficient motivation.

Alternatively, such employees may show some reactance, but in areas unrelated to performance. They may initiate conflict with others, insult the work or performance of other employees, or abuse sick or personal leave policies. Since they are unable to control the outcome of their own performance, these employees may try to build or maintain their self-esteem by seeking control over other aspects of the work situation, for example, interpersonal relations and attendance.

Individuals who differ in self-esteem also differ in how they attribute a particular outcome to external or internal causes. Individuals with high self-esteem attribute positive outcomes to internal causes and negative outcomes to external causes. They view success as a result of their own talent or effort; failure, as a consequence of events outside their control—the economy, the boss, the competition, the sales force. The result is that they maintain and protect their own self-esteem.

People with low self-esteem attribute successes to external factors: "I got lucky", "The job was easy", or "So-and-so really did all the work". To make matters worse, they attribute negative outcomes to internal causes: "I'm really not very good at my job" or "I don't know what I'm doing". By blaming themselves for negative outcomes, people with low self-esteem can maintain consistently negative perceptions of their own worth. They also believe that they lack the skills or lack the ability to "control" the situation.

Pay decisions and self-esteem

Because decisions about pay or bonuses are among the most significant feedback messages employees receive, managers need to pay special attention to two facts that complicate the sending and receiving of these powerful messages:

- Employees measure pay in both referent and absolute terms.
- Budget constraints limit resources available for merit pay, bonuses and so forth.

Employees evaluate pay increases or bonuses not only in absolute terms, but also by using referent persons or points. Referent individuals include fellow employees—and, to some extent, employees of other organizations—who are or are perceived to be similar in experience, job classification, skill, contribution to the organization and effort. Referent points include the employee's contribution to the organization, the cost of living, the state of the economy, and the financial position of the organization. When a pay decision is not consistent with employee expectations, the employee may view the decision as negative feedback regarding his or her performance.

Of course, performance-related rewards given to employees are not totally a function of individual performance. Budgets also constrain pay decisions. While employee expectations may stay constant over time, the resources available for merit pay or raises can vary from year to year, and even from quarter to quarter. If management fails to explain how resources constrain decisions, employees may view unmet expectations regarding pay as negative feedback.

Consider the first case of Bill Porter. Bill's behavior is typical for an individual with low self-esteem reacting to a negative feedback message: decreased motivation, depression and a lack of self-efficacy. But what evidence is there that Bill, or any other member of the group, was responsible for the failure of the project? Clearly the external environment—the recession and supplier problems—was the primary cause. Yet, the relatively small bonuses may have sent a failure message to group members, including Bill.

Bill's organization could have provided bonuses similar to those given in earlier years, despite the poor outcome of the project. There are situations when it may be appropriate to tie rewards to effort rather than actual performance. By doing so, organizations and managers avoid giving negative feedback to employees for performance outcomes that were beyond individual control.

In the second case, Julie Kandel also behaves in ways consistent with low self-esteem; she lacks motivation and direction, and is performing poorly. But Julie is a victim not only of her own low self-esteem but also of inconsistent feedback messages and budget constraints on pay decisions. Julie's manager, first, should have communicated clearly to Julie that her raise was more a function of the budget than of her performance. This would have helped Julie understand the pay decision and avoided the inconsistency. Second, Julie's manager could have offered other "goods", besides a higher salary, to reward her for her performance—days off, upgrades of equipment or office space, public recognition among her peers are examples. Non-monetary rewards would have provided a more consistent feedback message.

Managing Employee Reactions

Employees may respond in a variety of ways to negative feedback from pay decisions, but there are some steps that managers can take to lessen the possibility of negative outcomes.

- Take notice of the signs of low self-esteem—high needs for direction from superiors and approval from others, unwillingness to take risks or responsibilities, pointed criticism of others' behaviors and/or performance. Be particularly sensitive to the content and process of feedback messages when dealing with these employees. If possible, put your money where your mouth is.
- Phrases such as "great work", "super job", "outstanding" will be undercut by an average pay increase, because the pay message is likely to be interpreted as the most important one. Verbal strokes are important and valuable; most employees

appreciate such feedback, but the two messages should be consistent. If an employee has done a really outstanding job for an extended period of time, and has been told so, raise his or her pay.

- If pay messages are not consistent with other feedback, explain why. In many cases, there are legitimate reasons why merit pay or bonuses cannot match what an employee deserves. A simple way to deal with the inconsistency is to be honest. Tell employees through memos, one-to-one conversations, or group meetings about the constraints on pay. And tell them as soon as the problem becomes known, not during an appraisal session. If employees know beforehand that raises will be limited, they can evaluate pay feedback messages in terms of current conditions rather than those of previous years.
- Be aware of external constraints on performance. By acknowledging the many legitimate external reasons for failure, managers can help employees maintain their self-esteem.
- When pay is limited by budget constraints, consider alternative rewards—days off, increases in discretionary time or budgets to allow individuals to work on pet projects, upgrades in equipment or office space, and educational or personal development opportunities. Meaningful alternative rewards may require some thought and sacrifice by management. The reward must be something that employees will truly value and view as an acknowledgment of their performance. Otherwise, the reward may be regarded as just a ploy to buy their loyalty.
- Provide a legitimate process by which employees can challenge pay decisions. Managers are not always right and perfectly just. Mechanisms that allow employees to challenge pay decisions can give them the feedback they truly deserve.
- Remember that negative feedback is often unintended. Be aware that the same message may be

interpreted differently by different employees. Consider the individual to whom the feedback is directed and pay attention to the way the feedback is communicated.

Richard C. Ringer is a doctoral candidate at the University of Colorado, Boulder.

Talent Retention and Inculcating Loyalty

Some Facts

- Nearly 70% of organizations report that staff turnover has a negative impact.
- Approximate retention: 50% of organizations experience regular problems with employee.
- Over 50% of the people recruited into an organization will leave within 2 years.
- One in four people recruited will leave within 6 months.
- Over 70% of all employees respond to competitors' job offers during work hours?
- Voluntary resignations are at the highest level in over 20 years?
- Nearly 50% of all middle managers are either currently looking for another job or plan to do so?

Why is retention becoming one of the top issues in HR?

- The enormous cost associated with staff turnover.
- The difficulties experienced in replacing people.
- Each new recruit represents risk.
- Costs associated with training.
- The overall impact on the organizations ability to meet the needs of its customers.

Types of Talent Retention

Research Initiative

- To develop an objective understanding of issues relating to employee retention.
- Accurately diagnose the problem areas.

- Evaluate the effectiveness of retention interventions.

Issue of Retention

- Each new recruit represents risk.
- The enormous cost associated with staff turnover.
- The difficulties experienced in replacing people.
- Costs associated with training.
- The overall impact on the organizations ability to meet the needs of its customers.

Turnover Calculator

- Total cost of staff turnover.
- Total costs of recruitment.
- Total costs of training.
- Promotional Inputs.
- Average salary and expenses.
- Time to reach average performance level.

Cost of Employee Turnover

- Costs Due to a Person Leaving.
- New Hire Costs.
- Fresh Recruitment Costs.
- Fresh Training Costs.
- Lost Productivity Cost.
- Lost Sales Costs.

Rewarding Talent

- Be careful here. While rewarding good performance, once should ensure that it nourishes healthy competition.
- A manager should try to create balance while encouraging people to perform better.
- An employee's performance should be appreciated and rewarded, but in such a manner that is motivates his peers.

- It often happens that an employee is rewarded and it becomes a bone of contention between another employee and the organization.
- So don't go overboard, but also try not to be parsimonious.

Top Ten Talent Retention Tips

1. What do employees really want?
2. Work environment.
3. Challenging work.
4. Recognition and rewards.
5. Grow competencies, situationally. Look for opportunities to put people into challenging situations where their skills and competencies will grow.
6. Meet one-on-one, routinely. Conduct regular, but brief one-on-one meetings between manager/leaders and direct reports. Begin by asking, "What's on your mind?"—then listen and act.
7. Make retention everyone's responsibility. Encourage all members of the work group to feel responsible for the retention of their peers and to be alert to problems that can be fixed.
8. Be a career builder. Talk to people about their long-term career aspirations and help them use or build the skills and competencies they need for the future.
9. Help people get an "A". Give the gift of being clear about what an "A" level performance looks like.
10. Walk your talk. Be aware that people are always watching and assessing you and your actions as a leader.

Employee Retention Analysis

Retaining employees are crucial but not uncontrollable job if you are planned and ready with pros & cons. Retention manager should discus things in advance with employer to handle the situation confidently. The discussion stuff includes:

Name of employees, Date of joining, Designation, Gross Salary, Under paid/Over paid/balanced, Required level of skills, Any special skills, Punctuality, Personality, Attitude and behavior, Decision-making ability, Negotiation skills, Problem-solving techniques, Motivation ability, etc. you can put grade under each head like excellent, average or below average.

First, collect above said data with the consent of employer and prepare a list put your final grade to each of them like excellent, average or below average. For example, your employer is out of the country and on the moment he/she is not reachable and one of your excellent rank employees is going to resign or resigned but there is probability to retain him/her. This is really a crucial time for any retention manager. If you had discussed with your employer about all three segments of employees in advance then probably you could perform your job without any tension.

Then discuss with employer about all three types of employees. He/She might suggest you let them go to below average employees and he/she will give you some extra package to deal with the rest two segment and he may give the range to retain them incase they try to switch over.

You should redesign every time the package and compensation and benefits of excellent employees so that you won't give them chance to look beyond other wise there is a probability of loosing excellent employees.

16

Exit Interview

Exit Interview is a latest talent retention tool. In common parlance, exit interviews are conducted with employees leaving an organization. The purpose of the interview is to provide feedback on why employees are leaving, what they liked or didn't like about their employment and what areas of the organization they feel need improvement. Exit interviews are one of the most widely used methods of gathering employee feedback, along with employee satisfaction surveys. This is most beneficial for the employer as it is an eye-opener and a significant review to see how the company is doing. You may be surprised what you hear.

More recently, the concept of exit interviewing has been revisited and expanded as a knowledge management tool, as a way of capturing knowledge from leavers. Rather than simply capturing human resources information, the interview also aims to capture knowledge about what it takes to do the job.

In fact, anything that determines the quality of the organization, both in terms of its relationship with its staff, customers, suppliers, third-parties and the general public. Many employers ignore the opportunity that exit interviews offer, chiefly because exit interviews have not been practiced in the past, and starting them is a difficult initiative to undertake, given the potentially subjective and 'fuzzy' nature of the results; the time involved; and the unspoken corporate urge to avoid exposure to criticism. Exit interviews are nevertheless a unique chance to survey and analyze the opinions of departing employees, who generally are more forthcoming, constructive and objective than staff still in their jobs. In leaving an organization, departing employees are liberated, and as such provide a richer source of objective feedback than employed staff do when responding to normal staff attitude surveys.

As ever, corporate insecurity and defensiveness can be an obstacle to implementing exit interview processes, so if the organization finds it difficult to begin the practice as a matter of general policy, you can still undertake your own exit interviews locally with your own staff as and when they leave.

From the departing employee interviewee perspective, an exit interview is a chance to give some constructive feedback, and to leave on a positive note, with good relations and mutual respect. Recrimination, blame, revenge and spite are destructive feelings and behaviours, so resist any temptation you might have to go out all guns blazing. Be calm, fair, objective and as helpful as possible. In the future you may wish to return to the organization (situations and people change), and you may cross the paths of your ex-colleagues, managers in the future. The adage about treating people well on your way up because you might meet them on the way down applies just as well on your way out. The exit interview is an opportunity to shake hands and leave friends, not enemies.

Exit Interviews: Aims and Outcomes

- They provide an opportunity to 'make peace' with disgruntled employees, who might otherwise leave with vengeful intentions.
- Exit interviews are seen by existing employees as a sign of positive culture. They are regarded as caring and compassionate—a sign that the organization is big enough to expose itself to criticism.
- Exit interviews accelerate participating managers' understanding and experience of managing people and organizations. Hearing and handling feedback is a powerful development process.
- Exit interviews help to support an organization's proper HR practices. They are seen as positive and necessary for quality and effective people-

management by most professional institutes and accrediting bodies concerned with quality management of people, organizations and service.

- The results and analysis of exit interviews provide relevant and useful data directly into training needs analysis and training planning processes.
- Exit interviews provide valuable information as to how to improve recruitment and induction of new employees.
- Exit interviews provide direct indications as to how to improve staff retention.
- Sometimes an exit interview provides the chance to retain a valuable employee who would otherwise have left (organizations often accept resignations far too readily without discussion or testing the firmness of feeling—the exit interview provides a final safety net).
- A significant proportion of employee leavers will be people that the organization is actually very sorry to leave (despite the post-rationalization and sour grapes reactions of many senior executives to the departure of their best people). The exit interview, therefore, provides an excellent source of comment and opportunity relating to management succession planning. Good people leave often because they are denied opportunity to grow and advance. Wherever this is happening, organizations need to know about it and respond accordingly.
- Every organization has at any point in time several good people on the verge of leaving because they are not given the opportunity to grow and develop, at the same time, ironically, that most of the management and executives are overworked and stretched, some to the point of leaving too. Doesn't it therefore make good sense to raise the importance of marrying these two situations to provide advantage both ways—i.e. facilitate greater delegation of responsibility to those

who want it? Exit interviews are an excellent catalyst for identifying specific mistakes and improvement opportunities in this vital area of management development and succession.

- Exit interviews, and a properly organized, positive exit process also greatly improve the chances of successfully obtaining and transferring useful knowledge, contacts, insights, tips and experience, from the departing employee to all those needing to know it, especially successors and replacements. Most leavers are happy to help if you have the courage and decency to ask and provide a suitable method for the knowledge transfer, be it a briefing meeting, a one-to-one meeting between the replacement and the leaver, or during the exit interview itself.

Exit interviews are best conducted face-to-face because this enables better communication, understanding, interpretation, etc. and it provides far better opportunity to probe and get to the root of sensitive or reluctant feelings. However, postal or electronic questionnaires are better than nothing, if face-to-face exit interviews are not possible for whatever reason (although I remain to be convinced that there is never a proper excuse for not sitting down for 30 minutes with any departing employee...).

In some cases perhaps a particularly shy employee may prefer to give their feedback in a questionnaire form, in which case this is fine, but where possible, face-to-face is best.

In terms of managing the interview, listen rather than talk. Give the interviewee time and space to answer. Coax and reassure where appropriate, rather than pressurize. Interpret, reflect and understand (you can understand someone without necessarily agreeing). Keep calm, resist the urge to defend or argue—your aim is to elicit views, feedback, answers, not to lecture or admonish. Ask open 'what/how/why' questions, not 'closed' yes/no questions, unless you require specific confirmation about a point. 'When' and 'where' are also more specific qualifying questions, unless of course they are used in a general context rather than specific time or geographic sense?

'Who' should be used with care to avoid witch-hunts or defamatory risks. (Moreover many exit interviewees will be uncomfortable if asked to name people or allocate personal blame—exit interviews are not about 'blame', the allocation of which is not constructive and should be avoided for anything other than very serious complaints or accusations, which must then be suitably referred as follow-up would be beyond the normal exit interview remit.)

Prepare your exit interview questions and topics that you'd like to explore, especially when you believe that the interviewee has good experience, appreciation and understanding.

Take notes and/or use a prepared questionnaire form.

Remember simple planning aspects such as arranging a suitable time and place, avoiding interruptions, taking notes, preparing questions, being aware of the body-language and feelings of the interviewee and adjusting your own approach accordingly, etc.

Obviously the style of exit interview is different for someone who is being asked to leave, retiring, being made redundant, dismissed, or leaving under a cloud, compared to an employee leaving whom the organization would prefer to retain. However, everyone who leaves should be given the opportunity of an exit interview, and the organization can learn something from every situation. In certain situations (where appropriate), the exit interview also provides a last chance to change a person's mind, although this should not be the main aim of the exit interview situation.

When the interview is complete say thanks and wish the interviewee well. If there is some specific checking or follow-up to do then ensure you do it and report back accordingly. After the interview look at the answers and think properly—detached and objective—about what their meaning and implications.

Take action as necessary, depending on your processes for analysing and reporting exit interview feedback. If there's an urgent issue, or the person wants to stay and you want to keep them, then act immediately or the opportunity will be lost.

Exit Interviews: Responsibilities, Process and Outcomes

Participation in exit interviews by the employee leaving is voluntary. Do not compel departing employees to attend exit interviews. Offer a questionnaire form alternative, which again must be voluntary.

You cannot compel a departing employee to give you knowledge that is in their head, although the return of files, paperwork and material is normally something that an employer rightfully can insist happens. In any event, a positive constructive, grown-up approach is the best assurance of a happy outcome and an optimal transfer of knowledge and contact names, etc. should this be helpful, which often it will be.

If you hear any of your people using the ridiculously confrontational maxim "No-one is indispensable...", as a defence for not bothering to gather important knowledge from a departing employee it probably suggests that all opportunities for a cooperative hand-over have yet to be explored, so encourage people to explore them, or go explore them yourself.

Ideally, the organization should have a documented policy stating how exit interviews happen, when, and by whom. Some organizations hand the responsibility to a skilled interviewer in the HR or Personnel Department. Alternatively, line-managers or even supervisors can conduct the interviews. Interviewers need to be trained to interview, just as for normal job interviews. All types of interviews are sensitive emotional situations which require ability and maturity to manage properly, especially if interviewees are anxious or volatile.

In large organizations HR or Personnel Department should be responsible for designing the process, issuing guidelines and documentation, collecting results data, analysing and reporting findings, trends, opportunities and recommendations, especially including anything relating to health and safety, or employment law and liability.

If you design a questionnaire or exit interview form which will be used as an input document towards central analysis it is a good idea to convert questions wherever practicable into a 'scoreable' and/or multiple-choice format, which makes analysis far easier than lots of written opinions.

Actions resulting from exit interview feedback analysis, in any size or type of organization, fall into two categories:

- **Remedial and preventative**, for example, improving health and safety issues, stress, harassment, discrimination, etc.
- **Strategic improvement opportunities**, for example, improved induction, management or supervisory training, empowerment or team building initiatives, process improvement, wastage and efficiencies improvements, customer service initiatives, etc.

The head of HR or Personnel would normally be responsible for raising these issues with the board or CEO, and the conversion of exit interview feedback into action is a critical factor in justifying and maintaining a serious priority and operation of the process.

For many organizations, exit interviews provide a major untapped source of 'high-yield' development ideas and opportunities.

What are the Benefits?

- Vital knowledge is not lost to the organization when people leave.
- The learning curve of new people joining the organization is shortened.
- Exit interviews can be done relatively quickly and inexpensively.
- Exit interviews can result in the leaver having a more positive view of the organization.

Done correctly, exit interviews can be a win-win situation for both the organization and the leaver. The organization gets to retain a portion of the leaver's knowledge and make it available to others, while the leaver gets to articulate their unique contributions to the organization and to 'leave their mark'.

Who Benefits from an Exit Interview?

Responsible employers will use this information to improve their recruitment and retention policies. However, cynics may believe this information is solely captured incase of future litigation from the ex-employee. It's for this reason that advice differs on how to handle an exit interview well.

How do I do about it?

Traditional exit interviews can be conducted in a variety of ways: face-to-face, over the telephone, using a written questionnaire, or via the internet using an exit interview management system. In a knowledge-focused exit interview, a face-to-face interview is needed.

You will need to think carefully about the information you would like to gather before the interview and start your preparations early. While the traditional exit interview will tend to collect mainly human resources information, the primary focus of the knowledge-focused interview is on knowledge that would be helpful to the next person who will do the job or to others in the organization doing similar jobs.

Start planning the handover and exit interview as soon as you know a person is leaving. Identify who in the organization might benefit from that person's knowledge and what they will need to know. Then work out a plan to capture the leaver's knowledge during the time remaining before they leave. This should include both explicit knowledge (knowledge that is already documented such as in files and e-mails, and knowledge that can be easily documented), and tacit knowledge (knowledge that is less easy to capture and that needs to be explained or demonstrated).

In the case of explicit knowledge, make sure the leaver moves relevant files—both hard copy and electronic—into shared folders or a document library. Ask them to prune and organise these files and to create role and task folders or notes for their successor.

For tacit knowledge, you will need to interview the leaver face-to-face. Prepare for the interview by reviewing the key tasks the person does based on a job description or annual performance plan. You can then use that information as the basis for discussing how they go about those tasks, what knowledge and skills they need, any problems or pitfalls to be aware of etc. Find out about their network of contacts and sources of knowledge. If possible, create an overlap period between the leaver and their successor so that a 'live' handover can be done.

When conducting exit interviews, think carefully about who will be the interviewer. Traditional exit interviews are conducted by someone from human resources. However, this need not be the case in the knowledge-focused interview. Often a peer or a relevant subject expert will be most appropriate. Over and above the obvious interpersonal and interviewing skills needed, you will need to consider issues of trust and honesty. For example, if an employee has had a difficult relationship with a manager or colleague, that person might not be best placed to conduct the interview. Whoever you select, make sure they are appropriately skilled and trained.

Are there any Other Points I should be Aware of?

- Traditional exit interviews are usually only appropriate for employees who voluntarily resign or retire rather that those who are fired or made redundant. In the case of the knowledge-focused interview, much will depend on the extent to which the organization has a culture that encourages knowledge sharing.
- Be clear about who will use the knowledge gathered and how it will be used, before you begin to gather it; the purpose of the interview is not to gather knowledge per se, but to gather useful knowledge that will actually be used.
- The less you capture knowledge on a regular basis, the more you need to capture it at exit. However, you may decide that you could gain more value from capturing knowledge at more regular intervals. For example, The Post Office uses exit interviews as one

part of a series of 'cradle-to-grave' interviews to collect knowledge, using a method called 3E.

- The three Es are Entry, Expert and Exit. Entry interviews allow you to gather knowledge when employees first join the organization when they have 'new eyes' and a fresh perspective, and also to ask them what they would like to know to help them 'get up to speed'. Expert interviews are conducted as they develop skills and become experts in a particular role or field.

Must I Submit to an Exit Interview?

No. It's your right to decline an exit interview. A reputable employer will respect your decision. However, a not-so-reputable employer might resent that you didn't participate and file a "would not rehire" or similar adverse notation in your personnel records. The same employer might reveal the notation during a background check.

Should I Participate in an Exit Interview?

Naturally, the decision whether or not to participate in an exit interview is ultimately up to you. But there are varying opinions about whether or not you should participate. Some career experts think you should, because, although it doesn't help you much, it helps a sincere employer improve working conditions for remaining employees.

But other career experts question the usefulness of an exit interview. (A better time to conduct such a meeting is while an employee is committed, not while he or she is on the way out the door and concerned about burning a bridge.) Consequently, they don't think the risks for departing employees are worth it, so they advise against participating. Alternately, they advise participants to give "generic" responses only or at least think carefully before responding.

Besides potential bridge burning, risks for departing employees include the information falling into the wrong hands and ruining references, the employer revealing negative information during a background check, and as previously indicated, the employer submitting either positive or negative information as evidence in a lawsuit.

Some things to consider before participating in an exit interview are listed below:

- As a departing employee, will you benefit from an exit interview?
- Is the exit interview anonymous or must you sign a questionnaire or the HR rep's notes?
- Is the reason you're leaving any of the company's business or an invasion of your privacy?
- Why did your employer wait until you're leaving to ask your opinion?
- Will the HR department really use your comments for improvements or are they just trying to find out the "real" reason you're leaving?
- Might an exit interview burn a bridge, ruin a reference or cause an adverse background check for you?
- Might you sue your former employer down the road?

Ask the Right Question

While you have a lot of questions in mind, do not ask irrelevant questions regarding personal life. Offer to help them only if you can. You can ask thousands of question but here are some of the questions you may want to ask:

1. Why did you join this organization?
2. What did you like and dislike most about this company?
3. What prompted you to look for a new job?
4. What is most appealing about the new position?
5. How would you rate your supervisors and peers?
6. What has been frustrating/difficult/upsetting to you in your time with us?
7. How well do you think the appraisal system worked for you?

8. What suggestion would you make to improve working conditions, hours, shifts, amenities, etc?
9. What can the organization do to retain its best people (and not lose any more like you)?
10. Would you consider working again for us if the situation were right?
11. Are you happy to say where you are going (if you have decided)?
12. What are your suggestions for improving the organization?

The answers to the above will help you redefine some of your policies like appraisal, salaries, benefits, motivational tools, recruitment practices and so on.

Do not ask employees to fill questionnaire-like forms

Make it very short and precise. Also conduct a face-to-face interview or at the most a telephonic interview. But under no circumstances ask the employee to fill the form and drop it in an anonymous box as it's highly impersonal and infuriating.

The interview should be about them

Most people like talking about themselves and their achievements and accomplishments. Let them do so as talking about how one does their job and what they've accomplished can provide key information to the organization and make the person feel good at the same time.

Time the interview

There are two sides to this. When a person gives a notice that he/she may be leaving do an exit interview immediately. You may be able to change their mind. But if the person has been asked to go or is leaving due to some internal politics, there are chances that the person may be very agitated. So conduct the interview at a later date; may be two-three months later. During this period the person may have cooled off and will be able to give a more rational feedback.

Don't blow up

There are times you may not like what you are hearing about yourself or the organization. But please control yourself as saying anything that you don't really mean or hurting the departing employee will make him only feel that leaving the organization was after all the right decision.

Use the information collected

Once the interview is over, do not merely file the form in the personal record of the employee. Collate past information and understand why employees are leaving the organization and help change the internal policies and practices.

Brief Sample Exit Interview Questions

Exit interview forms vary widely, but here are some core questions you can expect:

- What is your main reason for leaving?
- Would you work for this employer again?
- Would you recommend this employer to friends or family?
- What did you enjoy/dislike about your job?
- What improvements would you suggest about your job/working conditions/management support?
- What do you think it takes to succeed at this company?
- What does your new employer offer different to this company?
- Any other comments?

How you handle these questions and how honestly you answer is entirely your decision.

If your main reason for leaving is to escape a tyrannical boss, carefully consider how you put this into words, particularly if you want to keep your options open for returning at a later date. Remember the HR person's notes will be on your file, for all to see. Although you may feel that reporting your boss is the "right thing to do" in an exit interview, consider whether this may be better conveyed in a private conversation with his or her superior.

Beware open-ended questions asking for improvement suggestions or generalizations. Keep your answers short and simple, and above all, remain calm if you've had less than ideal treatment. If you have any points to make, present your ideas constructively—your interviewer will appreciate this approach enormously.

Detail Sample Exit Interview Questions

These questions can be used in face-to-face exit interviews, or to compile exit interview proforma questionnaires or electronic feedback forms.

If using these questions to compile forms to be used for large scale analysis, take care to format the questions into a format which can be analysed numerically, as far as is reasonable (certain questions and answers will always be difficult to format in this way, for example, the 'how do you feel about...?' and open-ended questions seeking ideas and suggestions—such questions can only be analysed and reported 'by exception' when something of particular note crops up, or of a particular recurring theme is spotted).

In face-to-face interviews particularly, use the word 'why' if you want to probe, especially if the first answer is vague or superficial. Questions beginning with 'what' and 'how' are better for getting people to think and convey to you properly and honestly about their views. Some of these questions samples are more suitable for management employees, although always give people at all levels the chance to comment on issues normally 'above' their remit—you'll be surprised at how informed and insightful people can be. These questions examples are not in a sequential process, although broadly there is a logic to the order of the types of questions. There are lots more questions here than you would normally ask in a typical exit interview. Pick the questions that are most relevant to the leaving circumstances, the interviewee and your organization situation.

- Tell me about how you've come to decide to leave?

- What is your main reason for leaving?
- What are the other reasons for your leaving?
- Why is this important, or so significant for you?
- Within the (particular reason to leave) what was it that concerned you particularly?
- What could have been done early on to prevent the situation developing/provide a basis for you to stay with us?
- How would you have preferred the situation(s) to have been handled?
- What opportunities can you see might have existed for the situation/problems to have been averted/dealt with satisfactorily?
- What can you say about the processes and procedures or systems that have contributed to the problem(s)/ your decision to leave?
- What specific suggestions would you have for how the organization could manage this situation/these issues better in future?
- How do you feel about the organization?
- What has been good/enjoyable/satisfying for you in your time with us?
- What has been frustrating/difficult/upsetting to you in your time with us?
- What could you have done better or more for us had we given you the opportunity?
- What extra responsibility would you have welcomed that you were not given?
- How could the organization have enabled you to make fuller use of your capabilities and potential?
- What training would you have liked or needed that you did not get, and what effect would this have had?
- How well do think your training and development needs were assessed and met?

- What training and development that you had did you find most helpful and enjoyable?
- What can you say about communications within the organization/your department?
- What improvements do you think can be made to customer service and relations?
- How would you describe the culture or 'feel' of the organization?
- What could you say about communications and relations between departments, and how these could be improved?
- Were you developed/inducted adequately for your role(s)?
- What improvement could be made to the way that you were inducted/prepared for your role(s)?
- (For recent recruits of less than a year or so) What did you think about the way we recruited you? How did the reality alter from your expectations when you first joined us? How could we have improved your own recruitment? How could your induction training have been improved?
- How could you have been helped to better know/understand/work with other departments necessary for the organization to perform more effectively?
- What can you say about the way your performance was measured, and the feedback to you of your performance results?
- How well do you think the appraisal system worked for you?
- What would you say about how you were motivated, and how that could have been improved?
- What suggestion would you make to improve working conditions, hours, shifts, amenities, etc.?

- What would you say about equipment and machinery that needs replacing or upgrading, or which isn't fully/properly used for any reason?
- What can you say about the way you were managed?.... On a day to day basis?.... And on a month to month basis?
- How would you have changed the expectations/ objectives/aims (or absence of) that were placed on you?.... And why?
- What, if any, ridiculous examples of policy, rules, instructions, can you highlight?
- What examples of ridiculous waste (material or effort), pointless reports, meetings, bureaucracy, etc. could you point to?
- How could the organization reduce stress levels among employees where stress is an issue?
- How could the organization enabled you to have made better use of your time?
- What things did the organization or management do to make your job more difficult/frustrating/non-productive?
- How can the organization gather and make better use of the views and experience of its people?
- Aside from the reason(s) you are leaving, how strongly were you attracted to committing to a long and developing career with us?
- What can the organization do to retain its best people (and not lose any more like you)?
- Have you anything to say about your treatment from a discrimination or harassment perspective?
- Would you consider working again for us if the situation were right?
- Are you happy to say where you are going (if you have decided)?

- What particularly is it about them that makes you want to join them?
- What, importantly, are they offering that we are not?
- (If appropriate) Could you be persuaded to renegotiate/stay/discuss the possibility of staying?
- Can we be of any particular help to you in this move/deciding what to do next (we can't promise anything obviously)?

And, to address opportunities for knowledge-transfer prior to departure, possibly in advance of exit interview.

Exit Interviews and Knowledge Transfer

The days, weeks (or months in some cases) between the decision for the employee to leave, and the employee's actual departure date offer a crucial opportunity for the organization to gather important information and knowledge from the employee. This is especially relevant in roles where the employee has accumulated a significant amount of knowledge and personal connections, as typically applies in sales and buying roles, and obviously business unit management. The knowledge of the departing employee commonly has immense value, and the recovery of it is often overlooked altogether by the organization, until the employee has departed, or more likely been hurried out of the door holding the contents of their desk in a cardboard box.

When any employee resigns, or a decision is made for a person to leave for any reason, always ask: Should we spend some time thinking about how to enable some sort of knowledge transfer? In other words, if we place a value on the knowledge that the departing employee holds, isn't it worth thinking about how to enable this knowledge to be passed to the appropriate people remaining in the organization?

Instead of course all too often, senior management's response to all the head-scratching after a vital person has left, is to rationalise the loss of information (and vital personal contacts often) with the old cliché, "No-one is indispensable". The adage might ultimately be true, but that's not really the point. The fact is that most people who leave do actually possess useful (often critical) knowledge and experience. Moreover most departing employees are delighted to share this knowledge, to help a successor, or to brief a management team, if only the organization would simply ask them politely to do so (assuming their exit is handled decently of course, which the exit interview helps to enable).

This is another good reason for thinking properly about the exit procedure, and for properly organizing some form of exit interview process.

So much depends of course on the atmosphere surrounding the departure. Often, particularly in sales, there is suspicion and imagined threat on both sides, which rather weakens the chances of a helpful hand-over. This mistrust should be diffused—it really does nobody any good. In an ideal world the leaver should be encouraged and enabled (and arguably rewarded if necessary) to hold a briefing meeting, which all interested parties (and certainly the person's replacement if possible) can attend and learn what they need to know. Regrettably however, it is not unusual for traditional-type 'theory-X' sales directors and managers to be so intoxicated with testosterone and the taste of blood that such suggestions rarely make it off the stony ground of the board-room. I would urge you to take a more open constructive view. Give people the benefit of doubt, and discourage the kill'em and eat'em advocates from retaliating before there's any suggestion of being attacked. There are some suggested enabling questions below.

For organizations large and small, exit interviews therefore provide lots of advantages and opportunities:

Knowledge Transfer Questions

Start thinking about using these questions when the employee and the organization knows that the employee will be leaving. Don't leave these questions until the exit interview:

- How might we benefit from your knowledge, experience, introductions to your contacts, etc. prior to your departure?

- Would you be happy to take part in a briefing meeting with managers/replacements/successor/ colleagues so that we can benefit from your knowledge and experience, prior to your leaving?
- What can we do to enable you to pass on as much of your knowledge and experience as possible to your replacement/successor prior to your departure?
- How and when would you prefer to pass on your knowledge to your successor?
- I realise that you'll not be happy with the situation surrounding your departure, however, we would really appreciate it if you could help us to understand some of the important things you've been working on—how might we agree for this knowledge to be transferred?
- We'd be grateful for you to introduce (name of successor) to your key contacts before you go—are you happy to help with this?

As ever, you will derive most for the organization, and be able to give most help to the departing employee, by being positive, constructive, understanding and helpful, prior to and during the exit interview process. Treat people with integrity and decency, and generally they will respond in kind.

Exit Interview Checklist

Here's a mental checklist to run through to remind you how to behave in the exit interview:

- Have I chosen to attend this interview? It's not compulsory, so if you've decided to attend, do so with grace and dignity.
- Will anything change based on my comments? If so, let the feedback flow.
- Who will benefit from my honesty? Constructive feedback is useful to a company, even if it takes time to take action.

- Who will be harmed by my honesty? Remember that bland answers are an option if you're likely to get upset during the interview.
- Do I want to work for this employer again? Burnt bridges are difficult to repair!

The relationship with your employer can be more intense than with your romantic partner, because so many big emotions are involved—status, achievement, security, etc. When this relationship ends, for good or bad, it's better to handle the final good bye in your exit interview calmly. These sample exit interview questions, answers and checklist can help you maintain that focus.

Exit Interview Format

Dept:	Venue:
Name:	Designation:
Year or Period Covered:	Length of Service:
Exit Interview Date & Time:	Name of Interviewer:

Q.1. Why did you join this organization?

____

Q.2. What did you like and dislike most about this company?

____

Q.3. What prompted you to look for a new job?

____

Q.4. What is most appealing about the new position?

____

____

Q.5. How would you rate your supervisors and peers?

____

____

Q.6. What has been frustrating/difficult/upsetting to you in your time with us?

____

Q.7. What can the organization do to retain its best people (and not lose any more like you)?

____

Q.8. Would you consider working again for us if the situation were right?

____

Q.9. Are you happy to say where you are going (if you have decided)?

____

____

Q.10. What are your suggestions for improving the organization?

____

____

Sign of Executive

Conclusion and Suggestion (By Interviewer)
Sign of Interviewer

17

HR Policy

Human Resource Policy is made for the comforts of employees and employers and not for the discomfort. One of the major objectives of HR policy is to initiate and institutionalize globally competitive HR practices to become an employer of preferred choice.

To achieve this, we want to use modern methodologies to undertake organizational renewal exercise; identify and nurture talent; bring about changes in the mindsets of employees at all levels; to create performance-driven culture; to create a pool of entrepreneurial managers and business leaders of future; to inculcate strong and effective sales and service culture and to create a learning organization for employees' intellectual growth and creativity and to reskill the workforce to operate in a digitally-enabled modern core banking environment. All these aim at providing value to customers.

Why are Written Policies Important?

Sound employment policies provide the framework within which an organization governs its employee relations. A policies and procedures manual guides both managers and employees as to what is expected and can prevent misunderstandings about employer policy. In addition, supervisors and managers are more likely to consistently apply policies that are clearly communicated in writing.

It is true that written policies, like any record, can be used against an organization in a lawsuit. Poorly drafted policies often become the main evidence presented when employees allege that the policies were in fact a contract that the employer violated. However, policies that are carefully written so as not to be contracts actually should protect against these claims and not be a problem.

The simple act of putting policies in writing should not create a binding contract if the policies are written as guidelines that explain generally or typically what our requirements are and how employees normally will be treated. However, you can create a contract by using language that conveys rigid rules that must be followed exactly as written in all circumstances.

Why do I Need Written Policies?

Sound employment policies provide the principles by which an organization governs its employee relations in a fair and consistent manner. Having all policies and procedures in one manual helps employees be aware of what is expected and can prevent misunderstandings about employer policies. In addition, supervisors and managers are better able to implement policies that are clearly communicated in writing. Written policies also help employers document compliance with the unending tangle of employment laws and regulations. For example, the Supreme Court has indicated that employers can help protect themselves against liability for sexual harassment by having an effective policy against sexual harassment that includes a complaint procedure. (Instant HR Policies contains a harassment policy, called Productive Work Environment.)

In addition, the federal Family and Medical Leave Act requires employers to provide written information regarding the employee rights and employer obligations under the Act.

Supervisory Policy Manuals vs. Employee Handbooks

HR Policies are intended to help you create a supervisory policy manual. As a general rule, a supervisory policy manual is a guide for managers and supervisors and contains information that they need to implement the organization's policies. Accordingly, each policy provides a general statement of policy (identified as the "Policy") and is followed by several comments (identified as "Comments") that instruct managers how to apply the policy.

In contrast, an employee handbook is designed for broad distribution to all employees. It is typically intended to provide general information about the organization's practices, benefits, hours of work, pay policies, and work rules. It usually does not include information about supervisory procedures.

Although the *HR Policies*, as written, is designed to create a supervisory policy manual, it also can be easily modified to create an employee handbook.

How to Create a Supervisory Policy Manual Using *HR Policies?*

HR Policies model policies covering most employment situations that may arise, from hiring to termination, vacations, leaves of absence, and disciplinary procedures.

Each model policy is divided into two parts: Policy and Comments. The Policy section provides a short statement of the organization's policies. The Comments section offers details and explanations about how supervisors should implement the policy. You should use both the Policy and the Comments to create your final supervisory policy.

How to Create an Employee Handbook Using *HR Policies?*

An employee handbook serves a different purpose than a supervisory policy manual. Typically, an employee handbook focuses on the policies that affect employees and that govern their relationship with your organization.

Although the model policies in *HR Policies* are intended primarily to be used to create a supervisory policy manual, they also can be used in an employee handbook by removing the references to supervisory procedures.

Generally, you can use the Policy statements "as is". Review the "Comments" section and remove any references to what supervisors and managers are expected to do so that the information is more relevant to employees.

For example, the Comments section in the model Orientation and Training policy, let Policy 202B, includes several steps that the Human Resources Department and supervisors should take to develop and implement training programs. Most employers would not include any of this information in an employee handbook since it does not affect employees directly.

In contrast, the Policy statement and all of the Comments in the model harassment policy, let Policy 201A, should be used in both a supervisory manual and an employee handbook since they contain pertinent information on reporting sexual and other forms of harassment that all employees should know.

What Policies are Included?

HR Policies includes several model policies that cover most employment situations, from hiring to termination, vacations, leaves of absence, and disciplinary procedures.

Personnel Responsibilities

- Model Cover
- President's Letter
- Functions of this Manual
- Employee Supervision
- Personnel Manager
- Employer-Employee Relations
- Employment-at-Will

Employment

- Equal Employment Opportunity
- Productive Work Environment/Harassment
- Hiring
- Employment Agreements
- Orientation and Training
- Medical Procedures
- Serious Diseases
- Introductory Period
- Transfer
- Promotion

- Hours of Work
- Outside Employment
- Employee Classifications
- Layoff and Recall
- Termination of Employment
- Retirement

Pay Practices

- Salary Administration
- Performance Appraisals
- Severance Pay
- Job Evaluation

Reimbursement of Expenses

- Travel
- Automobile Usage
- Business Entertaining
- Meal Reimbursement
- Clubs/Civic Organizations
- Trade/Professional Assn.

Employee Benefits

- Disclosure of Benefits
- Vacations
- Holidays
- Lunch Facilities
- Educational Assistance
- Employee Counseling
- Recognition/Service Awards
- Company Products/Services
- Relocation
- Athletic & Recreational Programs

Work Areas

- Employee Safety
- Maintenance
- Personal Property
- Solicitation
- Parking
- Security
- Smoking

Absence from Work

- Attendance/Punctuality
- Short-term Absences
- Leaves of Absence
- Rest Breaks
- Meal Breaks

Personal Conduct

- Behavior of Employees
- Personal Appearance
- Personal Finances
- Customer Relations
- Communication Systems
- Conflicts of Interest
- Confidentiality
- Disciplinary Procedure
- Drugs, Narcotics, Alcohol

Miscellaneous

- Personnel Records
- Community Affairs
- Suggestion Program
- Dispute Resolution

Choosing Individual Policies

Not every organization needs several policies. If you currently have a supervisory manual or employee handbook, compare your policies to the *HR Policies* model policies to decide which policies you might want to add or update.

If you don't have a formal policy and procedures manual, you should begin by looking through the Table of Contents to determine which policies you want to include in your manual.

In choosing policies, you should consider the following issues:

- The culture of your organization and its recurring issues or problems;
- Any memos on policy topics (such as vacation and holiday schedules) and past practices (i.e. what you have done in the past to address a particular employee relations issue); and
- The HR practices followed by other organizations in your industry (including vacation lengths and leave allowances).

At a minimum, most employers develop policies on:

- At-will employment,
- Pay procedures,
- Benefits (including any paid vacation, sick leave, holidays, and other forms of leave),
- Meal and rest breaks,
- Personal conduct (work rules),
- Attendance and punctuality,
- Sexual and other forms of harassment,
- Equal employment opportunity,
- Disciplinary procedures, and
- Termination.

In addition, many employers include policies on:

- Performance appraisals,

- Smoking,
- Safety procedures,
- Appropriate dress and appearance,
- Use of communications systems (including telephones, computers, e-mail, internet access), and
- Drug and alcohol use.

Policy Writing and Updating: Myths and Truths

When was the last time you reviewed your organization's policies? If you're like many employers, writing or updating policies is at the bottom of a lengthy "to-do" list. And, you may even question the value of having written policies because of the apparently conflicting advice concerning their usefulness. On one hand, many HR experts advocate having written policies as a way of communicating your organization's values and practices to employees. Alternatively, a growing number of attorneys are warning their clients that poorly drafted policies may land them in court. So, who should you believe? The short answer is both groups. Upon closer consideration, these positions are not contradictory. Well-written policies can both serve as an effective communication device and help you stay out of court, or at least give you a better chance of prevailing. The following questions and answers will help define the underlying issues and make clear why written policies that are carefully developed, updated, and applied are an effective tool that you need.

1. Why are written policies important?

Sound employment policies provide the framework within which an organization governs its employee relations. A policies and procedures manual guides both managers and employees as to what is expected and can prevent misunderstandings about employer policy. In addition, supervisors and managers are more likely to consistently apply policies that are clearly communicated in writing.

It is true that written policies, like any record, can be used against an organization in a lawsuit. Poorly drafted policies often become the main evidence presented when employees allege that the policies were in fact a contract that the employer violated. However, policies that are carefully written so as not to be contracts actually should protect against these claims and not be a problem (See number 4, below). In addition, carefully written policies can be used to illustrate your commitment to a positive work environment and nondiscriminatory employment practices (See number 3, below).

2. Are we required to have written policies?

Although written policies in general are not legally required, certain policies may be required, or at least be considered an important component in helping employers establish good faith compliance with federal and state law. For example, the Supreme Court has indicated that employers may protect themselves against liability for sexual harassment by having clearly articulated policies against sexual harassment that include effective complaint procedures. In addition, the Family and Medical Leave Act requires covered employers to provide written information regarding employee rights and employer obligations under the Act. Similarly, certain federal contractors must have written equal employment opportunity policies. And finally, many state laws require written harassment policies and policies informing employees about compensation issues.

3. Does every organization need written policies?

As a general rule, every employer, except maybe those with fewer than 15 employees, should have written policies. Employers with 15 or more employees are covered by federal discrimination laws (such as Title VII and the Americans with Disabilities Act) and most state discrimination laws. Written policies are a good starting point to show your commitment to nondiscriminatory employment practices. For example, a performance review policy can show the job-related criteria used to evaluate employees and any safeguards used to ensure the process is conducted in a fair and objective manner.

Smaller employers should at least consider creating a handbook since it is likely they already have some policies in writing. For example, employment offer letters may explain vacation and sick leave accrual while other items, like a posted memo, may outline pay procedures. Thus, to ensure distribution to all employees, even the small employer is well advised to compile these memos into a handbook that is given to every employee.

4. Will we create a contract if we have written policies?

The simple act of putting your policies in writing should not create a binding contract if the policies are written as guidelines that explain generally or typically what your requirements are and how employees normally will be treated. However, you can create a contract by using language that conveys rigid rules that must be followed exactly as written in all circumstances.

Therefore, you should build flexibility into your wording and steer clear of any promises that could be interpreted as a contract. Your policies should not, for example:

- State that the organization will "only" or "always" do something or "must" act in a particular way;
- Describe employees as "permanent";
- State that employees will be terminated only for "cause";
- Make promises of job security; or
- Use all-inclusive lists, such as in disciplinary procedures or work rules.

Instead, you should use terms such as "generally", "typically", "usually", and "may" so that managers have flexibility in interpreting and applying the policies. In addition, you should specifically retain management's right to update, change unilaterally, and implement all policies as the organization sees fit. Finally, you should include a strong "at-will" statement that clearly specifies that all employees (who do not have contracts or collective bargaining agreements specifying otherwise) may quit at any time and for any reason or may be terminated at any time and for any reason.

5. What is the difference between a supervisory policy manual and an employee handbook? Which should we have?

A supervisory policy manual generally is intended as a guide for managers and supervisors and contains information that they need to implement the organization's policies. Thus, a supervisory policy usually provides a general statement of policy followed by several comments that instruct managers how to apply that policy.

In contrast, an employee handbook is designed for broad distribution to all employees. It is typically intended to provide general information about the organization's practices, benefits, hours of work, pay policies, and work rules. It usually does not include information about supervisory procedures.

At a minimum, you should have an employee handbook that explains your policies to employees. Many organizations, especially as they grow, also have a supervisory policy manual to ensure that their managers understand how to implement the policies. As a practical matter, having supervisory instructions may be especially prudent in today's legal climate where any inconsistent application of policy can result in a discrimination claim.

6. What policies should we include?

In choosing policies to include, you should consider the following points:

- The culture of your organization and its recurring issues or problems;
- Any memos on policy topics (such as vacation and holiday schedules) and past practices (i.e. what you have done in the past to address a particular employee relations issue); and
- The HR practices followed by other organizations in your industry (such as vacation lengths and leave allowances).

Most employers develop policies on the following topics:

- At-will employment,
- Pay procedures,

- Benefits (including any paid vacation, sick leave, and holidays, and other forms of leave),
- Meal and rest breaks,
- Personal conduct (work rules),
- Attendance and punctuality,
- Sexual and other forms of harassment,
- Equal employment opportunity,
- Disciplinary procedures, and
- Termination.

In addition, many employers include policies on performance appraisals, smoking, safety procedures, appropriate dress and appearance, use of communications systems (including the proper use of telephones, computers, e-mail, and Internet access), and drug and alcohol use.

Remember, your policies should be considered dynamic, not static. You may need to add to them, revise them, and even delete them as your organization grows and changes.

7. Is the job ever done?

Even when you've finished drafting or updating your policies, your job is not complete. The policies should be reviewed by your legal counsel to ensure that they comply with state and federal employment laws before they are finalized and distributed to employees. Further, you should review the policies on a regular basis to make sure they continue to comply with applicable law and the needs of your organization. New laws, regulations, and court cases can affect both policy language and how you implement the policies. Most experts suggest a thorough review of your policies at least once a year and the use of a notification service or publication to keep you posted during the interim. Finally, when policies are introduced or revised, you should distribute and thoroughly explain them to all employees. Clearly written policies that are regularly re-viewed can be both an effective employee relations tool and a good defense against employee lawsuits. In contrast, policies that are poorly drafted or applied can have exactly the opposite effect. They can lower morale and become evidence against you in court. The key question, therefore, becomes not whether to have written policies at all, but whether you are willing to invest the necessary amount of time and effort to make sure they are carefully drafted and properly applied.

Policy

It is the policy of the company to pay employees by check or direct deposit on a regular basis and in a manner so that the amount, method, and timing of wage payments comply with any applicable laws or regulations:

(1) Employees normally will be paid on the fifteenth day and the last day of the month. If the regular payday occurs on a Saturday, Sunday, or a holiday, employees will be paid on the last working day before the regular payday.

(2) Employees on each payday will receive, in addition to their check or deposit advice, a statement showing gross pay, deductions, and net pay. Local, state, federal, and Social Security taxes will be deducted automatically. No other deductions will be made unless required or allowed by law, contract, or employee obligation. Employees may elect to have additional voluntary deductions taken from their pay only if they authorize the deductions in writing.

(3) Employees who discover a mistake in their pay check, lose their pay check, or have it stolen should notify the Personnel Department immediately. In the case of a mistake, the error will be remedied promptly. In the case of loss or theft, the Personnel Department will attempt to stop payment on the check and reissue a new one to the employee. However, the employee is solely responsible for the monetary loss, and the company will not be responsible for the loss or theft of a check if it cannot stop payment on the check.

(4) Employees who are eligible for vacation may receive an advance on their vacation pay as long as an approved request for it is submitted to the Personnel Department at least one pay period before the beginning of the vacation. Under normal

circumstances, no other advances or loans for employees will be made without the prior approval of the Personnel Director.

(5) Nonexempt employees (those not exempt from the provisions of the Fair Labor Standards Act) will be paid overtime compensation at the rate of one and one-half times their regular hourly rate for work in excess of forty hours during their normal workweek.

(6) Nonexempt employees will receive premium pay at one and one-half their regular rate for work on Saturday and Sunday, regardless of the number of hours worked in the workweek, unless the normal workweek includes regular Saturday and Sunday work.

(7) Nonexempt employees will receive a shift differential calculated as follows:

(a) If the shift begins after noon and ends at 11:00 p.m. or earlier, 10 per cent of regular pay; or

(b) If the shift begins after 3:00 p.m. and ends after 11:00 p.m., 15 per cent of regular pay.

(8) Employees should discuss any questions or concerns regarding their rate of pay and other compensation issues with their department head or with the Personnel Department.

The Importance of an HR Policies and Practices Strategy

"Why," you may ask, "do I need a policies and practices strategy for my business?"

The simple answer is...because you have people working for you.

With human nature being what it is, employees will test limits and act "creatively" in workplace situations, so you need a strategy for developing, communicating and enforcing a set of policies and practices that reflect your standards of acceptable behavior.

But a successful policies and practices strategy does more than draw boundaries; it also recognizes and addresses people's needs.

There are many different types of people and, not surprisingly, they react differently to the need for policies and practices based on those differences. For example, some people prefer that there be a written policy for everything, while others favor having no policies at all and would leave everything open to interpretation as situations arise. Neither of these extremes contributes to a work environment that is conducive to high productivity levels. The answer is found in between, with the right number and types of policies and practices that are focused on a primary goal—improving individual performance in the workplace.

When you get to the heart of the matter, performance improvement is really about the process of setting expectations and meeting them. The focus in business is not just about meeting specific goals, but also how you achieve them. And the "how" affects the liabilities you create in the process.

So, how will you make sure your employees have clear expectations and are treated fairly as they work to help build your company?

The answer is found in the way you address four key elements related to the development and deployment of your policies and practices—roles, rules, consequences and tools.

Roles

People like to have a clear understanding of their role in an organization and the roles of others. Every successful team has well-defined positions for its members. Everyone knows what he or she is to do, how to do it and how their performance can impact those around them. In business, this means you need to have clear reporting structures that spell out who is in charge and how tasks are to be accomplished in the organization.

This approach applies not only to intradepartmental structures, but also to company-wide or interdepartmental projects. In addition, role definition is a foundational part of establishing clear performance expectations for each employee.

Rules

Managers and employees need to share a clear understanding of what is and what is not acceptable behavior within the organization. Unfortunately, in today's workplace, an employer can be held liable for the bad behavior of an employee, especially when that bad behavior affects other employees, clients or individuals. Having a clear set of behavioral expectations is critical to establishing that you are not contributing to that bad behavior as an employer.

Setting clear and specific behavioral standards in the form of rules establishes a framework for spotting and addressing violations of those standards. If you rely on loosely defined general standards that are not properly documented, then violations become subjective and open to interpretation. The result of such ambiguousness is often litigation.

Consequences

It is important that you clearly state consequences for violations of your behavioral standards, so that employees know what to expect and have fair warning of those expectations. In addition, clear consequences help to ensure that you are not limited in your options for dealing with improper behaviors. To establish these standards and violation consequences, sit down with your management team and think through the over-the-line behaviors that will not be permitted in your organization. It is essential that you know ahead of time what employee actions require an immediate dismissal. Similarly, you want to know what performance issues may qualify for a more progressive disciplinary approach, and then define the steps involved in that approach. As I said earlier, people are by nature complex beings who will confound you one minute and astound you the next. And, except for violations that warrant immediate firings, it is usually a wise, compassionate and financially prudent course to help people strengthen their character by overcoming their weaknesses. Also, this approach provides you with a way to retain experienced employees and recover your investment in their training.

I have found that in many instances, managers are disappointed in an employee's performance, although the manager never clearly communicated his or her expectations to the employee. If you do not take steps to set clear expectations, the consequences you administer for failure to meet those expectations can seem unfair. This is extremely important because an employee who feels that they have been treated unfairly can create a great deal of liability. In many cases, the key issue is not whether they were actually treated unfairly, but whether the employee feels or perceives that he or she was treated unfairly. And it doesn't stop with the affected employee. If you or your managers have not clearly communicated your expectations to one employee, chances are you have not done so with other employees and they can be quick to empathize with any affected workers. It is natural for employees to wonder, "What if that happened to me?" To avoid the negative effect such a chain-reaction can have on your workplace, be clear about your expectations with all employees at all times. Most employees will appreciate and respect your forthright clarity.

Building a great company has a lot to do with how people work together. Policies and practices can improve the way your employees interact, while minimizing the personnel obstacles that often arise in today's workplaces.

Tools

Tools address the question of how you support the supervisors in your company who manage employees. When faced with a specific personnel issue, what resources are available to them? Do they have an employee handbook or a policy guide? What about regular training in company policies and practices, coupled with simple, easy-to-use forms to guide them when dealing with particular issues? Are you giving them a clear directive on working with your human resources personnel or legal representatives? Are your resources available online?

Tools like these are vital not just to help avoid litigation, but also to minimize the time it takes for you to deal with productivity-draining people issues instead of core business matters. Because many small business owners lack these resources and are not sure where to turn for help, they call on professional employer organizations like Administaff to provide the support of a full-service human resources department. Other businesses may use attorneys and HR consultants on an *la carte* basis to address such issues.

Whatever the approach, the key to success is to devote the time and resources to develop a policies and practices strategy for your organization before the need arises. It is an investment that can pay large dividends in increased productivity and minimized litigation. And it is an essential component of your comprehensive people strategy.

Conclusion

Rules are made for better services and comforts of the employees and employer and not for discomfort for any of them. Rules are made to safeguard to the employees and employer's benefits and risk. It is very important for in smooth functioning of the company. For example, you have got a good break somewhere else then you have to give one month notice to the organization so that any one can take charge of your assigned job responsibility. And if you couldn't inform to the company in any case one moth advance then you have to pay one month salary to the employer. Similarly, if a company wants to relieve you from the services then HR manager will let you know one month advance or will pay you one month salary in lieu of.

18

Leadership Development

Leadership is the ability of an individual to influence, motivate, and enable others to contribute toward the effectiveness and success of the organizations. Organizationally, leadership directly impacts the effectiveness of costs, revenue generation, service, satisfaction, earnings, market value, share price, social capital, motivation, engagement, and sustainability. Leadership is the ability of an individual to set an example for others and lead from the front. It is an attitude that influences the environment around us.

Good leaders are made, not born. If you have the desire and willpower, you can become an effective leader. Good leaders develop through a never ending process of self-study, education, training, and experience. This guide will help you through that process.

To inspire your workers into higher levels of teamwork, there are certain things you must be, know, and, do. These do not come naturally, but are acquired through continual work and study. Good leaders are continually working and studying to improve their leadership skills; they are not resting on their laurels.

Before we get started, let's define leadership. Leadership is a process by which a person influences others to accomplish an objective and directs the organization in a way that makes it more cohesive and coherent. Leaders carry out this process by applying their leadership attributes, such as beliefs, values, ethics, character, knowledge, and skills. Although your position as a manager, supervisor, lead, etc. gives you the authority to accomplish certain tasks and objectives in the organization, this power does not make you a leader...it simply makes you the boss. Leadership differs in that it makes the followers want to achieve high goals, rather than simply bossing people around.

Bass' (1989 and 1990) theory of leadership states that there are three basic ways to explain how people become leaders. The first two explain the leadership development for a small number of people. These theories are:

- Some personality traits may lead people naturally into leadership roles. This is the Trait Theory.
- A crisis or important event may cause a person to rise to the occasion, which brings out extraordinary leadership qualities in an ordinary person. This is the Great Events Theory.
- People can choose to become leaders. People can learn leadership skills. This is the Transformational Leadership Theory. It is the most widely accepted theory today and the premise on which this guide is based.

When a person is deciding if she respects you as a leader, she does not think about your attributes, rather, she observes what you do so that she can know who you really are. She uses this observation to tell if you are a honorable and trusted leader or a self-serving person who misuses authority to look good and get promoted. Self-serving leaders are not as effective because their employees only obey them, not follow them. They succeed in many areas because they present a good image to their seniors at the expense of their workers.

The basis of good leadership is honorable character and selfless service to your organization. In your employees' eyes, your leadership is everything you do that effects the organization's objectives and their well being. Respected leaders concentrate on what they *are [be]* (such as beliefs and character), what they *know* (such as job, tasks, and human nature), and what they do (such as implementing, motivating, and provide direction).

What makes a person want to follow a leader? People want to be guided by those they respect and who have a clear sense of direction. To gain respect, they must be ethical. A sense of direction is achieved by conveying a strong vision of the future.

Definition of a Manager and a Leader

A manager basically directs resources to complete predetermined goals or projects. For example, a manager may engage in hiring, training, and scheduling employees in order to accomplish work in the most efficient and cost effective manner possible. A manager is considered a failure if he/she is not able to complete the project or goals with efficiency or when the cost becomes too high.

On the other hand, a leader within a company develops individuals in order to complete predetermined goals and projects. A leader develops relationships with his/her employees by building communication, evoking images of success, and by eliciting loyalty. In simple words, leader leads and manages man whereas a manager manages process.

Leadership is a Facet of Management

Leadership is just one of the many assets a successful manager must possess. Care must be taken in distinguishing between the two concepts. The main aim of a manager is to maximise the output of the organization through administrative implementation. To achieve this, managers must undertake the following functions:

- Organization
- Planning
- Staffing
- Directing
- Controlling.

Leadership is just one important component of the directing function. A manager cannot just be a leader, he also needs formal authority to be effective. "For any quality initiative to take hold, senior management must be involved and act as a role model. This involvement cannot be delegated."

In some circumstances, leadership is not required. For example, self-motivated groups may not require a single leader and may find leaders dominating. The fact that a leader is not always required proves that leadership is just an asset and is not essential.

Differences in Perspectives

Managers think incrementally, whilst leaders think radically. "Managers do things right, while leaders do the right thing". This means that managers do things by the book and follow company policy, while leaders follow their own intuition, which may in turn be of more benefit to the company. A leader is more emotional than a manager. "Men are governed by their emotions rather than their intelligence". This quotation illustrates why teams choose to follow leaders.

"Leaders stand out by being different. They question assumption and are suspicious of tradition. They seek out the truth and make decisions based on fact, not prejudice. They have a preference for innovation."

Subordinate As a Leader

Often with small groups, it is not the manager who emerges as the leader. In many cases it is a subordinate member with specific talents who leads the group in a certain direction. "Leaders must let vision, strategies, goals, and values be the guide-post for action and behaviour rather than attempting to control others."

When a natural leader emerges in a group containing a manager, conflict may arise if they have different views. When a manager sees the group looking towards someone else for leadership he may feel his authority is being questioned.

Loyalty

Groups are often more loyal to a leader than a manager. This loyalty is created by the leader taking responsibility in areas such as:

- Taking the blame when things go wrong.
- Celebrating group achievements, even minor ones.
- Giving credit where it is due.

"The leader must take a point of highlighting the successes within a team, using charts or graphs, with little presentations and fun ideas."

"Leaders are observant and sensitive people. They know their team and develop mutual confidence within it."

The Leader is Followed: The Manager Rules

A leader is someone who people naturally follow through their own choice, whereas a manager must be obeyed. A manager may only have obtained his position of authority through time and loyalty given to the company, not as a result of his leadership qualities. A leader may have no organizational skills, but his vision unites people behind him.

Management Knows How It Works

Management usually consists of people who are experienced in their field, and who have worked their way up the company. A manager knows how each layer of the system works and may also possess a good technical knowledge. A leader can be a new arrival to a company who has bold, fresh, new ideas but might not have experience or wisdom.

Conclusion

Managing and leading are two different ways of organizing people. The manager uses a formal, rational method whilst the leader uses passion and stirs emotions. William Wallace is one excellent example of a brilliant leader but could never be thought of as the manager of the Scots!

Leadership vs. Management

What is the difference between management and leadership? It is a question that has been asked more than once and also answered in different ways. The biggest difference between managers and leaders is the way they motivate the people who work or follow them, and this sets the tone for most other aspects of what they do.

Many people, by the way, are both. They have management jobs, but they realize that you cannot buy hearts, especially to follow them down a difficult path, and so act as leaders too.

Managers have subordinates

By definition, managers have subordinates—unless their title is honorary and given as a mark of seniority, in which case the title is a misnomer and their power over others is other than formal authority.

Authoritarian, transactional style

Managers have a position of authority vested in them by the company, and their subordinates work for them and largely do as they are told. Management style is transactional, in that the manager tells the subordinate what to do, and the subordinate does this not because they are a blind robot, but because they have been promised a reward (at minimum their salary) for doing so.

Work focus

Managers are paid to get things done (they are subordinates too), often within tight constraints of time and money. They thus naturally pass on this work focus to their subordinates.

Seek comfort

An interesting research finding about managers is that they tend to come from stable home backgrounds and led relatively normal and comfortable lives. This leads them to be relatively risk-averse and they will seek to avoid conflict where possible. In terms of people, they generally like to run a 'happy ship'.

Leaders have followers

Leaders do not have subordinates—at least not when they are leading. Many organizational leaders do have subordinates, but only because they are also managers. But when they want to lead, they have to give up formal authoritarian control, because to lead is to have followers, and following is always a voluntary activity.

Charismatic, transformational style

Telling people what to do does not inspire them to follow you. You have to appeal to them, showing how following them will lead to their hearts' desire. They must want to follow you enough to stop what they are doing and perhaps walk into danger and situations that they would not normally consider risking.

Leaders with a stronger charisma find it easier to attract people to their cause. As a part of their persuasion they typically promise transformational benefits, such that their followers will not just receive extrinsic rewards but will somehow become better people.

People focus

Although many leaders have a charismatic style to some extent, this does not require a loud personality. They are always good with people, and quiet styles that give credit to others (and takes blame on themselves) are very effective at creating the loyalty that great leaders engender.

Although leaders are good with people, this does not mean they are friendly with them. In order to keep the mystique of leadership, they often retain a degree of separation and aloofness.

This does not mean that leaders do not pay attention to tasks—in fact they are often very achievement-focused. What they do realize, however, is the importance of enthusing others to work towards their vision.

Seek risk

In the same study that showed managers as risk-averse, leaders appeared as risk-seeking, although they are not blind thrill-seekers. When pursuing their vision, they consider it natural to encounter problems and hurdles that must be overcome along the way. They are thus comfortable with risk and will see routes that others avoid as potential opportunities for advantage and will happily break rules in order to get things done.

A surprising number of these leaders had some form of handicap in their lives which they had to overcome. Some had traumatic childhoods, some had problems such as dyslexia, others were shorter than average. This perhaps taught them the independence of mind that is needed to go out on a limb and not worry about what others are thinking about you.

Summary

This table summarizes the above (and more) and gives a sense of the differences between being a leader and being a manager. This is, of course, an illustrative characterization, and there is a whole spectrum between either ends of these scales along which each role can range. And many people lead and manage at the same time, and so may display a combination of behaviors.

Leader Manager Chart

Subject	Leader	Manager
Seeks	Vision	Objectives
Focus	Leading people	Managing work
Have	Followers	Subordinates
Horizon	Long-term	Short-term
Essence	Change	Stability
Approach	Sets direction	Plans detail
Decision	Facilitates	Makes
Credit	Gives	Takes
Blame	Takes	Blames
Energy	Passion	Control
Dynamic	Proactive	Reactive
Persuasion	Sell	Tell
Style	Transformational	Transactional
Exchange	Excitement for work	Money for work
Likes	Striving	Action
Wants	Achievement	Results
Truth	Seeks	Establishes
Rules	Breaks	Makes
Conflict	Uses	Avoids
Direction	New roads	Existing roads

Do you want to be a leader or a manager? You need to make a choice as there is a huge difference. "The world is full of managers and desperately short of leaders—real leaders."

Today's World Realities

In today's new economy, the old ways of management no longer work and will never work again. The magnitude and pressure of environmental, competitive, and global market change we are experiencing is unprecedented. It's a very interesting and exciting world, but it's also volatile and chaotic. You cannot address these new challenges with more of the same management solutions—successful change requires leadership.

Psychological research has shown that "under circumstances of uncertainty or unusual challenge and difficulty, people look for help in understanding questions about what matters, what to do, what direction to take, and what they should not do. Providing people with the answers that help them with these difficult questions is the essence of leadership".

Leadership-Management Synergy

To Lead or To Manage?

You need both. The old proverb says that leadership is doing the right thing; management is doing things right. The difference between the two is not as sharp as the saying would suggest, and both are required for effective corporate growth: leadership risk creates opportunities while management strictness turns them into tangible results.

However, "if your organization is not on a journey don't bother about leadership—just settle for management", advises John Adair.

"There is a direct correlation between the way people view their managers and the way they perform. Strong leadership is imperative for shaping a group of people into a force that serves as a competitive business advantage."

Leading Change

Leadership is about getting people to abandon their old

habits and achieve new things, and therefore largely about change—about inspiring, helping, and sometimes enforcing change in people. "While there can be effective management absent ideas, there can be no true leadership."

Leadership and Management

- Leaders seize opportunities; Managers avert threats. Both together progress more.
- Leaders amplify strengths; Managers reduce weaknesses. Both together develop more.

Why Inspirational Leadership?

Do you want to encourage extraordinary performance from your people? Do you want them to do great things? If yes, then you must create an inspiring corporate culture that inspires, empowers and energizes them. People do what they have to do for a manager, they do their best for an inspirational leader.

To inspire, you must both create resonance and move people with a compelling vision. You must embody what you ask of others, and be able to articulate a shared vision in a way that inspires others to act. You must offer a sense of common purpose beyond the day-to-day tasks, making work exciting, advises Steve Farber.

Inspirational Leadership: 10 Roles

Inspirational leaders create an inspiring culture within their organization. They supply a shared vision and inspire people to achieve more than they may ever have dreamed possible. They are able to articulate a shared vision in a way that inspires others to act. People do what they have to do for a manager; they do their best for an inspirational leader.

1. Provide an inspiring vision and strategic alignment, launch a crusade. As a leader, you must envision the future, passionately believe that you can make a difference, and inspire people to achieve more than they may ever have dreamed possible. You must see a changed world beyond the time horizon, create an ideal and unique image of what it could become, open your followers' eyes and lift their spirits. You must believe that your dreams can become reality and, through your attitude, get people to see exciting opportunities and possibilities for the future. People change and unlock their inner power when they are emotionally engaged and committed.

2. Help people connect their personal goals to business goals. Leadership is essentially about helping people to achieve a better life. An important measure of your own success as a leader is the success of your followers. Talented and empowered employees are the prime ingredient of organizational success and they need to be able to lead themselves. Provide strategic alignment and be a coach to your people to help each of your followers to develop into an effective self-leader. Establish an attitude of relentless growth to enable your organization and people to achieve their stretch goals.

3. Make relentless innovation a religion. Lead innovation, emphasize opportunities, not problems, and encourage innovative behavior. Establishing the culture of innovation requires a broad and sustained effort. Questions are critical to innovation, so start with creating a culture of questioning. Exploration of possibilities, discoveries, innovation, and progress start with challenging assumptions, asking searching "Why?" and "What if?" questions, and plying "What if" scenarios. Encourage your people to challenge assumptions, and run "The Best Question" contests. Reward both individual and collective contributions. Celebrate success.

4. Encourage entrepreneurial creativity and experimentation. Develop entrepreneurial staff and create a corporate climate that encourages rule-breakers and outside-the-box thinkers. Experimentation by definition is a trial-and-error process, but experimentation is also the key to discovery. Without action, you cannot know whether or not your innovative ideas will actually work.

5. Involve everyone, empower and trust employees. Talented and empowered human capital is the prime ingredient of organizational success. A critical feature of successful teams, especially in knowledge-driven enterprises, is that they are invested with a significant degree of empowerment, or decision-making authority. Formulate stretch goals, provide resources, and empower your people. Find a delicate balance between laissez-faire and overly controlling styles.

6. Coach and train your people to greatness. Empowerment alone is not enough. You must train and coach your people to enhance their learning ability and performance. Coaching is the key to unlocking the potential of your people, your organization, and yourself. It increases your effectiveness as a leader. As a coach, you must help your people grow and achieve more by inspiring them, asking effective questions and providing feedback. Find the right combination of instructor-led training and coaching follow-ups to achieve success.

7. Build teams and promote teamwork, leverage diversity. Teamwork is essential for competing in today's global arena. Build a star team, not a team of stars. Diversity of thought, perception, background and experience enhance the creativity and innovation. A team should not just be diverse; it has to make the most of it. Involve everyone, facilitate cross-pollination of ideas, build and empower cross-functional teams if you wish to harness the power of diversity. Challenge people from different disciplines and cultures to come up with something better together and achieve creative breakthroughs.

8. Motivate, inspire and energize people, recognize achievements. Financial rewards do encourage people to produce results. But the kind of ownership that really generates energy is not financial. It is emotional. Set stretch goals—they energize people. Become a positive, encouraging person. Give people a sense of responsibility and make them feel that their actions make a difference. Communicate with people frequently and praise them.

9. Encourage risk taking. Take risks. Don't play it safe. Making mistakes is essential to innovation and organizational growth, as long as systems are developed to learn from failures and to avoid making the same mistake twice. The more people fail, the more they succeed. They learn from taking action, from mistakes, from feedback, from getting going. Treat failures as learning opportunities. Develop a tolerance for mistakes and give your people freedom to fail, learn from failures, and start again more intelligently.

10. Make business fun. As business today is about passion and creating new things, fun has become a big element in the business strategy of many highly successful businesses. Make fun an important part of your corporate culture to enable relentless innovation and create an inspiring culture. "What's really driving the new economy—and confounding the grand pooh-bahs of the old one—is that individuals are having a huge impact. And an awful lot of fun," writes Edward O. Welles in *The Fun Factor*. People should be happy at work and have fun. Encourage just-for-fun programs. "Find some humor in your failures. Don't take yourself so seriously. Loosen up, and everybody around you will loosen up. Have fun. Show enthusiasm—always," advised Sam Walton.

Can a Manager be a Leader and a Leader be a Manager?

The answer to the question is "yes". The skills to be a leader or a manager are not exclusive in nature. A leader who only displays leadership skills will be ineffective when it comes to checking time cards, completing employee reviews, and scheduling employee vacation time; things that employers require their managers to do on timely basis. Similarly, a manager who spends all his/her time completing paperwork and reading reports; only creates more problems for him or her because they lack a developing relationship with their employees.

If you are a manager who has spent too much time managing and not leading his/her employees, start spending 10 per cent of your time each week leading until you can establish 25 per cent of your time in leadership practices. If you are a leader who only likes to lead, either become a politician, hire an assistant to be the manager, or start spending 50 per cent of your time getting the paperwork done.

Environment

Every organization has a particular work environment, which dictates to a considerable degree how its leaders respond to problems and opportunities. This is brought about by its heritage of past leaders and its present leaders.

Goals, Values, and Concepts

Leaders exert influence on the environment via three types of actions:

1. The goals and performance standards they establish.
2. The values they establish for the organization.
3. The business and people concepts they establish.

Successful organizations have leaders who set high standards and goals across the entire spectrum, such as strategies, market leadership, plans, meetings and presentations, productivity, quality, and reliability.

Values reflect the concern the organization has for its employees, customers, investors, vendors, and surrounding community. These values define the manner in how business will be conducted.

Concepts define what products or services the organization will offer and the methods and processes for conducting business.

These goals, values, and concepts make up the organization's "personality" or how the organization is observed by both outsiders and insiders. This personality defines the roles, relationships, rewards, and rites that take place.

Roles ad Relationships

Roles are the positions that are defined by a set of expectations about behavior of any job incumbent. Each role has a set of tasks and responsibilities that may or may not be spelled out. Roles have a powerful effect on behavior for several reasons, to include money being paid for the performance of the role, there is prestige attached to a role, and a sense of accomplishment or challenge.

Relationships are determined by a role's tasks. While some tasks are performed alone, most are carried out in relationship with others. The tasks will determine who the role-holder is required to interact with, how often, and towards what end.

Also, normally the greater the interaction, the greater the liking. This in turn leads to more frequent interaction. In human behavior, its hard to like someone whom we have no contact with, and we tend to seek out those we like. People tend to do what they are rewarded for, and friendship is a powerful reward. Many tasks and behaviors that are associated with a role are brought about by these relationships. That is, new task and behaviors are expected of the present role holder because a strong relationship was developed in the past, either by that role holder or a prior role holder.

Culture and Climate

There are two distinct forces that dictate how to act within an organization: culture and climate.

Each organization has its own distinctive culture. It is a combination of the founders, past leadership, current leadership, crises, events, history, and size. This results in rites: the routines, rituals, and the "way we do things". These rites impact individual behavior on what it takes to be in good standing (the norm) and directs the appropriate behavior for each circumstance.

The climate is the feel of the organization, the individual and shared perceptions and attitudes of the organization's members. While the culture is the deeply rooted nature of the organization that is a result of long-held formal and informal systems, rules, traditions, and customs; climate is a short-term phenomenon created by the current leadership. Climate represents the beliefs about the "feel of the organization" by its members. This individual perception of the "feel of the organization" comes from what the people believe about the activities that occur in the organization. These activities influence both individual and team motivation and satisfaction, such as:

- How well does the leader clarify the priorities and goals of the organization? What is expected of us?
- What is the system of recognition, rewards, and punishments in the organization?
- How competent are the leaders?

- Are leaders free to make decision?
- What will happen if I make a mistake?

Organizational climate is directly related to the leadership and management style of the leader, based on the values, attributes, skills, and actions, as well as the priorities of the leader. Compare this to "ethical climate"—the "feel of the organization" about the activities that have ethical content or those aspects of the work environment that constitute ethical behavior. The ethical climate is the feel about whether we do things right; or the feel of whether we behave the way we ought to behave. The behavior (character) of the leader is the most important factor that impacts the climate.

On the other hand, culture is a long-term, complex phenomenon. Culture represents the shared expectations and self-image of the organization. The mature values that create "tradition" or the "way we do things here". Things are done differently in every organization. The collective vision and common folklore that define the institution are a reflection of culture. Individual leaders, cannot easily create or change culture because culture is a part of the organization. Culture influences the characteristics of the climate by its effect on the actions and thought processes of the leader. But, everything you do as a leader will effect the climate of the organization.

Leadership Styles Overview

When developing your leadership skills, one must soon confront an important practical question, "What leadership styles work best for me and my organization?" To answer this question, it's best to understand that there are many leadership styles from which to choose.

Three Classic Leadership Styles

One dimension of it has to do with control and one's perception of how much control one should give to people. The laissez-faire style implies low control, the autocratic style high control and the participative lies somewhere in between.

The Laissez-Faire Leadership Style

The style is largely a "hands off" view that tends to minimize the amount of direction and face time required. Works well if you have highly trained and highly motivated direct reports.

The Autocratic Leadership Style

The style has its advocates, but it is falling out of favor in many countries. Some people have argued that the style is popular with today's CEOs, who have much in common with feudal lords in Medival Europe.

The Participative Leadership Style

It's hard to order and demand someone to be creative, perform as a team, solve complex problems, improve quality, and provide outstanding customer service. The style presents a happy medium between over controlling (micromanaging) and not being engaged and tends to be seen in organizations that must innovate to prosper.

Determining the Best Leadership Style

Situational Leadership. In the 1950s, management theorists from Ohio State University and the University of Michigan published a series of studies to determine whether leaders should be more task or relationship (people) oriented. The importance of the research cannot be over-estimated since leaders tend to have a dominant style; a leadership style they use in a wide variety of situations.

Surprisingly, the research discovered that there is no one best style: leaders must adjust their leadership style to the situation as well as to the people being led.

The Emergent Leadership Style

Contrary to the belief of many, groups do not automatically accept a new "boss" as leader. We see a number of ineffective managers who didn't know the behaviors to use when one is taking over a new group.

The Transactional Leadership Style

The approach emphasizes getting things done within the umbrella of the status quo; almost in opposition to the goals of the transformational leadership. It's considered to be a "by the book" approach in which the person works within the rules. As such, it's commonly seen in large, bureaucratic organizations.

The Transformational Leadership Style

The primary focus of this leadership style is to make change happen in:

- Our Self,
- Others,
- Groups, and
- Organizations.

Charisma is a special leadership style commonly associated with transformational leadership. While extremely powerful, it is extremely hard to teach.

Visionary Leadership. The leadership style focuses on how the leader defines the future for followers and moves them toward it.

From the short review above, one can see that there are many different aspects to being a great leader; a role requiring one to play many different leadership styles to be successful.

Other leadership styles include:

Strategic Leadership is practiced by the military services such as the Indian Army, Indian Air Force, and many large corporations. It stresses the competitive nature of running an organization and being able to out fox and out wit the competition.

Team Leadership. A few years ago, a large corporation decided that supervisors were no longer needed and those in charge suddenly were "team leaders". Since there also were no departments; workers suddenly became "a team". Today, companies have gotten smarter about teams, but it still takes leadership to transition a group into a team.

Influence Oriented Leadership Styles. Here one looks at the behaviors associated how one exercises influence. For example, does the person mostly punish? Do they know how to reward?

Cross-Cultural Leadership. Not all individuals can adapt to the leadership styles expected in a different culture; whether that culture is organizational or national.

Coaching. A great coach is definately a leader who also possesses a unique gift—the ability to teach and train.

Level Five Leadership. This term was coined by Jim Collins in his book *Good to Great: Why Some Company's Make the Leap and Other Don't.* As Collins says in his book, "We were surprised, shocked really, to discover the types of leadership required for turning a good company into a great one".

Servant Leadership. Some leaders have put the needs of their followers first. For example, the motto of the Los Angeles Police Department, "To Protect and Serve". reflects this philosophy of service. One suspects these leaders are rare in business.

The Two Most Important Keys to Effective Leadership

A Hay's study examined over 75 key components of employee satisfaction. They found that:

- Trust and confidence in top leadership was the single most reliable predictor of employee satisfaction in an organization.
- Effective communication by leadership in three critical areas was the key to winning organizational trust and confidence:
  1. Helping employees understand the company's overall business strategy.
  2. Helping employees understand how they contribute to achieving key business objectives.
  3. Sharing information with employees on both how the company is doing and how an employee's own division is doing—relative to strategic business objectives.

So in a nutshell—you must be trustworthy and you have to be able to communicate a vision of where the organization needs to go. The next section, "Principles of Leadership", ties in closely with this key concept.

Principles of Leadership

To help you be, know, and do; (U.S. Army, 1973) follow these eleven principles of leadership (later chapters in this guide expand on these and provide tools for implementing them):

Know yourself and seek self-improvement—In order to know yourself, you have to understand your be, know, and do, attributes. Seeking self-improvement means continually strengthening your attributes. This can be accomplished through self-study, formal classes, reflection, and interacting with others.

1. **Be technically proficient**—As a leader, you must know your job and have a solid familiarity with your employees' tasks.
2. **Seek responsibility and take responsibility for your actions**—Search for ways to guide your organization to new heights. And when things go wrong, they always do sooner or later—do not blame others. Analyze the situation, take corrective action, and move on to the next challenge.
3. **Make sound and timely decisions**—Use good problem solving, decision-making, and planning tools.
4. **Set the example**—Be a good role model for your employees. They must not only hear what they are expected to do, but also see. *We must become the change we want to see*—Mahatma Gandhi.
5. **Know your people and look out for their well-being**—Know human nature and the importance of sincerely caring for your workers.
6. **Keep your workers informed**—Know how to communicate with not only them, but also seniors and other key people.
7. **Develop a sense of responsibility in your workers**—Help to develop good character traits that will help them carry out their professional responsibilities.

8. **Ensure that tasks are understood, supervised, and accomplished**—Communication is the key to this responsibility.
9. **Train as a team**—Although many so called leaders call their organization, department, section, etc. a team; they are not really teams...they are just a group of people doing their jobs.
10. **Use the full capabilities of your organization**—By developing a team spirit, you will be able to employ your organization, department, section, etc. to its fullest capabilities.

Factors of Leadership

There are four major factors in leadership:

Follower

Different people require different styles of leadership. For example, a new hire requires more supervision than an experienced employee. A person who lacks motivation requires a different approach than one with a high degree of motivation. You must know your people! The fundamental starting point is having a good understanding of human nature such as needs, emotions, and motivation. You must come to know your employees' be, know, and do attributes.

Leader

You must have a honest understanding of who you are, what you know, and what you can do. Also, note that it is the followers, not the leader who determines if a leader is successful. If they do not trust or lack confidence in their leader, then they will be uninspired. To be successful you have to convince your followers, not yourself or your superiors, that you are worthy of being followed.

Communication

You lead through two-way communication. Much of it is nonverbal. For instance, when you "set the example", that communicates to your people that you would not ask them to perform anything that you would not be willing to do. What and how you communicate either builds or harms the relationship between you and your employees.

Situation

All are different. What you do in one situation will not always work in another. You must use your judgment to decide the best course of action and the leadership style needed for each situation. For example, you may need to confront an employee for inappropriate behavior, but if the confrontation is too late or too early, too harsh or too weak, then the results may prove ineffective.

Various forces will affect these factors. Examples of forces are your relationship with your seniors, the skill of your people, the informal leaders within your organization, and how your company is organized.

Attributes

If you are a leader who can be trusted, then those around you will grow to respect you. To be such a leader, there is a Leadership Framework to guide you:

Leadership Models

Leadership models help us to understand what makes leaders act the way they do. The ideal is not to lock yourself in to a type of behavior discussed in the model, but to realize that every situation calls for a different approach or behavior to be taken. Two models will be discussed, the Four Framework Approach and the Managerial Grid.

Four Framework Approach

In the Four Framework Approach, Bolman and Deal (1991) suggest that leaders display leadership behaviors in one of four types of frameworks: Structural, Human Resource, Political, or Symbolic. The style can either be effective or ineffective, depending upon the chosen behavior in certain situations.

Structural Framework

In an effective leadership situation, the leader is a social architect whose leadership style is analysis and design. While in an ineffective leadership situation, the leader is a petty tyrant whose leadership style is details. Structural Leaders focus on structure, strategy, environment, implementation, experimentation, and adaptation.

Human Resource Framework

In an effective leadership situation, the leader is a catalyst and servant whose leadership style is support, advocate, and empowerment. While in an ineffective leadership situation, the leader is a pushover, whose leadership style is abdication and fraud. Human Resource Leaders believe in people and communicate that belief; they are visible and accessible; they empower, increase participation, support, share information, and move decision-making down into the organization.

Political Framework

In an effective leadership situation, the leader is an advocate, whose leadership style is coalition and building. While in an ineffective leadership situation, the leader is a hustler, whose leadership style is manipulation. Political leaders clarify what they want and what they can get; they assess the distribution of power and interests; they build linkages to other stakeholders, use persuasion first, then use negotiation and coercion only if necessary.

Symbolic Framework

In an effective leadership situation, the leader is a prophet, whose leadership style is inspiration. While in an ineffective leadership situation, the leader is a fanatic or fool, whose leadership style is smoke and mirrors. Symbolic leaders view organizations as a stage or theater to play certain roles and give impressions; these leaders use symbols to capture attention; they try to frame experience by providing plausible interpretations of experiences; they discover and communicate a vision.

This model suggests that leaders can be put into one of these four categories and there are times when one approach is appropriate and times when it would not be. Any one of these approaches alone would be inadequate, thus we should strive to be conscious of all four approaches, and not just rely on one or two. For example, during a major organization change, a structural leadership style may be more effective than a visionary leadership style; while during a period when strong growth is needed, the visionary approach may be better. We also need to understand ourselves as each of us tends to have a preferred approach. We need to be conscious of this at all times and be aware of the limitations of our favoring just one approach.

For an activity, see Bolman and Deal's Four Framework Approach.

Managerial Grid

The Blake and Mouton *Managerial Grid* (1985) uses two axis:

1. "Concern for people" is plotted using the vertical axis.
2. "Concern for task" is along the horizontal axis.

They both have a range of 0 to 9. The notion that just two dimensions can describe a managerial behavior has the attraction of simplicity. These two dimensions can be drawn as a graph or grid:

Most people fall somewhere near the middle of the two axis. But, by going to the extremes, that is, people who score on the far end of the scales, we come up with four types of leaders:

- **Authoritarian** (9 on task, 1 on people)
- **Team Leader** (9 on task, 9 on people)
- **Country Club** (1 on task, 9 on people)
- **Impoverished** (1 on task, 1 on people).

Authoritarian Leader (high task, low relationship)

People who get this rating are very much task oriented and are hard on their workers (autocratic). There is little or no allowance for cooperation or collaboration. Heavily task oriented people display these characteristics: they are very strong on schedules; they expect people to do what they are told without question or debate; when something goes wrong they tend to focus on who is to blame rather than concentrate on exactly what is wrong and how to prevent it; they are intolerant of what they see as dissent (it may just be someone's creativity), so it is difficult for their subordinates to contribute or develop.

Team Leader (high task, high relationship)

This type of person leads by positive example and endeavors to foster a team environment in which all team members can reach their highest potential, both as team members and as people. They encourage the team to reach team goals as effectively as possible, while also working tirelessly to strengthen the bonds among the various members. They normally form and lead some of the most productive teams.

Country Club Leader (low task, high relationship)

This person uses predominantly reward power to maintain discipline and to encourage the team to accomplish its goals. Conversely, they are almost incapable of employing the more punitive coercive and legitimate powers. This inability results from fear that using such powers could jeopardize relationships with the other team members.

Impoverished Leader (low task, low relationship)

This leader uses a "delegate and disappear" management style. Since they are not committed to either task accomplishment or maintenance; they essentially allow their team to do whatever it wishes and prefer to detach themselves from the team process by allowing the team to suffer from a series of power struggles.

The most desirable place for a leader to be along the two axis at most times would be a 9 on task and a 9 on people—the Team Leader. However, do not entirely dismiss the other three. Certain situations might call for one of the other three to be used at times. For example, by playing the Impoverished Leader, you allow your team to gain self-reliance. Be an Authoritarian Leader to instill a sense of discipline in an unmotivated worker. By carefully studying the situation and the forces affecting it, you will know at what points along the axis you need to be in order to achieve the desired result.

For an activity, see The Leadership Matrix.

The Process of Great Leadership

The road to great leadership (Kouzes & Posner, 1987) that is common to successful leaders:

- **Challenge the process**—First, find a process that you believe needs to be improved the most.
- **Inspire a shared vision**—Next, share your vision in words that can be understood by your followers.
- **Enable others to act**—Give them the tools and methods to solve the problem.
- **Model the way**—When the process gets tough, get your hands dirty. A boss tells others what to do...a leader shows that it can be done.
- **Encourage the heart**—Share the glory with your followers' heart, while keeping the pains within your own.

The Enneagram is the single most powerful tool I have encountered to help leaders face and work through their limitations in order to achieve their full potential. I agree with Robert Kaplan (*Beyond Ambition*) that we are all somewhat ambivalent about knowing ourselves better because we're invested through long habit—however unfortunate its outcomes—in the self-image we find familiar. But coming to know your Enneagram style can be a powerful catalyst for personal change that will also enhance your effectiveness as a leader.

Because this is a *motivational* model, however, and not a *behavioral* model, it is best to determine your character type through a process of discovery, focusing on the *compulsion* or "driving force" of each style (vs. relying on any of the available questionnaires). If you focus only on the *behaviors* that are emphasized for each, you will see yourself in a number of them, which would be unnecessarily confusing. Friends and co-workers may offer useful feedback about behaviors that *seem* to identify your style. But only you can make the final judgment—one of the styles will characterize these key aspects more fully than the others:

- What is your **driving force** or "compulsion"?
- What is the **behavior set** or "fixation" that arises from your driving force?
- What **talk style** is typical of you?
- How do you react **under stress**?
- What is your key **development** need?

Once you make those distinctions you will understand why Michael Goldberg (The *Nine Ways of Working*) suggests that the nine styles might as well come from different planets: each views the world differently and wants something different from life. At work, each has a characteristic agenda and operates within a particular decision-making frame. My book with Clarence Thomson, *Out of the Box*: *Coaching with the Enneagram*, is full of business-related cases that bring all nine Enneagram styles to life.

In my experience as a leadership development coach, all of the Enneagram styles, when driven by compulsive forces, protect their self-image at great cost to their full potential as organizational leaders. With awareness of their underlying character and a commitment to self-development, all of the nine are also capable of great contributions and gifts to the organization and to the people they manage.

Leadership Style One: The Idealist

A self-observing *Idealist* can be a wonderful leader: wise, tolerant, balanced, and focused on standards of excellence in ways that provide an exemplary vision for followers. Ones are often the purveyors of quality in an organization.

When less well-developed, they show their fixation on perfectionism. They carry an internal judging voice, which chastises themselves (or others) for falling short of perfection (preaching) or, in a very healthy individual, invokes higher attainment (teaching). Their driving force is anger, which is typically over-controlled until it erupts as resentment when someone has failed to live up to their expectations. They're good at moral tirades, yet they also show a "running amok" side that allows them to escape their own high standards.

Developmental skills include reducing the power of their internal critic, channeling anger more effectively, learning to respond to criticism non-defensively, and moving away from black-and-white thinking with positive reframing and creative problem-solving. The key development need for this leadership style is patience, the willingness to accept conditions that do not conform to one's ideal.

Leadership Style Two: The Mentor

The most interpersonally oriented of all the leadership styles, healthy *Mentors* are unconditionally caring leaders who derive deep satisfaction from seeing and encouraging the development of others; they are typically great supporters of customer service. Well-developed Twos will also be aware of their own needs, which provides balance in their lives and allows them to give freely, without expectation of return.

Their *driving force* is pride, which is attached to their self-image as helper; out of this they tend to be in the middle of things, giving help and advice whether others want it or not. When less developed they have a fixation on entitlement and can use manipulation to influence people. If they feel betrayed they may even become vindictive ("after all I've done for you!"). Their key development need is humility, which accompanies true compassion without expectation.

Developmental skills include acknowledging their own needs, seeing how they contribute to their own workload and saying no, setting clearer boundaries, and asserting their interpersonal power more directly.

Leadership Style Three: The Star

Star leaders are often expansive, risk-taking go-getters who ensure high productivity for their organizations. Formidable models for others, they are efficient and supremely goal-oriented; consequently, they tend to rise to top organizational levels, or to run their own companies.

What under-developed threes personify for all of us is our image-making. They're good at self-promotion and can be perceived as showcasing themselves at the expense of the team. Threes tend to look outward for their reflection in the eyes of others—and their inner life can be lacking. Their driving force is vanity, which shows up in the fixation of self-deception (e.g. convincing oneself that a failure to involve the team in a major business coup was not important because of the results achieved).

Developmental skills include learning to collaborate instead of compete, clarifying their own values/developing internal criteria (vs. external validation), learning from failure, and accessing their feelings. Their key development need is truthfulness, speaking from the essential self and not through personality needs.

Leadership Style Four: The Innovator

Innovators are vital to the health of an organization because they are able to view things from a new slant and are not bound by tradition; they can keep an organization from slowly dying out of untested and outdated assumptions.

More in touch with their feelings than other types, they are in danger of sinking into moodiness if they meet with resistance to their ideas. The same talent that allows fours to "look outside the box" can lead them to wonder why they never see things the way others do, and subsequently to question if they are flawed—their conversation is ripe with sad stories. Their *driving force* is envy, which shows up in the *fixation* of dissatisfaction, a perception that "the grass is always greener somewhere else".

Developmental skills include focusing more on strengths and resources and less on the "tragedy" of life, learning to develop the possibilities of their current jobs, shifting their moods through physical exercise or creative outlets, reframing self-criticism in more positive ways, and championing a program or process they believe in. Their key development need is equanimity, the ability to live in the moment.

Leadership Style Five: The Synthesizer

Because of their ability to take in the whole picture and integrate its components in creative ways, well-developed

Synthesizers can be consummate strategists and visionaries. Often very bright, they are extremely capable of influencing others through their knowledge.

Sometimes they sound like they're giving a dissertation. Although fives can be profound and passionate leaders, they tend to disdain the role of emotions in human interaction. They are the most independent of the nine styles and prefer to be surrounded by other highly capable people who need no direction or external reinforcement. Their driving force is hoarding, which shows up particularly in their fixation on detachment from emotions, a "stinginess" of feelings.

Developmental skills include debating less and probing/listening more with the goal of mutually satisfying solutions, taking their role as coach more seriously—including giving attention to group process (meetings, teamwork, etc.), and affirming others' positive efforts. Their key development need is nonattachment, engaging with others without fear of being overwhelmed.

Leadership Style Six: The Partner

Partners at their best are highly team-oriented leaders and excellent managers who bring out the best in everyone. These are energetic executives who attend to interdependent organizational needs, which shows up in their language as thoughts about the group.

Their *driving force* is fear, which is manifested in less well-developed sixes as a fixation on accusation of others (particularly those in authority). Sixes also look for hidden agendas, and experience self-doubt. They may procrastinate and/or blurt out their feelings with a kind of reckless courage (driven by their anxieties), and then worry that they've shot themselves in the foot—and they may have. The good news is that they challenge others in ways that hold them accountable; the bad news is that they're always looking for the bad news!

Developmental skills include getting a reality check on their fears, empowering themselves vs. blaming others, focusing more on possibilities vs. worries, and centering their verbal presentations on a central theme and several key points.

Their key development need is courage, consistent with a certain kind of "morality": recognizing their own contribution to situations instead of playing "victim".

Leadership Style Seven: The Futurist

Charming and easy to talk to, highly evolved *Futurists* are the organization's cheerleaders because of their natural optimism. They focus on long-term perspective and possibilities. Equality is important to them, so sevens sometimes have to work around organizational constraints.

Less developed leaders of this type can seem egotistical because they love to tell anecdotes and may forget to invite others to talk. They're sometimes perceived as lacking analytical ability because of oversimplifying or skating over the surface. The Seven's *driving force* is gluttony, a seeking of pleasure in order to avoid pain; consequently they are overfocused (*fixated*) on enthusiasm (the "bad" news is that they only want to hear the good news) and uneasy activity.

Developmental skills include contingency planning for problems, eliciting and accepting feedback, using negative reframing to counter their optimism, and—particularly—disciplining themselves to follow through on their own development (it's hard work)! Their key development need is temperance: seeking moderation and letting go of materialism.

Leadership Style Eight: The Advocate

Advocate leaders who have paid attention to their own development are able to shoulder huge responsibility without having to control everything. Right beneath the surface they are soft-hearted; when this is tempered with their typical self-confidence, they have loyal followers and can truly move mountains.

Unfortunately, eights have the reputation of power mongers and tyrants because it is difficult for them to feel enough trust to acknowledge any vulnerability. Their *driving force* is lust/excess. Often, they feel it is their responsibility to intervene in and direct situations, and they pursue power and control (their fixation) aggressively. They hold a value for justice—as self-defined! *Advocates* can have a "bull-in-the-china-shop" approach because they speak in imperatives.

Developmental skills include enhancing their ability to put themselves in others' shoes, collaborative negotiation and active listening skills, and respecting and mentoring others. Their key development need is innocence—a regaining of the child they never were, accompanied by a shift to more altruistic and benign modes of operating, a focus on service to the world.

Leadership Style Nine: The Diplomat

Serene and centered, well-developed *Diplomats* bring cooperation to any organization; they are highly capable of dealing with others' problems and building consensus. They have a natural tendency to honor diversity, and can get along with almost anyone.

Unexamined nines tend to merge with others' preferences, however, and to forget their own. Taking a strong position is particularly difficult for them, because they see all sides of an issue and because they are essentially non-aggressive. Their *driving force* is indolence—not that they're lazy (they're very hard workers) but that they are out of touch with their own wishes, a *fixation* on self-forgetting. Though quiet, once they get started they tend toward epic tales (they hold so many alternative views it's hard to focus).

Developmental skills include learning to speak up/confront others, recognizing passive-aggressive behavior/becoming more assertive, setting priorities/sticking to them, staying focused, and initiating change. Their key development need is active engagement, the willingness to stay focused on their own purpose, without distraction.

Are You A Leader? Part II: Leadership Self Test Answers and Discussion

The little "Self Test" printed in Part I of this article is meant to provoke thought, and there are no standards here for how many "leader" responses would make you a "true leader".

The answers and ideas offered come from experience with assessments involving hundreds of leaders and managers over time, but this is not a standardized test. I hope you find the discussion below interesting and educational.

Remember, most managerial jobs require some leadership practice, and executives need both strong management and leadership skills. The idea that real people are either "leaders" or "managers" is false—different jobs require different balances of each.

Self Test Answers and Discussion

1. **TRUE or FALSE: I think more about immediate results than I do about mentoring others.** Managers focus on the process and immediate efficiency more than leaders do. Leaders think about how they invest their time to develop the strongest talent so that those people can grow and do more and more over time. Leaders figure if they do that, those people will do a better job of watching and improving processes than they themselves will. "True" is more of a manager's response, and "False" is more of a leader's response.

2. **TRUE or FALSE: People will be motivated if you pay them enough.** Leaders understand that pay is a satisfier, not a true motivator. Once the satisfier is in place at an acceptable level, people are motivated by the nature of the work and challenges, opportunities to learn and grow, and based on whether or not they feel their bosses support or care about them. "True" is more of a manager's answer, and "False" is more of a leader's answer.

3. **TRUE or FALSE: It's nice to know about people's long-term goals, but not necessary to get the job done.** Someone once said that managers get "work done through people", but leaders get "people done through work". Since leaders need to know what makes individual people tick, they want to know long-term goals and aspirations, so they can craft ways to combine personal goals with the work at hand, or even the organization's goals. For a given project, it may be less important to know people's long-term goals, but for organizational success and growth, it is necessary. "True" is

more of a manager's answer, and "False" is more of a leader's answer.

4. TRUE or FALSE: If you have a consistent recognition system that rewards everyone in the same way, then that is enough. Leaders' recognize that everyone is motivated a little differently, and so consistency is not an absolute virtue in recognizing people. Some people may like public praise, and others may emphasize more the opportunity to have flexible family time, for example. Since managers emphasize systems more than they do people or personalities, "True" is more of a manager's response, and "False" is more of a leader's response.

5. TRUE or FALSE: The best way to build a team is to set a group goal that is highly challenging, maybe even "crazy". Manager's tend to think more in terms of what has been done before and try to make more incremental improvements, while leaders like to challenge people to bring out their best in ways they themselves may not have imagined possible. The best way to build team coherence is to take people through a shared, difficult challenge—something any military platoon leader can tell you. "True" is more of a leader's response, and "False" is more of a manager's response.

6. TRUE or FALSE: My greatest pleasure in my job comes from making the work process more effective. This is a classic manager's priority, deriving most pleasure from process and efficiency. Leaders enjoy that a lot too, but they tend to enjoy most when they can help people and organizations grow. "True" is more of a manager's response, and "False" is more of a leader's response.

7. TRUE or FALSE: I spend more of my time and attention on my weaker performers than I do on my top performers, who basically take care of themselves. Leaders use their time as a reward, and seek to invest their attention where it can have the most upside impact. Generally speaking, people have the most opportunity to grow and become truly great where they already demonstrate strong performance, and so leaders tend to avoid remedial projects or the constant oversight of weaker performers. Instead, they spend more of their attention on the people who are the best at what they do, since those are the people who will bring invent the greatest process and performance improvements in the future. Managers tend to focus more on problems to solve than they do on opportunities to boost people toward previously unachieved levels of excellence. "True" is more of a manager's response, and "False" is more of a leader's response.

8. TRUE or FALSE: It's better not to know anything about the personal lives and interests of the people who report to me. Leaders try to learn what makes each person tick, so that means knowing getting to understand them in a more personal way, without being invasive or inappropriate. Managers tend to be more cut-and-dried in their work relations. "True" is more of a manager's response, while "False" is more of a leader's response.

9. TRUE or FALSE: Sometimes, it's almost as if I'm a "collector of people" because I'm always recruiting and getting to know new people. Some of the best managers are very good at studying best practices—ways to "build a better mousetrap" to improve performance and efficiency. Leaders tend to look more for the "Einsteins" and star performers of the world who are more likely to invent those better mousetraps in the first place. Leaders think about people and their talents as if they were investment opportunities, and so "True" is more of a leader's response, and "False" is more of a manager's response.

10. TRUE or FALSE: I like to surround myself with people who are better at what they do than I am. This is a classic leadership statement, since leaders are all about finding and cultivating talent, and are not threatened by it. Managers may tend to want to feel more in control of their surroundings—not least of all because highly talented people can be very independent and difficult to "manage!" Since leaders tend to have stronger social skills than managers do, and so are better prepared to deal with other strong egos, "True" is more of a leader's response, and "False" is more of a manager's response.

11. TRUE or FALSE: I am a lifelong student of what makes other people tick. "True" is more of a leader's response, and "False" is more of a manager's response, for reasons already discussed.

12. TRUE or FALSE: People talk about "mission" too much—it's best just to let people do their work and not try to bring values into the conversation. While it's true that "mission" and "vision" are concepts that have become watered down by careless misuse, leaders still understand that it is best to connect daily work and projects into a larger framework that gives work a sense of purpose and meaning. People would rather feel that their work has some purpose and meaning in order to do their work well and care about results. "True" is more of a manager's response, and "False" is more a leader's response.

13. TRUE or FALSE: It's my job to know everything that goes on in my area. Since leaders focus more on knowing the people who know what is going on, rather than on the details of everything that is going on. "True" is more of a manager's response, and "False" is more of a leader's response.

14. TRUE or FALSE: I pay close attention to how and where I spend my time, because the priorities I put into action are the ones that other people will observe and follow. Leaders realize that the little things they do ripple out in wider and wider ways, and that their actual priorities will be mimicked throughout an organization. As a result, they make their choices wisely, knowing that people, and other managers or supervisors, do imitate the "boss", who sets the ultimate tone. "True" is more of a leader's response, and "False" is more of a manager's response.

15. TRUE or FALSE: I've worked hard to get along with or understand people who are very different from me. As headstrong as many leaders can be, they know from experience that being so headstrong can be a liability, and they have learned to work hard at accepting and listening to other points of view. Managers may be more focused on what they believe to be the "right way" to do some job or work process, and may be less open to widely divergent views. Leaders may not always enjoy hearing other views, but they often have learned the critical importance of the saying, "Let the best idea win!"

"True" is more of a leader's response, and "False" is more of a manager's response.

Ten Rules to Live by to Achieve Success

1. ***Feed Your Strengths!*** Do things that allow your excellent organizational and logical abilities to flourish. Explore the worlds of business management, accounting, and medicine.

2. ***Face Your Weaknesses!*** See your weaknesses for what they are, and seek to overcome them. Especially, strive to use your judgment against your internal store of knowledge, rather than as a means of disregarding other people's ideas.

3. ***Talk Through Your Thoughts.*** You need to step through your vast amount of information in order to put things into perspective. Give yourself appropriate time to do this, and take advantage of discussing ideas with others. Some find that externalizing your thoughts is a valuable exercise, as is expressing your ideas clearly in writing.

4. ***Take in Everything.*** Don't dismiss ideas prematurely because you don't respect the person generating the ideas, or because you think you already know it all. After all, everybody has something to offer, and nobody knows everything. As Steven Covey says, "Seek first to understand, and then to be understood."

5. ***Quench Your Desire to Control Others.*** Remember that most people do not want to be controlled. Again, turn your controlling tendencies inwardly rather than outwardly. You can only really control yourself.

6. ***Be Aware of Others.*** Take time to notice where others are coming from. What is their personality type? How are they currently feeling?

7. ***Be Accountable for Yourself.*** Don't blame the problems in your life on other people. Look inwardly for solutions.

8. ***Be Gentle in Your Expectations,*** and judge yourself at least as harshly as you judge others.

9. ***Assume the Best.*** Don't distress yourself and others by dwelling on the dark side of everything. Just as there is a

positive charge for every negative charge, there is a light side to every dark side. Remember that positive situations are created by positive attitudes, and vice versa. Expect the best, and the best will come forward.

10. There is Nothing to Fear but Fear Itself. Sometimes it's necessary to take a risk to initiate change. Don't be afraid to do so when that time comes. In most cases, the obstacles and burdens standing in the way of your goal are not really there—they just exist in your perspective. Change your perspective—change your life.

The Difference between Management and Leadership

It sounds great. "You lead people, and you manage things." It's salient. Even philosophical. But it's wrong.

Before I defend my position, some definitions would probably help. In the words of Peter Drucker and Warren Bennis, two of the most respected names in business, leadership is doing the right things; management is doing things right.

In other words, *leadership*—doing the right things—is deciding the best course of action to take. What are the things we should be doing to get us to where we want to go? What direction or course of action should we take? Where do we want to be in the end?

The act of management then follows the act of leadership. Once the best course or direction has been decided, *management*—doing things right—picks up the ball, looks at the objectives established by leadership and says, "Okay, here's the best way to get there".

Shall the twain ever meet? You bet. Leaders must use some management skills and managers must use some leadership skills. But understanding the differences and working within their basic framework can make the workplace a whole lot more productive.

In an example offered by Stephen Covey, one corporate leader had his eyes opened when he was shown the leadership/management differences. He was spending a huge percentage of his time *managing* day-to-day operations. He worked closely with managers to help ensure production was optimal. But after he learned the definition of leadership, he took his hands off the day-to-day operations and began spending time looking at the direction of his company. He spent considerably more time examining trends and data, discovering what his company should be doing to stay competitive down the road. Then, armed with that information, he set strategic objectives for growth. The result? After years of stagnant growth, corporate profits rose more than 50 per cent within a year.

Does this mean the person was a bad manager? Not at all. He may be great in a manager's role. But he was trying to do a manager's job while filling a leader's role. The double focus resulted in diminished leadership. Once he understood the role of a leader, he shed his management tasks and focused on leading, with great results.

To give my professor credit, yes, we lead people and we manage things, but we cannot neglect the management of people.

Managing people involves understanding the strengths and weaknesses of individuals within a work team and assigning people tasks for optimal efficiency. In fact, another way to look at these differences is to equate leadership with effectiveness and management with efficiency.

Effectiveness (leadership) has to do with quality—the right direction; and efficiency (management) has to do with time.

Jim is a manager I know at factory in the Midwest. He has five people in his department, and he is well-aware of each person's strengths and weaknesses. When sales are off and work is slow, Jim let's his team work wherever they want at the various workstations in the department. But when sales are up or when rush orders come in, Jim is quick to assign people to specific workstations.

Jim knows that everyone in his department can do every task, but he also recognizes that some people have a natural ability to do better in some tasks than others. Matching a person's skills to fit the job is management. It's putting the right people in the right places to get things done correctly and efficiently.

On a construction site, it may be that a carpenter knows how to wire a house, and an electrician knows how to cut wood, but it would be bad management to have them do each other's jobs. Good managers put people in positions best suited to their skills.

With all due respect to my professor and my student last week, we lead people and we manage people. It just depends on our role within the organization whether we should focus our efforts on one or the other.

Leader's Insight: Leaders' Top Three Mistakes

The first big mistake I made as a leader was to fail to ask what mistakes I was making.

I was curious what Ron Potter, my friend and the president of Team Leadership Culture, would say are the top three mistakes most leaders make. After all, he has spent the last twelve years of his professional life consulting with top leaders of national and international organizations helping them recognize and correct their mistakes.

1. Managing instead of leading. Ron didn't even have to think about the first mistake. "Managing has more to do with directing day-to-day tasks, whereas leading has more to do with casting a vision, goal setting, and motivation," he said.

When a leader spends more time managing than leading, morale suffers among the troops. Most people would prefer a goal to shoot for and some freedom to figure out how to reach that goal. "We all crave at least a partial sense of control," Ron said.

In a study several years ago, two teams of leaders were given a difficult problem to solve. The complex problem involved mental gymnastics, difficult decisions, and intense concentration. Both teams participated in the project in a room where distracting sounds were piped in through speakers. The music, noise, and voices were enough to drive you to distraction. Which, of course, was the point.

Team A couldn't do anything about the distracting sounds. They just had to put up with them. Team B was told that by pushing a button they could silence the distractions for five minutes. The only catch was that they could only use the button once each hour. Each team was then scored on various phases of their group task.

Not too surprisingly, Team B consistently outscored Team A. The kicker is, *Team B never pushed the button.* Team B at least *thought* they had control over their environment. Just knowing that they had a little freedom within their boundaries boosted their confidence level.

When leaders micromanage, they take away that sense of control vital to team dynamics and problem-solving. Former U.S. President Dwight D. Eisenhower summed this up when he said, "Pull the string, and it will follow wherever you wish. Push it, and it will go nowhere at all."

2. Mistaking individual loyalty for team building. Have you seen that little desk toy that has several steel balls hanging from a crossbeam, all in a row? If you pull one of the balls away from the others and let it go, when it strikes the row of spheres the one on the opposite end swings away from the rest in direct response to the force of the first ball. It's called "Newton's Cradle".

The next mistake is a bit more subtle and difficult to detect. Ron calls it, "The Newton's Cradle approach to leadership".

Let's say that you are the person at the top of the leadership chain in your organization. You are the crossbeam. Those steel spheres hanging beneath the crossbeam are the people who work closely with you. The plastic connectors are the individual relationships you make with those people.

You, the leader, pull one of your team members away from the others and get him pumped up about a change that needs to be made. That's like pulling one of the steel balls and holding it there. Then when you let him go, you expect him to return to the rest of the team, where they will all function with superb team dynamics, solving the current problems, achieving team goals, and making changes.

Ron explained what really happens. "The leader lets that team member go, and he just bangs against the other team member closest to him, and that one bangs quickly into the team member next to him, and so on. So all that really happens is that this one team member bangs into the others, and they swing back and forth, bumping into each other."

We shouldn't neglect the individual relationships with those who work closely with us. We also can't miss the important steps necessary to putting those people together in team situations where they learn what it means to work together.

3. Failing to apply what motivates us. "What motivates you?" Ron asked. "The ability to create? The freedom to apply what you know in order to solve problems? The thrill of a new challenge? Ask most leaders what motivates them and those items will surface. But when we get our jobs down to a science and there are no new challenges, we get bored or lose interest."

A leader may know what motivates him, but he forgets that the same things motivate those who work for him.

We want our people to be competent so that everything always runs smoothly. But when we lock people into the routine of sameness, we wind up killing their motivation. When we stretch people into new areas of challenges, we know they are going to make mistakes. But when we keep them "safe". We take the motivational wind out of their sails.

It means we have to risk other people's failure. It means we have to bite our lips and let some people toddle out into the unknown world. Yet they'll thank you for allowing them to tackle a new challenge, even if they stumble a few times.

Like a parent who prays harder when the teenager begins to drive, a leader must accept that new challenges are frightening to us but freeing to others.

Hearing this assessment of the top three mistakes leaders make, I recalled my first big mistake in leadership: failure to ask where I was making mistakes.

I need to discover where I am guilty of managing more than leading. I need to build into my leadership training calendar specific times to work on team building. And I need to motivate my leadership team by allowing them to tackle new challenges. Most of all, I need to remain courageous enough to keep asking what mistakes I'm making.

Personality Compatibility Analysis

Individual Attributes

An old proverb states that a tiger cannot change its stripes. Individual attributes, for the most part, are that part of our personality that cannot be altered much. We cannot become more intelligent, but we can become more educated. We cannot become more attentive, or less impatient, or more optimistic. These are physical characteristics that are determined by our brain structure and our body chemistry. Drugs such as alcohol, tobacco, caffeine, etc. can affect our brain chemistry and our personality. Some changes are reversible, but others are permanent and may result in addiction, flashbacks, hallucinations, and other abnormal conditions. Strokes and head injuries can also cause personality changes.

The following table lists ten Individual Attributes and some characteristics of the attributes. The characteristics are divided into positive and negative columns. The labels "positive" and "negative" do not mean that the characteristics are desirable or undesirable; they represent the degree of particular traits. It is not necessarily bad to be moderate, impatient, or passive. Compatible persons will generally share a substantial number of characteristics from the same column for each attribute, but sometimes a relationship is more stimulating when two people have characteristics from opposite columns. If a person is slow (i3–) and the other one energetic (i3+), they will not be very compatible. One person will always want to go and the other one will want to rest. However, if one is mature (i6+) and the other one inexperienced (i6–), the relationship may work if the mature person has the patience to teach the inexperienced person and the inexperienced person is willing to learn.

Individual attributes	Characteristics	
	Positive +	**Negative –**
i1. Achievement attitudes—degree of motivation.	persistent, ambitious, obsessive	easy-going, moderate, unmotivated
i2. Emotional temperament—emotions that rule our lives.	confident, stable, calm, relaxed, patient	insecure, erratic, angry, dissatisfied, impatient
i3. Energy level—pace of our daily life.	active, energetic, fast	passive, lethargic, slow
i4. Intellectual factors—characteristics of our minds.	alert, inquisitive, intelligent	inattentive, dull-witted
i5. Material attitudes—how we regard our environment.	frugal, thrifty, materialistic	spendthrift, wasteful, spiritual
i6. Maturity—our level of experience and wisdom.	mature, knowledgeable, wise	immature, inexperienced, ignorant
i7. Philosophical attitudes—our ways of thinking.	optimistic, positive, flexible	pessimistic, negative, inflexible
i8. Physical attributes—how we regard our body.	youthful, healthy, strong, sane	old, sick, weak, mentally sick
i9. Risk attitudes—degree of concern for oneself.	conservative, cautious, calculating	adventurous, impulsive, daring, drug user
i10. Task performance—attitudes toward problem solving.	organized, accurate, skillful, methodical	error-prone, disorganized, blunderer, careless

The following paragraphs discuss details of ten Individual Attributes of personality. In some cases, it is possible to anticipate how these characteristics affect relationships.

i1. Achievement Attitudes. How motivated are you to reach your goal? Are you indifferent or are you obsessive?

Sometimes personal goals do not become evident until age 25 or 30. Once you decide to have a family, further your professional career, or establish a business, you have a different degree of motivation than before you made this decision. Whereas you may have been indifferent before, your new perspective of life motivates to reach your goals. Or, if you have already achieved some of your goals, it may be more important to relax and enjoy life. In this case, your zest for accomplishment may diminish.

Ambitious and moderate people are often incompatible because they have different perceptions of what is important. The ambitious person feels that he cannot waste time on trivial things, and the moderate individual will be more contemplative and not make as much effort to achieve goals. A persistent person matched with a moderate or easy-going person will tend to nag. Nobody likes to hear "Why don't you do this? Why don't you do that?" over and over again.

i2. Emotional Temperament. How patient are you? Do you get restless when you have to wait? How do you react to frustration? Does your temper explode when your car is not delivered on time from the auto shop or do you try to look for alternatives calmly? Your emotional temperament is a measure of the degree and duration of your outbursts of frustration and of your ability to remain calm under pressure. If you are irascible, you are likely to do and say things that will ruin a relationship. Many relationships end with the phrase "If that is what you think, then it is over!" Relationships endure better when the reaction to an unpleasant surprise is more logical and less emotional. However, an extreme disappointment or an unfortunate accident can cause great emotional grief that cannot be controlled. Two angry and impatient people are more likely to get into a fight than an angry and a patient person. A habitually angry person and a calm person cannot have a very good relationship even if the calm person tries to adapt to the angry person.

i3. Energy Level. Do you like physical activities and sports, or would you rather sit down in a theater? Do you like to spend an hour at the gym or is it enough for you to walk around the block? Your energy level determines the rhythm of your life. Some people get up early and have already done many things before breakfast while others would rather stay in bed and sleep late. Human dynamos and slow, passive people can only frustrate each other. The energetic individual needs to be active to be happy. The slow individual will be miserable and exhausted with an active life style. Can such opposites manage to make good partners? Yes, but only if they do things separately. This can be completely unacceptable to a person with great libido because it demands mutual participation. Partners with similar levels of energy can have more satisfying relationships.

i4. Intellectual Factors. Intelligent gentleman seeks dumb blonde for a serious relationship. Not very likely! Successful relationships require similar levels of intellect. When we have a personal problem, we need someone who can understand us. A dull-witted person may be very kind and loving, but this may not be enough for an alert, intelligent person. Intelligent persons understand each other better. Persons with lower intellect will feel more at ease with a person of their own caliber; they will not feel dumb or intimidated.

If you are of average intelligence, you should not be looking for a genius. You will end up in second place. Your decisions will always be subjected to analysis by a greater intellect that will make you feel inferior. Relationships between people with different intellectual levels generally end up like a parent/child relationship.

i5. Material Attitudes. Are you economical or extravagant? Do you prefer to save for the future or would you rather spend what you have now? Do material possessions matter to you, or are you more interested in spiritual pursuits? Many relationships fail because of conflicts about money and possessions. "You make twice as much money as I do, why do we have to split the expenses half and half?", "I am the wife and you are supposed to support me", "Why do you give so much money to your mother when I don't have anything to wear?"

Financial advisors and marriage counselors suggest that you discuss financial matters and obligations *before* you get married. The average marriage in the United States lasts an average of seven years (it is not "till death do us part"). Your plans should include a prenuptial agreement that describes what each will take in case of a divorce. This is particularly important for second marriages when there are substantial assets or children from previous marriages. You should also agree on how to handle expenses when both people work, when one loses a job, or when the woman becomes pregnant and cannot work. You also need to discuss about savings goals, life insurance, wills, and revocable trusts. Agree on how previous debts will be handled. Marriage makes you legally responsible for your partner's debts. Are you uncomfortable talking about divorce and finances before getting married? You don't need to do it, but be prepared for unpleasant surprises.

i6. Maturity. Maturity is a personality attribute that describes good judgement. Do you do something without thinking about the consequences? Are your actions well thought out and premeditated? Maturity cannot be equated to education, but education provides maturity. Maturity is the ability to judge whether something is safe or dangerous, good or evil, or prudent or foolish. It is said that wise people learn from the mistakes of others, whereas fools learn from their own mistakes.

Can two people of different maturity levels have a successful relationship? As stated earlier, the relationship may work if the mature person has the patience to teach the inexperienced person and the inexperienced person is willing and able to learn. These are typical teacher/student relationships. The inexperienced person may initially feel inferior to the mature person, but as long as the level of intelligence is compatible, the relationships may be successful. In the long term, these relationships have the risk of failing when the inexperienced person matures and demands an equal relationship with the partner. At this point the person who had previously been superior may resent the change of status.

i7. Philosophical Attitudes. Are you optimistic or pessimistic? Is the glass half full or half empty? Do you think that we are animals that have evolved on the earth as an accident of nature, or do you think that man was put on earth by a Divine Creator? Are you willing to consider changing your point of view? To what degree are you willing to fight to defend your point of view? Why do you think that you are right? The philosophical attitude of our personality develops from our education and our internal conception of how the world works. A positive philosophical attitude gives you hope when life is hard, whereas a negative attitude may even lead you to suicide.

How likely is it that two people with different philosophical attitudes are compatible? The chances are very small. Most relationships between people of different religions reach a crisis when it is time to educate their children. "Should we raise the children as Jews, Muslims, Christians, etc.?", "Should the children go with me to church and to the mosque with you?", "Will you change your religion for me? If you love me enough you will convert to my religion." So many people have been killed in the name of religion over the centuries that it is very evident that successful relationships cannot exist between people of different creeds. Even if your partner supports you, his or her family may object to your beliefs. You will not be a whole family.

As partners, optimists and pessimists face similar problems, but the tensions surface in different ways. An optimist may feel that he has a new business opportunity that will be financially rewarding, whereas a pessimist is sure that the investment money will be wasted without any results. In the end, they will fight about money. Successful relationships require similar philosophical attitudes.

i8. Physical Attributes. The physical attributes of your personality are a combination of your age and your physical fitness. Some people at age 50 are ready for the grave, whereas some in their 80's may be getting ready for a party. You are as young as you feel. Can an older person have a successful relationship with a younger person? The answer is yes, unless the age difference is very great. The average life expectancy in the United States is 84. If there are no health problems, age is not a deterrent to a good relationship. If you are thinking of raising a family, it is better that you and your partner are both young. This will give you time to raise the children and put them through school until they are independent.

When one of the persons is healthy and the other one is sick, the healthy person has to understand the level of effort that will be needed to take care of the sick person. This is not an obligation that should be taken lightly and it can stress the relationship. If a person has a mental illness, it is seldom possible to have successful relationship. The sane partner will always have doubts about whether offensive behavior or actions from the other person are intentional or a result of the illness.

i9. Risk Attitudes. Hundreds of automobile accidents happen everyday. You are taking a risk when you drive to work. You need to pay for your house and your food, so you take the risk everyday. You do this not because you lack maturity, but because for you it is a necessity. You try to minimize your risk of injury by using seat belts and driving carefully. You are a cautious person. What about the person who goes mountain climbing or diving for the weekend? Is he or she more adventurous or daring? How about the hang glider or amateur pilot?

The level of risk of an activity can be assessed by asking your life insurance agent how much the insurance will cost for a diver, a pilot, etc. The death rates associated with each activity are a real measure of the risk. If you do something knowing that it is dangerous, you are a risk taker. If you know that the casino always makes a profit and you gamble anyway, you are a risk taker. If you smoke, drink alcohol excessively, or take drugs, you are a risk taker even if you think that you will not be harmed by your actions. The statistics are not in your favor.

Can two people with different risk attitudes have a successful relationship? Not always. People who are cautious do not like the stress of taking risks, whereas the risk-takers find it boring to do something less exciting.

i10. Task Performance. Task performance describes the accuracy and organization with which we solve problems. Methodical people organize and schedule their work to know which things will be done when. Disorganized people do not have systematic ways of approaching problems and may not be able to solve some problems. Error-prone and disorganized people do not have much in common with accurate, methodical people. Relationships between these individuals are subject to stress because the disorganized person cannot meet the expectations of the methodical person. Disorganized persons are not neat and this is irritating to methodical persons. It is possible for a disorganized person to become more organized, but this requires great effort and changing established habits.

Succession Planning

A change in executive leadership is inevitable for all organizations and can be a very challenging time. A succession plan policy is a tool to help an organization be prepared for planned or unplanned absences of the director, clarifying authority and decision-making, and thereby maintaining accountability and ensuring stability.

The following sections outline the key components of succession plan policy and provide a brief sample policy. For practical advice on how to develop a policy, see the July 2003 issue of *Transition Leader*, which includes a case study on emergency succession planning.

Elements of a Succession Plan Policy

- Statement of commitment to prepare for inevitable leadership change.
- Statement of commitment to assess leadership needs before beginning a search.
- Plan to appoint interim leadership to ensure smooth operations and compliance with contractual obligations.

- Outline of succession procedures including:
  * internal management succession to the interim position,
  * time frame for making the interim appointment,
  * time frame for appointing a board transition committee, and
  * roles of the transition committee, e.g. communication with stakeholders, identifying a transition management consultant, conducting an organizational assessment and designing the search plan.

Sample Executive Succession Plan Policy

Policy Statement: A change in executive leadership is inevitable for all organizations and can be a very challenging time. Therefore, it is the policy of the [ORGANIZATION] to be prepared for an eventual permanent change in leadership—either planned or unplanned—to ensure stability and accountability of the organization until such time as new permanent leadership is identified. The board of directors shall be responsible for implementing this policy and its related procedures.

It is also the policy of the board to assess the permanent leadership needs of the organization to help ensure the selection of a qualified and capable leader who is representative of the community, a good fit for the organization's mission, vision, values, goals and objectives, and who has the necessary skills for the organization. To ensure the organization's operations are not interrupted while the board of directors assesses the leadership needs and recruits a permanent executive officer, the board will appoint interim executive leadership as described below. The interim chief executive officer shall ensure that the organization continues to operate without disruption and that all organizational commitments previously made are adequately executed, including but not limited to, loans approved, reports due, contracts, licenses, certifications, memberships, obligations to lenders or investors of the [ORGANIZATION], and others.

It is also the policy of the [ORGANIZATION], to develop a diverse pool of candidates and consider at least three finalist candidates for its permanent CEO position. The [ORGANIZATION], shall implement an external recruitment and selection process, while at the same time encouraging the professional development and advancement of current employees. The interim CEO and any other interested internal candidates are encouraged to submit their qualifications for review and consideration by the transition committee according to the guidelines established for the search and recruitment process.

Procedures for Succession: For a temporary change in executive leadership (i.e. illness or leave of absence) refer to the organization's Personnel Guidebook. In the event the chief executive officer (CEO) of the [ORGANIZATION], is no longer able to serve in this position (i.e. leaves the position permanently), the executive committee of the board of directors shall do the following:

1. Within five business days appoint an interim CEO according to the following line of succession:
   a. chief operating officer (COO) of [ORGANIZATION],
   b. senior vice president of the parent affiliate of the [ORGANIZATION],
   c. external consultant (with experience as an interim executive director).
2. Within fifteen business days appoint an executive transition committee, in the event that a permanent change in leadership is required. This committee shall be comprised of at least one member of the executive committee and two members of the board of directors. It shall be the responsibility of this committee to implement the following preliminary transition plan:
   a. Communicate with key stakeholders regarding actions taken by the board in naming an interim successor, appointing a transition committee, and

implementing the succession policy. The organization shall maintain a current list of key stakeholders who must be contacted, such as lenders and investors of the [ORGANIZATION], foundations, government agencies, and others.

b. Consider the need for consulting assistance (i.e. transition management or executive search consultant) based on the circumstances of the transition.

c. Review the organization's business plan and conduct a brief assessment of organizational strengths, weaknesses, opportunities and threats to identify priority issues that may need to be addressed during the transition process and to identify attributes and characteristics that are important to consider in the selection of the next permanent leader.

d. Establish a time frame and plan for the recruitment and selection process.

e. Refer to the CEO Hiring Policy and Procedures in the Personnel Guidebook for additional procedures.

The board should use similar procedures in case of an executive transition that simultaneously involves the chief executive officer and other key management. In such instance, the board may also consider temporarily subcontracting some of the organizational functions from trained consultant or other organizations.

"A succession plan policy is a tool to help an organization be prepared for planned or unplanned absences of the director."

How Succession Planning Helps?

Succession planning establishes a process that recruits employees, develops their skills and abilities, and prepares them for advancement, all while retaining them to ensure a return on the organization's training investment. Succession planning involves:

- Understanding the organization's long-term goals and objectives.
- Identifying the workforce's developmental needs.
- Determining workforce trends and predictions.

In the past, succession planning typically targeted only key leadership positions. In today's organizations, it is important to include key positions in a variety of job categories.

With good succession planning, employees are ready for new leadership roles as the need arises, and when someone leaves, a current employee is ready to step up to the plate. In addition, succession planning can help develop a diverse workforce, by enabling decision-makers to look at the future make-up of the organization as a whole.

How Effective is your Succession Plan?

Succession planning is an essential part of corporate strategy in most IT organizations. While the design of the succession chart looks good on paper, it has often been found that the planning process fails to meet requirements at the time of filling a key position that has just been vacated. It is not an easy task dealing with the ever-changing equations of the leadership pipeline. According to a report by US-based business research firm Cutting Edge, while many companies have succession plans, very few follow through with the rigorous implementation required. In fact, 70 per cent of succession plans fail due to bad execution.

Succession planning has to ensure that the right people with the right skills are in the right place at the right time. It can be done in three ways: role-based, individual-based and team-based. The first is about identifying key positions, the second focuses upon key people, and the last involves replacing a section of people or resources.

Reviewing Talent

One of the challenges in all organizations is planning for HR needs. It is essential to adopt a disciplined approach to match HR resources with the anticipated needs of an organization. This includes aligning the succession planning process with business strategy.

"The purpose of the talent review is to figure out the talent required to implement the business strategy and constantly strengthen the talent pool. The talent review and planning process helps us identify talent for emerging roles in the organization," says Bijay Sahoo, vice-president (talent engagement and development) and head of HR, Wipro Technologies. Commitment from the top management is another key factor for ensuring the success of succession planning. Sahoo reveals that in Wipro, the chairman (Azim Premji) and vice-chairman and CEO (Vivek Paul) give enormous importance and their personal time for talent review and planning, and personally supervise the development and implementation of the talent plan for key roles.

According to Sahoo, the other essential factors are: (a) Accountability, as the succession planning program requires ownership at all levels in the organization. Each manager should be responsible for assessing and developing the talent in his or her team. (b) Constant attention, as it can be tempting to overlook the need for succession planning in the face of more immediate needs.

Planning the Process

The bench strength of current and future leaders gives a competitive edge to every organization. At Wipro, the succession planning programme is called Talent Review and Planning (TRP), and it is the most critical part of the organization's leadership building and talent management process. "Once our business strategy for the year is finalised, we identify the critical roles to execute it. We review the talent available for those roles internally as well as externally. We plan for the succession of existing critical roles, including that of the CEO, and identify employees who are ready to take over the roles immediately and over the next 1-2 or 2-3 years," informs Sahoo. He adds that the company does developmental planning for each identified internal candidate in terms of job rotation, training, coaching and performance counselling. They also keep track of potential external candidates, and establish touch points for attracting them at the appropriate time.

The respective SBU heads and the SBU HR heads do the TRP for the top three levels of their business. This contributes to the TRP at the Wipro Technologies level, where the chairman and vice-chairman, along with the HR head, get involved in talent planning for the top three levels. Next is the implementation of the talent strategies by developing and reviewing the action plan.

At Infinite Computer Solutions (ICS), which has a global headcount of 1,800, employees have also taken up higher roles without a change in designation, with support from functional heads and senior management teams. A skill-gap analysis is done of the candidates, and requisite training provided to make them able successors.

Clear Focus

It is a known fact that while most managements are interested in developing a pool of successors for key positions, they find it a difficult task to ensure the success of their efforts. Succession planning can get very complicated. Organizations must, therefore, have a clear focus.

Wipro has quarterly talent engagement and development (TED) reviews, and action points of each SBU and vertical are tracked. "We also track the number of senior positions that are filled internally, which gives an indication of the success of the programme. At the macro level, the retention figure also reflects the effectiveness of the succession planning programme, since one of the objectives of the programme is to help employees realise their career aspirations and thus retain them in the organization. Systematic succession planning does generate leadership talent, and an organization can measure its effectiveness by looking at the leadership talent it has created and provided to the industry. Wipro is one of the top companies when it comes to creating top-class leaders in the IT industry. "Many of our ex-employees are heading successful IT companies," says Sahoo with apparent pride.

The Training Difference

Organizations are less vulnerable to leadership crises when there's a shadow group of successors who are able and available to step into their shoes. Training plays a key role in succession planning. It is imperative to strategise, design and implement programmes to train future leaders.

Wipro has its lifecycle leadership development programmes, which are synchronised with the roles employees play at different stages of their corporate life. These include the New Leaders Programme, Wipro Leaders Programme, Business Leaders Programme and Strategic Leaders Programme for different leadership positions that an employee will assume in the organization.

"Most organizations do skill-gap analysis of the selected candidates. A schedule is drawn for the prospective individual to acquire the knowledge, skills and competencies within a time-frame," says Sunder Rajan, general manager, HR and administration, ICS. He adds that the training could be through internal programmes or on-the-job (local as well as global) to gain cross-functional or cross-geographical exposure for better maturity of the expertise that would enhance the confidence level of the person.

Just-in-time Succession

Then there's just-in-time succession, which maps existing competencies of the staff to fill an important position. Succession planning software uses competency analysis which lets companies understand the demand side of the equation with what their staff have to offer. "Succession planning is not an issue of a position; you can plan for two or three years, but by that time the to-be-successor may have already left the organization; consequently it is not relevant. Instead of looking at a job to fill, organizations should profile it in terms of competencies, go to the data bank, and find whose competency profile matches the job," advises Stephen Martin, president of ITAP Europe. The key to this is competency development across the organization; ITAP has done succession planning for many global organizations through competency development.

Whatever be the methodology, measuring the effectiveness of a succession planning programme is critical to every organization, irrespective of its size. After all, it is more than just the passing of power and responsibility—it is about survival and continuity.

19

Indian Mentors

India has emerged as second fastest growing country in the world and Indian has become global unemployment solver. You can find 4-5 Indians in top 10 global billionnaire list and you can get 1, 2, 3 Indian teens in global teens billionnaire club. Some great Indian business tycoon always interact with intellectual group and try to reflect light back to the society. They are the role model who gives insight, vision, direction and motivation to get success in this fastest moving world. Hence we can have a look on summarized view of those eminent, Indian businessmen's success story.

Eight Steps to Excellence

Among others, Wipro has recently won the prestigious 'Risk Management Award', instituted by the *Financial Times-The Banker* magazine. What is that which makes this company so successful? "An obsession for excellence", says Azim Premji, Chairman and Managing Director, Wipro Limited.

Chairman and Managing Director of Wipro, Premji is credited with transforming Wipro, his family's vegetable oil business, into one of the world's foremost software company.

Although one of the richest Indians, he flies economy class and is happiest when hiking, reading or discussing the foundation he has set up to promote primary education.

These are changing times. Yet in the middle of all the changes there is one thing that constantly determines success. Some call it leadership. But to my mind, it is the single-minded pursuit of excellence.

Excellence endures and sustains. It goes beyond motivation into the realms of inspiration. Excellence can be as strong a uniting force as solid vision.

Excellence does not happen in a vacuum. It needs a collective obsession as I have experienced the benefits of excellence in my own life. Excellence is a great starting point for any new organization and also an unending journey. What is excellence? It is about going a little beyond what we expect from ourselves. Part of the need for excellence is imposed on us externally by our customers. Our competition keeps us on our toes, especially when it is global in nature.

But the other driver of excellence is internal. I have found that excellence is not so much a battle you fight with others, but a battle you fight with yourself, by constantly raising the bar and stretching yourself and your team. This is the best and the most satisfying and challenging part about excellence.

How does One Create Excellence in an Organization?

First, we create an obsession with excellence. We must dream of it not only because it delivers better results but because we truly believe in it and find it intrinsically satisfying to us.

We must think of excellence not only with our mind but also with our heart and soul. Let us look outside, at the global standards of excellence in quality, cost and delivery and let us not rest till we surpass them.

Second, we need to build a collective self-confidence. Organizations and people who pursue excellence are self-confident. This is because excellence requires tremendous faith in one's ability to do more and in a better way. Unless, we believe we can do better, we cannot.

Third, we must understand the difference between perfection for its own sake and excellence. Time is of essence. Globalization has made the customer only more impatient. This may seem like a paradox: should we aim for excellence or should we aim for speed?

Excellence is about doing the best we can and speed lies in doing it quickly. These two concepts are not opposed to each other; in fact, speed and timeliness are important elements of quality and excellence.

Fourth, we must realise that we cannot be the best in everything we do. We must define what we are or would like to be best at and what someone else can do better.

Excellence is no longer about being the best in India. It is about being the best in the world. We have to define what our own core competencies are and what we can outsource to other leaders. Headaches shared are headaches divided.

Fifth, we must create processes that enable excellence. Today, there are a number of global methods and processes available whether it is Six Sigma, CMM or ISO. Use them because they are based on distilled wisdom collected from the best companies in the world.

Also, we must build a strong foundation of information technology, because in this complex, dynamic world, it is imperative that we use the most modern tools to keep processes updated.

Sixth, we must create a culture of teaming. I have found that while great individuals are important, one cannot have pockets of excellence. Quality gives ample opportunities to build a culture of teaming. Cross-functional teams that are customer facing can cut through an amazing amount of bureaucracy, personal empire building and silos and deliver savings that one would not have imagined possible.

The other advantage of building teams focussed on quality is that the teaming culture eventually spreads to the rest of the organization and teaming becomes a way of life.

Seventh, invest in excellence for the future. Future always seems to be at a distance. But it comes upon you so suddenly that it catches you by surprise, if not shock. What constitutes excellence in the future will be significantly different from what it is today.

In these days of severe market pressures, there is big temptation to sacrifice the future to look good in the present. We must certainly trim our discretionary expenses, but we must ensure that our investments in strategic areas that lead to excellence in the future are protected.

Finally, excellence requires humility. This is especially needed when we feel we have reached the peak of excellence and there is nothing further we can do. We need an open mind to look at things in a different way and allow new inputs to come in.

Otherwise, there is a real danger of becoming complacent or even downright arrogant. I would like to end my talk with a story that illustrates this very well.

A brilliant young professor went to meet a famous Zen master to have a discussion with him on Zen. He found himself in front of a modest house. He rang the doorbell and waited. A while later, he heard shuffling footsteps and the door was opened by the Zen master.

He invited the professor to sit with him on the dining table. The professor was a little disappointed with the shabby appearance of the Zen master. He started quizzing him immediately on comparative philosophies and the Zen master gave some brief answers.

When the professor began to debate with him on those answers, the Zen master stopped speaking and kept smiling at him. Finally, the professor got angry. He said, "I have come from a long distance just to understand the relevance of Zenism. But apparently you have nothing to say. I have not learnt anything from you at all."

At this point, the Zen master asked the professor to have some tea. When the professor held the cup, the Zen master started pouring tea into it. After some time, the tea started spilling and the professor shouted, "Stop! The cup can contain no more."

The Zen Master stopped and then, once again smiling, he said, "A mind, full of itself can receive nothing. How can I speak to you of Zenism until you empty your mind to learn." The professor understood and apologized to the Zen master. He parted from him, the Zen master—a wiser man.

Mantra of Corporate Governance by Narayan Murthy

A leader is an agent of change, and progress is about change. In the words of Robert F. Kennedy, 'Progress is a nice word; but change is its motivator.'

Leadership is about raising the aspirations of followers and enthusing people with a desire to reach for the stars. For instance, Mahatma Gandhi created a vision for independence in India and raised the aspirations of our people.

Leadership is about making people say, 'I will walk on water for you.' It is about creating a worthy dream and helping people achieve it.

Robert Kennedy, summed up leadership best when he said, 'Others see things as they are and wonder why; I see them as they are not and say why not?'

Adversity

A leader has to raise the confidence of followers. He should make them understand that tough times are part of life and that they will come out better at the end of it. He has to sustain their hope, and their energy levels to handle the difficult days.

There is no better example of this than Winston Churchill. His courageous leadership as prime minister for Great Britain successfully led the British people from the brink of defeat during World War II. He raised his people's hopes with the words, 'These are not dark days; these are great days—the greatest days our country has ever lived.'

Never is strong leadership more needed than in a crisis. In the words of Seneca, the Greek philosopher, 'Fire is the test of gold; adversity, of strong men.'

Values

The leader has to create hope. He has to create a plausible story about a better future for the organization: everyone should be able to see the rainbow and catch a part of it.

This requires creating trust in people. And to create trust, the leader has to subscribe to a value system: a protocol for behavior that enhances the confidence, commitment and enthusiasm of the people.

Compliance to a value system creates the environment for people to have high aspirations, self-esteem, belief in fundamental values, confidence in the future and the enthusiasm necessary to take up apparently difficult tasks. Leaders have to walk the talk and demonstrate their commitment to a value system.

As Mahatma Gandhi said, 'We must become the change we want to see in the world.' Leaders have to prove their belief in sacrifice and hard work. Such behavior will enthuse the employees to make bigger sacrifices. It will help win the team's confidence, help leaders become credible, and help create trust in their ideas.

Enhancing Trust

Trust and confidence can only exist where there is a premium on transparency. The leader has to create an environment where each person feels secure enough to be able to disclose his or her mistakes, and resolves to improve.

Investors respect such organizations. Investors understand that the business will have good times and bad times. What they want you to do is to level with them at all times. They want you to disclose bad news on a proactive basis. At Infosys, our philosophy has always been, 'When in doubt, disclose'.

Governance

Good corporate governance is about maximising shareholder value on a sustainable basis while ensuring fairness to all stakeholders: customers, vendor-partners, investors, employees, government and society.

A successful organization tides over many downturns. The best index of success is its longevity. This is predicated on adhering to the finest levels of corporate governance.

At Infosys, we have consistently adopted transparency and disclosure standards even before law mandated it. In 1995, Infosys suffered losses in the secondary market. Under Indian GAAP (generally accepted accounting principles), we were not required to make this information public. Nevertheless, we published this information in our annual report.

Fearless Environment

Transparency about the organization's operations should be accompanied by an open environment inside the organization. You have to create an environment where any employee can disagree with you without fear of reprisal.

In such a case, everyone makes suggestions for the common good. In the end, everyone will be better off.

On the other hand, at Enron, the CFO was running an empire where people were afraid to speak. In some other cases, the whistle blowers have been harassed and thrown out of the company.

Managerial Remuneration

We have gone towards excessive salaries and options for senior management staff. At one company, the CEO's employment contract not only set out the model of the Mercedes the company would buy him, but also promised a monthly first-class air ticket for his mother, along with a cash bonus of $10 million and other benefits.

Not surprisingly, this company has already filed for bankruptcy.

Managerial remuneration should be based on three principles:

- Fairness with respect to the compensation of other employees;
- Transparency with respect to shareholders and employees;
- Accountability with respect to linking compensation with corporate performance.

Thus, the compensation should have a fixed component and a variable component. The variable component should be linked to achieving long-term objectives of the firm. Senior management should swim or sink with the fortunes of the company.

Senior management compensation should be reviewed by the compensation committee of the board, which should consist only of independent directors. Further, this should be approved by the shareholders.

I've been asked, "How can I ask for limits on senior management compensation when I have made millions myself?" A fair question with a straightforward answer: two systems are at play here. One is that of the promoter, the risk taker and the capital markets; and the other is that of professional management and compensation structures.

One cannot mix these two distinct systems, otherwise entrepreneurship will be stifled, and no new companies will come up, no progress can take place. At the same time, there has to be fairness in compensation: there cannot be huge differences between the top most and the bottom rung of the ladder within an organization.

PSPD Model

A well run organization embraces and practices a sound Predictability-Sustainability-Profitability-Derisking (we call this the PSPD model at Infosys) model. Indeed, the long-term success of an organization depends on having a model that scales up profitably.

Further, every organization must have a good derisking approach that recognises, measures and mitigates risk along every dimension.

Integrity

Strong leadership in adverse times helps win the trust of the stakeholders, making it more likely that they will stand by you in your hour of need. As leaders who dream of growth and progress, integrity is your most wanted attribute.

Lead your teams to fight for the truth and never compromise on your values. I am confident that our corporate leaders, through honest and desirable behavior, will reap long-term benefits for their stakeholders.

Two Mottos

In conclusion, keep in mind two Sanskrit sentences: *Sathyannasti Paro Dharma* (there is no *dharma* greater than adherence to truth); and *Satyameva jayate* (truth alone triumphs). Let these be your motto for good corporate leadership.

Importance of Talent in Global India by Aditya Birla

Few would argue with the statement, "It's tough being a Birla." Expectations are high, the stakes even higher. Yet over the past few years, Kumar Mangalam Birla, Chairman of the Aditya Birla Group, one of India's largest business houses, has earned his kudos. He is both a chartered accountant and an MBA.

Kumar Mangalam Birla focuses on two pertinent questions:

- We are a country of over a billion people, about one-sixth of humanity. Do Indians constitute the universe of talented people in equal proportion?
- Are we doing everything we can to help people be the best they can be?

In this article, I want to share some thoughts with you on 'talent', given that it is a subject presently occupying the attention of managers the world over, given that it is in extremely short supply, and given that the need to attract it and nurture it in sufficient numbers, is very real.

It is a management problem that is immediate, here and now.

A Key Resource

In any attempt to define our times, words and phrases such as 'accelerating pace of change', 'discontinuity' and 'complexity' figure often. Everything, however, somehow boils down to change and speed, mixed with a generous dose of confusion and chaos. Conventional truths and guideposts are now meeting their nemesis.

In such conditions, business survival and prosperity are clearly not a function of capital resources alone. Nor are they as dependent critically on scale or technology or labour, in the conventional sense of the word.

Even the newer strategic models do not give us sufficiently clear bearings on how to run our business. The point is, that when everyone in a Grand Prix drives a Ferrari, it is clearly the driver—and his skills, attitude, temperament and sense of purpose—that make the difference!

The one, single dominant force that has then emerged is talent. Management means attracting talented people, nurturing them, developing them, and giving them space.

People no longer want to just work, but are equally engaged in a search for their own identity and for a holistic meaning to their life.

The sharp focus on talent today stands out clearly. Microsoft employs around 200 full time recruiters. A recent survey by a leading international consulting firm (Amrop) revealed that 40 per cent of top management's time is spent on HR or talent related issues.

Another survey by the Harvard Business School identified the ability to spot talent and develop it as being the third most sought after attribute for a successful CEO.

Customers, yes. Shareholders, yes. But businesses will also have to embrace this stakeholder just as well—the employee, the talent pool, the intellectual capital, the resource that is the most fungible, the one that can easily walk out the door.

Every organization has to create a sense of ownership among people who will not be owned. A business of any worth today has to grapple with this compulsion. Talent is, in fact, central in the new paradigm. Without 'people power' even the best of operational and strategic thinking will come to naught.

What is Talent?

Let's reflect a bit about what exactly 'talent' means. I believe the term has become too complex to define. Instead, let me quote from the book Excellence, written by John W. Gardner, the American social reformer. According to him, 'There are those who perform great deeds and those that make it possible for others to perform great deeds. There are pathfinders and path preservers. There are those who nurture and those who inspire. There are those whose excellence involves doing something well and those whose excellence lies in being the kind of people they are, lies in their kindness or honesty or courage.'

Going a step further, the term 'talent' has developed some broader connotations. Earlier 'talented' might have referred to a person with expertise in a given functional area or a given business, or even a person who had achieved a pre-determined objective.

Today, these 'talents' are almost taken for granted. We now take stock of a person's managerial and leadership potential, the ability to straddle different functional areas, businesses, cultures and geographic boundaries—all in a seamless manner. We need to assess not only intellectual skills, but also softer skills such as emotional intelligence, values, creativity, the ability to work in teams, to think out of the box, entrepreneurial abilities, and also, importantly, the willingness to learn and share.

A recent study by Janice McCormack, Professor at Harvard Business School, aptly describes topnotch talent today as someone 'having the vision of an architect, the theoretical mindset of a physicist, the attention to detail of an engineer and the financial acumen of an investment banker.'

In short, the ability to not get cowed down by 'competing imperatives'.

Why Now?

People have always been important, so one may legitimately ask, why all this commotion now? Let us try to answer this question.

First, there is no doubt that the supply-demand imbalance in the talent area has become acute, not only in India, but also globally, and is getting more so. In India, a host of new industries—information technology, financial services, media and entertainment—are vying for the best people.

A flood of multinational companies is out to attract the best brains, not just for their operations in India, but for their overseas needs. The outstanding success of India's leading educational institutions, especially the IITs and IIMs, has drawn them to take a pick from our brains and capabilities. India has, in effect, become the world's scouting ground for talent.

Second, the desire to 'be one's own boss' is more common. More and more talented people want to strike out on their own, or work in a company which offers a significant entrepreneurial environment. So the pool of people from which to select is contracting, relative to the demand for them.

There is a third factor behind the scarcity of talent. Until recently, our preoccupation with talent was confined largely to the higher levels of an organization. Today, every level of a company's operations requires talented people. In the wake of intense competition, and the consequent need for speed, the top-down approach to managing is increasingly proving ineffective.

Dispersal of decision-making is also being driven by complexity—the sheer geographic spread of companies, the diversity of product lines and the need to be close to the customer. Decisions need to be made at every level and decisions need to be quick. So, we have to spot, incubate and groom talent at every level of the organization, because more people need to be making high quality decisions.

And finally, much higher degrees of business complexity result in a much larger premium on talent. Complexity calls for an integrated approach, the ability to look at a problem from different perspectives, and a high degree of creative and non-linear thinking.

Coupled with that, there is the need for heightened cultural sensitivity as national boundaries are becoming hazy and business is becoming truly global.

India Well Placed to Nurture Talent

I have tried to identify some of the key factors driving the demand for talent, which has now come to be the strategic resource. However, despite the scarcity, we are fortunate that

India has many of the right ingredients that help to nurture talent.

We just have to look at our present times to realise the considerable advantages we possess as regards talented people. I am sure we all must have been taken aback with the surge in the globalization of Indian talent. We all knew it was there—but today the entire world recognises it, and how.

As the joke in Silicon Valley runs, if a person's name is Shreedhar, don't bother checking his IT skills! Across a range of areas—engineering, computer programming and financial services—the Indian brain has begun to command the highest brand equity.

Indians are breaking the glass ceiling and staking their claim at the upper levels of global firms, in increasing numbers.

How did this happen? Unlikely as this may seem, India does seem to have some of the prerequisites that can be leveraged to nurture talent. We have the much sought after facility with today's Lingua Franca, the English language, as also a relatively high degree of numerical aptitude.

And, we have an innate capacity to adapt, without which it would not have been possible for Indians to strike roots overseas and become among the more successful of the immigrant communities, in a number of countries.

Of course, competition also does much to nurture talent. And we in India, work in a very competitive environment, pretty much from childhood. We even have interviews to get admitted to a nursery school!

Even leaving aside this extreme, we are constantly being graded, scored, evaluated and ranked. The admissions-to-applicants ratio at our premier educational institutes is more demanding than that of even the most elite universities abroad. The same is true of our Civil Service.

What Retards Talent in India?

On the flip side, we need to recognise and deal with some of the powerful attitudes and forces that not only retard talent, but also are hostile to it.

For one, there is the fear of failure. There is an almost indelible stigma attached to failure, much more than in the West. The family, the peer group, the society, the banker—all still frown on failure—of any sort, no matter how heroic and daring the effort that preceded it.

This attitude thwarts experimentation and stifles innovation. Better to be 'mediocrely' right than 'stunningly' wrong. The possibility of getting a second chance is rare.

It is difficult to think of the exploits of a Thomas Alva Edison happening here: the daring experiments, the failures, the bankruptcy, and then the success, the most well known of which is the electric bulb.

A second obstacle to talent is conformity. There is less acceptance of the offbeat. Dissidence is not looked upon too favorably: it's the nail that sticks out that invariably gets hammered down. Conformity is all around us: in the dress code, in the jargon of our times, in our patterns of strategic thinking, at a point in time.

The herd instinct is evident even in the way we invest, with everyone running after the same scrips, in the same industries, at a particular moment. Being different is difficult. Where are the contrarians?

Finally, I believe that our educational system contributes, in substantial measure, to our inability to draw out the store of talent latent in us. Students at the school level are overburdened with rote learning. Listening and being talked to is the norm.

Questioning, discourse, the spirit of discovery, curiosity and inquiry are rare. The curriculum is narrow and outdated and, to a large extent, 'memory-centric'. Unlike in the West, the options offered are few.

Talent Issues in Indian Organizations

At this point, I would like to share my thoughts on some of the critical talent related issues that we in Indian organizations need to address. No doubt, many readers are already working to tackle similar issues, and you would be having your own unique perspectives.

In my own organization, although we have been putting in a lot of effort, in these and related areas, we are some distance away from having all the right answers. Perhaps, many of these are fuzzy issues and there are no definitive answers. Each organization must chart out its own approach and course, given the specific context in which it operates.

Adrenaline: The first major issue is how to keep the adrenaline flowing in talented people. The game does not stop at identifying talent or inducting it. Talented people get bored easily and so they have to be kept constantly challenged.

In our organization, we address this issue by fast tracking deserving talent, offering definite career paths, providing cross functional exposure across different businesses, and secondments to our operations abroad.

The objective is to offer a high quality of exposure, faster, thus enabling the manager to increase his overall intrinsic worth and to take on higher responsibilities, much earlier in his career.

Integration: A second issue concerns how best one can integrate talented people into the organization, in a way that there is no undue disruption. I bring this point up because, quite often, mediocrity tends to drive out talent or make it ineffective.

Integrating talented people into the organization involves handling a host of sensitive issues and this is a task that will fully test the leadership abilities of senior management.

At the same time, as we move about with the process of integrating talent, we do need to subject ourselves—and talented people—to some kind of a reality check, every now and then. The best of talent has to operate, ultimately, within the boundaries of organizational objectives, and talent, no matter how highly regarded, cannot become dysfunctional.

Creating an ivory tower is not desirable. In the same vein, we have to keep in mind that talent means much more than 'white collar'. We cannot glorify a certain kind of talent, at the cost of talent in other areas. As always, maintaining the right balance is the challenge.

Compensation: The third issue I would like to touch upon is one very much in the spotlight today: the growing divergence in compensation and reward levels between the talented and those less so. This differential is widening by the day—in absolute and relative terms.

How we handle this divergence is again absolutely critical to an organization's health. Today, the clamour for stock options runs high. Incorporating a significant performance-based component in the compensation package is almost mandatory. Again, there are no clear cut solutions. It goes much beyond the criteria of affordability.

We have to look at larger and fundamental issues such as equity, value systems and organizational morale.

Until we find an answer to this dilemma, let me read out this very interesting text of an advertisement, which appeared in the London newspapers in the year 1900. Ernest Shackleton, the famous explorer, inserted this advertisement when recruiting team members for the National Antarctic Expedition.

The advertisement read as follows: 'MEN WANTED FOR HAZARDOUS JOURNEY. Small wages, bitter cold, long months of complete darkness, constant danger, safe return doubtful. Honour and recognition in case of success.'

Shackleton later said of the call for volunteers that, 'It seemed as though all the men in Great Britain were determined to accompany me, the response was so overwhelming.' Perhaps, taking the cue from this, the real challenge lies in striking the right balance between material rewards and the larger sense of mission.

What per cent?

In conclusion, I believe that making India talent-friendly will require actions at the macro level also. Nurturing talent and keeping it here and putting it to good use requires resolving some tough quality of life issues.

For instance, India ranks low in any human development or quality of life index. Talent cannot flourish if the enabling social and physical infrastructure is not in place. Only then can we reverse the brain drain decisively. This is a task that needs the involvement of all of us—in business, in government, in our educational institutions, in our professional bodies.

Attracting brains is a lot more difficult than attracting FDI or portfolio investments. But then that is also what will make us really competitive.

At the end of it all, we have to ask ourselves not only whether we have talented people, but also whether we have enough of them; and whether we are doing everything we can to nurture them in greater numbers.

We are a billion Indians, about one-sixth of humanity. Do Indians constitute the universe of talented people, in equal proportion?